DIRTY JOKES AND BAWDY SONGS

FOLKLORE STUDIES
IN A MULTICULTURAL
WORLD

The Folklore Studies in a Multicultural World series is a collaborative venture of the University of Illinois Press, the University Press of Mississippi, the University of Wisconsin Press, and the American Folklore Society, made possible by a generous grant from the Andrew W. Mellon Foundation. The series emphasizes the interdisciplinary and international nature of current folklore scholarship, documenting connections between communities and their cultural production. Series volumes highlight aspects of folklore studies such as world folk cultures, folk art and music, foodways, dance, African American and ethnic studies, gender and queer studies, and popular culture.

DIRTY JOKES AND BAWDY SONGS

THE UNCENSORED LIFE OF GERSHON LEGMAN

SUSAN G. DAVIS

UNIVERSITY OF ILLINOIS PRESS
Urbana, Chicago, and Springfield

© 2019 by the Board of Trustees
of the University of Illinois
All rights reserved
Manufactured in the United States of America

1 2 3 4 5 C P 5 4 3 2 1
⊚ This book is printed on acid-free paper.

Publication of this book was supported in part by a
grant from the L. J. and Mary C. Skaggs Folklore Fund.

Library of Congress Cataloging-in-Publication Data
Names: Davis, Susan G., 1953– author.
Title: Dirty jokes and bawdy songs : the uncensored life
   of Gershon Legman / Susan G. Davis.
Description: [Urbana] : University of Illinois Press,
   [2019] | Series: Folklore studies in a multicultural
   world | Includes bibliographical references and index.
Identifiers: LCCN 2019005760| ISBN 9780252042614
   (hardcover : alk. paper) | ISBN 9780252084447 (pbk. :
   alk. paper)
Subjects: LCSH: Legman, G. (Gershon), 1917–1999.
   | Folklorists—United States—Biography. | Sex—
   Folklore—Research—History—20th century.
Classification: LCC GR55.L44 D39 2019 | DDC 398.2092 [B]
   —dc23
   LC record available at https://lccn.loc.gov/
   2019005760

E-book ISBN 9780252051456

To the librarians

CONTENTS

Preface   ix

Acknowledgments   xiii

Introduction   1

1   The Stranger   11

2   Sex Researcher   37

3   Kinsey's Bibliographer   65

4   *Love & Death*   87

5   *Neurotica*   112

6   Advanced Studies in Folklore   141

7   "The Ballad" and *The Horn Book*   161

8   The Key to the Fields   174

9   The Hell Drawer   194

10   Under Mt. Cheiron   223

Notes   243

Works Consulted   295

Index   297

PREFACE

This book began when I read Gershon Legman's obituary in the *New York Times* in 1999, and stories I had heard about him in the 1970s came back to me. I remembered reading his anthologies of dirty jokes, and seeing announcements for "Kryptadia," Legman's planned yearbook of erotic folklore. I had heard stories from some of my own teachers about his troubles with the United States Post Office. Thinking I might write an article on Legman and his erotic folklore research, I looked up his work in the Library of Congress catalog and saw that his career went far beyond joke collecting. It turned out that Legman was a sturdy digger and agitator on all kinds of topics beyond folklore. Not only had he published enormous collections of raunchy limericks, as I remembered, but he had also worked for Alfred Kinsey and dissented vociferously from his epic report, *Sexual Behavior in the Human Male*. In the late 1940s, Legman published an influential analysis of comic books and detective stories, and in the 1960s he fired a broadside at "the LSD and happening hippie crap," the counterculture of the time. He had rescued and published lost obscene manuscripts by Mark Twain and Robert Burns. He fostered the bawdy song and story collections of the legendary Ozark folklorist Vance Randolph. The list went on: He compiled multilanguage bibliographies of centuries of suppressed erotica and tried to uncover the anonymous authors of Victorian pornography. He wrote some pornography of his own. I started a Legman reading project, although a few years after his death, his books were all out of print and many of his articles were published in hard-to-find journals.

There was always a scent of the disreputable about Legman's work, and indeed even today university libraries keep some of his books in controlled circulation to protect them from the reading public (and vice versa). In a way, Legman's reputation had been dragged down by the prudishness he spent his whole life fighting. Even after eighty years, Legman's books are still outrageous. For instance, his first book, *Oragenitalism: Oral Techniques in Genital Excitation,* is an odd combination of how-to manual and free-love tract. If it seemed weird in 2000, what was it like to publish it in 1939?

Legman's books are not easy on the reader. As his friend Bruce Jackson put it, "Legman's style can seem as old fashioned as an elocution lesson, but it is vigorous, learned, and intense. His slowly unfolding paragraphs are furiously cross referenced and packed with fascinating (sometimes distracting) detours and details." He did not care to make his readers like him or even agree with him. The blasts he delivers are refreshing and alarming at the same time. Jackson again: "One must be willing to argue many of the things Legman asserts, work through in one's own mind the anger that rises suddenly at many of his apparently outrageous remarks. Few scholars force that kind of work."[1] Even Legman's folklore collections were vehicles for his polemics against the modern world and what he called "the bloodlust" that surrounds us.[2]

Legman's work is so different from the writers we read to today that it can be baffling; it is difficult to understand where his wild projects and ideas came from. He rarely cared to show his debt to other thinkers, and he only occasionally gave out bits of (not always accurate) personal information. Studying his texts, I realized, would not be enough. I had to find people who knew and worked with him who could bring him into focus, but by the early twenty-first century, much of Legman's American network was fragile. The sources best informed on his early life are dead, and his old neighborhoods are changed beyond recognition. The literary world of 1940s Manhattan has vanished, and so has the Beat movement he is credited with starting. His younger friends, with the exception of his widow, Judith Legman, knew him mostly at a distance. But still, as I posted requests for leads to people who had known him, it became clear that he was very much alive in oral tradition. People who had met or corresponded with him, or even just heard about him, sent me vivid descriptions of his astounding pronouncements and obnoxious behavior.

After several years of digging into Legman's opus, I was able to visit his personal archive in Opio, France, and interview members of his family. With the help of Judith Legman (who has carefully preserved and indexed his letters and document files), I began to see the outline of his rich network of friends and coworkers and to appreciate how ambitious his projects were. As an outline of Legman's writing life emerged from more than fifty years of correspondence and collecting, I could see how he bootstrapped himself from poverty into a tenuous contrarian niche. From early adulthood, Legman was fully engaged in an intellectual battle against his world, in work on issues that endure today, including sexual freedom, feminism, and militarism. And he did this work, in large part, in the field of folklore.

It became clearer to me that Legman is ill-remembered today not because he failed to have an impact: he certainly was influential upon his fans and enemies, as I have tried to show. Nor has he been neglected because editors found him difficult to work with. This is true of plenty of ambitious writers. Legman has been hard to assimilate because he belongs to a long American tradition of cultural dissent that is usually held far from the academic and publishing mainstream. He simply would not say that Americans live in the happiest era, in the best of all possible countries. I am convinced our intensely commercial and conformist culture needs alienated denunciation as much now as it did when Legman began his projects.

Folklore, one of the fields Legman wished to speak to, has been wary of him. Prudishness and distaste for his insistence on sexual and obscene subjects drew attention to Legman's work while keeping him at academic folklore's margins. So too did his attacks on scholarly manners and fashions. Legman's use of Freudian theory in his approach to expressive culture was regarded with suspicion when his works appeared, and it remains largely unassimilated.

Overall, Gershon Legman's life and work help show the contradictions of folklore as a way of thinking about culture. As we continue to examine folklore's two-hundred-year-old intellectual legacies, Legman's work can throw a harsh but helpful light upon our field of discovery and work. In his opus, there is something "to offend everyone," but as he saw it, he was always "telling the rock-hard truth."[3]

ACKNOWLEDGMENTS

Even a nontraditional biography is an enormous amount of work, and expensive. I could not have completed the research this book demanded without extensive support from the University of Illinois, especially the Research Board, the Institute for Communication Research, the Graduate School of Library and Information Science, and the Department of Communication. Also at the University of Illinois, I had research assistance from Kassie Lamp, Ted Gournelos, Diem-My Bui, Roswell Quinn, Maritza Quinones, Allie Cavallaro, and Jess Cavallaro. Kate McQueen and Jermaine Martinez provided expert research assistance in the final phases.

Gershon Legman's last years of good health were spent writing "Peregrine Penis: An Autobiography of Innocence," prospectively eight books, recounting his sexual, intellectual, and literary adventures, "Like Casanova, with laughs!" As I completed my own study, Legman's widow, Judith, was able to publish the first six volumes of "Peregrine Penis." I have drawn on published and unpublished parts of the memoir, which is as much a document of a marginal intellectual world in midcentury Manhattan as it is a collection of remembered erotic encounters. In addition to Legman's big scholarly books, I have used his staggering collection of personal letters and reference cards and extensive interviews with his family, friends, and colleagues. The formidable work Judith Legman did to sort and organize her husband's papers, and to bring his manuscripts to publication, a promise she was keeping to Gershon, was indispensable to me. She has been a generous and important source as well, sharing insights and memories and offering extensive practical help. So too have Gershon's children, especially David Berenger and Ariëla Legman.

xiv — *Acknowledgments*

Throughout his life, Gershon Legman depended upon libraries, bookstores, and book lovers, as I have. Although Legman's relationship to librarians was sometimes antagonistic, they were central and nourishing to his work, as they have been to mine. Thus, the dedication of this book. At Bloomington, Indiana, the Kinsey Archive and Library at the Institute for Research into Sex and Gender was an indispensable resource. My warmest thanks to Liana Zhou and her staff. I also relied heavily on the University of Illinois's superb library and reference services; the Western Historical Collection of the Missouri State Historical Society at the University of Missouri, St. Louis; the American Folklife Center at the Library of Congress; the Santa Fe Public Library; and the library of the School for Advanced Research.

Many of Legman's friends and my colleagues helped as well. My thanks go to James Leary, Simon Bronner, John Szwed, Alan Dundes, Roger D. Abrahams, Ed Cray, Martha Cornog, Timothy Perper, James Gilbert, Eric McLuhan, Barbara Kirshenblatt-Gimblett, Bruce Jackson, Diane Christian, Archie Green, Reinhold Aman, Frank Hoffman, David Taylor, Deborah Kodish, Eric Laursen, Mary Dearborn, John McLeish, Jay Gertzman, Michael Neal, and many others. Some of these colleagues kindly gave me originals or copies of their Legman correspondence to use, and I am grateful. Bruce and Ling Anderson helped me locate the letters of some of Legman's far-flung California admirers, including the mysterious "Wanda Tinasky." Jeffrey St. Clair and Alexander Cockburn published an early piece of my work on Legman's encounter with the Post Office in *CounterPunch,* which in turn brought me new leads. John Dorst, Mario Montaño, and Sam Schrager offered sympathetic counsel over many years. Diana Undercuffler generously read and commented on the final draft. Louisa Dewey at the University of Iowa provided a thorough manuscript cleanup.

At the University of Illinois Press, Willis Regier and James Engelhardt were encouraging through this long process and provided astute advice. Also at Illinois, Tad Ringo and Kevin Cunningham shepherded the manuscript through production, and Annette Wenda gave it a gentle, expert copy editing.

My friends at the University of Illinois, especially Inger Stole, Michéle Koven, Megan McLaughlin, and Harriet Murav, listened and offered creative suggestions. Jim and Jenny Barrett were a sturdy source of criticism, encouragement, and historical perspective. Janice Dulak, Douglas Nelson, and Julia Kling in Champaign and Dr. Eric Terman in Chicago helped me cope with a serious injury and continue to write.

Peggy Miller and Dan Schiller each read the whole book and discussed my interpretations with me at length. My friendship with Peggy, an ethnographer of childhood, goes back to a course we taught together on narrative theory, and from that time her clear-eyed insights and thoughtful comments on

Acknowledgments   **XV**

childhood, story, and research at the margins have informed my work. Dan supported this project from the beginning and lived, off and on for years, with its sprawl across our dining room table. He believed when my confidence flagged and always, devotedly, made more coffee. My children, Lucy Schiller and Ethan Schiller, have been tolerant of the mental and physical space Gershon Legman occupied in my life. Lucy offered skilled and thoughtful editorial suggestions on chapters 9 and 10. Thank you all.

¡No Pasaran!

DIRTY JOKES AND BAWDY SONGS

INTRODUCTION

There are a few old roads that may be trodden with profit.
—Henry David Thoreau, "Walking," *Atlantic*, June 1862

Gershon Legman (1917–99), known as G. Legman to his readers, was a collector of the erotic, the obscene, and the banned. The secret things everyone did or thought about doing, the desires people were afraid to acknowledge, Legman was compelled to document and write about profusely. He reveled in the profane words expunged from polite dictionaries.

Folklorists claim Legman and many of his works, but he saw himself more broadly as a social critic, a leader in the battle to destroy American sexual censorship. Coming of age in the Great Depression, he connected early-twentieth-century atheist and free-speech traditions with a post–World War II attack on prudery. He was determined to excavate the country's "hell drawer," the newspaperman's name for the secret cabinet where unpublishable submissions ended up. Legman was at the height of his powers as a fighter against his world just as the intellectual openness of America in the 1930s shut down in the dark period of Cold War reaction. In a nation that stressed conformity and patriotism, Legman tried to use the suppressed contents of its hell drawer in a humanistic critique of mass culture and militarism. In his audience were the forerunners of the 1960s counterculture.

At midcentury Legman asserted that the country was headed for a nervous breakdown, and his diagnosis of the collective crazy was that sexual repression fed American violence. Legman's prescription, a loosening of American attitudes toward sex, had been offered from the early twentieth century. But sexual frankness horrified respectable opinion, and in practice sexual freedom was available only to the very protected and privileged.[1]

Emptying out the secret archives and listening to living erotic folklore could liberate literature and Americans from prudery, Legman argued. But until the 1930s, the study of folklore had been largely the province of gentlemen and ladies who were concerned with protecting the reading public from scabrous materials. Almost alone in this period, Legman was a fascinated, driven advocate of English-language erotic traditions. His goal was to put them in print uncensored and unexpurgated. To do this, he reached back into an age he thought of as less "neutered" and more open, the fifteenth and sixteenth centuries. His aim was to find the most antirespectable, antibourgeois relics and show that in folklore, the property of the people, they still lived. By itself, this would have been an ambitious project, but Legman also amassed enormous archives of unpublishable contemporary lore he thought revealed Western civilization's sexual predicaments.

In 1953 America's censors and the Red Scare forced Legman to leave the United States. As he understood it, he had no hope of doing his work in his own country. From France, he reconstructed his scholarly life and pursued decades of deep research. Except for a few brief visits to the United States, he remained in a self-imposed exile and penury that most scholars would have found unendurable. But by the time of his death in 1999, he had used his remarkable library and archive to publish a series of advanced studies in folklore, documenting his case against censorship and arguing for the importance of attending to the erotic in everyday culture. Without an academic job and often outside legitimate publishing circles, Legman laid down trails that are still being explored today.

By the 1960s, although he was rarely in the United States, G. Legman was a name to conjure with. Legman was familiar to countercultural types through *Ramparts*, the *Realist*, and the *Village Voice*, as well as mass-circulation magazines like *Playboy* and *Screw*. He even made the occasional appearance in *Time*. Beats and offbeat intellectuals, folk singers, and English professors knew his name, although most knew little about the man. Mostly he was famous as the world expert on dirty words, curses, jokes, and filthy songs—in short, the man who knew everything about the underground traditions of sex.

From the late 1960s to the mid-1970s, Legman published *The Rationale of the Dirty Joke: An Analysis of Sexual Humor (First Series)* and its companion, *No Laughing Matter: The Rationale of the Dirty Joke (Second Series)*, composing his study of the thousands of jokes he collected over more than thirty years and analyzed, "more in tears than laughter," for what they showed about humanity. A friend from the 1940s, novelist John Clellon Holmes, wrote of Legman as a "Representative Man" from a postwar literary world the sixties were rapidly forgetting.

Clellon Holmes used the metaphor of a spelunker for Legman, describing him absorbed in a "stubborn and exhaustive attempt to limn the underwater part of our society's psychological iceberg."[2] The image of a lone figure descending into an invisible terrain captures Legman, in part. The archaeologist is another image for Legman, the person who painstakingly lays bare and interprets the buried and forgotten. And so is the keeper of the geniza, the secret room where a community's sacred trash is piled and stuffed.[3] But these images emphasize solitude. It is true Legman loved to study orphan phenomena, subjects few would seriously tackle, and he did isolate himself to get his work done. But he inhabited many intellectual circles, and he had hundreds of friends who shared his interest in the same problematic materials.

Legman and his work are little acknowledged today. Some of his obscurity flows from anachronism, a misunderstanding of the relationship between the past and the present. We tend to imagine the passing of time as progressive and to believe that old-fashioned scholarship and erroneous ideas of the past are steadily replaced by better methods and concepts in the always improving present. But history is as much about forgetting as it is about progress, and culture is as much about rejection as it is about acceptance and assimilation. Legman's work has received some cursory attention since his death but no sustained exploration of his intellectual history and landscape.[4] One of the aims of this biography is to reinsert Legman into times and places that can help us make sense of his sprawling and challenging body of work.

His overt political stances are divergent also. Between about 1936 and 1953, when Legman worked at the hungry edges of New York's intellectual life, he developed a heated and bracing polemical style. His cantankerous early voice made arguments that have seeped into our broader culture. His self-proclaimed Marxism and his self-taught Freudianism are unusual among folklorists, who for most of the century have described themselves as documentarians rather than activists or diagnosticians. But examined closely, we can see Legman as an early popular proponent of taking the insignificant seriously. His heated polemical attacks on every commonsense understanding of the way the world worked fused political critique with the study of popular culture. Familiar now, his orientation was unusual from the 1940s through the 1960s.

Here is one of his alienated positions that have become common sense: his favorite among his own works, *Love & Death: A Study in Censorship* (1949), was Legman's bleak assessment of mass culture, here presented in his analysis of murder mysteries: "We are faced in our culture by the insurmountable schizophrenic contradiction that sex, which is legal in fact, is a crime on paper, while murder—a crime in fact—is, on paper the bestseller of all time."[5] Replace "murder on paper" with "murder in film and television," and we can find this formulation in today's newspapers, where critics compare the extremes of violence offered for enjoyment with the timid, not to say prudish, way that nonviolent, consensual sexuality is presented. The reader will have to test whether this idea holds up, but Legman's formulations "no longer seem so radical or outrageous . . .," as John Clellon Holmes noted in 1965. "To some degree, at least, the world has grown up to them."[6]

Legman was far ahead of his time on many topics, and he developed his own mode of cultural documentation and interpretation, much of which his fellow folklorists could not take on board. When Legman is reinserted in his times, we can see how his interests in folklore connect to other submerged and dissident American intellectual traditions. His work offers a view of the underside of the American discovery of folklore and the way popular traditions have been studied.

While Legman was an intellectual outlier, Clellon Holmes pointed out that we miss a great deal when we categorize him as an eccentric or an obsessive. He appears to have found his way on his own, synthesizing his view of the world from indefatigable reading, long-standing traditions of heresy, and his own experiences, particularly the kinds of economic and personal disasters common to immigrant families. But his feelings were shared. The position Legman, Clellon Holmes, and their friends formulated in the little magazine *Neurotica* and other experiments gave voice to a complex sense of betrayal by old values and loathing for the new, consumerist America. Their ideas were unpopular then but have become better known to American intellectuals through the work of the Frankfurt School and its fusion of Marxism with psychoanalysis.

Legman's reading background was common to the generation of children of eastern European immigrants. He seems to have integrated eastern European anarchism, with its love of Jewish culture and adamant rejection of religion, with eclectic strains of American radicalism. Although Legman was of the Left, he was not on the Left. Asked about his politics for an entry in a dictionary of literary biography, Legman wrote "Marxist," but he did not take part in organized politics.[7] He was constitutionally unable to sit through meetings, and he certainly did not have the personality to accept movement discipline. Although he saw the world as dangerously imperfect, like many of his generation he saw hope and potential for change. Legman had many friends who joined or sympathized with working-class movements, and in the 1930s some of them tried to recruit him to the American Communist Party. But when the Federal Bureau of Investigation (FBI) snooped through Legman's personal and political closets in 1949, they found no political ties at all.

While Legman's personal blend of old and new European and American left radical politics was not unheard of for a bright, self-educated young man

Introduction

of the Depression generation, he was unique in bringing this intellectual stance together with folklore and sex radicalism. No one had pulled this off before—nor, really, have they since. For Legman, erotic folklore was a way to be in touch with something more real than the stuffy life of parlor, school, and synagogue, while sex advocacy let him fuse politics and love.

Legman's discovery in adolescence that he wanted to dedicate his life to the theory and practice of sexual freedom seemed to him predestined. The legacy of the early movement for "free love and anarchism" had been destroyed in 1917; it was not at the forefront of political agitation during the Depression. Almost no one in Depression-era America was publicly connecting sex to left politics. (The exceptions would be the mostly forgotten V. F. Calverton, editor of the *Modern Quarterly*, and novelist Floyd Dell.) Legman wrote as if the crusade for sexual openness was his own unique and hormonally driven discovery, but he was aware of the work of earlier American bohemians and the tiny handful of nineteenth-century social thinkers who argued for the sexual liberation of women and men. In this way, his writings were a bridge between nineteenth- and twentieth-century radicalisms. Certainly, Emma Goldman's denunciations of plutocrats and her advocacy for the rights of poor and working people would have resonated with a young man who grew up among coal miners and railroad men. Goldman's and Margaret Sanger's advocacy of sexual freedom and birth control in the cause of women's pleasure struck a chord with Legman, too.

Hostile in his very bones to sexual repression, Legman zeroed in on a basic principle. If the world was to be made into a sane, humane place, erotic language and images had to be unfettered and uncensored. This was not an easy position to espouse in the 1930s. Although America's leading censor, Anthony Comstock, was dead, his legacy persisted in law and practice. Legman's enemies would be the same powerful forces who had harassed the sex radicals seventy-five years earlier: the vice squad and the police chief, and their allies in the Catholic Church, the U.S. Post Office Department, and the Customs Office, all of whom upheld the American regime of censorship.

Legman's other bold move was to fold his sexual politics into his love of folklore. He loved traditional verbal arts. His father, Emil, was an excellent raconteur of traditional tales, who specialized in explaining the family's long history of rotten luck. The Legmans were familiar with the power of Hungarian proverbs, and from his earliest years Gershon was fascinated by slang, catchphrases and jokes, and old songs. From childhood, he was delighted that sex had its own, often underground, traditions and lore.

Legman didn't spend a lot of time theorizing folklore, but his thinking about vernacular traditions was clear enough. All the kinds of knowledge that people share and pass around informally counted as folklore for Legman.

6 *Introduction*

Anything passed along by word of mouth or example, shaped by people who told it over and over again, delivered into the present by centuries of ordinary living and struggle to survive: it all fascinated him. For Legman, "folk" were not just peasants and members of isolated, rural communities but the ordinary, laboring, and poor people of the country and the city—the people with whom he had grown up in Depression-era Scranton. In contrast with many of his contemporaries, for Legman "lore" was not the property of a race, region, or nation but belonged to those with little social and economic power. Because it existed outside and in opposition to the language of the schoolroom, the church or temple, and the courthouse, he found that folklore had a rare psychological realism.

By the late 1940s, Legman was calling his specialty erotic folklore, and in some way he was simply retrospectively naming his longtime fascination. By erotic folklore Legman meant any traditional material having to do with sexual behavior, ideas, or concepts.[8] The folklore of sex could be as simple as a finger scratched across a palm, a nonverbal sexual invitation Legman remembered from his Scranton boyhood, contemporary and ancient, local and universal. From the time he was eight years old, he snipped bawdy jokes from pulp magazines, pasted them to index cards, and kept them in a shoe box. (This box was the beginning of his *Rationale* books.) A bit later, he began a scrapbook of erotic photos, some homemade and some bought under the drugstore counter and swapped with friends. But in typical Legman style, over the years both card file and scrapbook expanded to account for every sexual possibility, position, and problem, becoming an exhaustive collection.

He was attentive to the sexual words people used in everyday talk. Where the language of sex was reviled and excised by ordinary dictionary makers, in fugitive lexicons Legman saw a rich history that expressed real, if impolite, perspectives and emotions. These words deserved serious examination and tracing. They needed to be reconnected to the history of the English language, because they bore evidence of ordinary people's erotic experiences and problems.

He collected names for genitals. For thousands of years, people had named genitals with humor and creativity: "Big John," "Mr. Johnson," "the wrinkle," and "my little ball of yarn." People gave folk terms for genitals to places (and birds and animals) in their familiar landscapes. Vernacular place-names like "The Parson's Prick" and "Cunt-Tickle Creek" were routinely erased by mapmakers.[9]

Everywhere, there were sexual colloquialisms. There were turns of phrase: "I bet she'd bounce like a rubber ball!" or "He's a real piss-cutter." There were proverbs, such as "A woman kissed is a woman half-fucked," and proverbial expressions, like "That woman is cunt *all over*." Spooneristic conundrums asked, "What's the difference between a nun and a woman taking a bath?" (One has a soul full of hope.) Wellerisms juxtaposed benign catchphrases with disturbing images: "'They're off!' said the Monkey as he backed into the lawnmower" or "'That remains to be seen,' said the Elephant as he shat on the sidewalk." Legman was intrigued by verbal abuse, which he sometimes compared to an ancient form of magic. He collected curses like "Tor ass clot!" ("Your ass cloth!"), a West Indian reference to menstruation. He pondered the "flyttings," battles in insults, of the ancient Scots. He puzzled over enigmatic insults, like "You don't make my Sunday asshole!" which he probably heard from a male prostitute in Harlem in 1940.[10]

The imaginative world of folklore jostled with traditional and rumored sex positions and lovemaking customs (what was a sleeve job, anyway?), vernacular birth control techniques, and deeply held beliefs about parts of the body. Legman was fascinated with ideas about the power and vulnerability of the head in American and African cultures, and he expanded on this topic in theses on the practice of oral sex. There were the European and central Asian folktales with their amazing exaggerations of sexual organs and feats. He traced folk ideas about sex through ancient epics, the Bible, Boccaccio's jest books, and Shakespeare's plays.

There were ballads, "songs sung in the streets" about sexual love and enthusiasm and cuckoldry, from the tiresomely filthy "Bollocky Bill the Sailor" to the (before Legman) unmentionable "Brinzi O'Flynn," which "contains almost the only reference to oral sexuality" in English folk song and "has the most beautiful minor-key air." And there were the jokes, always old and new at the same time, the folktales of the industrial world. All this was the geniza Legman excavated and analyzed, a labor of more than fifty years.

Although sex and sexual folklore are not in any sense innocent, Legman thought they were "natural and necessary, in fact indispensable" to human life. Unlike the stifling culture of the middle-class parlor and classroom, folklore uncensored offered a celebration of the body and frankness about erotic life. For Legman, folklore's irreverent quality allowed a window onto what people really think, feel, and do. It persisted as a necessary antidote to the cruel and mealymouthed ways ordinary people are described and prescribed from above. But as he saw when he laid out his analysis of dirty jokes, the American hell drawer mingled hilarity with hostility, anger and fear. In Legman's view, what people do to each other in the name of civilization is often so horrific that even while they must look at it, they also must explain it away. For Legman, folklore is one way people express hostility and rationalize the unbearable, and so an accurate record of erotic folklore is essential to understanding the pain of being human in an exploitative civilization.

He also thought folklore was in danger from its collectors. The arbiters of culture, Legman wrote, not only neglect folklore but also despise it for its psychological realism. And so they alter and expurgate it and try to own it. He was, in his own view, the rare honest and completely scientific recorder of ordinary people's imaginations, since he never cleaned up his collections, even if it meant rejection by every publisher in the United States. Another of his lifelong projects was gathering irrefutable documentary evidence of the censorship processes, proving that erotic lore's very existence was denied out of fear as much as prudery. Legman was also implacably angry at academic folklorists who collaborated with mass culture, "improving" and copyrighting folk songs, lining their pockets while sucking on the university teat. "All the wrong people are sniffing around folklore," he wrote to Richard Dorson, as they discussed the popularity of folklore books. When folklore was cleaned up for a middle-class market, it met a horrible fate. Legman put his finger on it: to purify folklore was to adulterate it.

In his way, Legman was a romantic and a modernist. While he believed in destroying old ways to broaden personal and sexual freedoms, he reached back into a past to argue that folklore was a bulwark against standardized and industrially produced emotion for the masses. While he said yes to the pleasures of the body, he bellowed a defiant no to much of contemporary life. He snarled at the notion that modern life was "civilized." With most folklorists of his time, he held the conventional view that the old folk songs and folktales—at least in their English-language versions—were near extinction because of the pace of change in the twentieth century. The mass media were partly to blame. Folk songs and folktales that had been transmitted orally and in print for centuries were now being commercialized, marketed, and "kitsch-ified" by the publishing and recording industries that sold them back to the people who created them in the first place. But Legman never stopped suspecting and hoping that there was something realer, truer, behind the surfaces of mass culture.

At the same time, and with reasonable inconsistency, Legman acknowledged that folklore, and especially erotic folklore, was not really withering in the face of modern life. It was adapting. For at least sixty years, he was an active participant in the world of limerick rhymers, obscene graffito writers, and singers of bawdy songs, and he had collected enough dirty jokes to realize that although the shapes of jokes changed, people had not stopped telling them. He had listened to enough children playing the dozens to know that even the most determined school principal could not eradicate obscenity on the playground. Late in life he developed an enthusiasm for the photocopy machine, recognizing it as a popular means of circulating old insults and new workplace grievances. He used photocopies this way himself—to attack fads among folklorists.[11]

The difficulty of seeing Gershon Legman today shows how hard it is to imagine the self-taught, unauthorized intellectual. Uncovering his career and his extrusion from American letters lets us wonder about how much room there is now for nonconformist intellectual work. In the twenty-first century, most scholars work in the enormous bureaucracies of universities or the plush offices of corporately funded think tanks. These environments are designed to keep out cranky, prophetic remnants, not support them. They tame humanist thought, and even hope to quantify it, in what Legman would see as a new kind of censorship. But in Legman's early days, at least, one could be an influential thinker without the safety of a university academic job or the padding of a grant. A writer did not need a master's degree to produce a regular magazine column, to be heard.

Legman belongs to a small group of writers of his generation, mostly men, who found an independent intellectual life possible and desirable; he belongs to an even smaller group of visionaries and collectors of the cultural strange who made such a life without patronage or inheritance and who paid accordingly. Among Legman's fellows in this cohort were Harry Smith, the experimental filmmaker and folk music collector, and Hamish Henderson, the radical Scottish poet and folklorist. Again, there was Vance Randolph, the writer who spent his adult life collecting Ozark stories and songs, independent of the academic world. Like Legman, these scholars counted the benefits and the material and psychic costs of being outsiders, even while they generated remarkable collections of traditional arts.

It is not that Legman would not have welcomed success. While he enjoyed recognition and needed any money his publications could bring, he had little desire to be popular. Certainly, he sold books, and by the late 1960s he had a small circle of devoted coworkers and a crew of enthusiastic fans, but he deplored commercially salable subjects. It would gall him, but perhaps the best evidence of the popularity he achieved without advertising or marketing is the frequency with which publishers pirated his books and pocketed his royalties. He felt, not without some justification, that other writers stole his ideas. While shockingly unfair, the piracy, plagiarism, and recycling of his writings helped Legman's ideas filter into the culture at large.

The account that follows is not a biography in the traditional sense. I have tried to construct a writer's life in slices, looking at the major pieces of Legman's work on folklore and sex. Presenting Legman's writings against the discoverable events of his life, and in the spirit of his times, I have tried to de-isolate him, considering what he was doing as he wrote and reconnecting him to the world events and shifting cultural winds he was gauging as he worked. Intellectual friendships, love affairs, and personal tribulations—there were always plenty of these—are here, too. But my focus remains on what he thought he was doing with folklore and why. In some ways, this question must be answered from his published works, although the letters he wrote for hours every day are also important. My reading history into Legman's work and his work into history is sometimes an oblique process. Again, he is hard to see, in part because our world is centered so differently from his. There is some guesswork here about events and their meaning for Legman here, but not wild guesses.

I should note that Legman's opus was so big that I have not been able to address all of it. I have had very little to say about his contributions to paper folding and his role in introducing the Japanese folk art of origami to Europe and America. His work is considered important by paper-folding experts, but I have left it to them to examine and interpret. I have not had the space to account for his many friendships with people interested in magic and puzzles, including prominent Americans like mathematician Martin Gardner. I have not examined in detail his work on the Knights Templar or on Shakespeare. Nor have I taken up his attacks on L. Ron Hubbard and Dianetics (the Church of Scientology) or his polemical essays on cybernetics and computerization. I have not looked at his unpublished attempts at novels or tracked down all the works he ghostwrote for others. But many of these topics connect back to the oral traditions he spent so much time on, and they can bear some serious study by others.

The reader will probably want to know if I ever met G. Legman. I had chances, and our paths nearly crossed several times, but I never encountered him. I think I can say, while meaning no disrespect, that this was probably a good thing.

1
THE STRANGER

Isn't it a terrible thing to grow up in the shadow of another person's sorrow?

—Grace Paley, "The Immigrant Story," in *Enormous Changes at the Last Minute: Stories* (1974)

Gershon Legman's parents were immigrants, part of the mass migration of poor Jews from Eastern Europe to the United States in the early twentieth century. His mother and father came to the United States from small towns, as Legman recounted, "in the Carpathian Mountains of Transylvania," on the shifting border "between Romania and Hungary."[1]

Emil Mendel Legman was from Retteag, Hungary, now Cluj, Romania, near the city of Dej. According to Gershon's genealogical research, the Legman ancestors had been in Hungary from at least the late sixteenth century, but the name Legman is Jewish, not Hungarian, he points out, and this indicates that his forebears probably migrated east from Germany. Gershon wrote that his grandfather Yomtov Legman was a butcher from a long line of butchers, who were also horse traders "selling to the various landowners and small nobility" for centuries. As will become clear, Gershon had reason to tell people his father had been a butcher, but Emil failed in his ambition to be a kosher butcher.[2]

Emil told different versions of his immigration story. As the account came down in the family, he landed at Ellis Island in New York in 1907 and like so many greenhorns was immediately hustled out of all his money by immigrant swindlers protected by the Tammany machine. His last resort was a Jewish immigrant aid society that pinned a ticket to his jacket and put him on a train to Scranton, Pennsylvania, near the booming coalfields and factories. A friend of his family gave him work in a butcher shop, and in Scranton he settled and stayed.[3]

In another version of events given to a Scranton newspaper, Emil said he worked in New York for a year after arriving, painting the Brooklyn Bridge. Then he was recruited to teach at a new heder, a Hebrew elementary school, in Scranton. The new immigrant Jews from Eastern Europe tended to be Orthodox and more devout than earlier generations from Germany, and they were busy designing religious education for their children.[4]

Gershon's mother, Yolande Friedman (called Julia), was from "another little town of the Transylvania, Mono, near Debrecen," although she did not meet Emil until she got to Scranton.[5] The Friedmans were more affluent and more secular than the Yomtov Legmans. Julia and her sisters were sent to

Julia Friedman at the time of her arrival in America from Romania, about 1910. Courtesy of the Legman Archive.

school, possibly even to high school, unusual for Orthodox girls. The family maids would sometimes smuggle books to Julia and her sisters, perhaps the novels of Balzac and Zola and other suggestive contraband materials.[6] Julia was rebellious from the beginning. Family tradition had it that she refused an arranged marriage and that she found the Orthodox injunction to cut her beautiful, dark hair unbearable. She engineered an escape from Mono to France, slipping out of the betrothal during a visit with her aunt and uncle. All three moved to Scranton in 1908, where Julia's *tante* (aunt) and uncle Phillips (or Fulops) started "a candy store in the north part of town, called Green Ridge."[7] A photograph of Julia, likely before her marriage, shows her fully corseted and elegantly dressed in a wool traveling outfit.

Julia and Emil Legman on their wedding day, Scranton, Pennsylvania, 1910. Courtesy of the Legman Archive.

Emil and Julia "met first at a party at the synagogue in Scranton, in a depressed part of town . . . known as The Flats," where no one would live but the poor and newly arrived. The couple married in 1910, and Julia "was pregnant with her first baby, a girl [Ruth], before she dared to inform her parents back in Romania what she had done."[8] The wedding photograph shows a tall and beautiful Julia, her magnificent hair swept up in a pompadour, wearing a handmade lace dress. Emil is seated in a black morning coat, a white cravat, white gloves, a beaver hat, and a lily-of-the-valley boutonniere. The couple is clearly becoming American: Emil's hair is cropped, and he is sporting a carefully trimmed mustache on a prominent upper lip. They may have been struggling, but they did not have to look poor for their marriage day.

Scranton was the most important city in America's anthracite coal belt, and Emil and Julia had arrived in one of its boom times. In the years between about 1900 and the stock market crash that caused the Great Depression, Scranton was one of the fastest-growing cities in the United States. From a coal-mining and iron-smelting town, it expanded into an important northeastern railroad hub and quickly transformed into a moderate-size "electrical" industrial and commercial city. Well-located Scranton fed coal to the furnaces and steel mills of Allentown, Easton, and Bethlehem, and its railroad shops and textile mills tied the region to the larger industrial expansion of New York, northern New Jersey, and Philadelphia. There was a diversity of industry: garment making, harness making, silk factories, a correspondence-course empire, and the Woolworth's dry-goods chain were nestled in the hills around the Lackawanna River.[9] Enormous wealth was on display in Scranton's commercial and residential neighborhoods, and the city's elite built an elegant railroad station, imposing hotels, a board of trade, hospitals, asylums, schools, and libraries. But it was also a laboring city, heavily dependent on its poor immigrant working class.

Until the close of immigration in 1918, Scranton's poor neighborhoods filled with men and women from southern and Eastern Europe, all looking for work. In 1927 about 20 percent of the 250,000 people in the metropolitan area were foreign born; another 40 percent were the American children of recent immigrants. A contemporary geographer noted that in neighborhoods like the Flats and the mine patches, "where foreign families predominate, English is seldom heard, unsanitary living conditions prevail, houses are painfully primitive." Jewish immigrants were among these "poorest of the poor," working as miners and factory hands but also as peddlers and street vendors.[10]

Like many of their fellows, Julia and Emil Legman relied on relatives and institutions to help them start their family life.[11] In 1901 Scranton had at least six Orthodox synagogues whose members differed from each other "to a degree in socio-economic status and religiosity, but mostly according to language and country of origin."[12] In the 1920s, four more synagogues were built. The city's ethnic service industries were thriving: Jewish shopkeepers tended to serve their countrymen and coreligionists, but they also created a niche for themselves supplying the Christian immigrants who worked in mines and factories.[13] There were "kosher butchers, bakers, and places to eat," Jewish bookstores, and a parallel charitable structure of orphanages and poor people's and old folks' homes. For the education of young children, there were *hadarim* (Hebrew religious schools) "resembling those of Eastern Europe."[14] As in Europe's small towns, these schools were cramped and chaotic and had few trained teachers.

Emil and Julia Legman were relatively advantaged newcomers. As Austro-Hungarian Jews, they were in the minority among immigrants, but both were literate. Both the Legman and the Friedman families had registered the effects of the emancipation and Jewish enlightenment.[15] On arriving in the United States, Emil could read Hungarian, German, Yiddish, and Hebrew, and he quickly learned to write and read English. Julia certainly read a great deal, too: Gershon remembered that she always had a library book at hand and that she preferred long Russian novels.[16] Emil's own education had been intense—Hebrew and Torah study at heder from early in the morning, then Hungarian secular school (and later high school), followed by more Torah school until near midnight. He claimed to have been a student of the Bible from age four, which was neither impossible nor unlikely for a young Orthodox man of his generation.[17] In 1910 and 1920, federal census takers recorded that the Scranton Legmans spoke Magyar (Hungarian) at home. They did not speak a word of Yiddish, although in immigrant Scranton that would have been the lingua franca for most Jews. Their children grew up speaking English, the language of the public schools and the secular world.

For a few years, the newly married couple remained in Emil's lodgings on Washington Avenue, across the street from "Ahavas Achim," the Hungarian-Jewish temple and its Talmud-Torah, the Southside Hebrew School.[18] In 1910 they shared lodgings with Isaac Friedman, a "laborer," probably Julia's cousin.[19]

Emil fiercely wanted to be a rabbi and a scholar, the highest position of honor and prestige in an Orthodox community. But under the circumstances of an incomplete religious education, the disruption of emigration, and with a new family to support, the best he could do was to be a heder teacher. The schools were informally organized and conducted in the teachers' rooms, where the young boys learned the prayers and texts they would need to be observant Jews. Emil had loved his own Torah school training and throughout his life devoted himself to intense word-by-word, syllable-by-syllable study. But he was temperamentally ill-suited to teaching. According to Gershon,

Emil lost his first teaching job for "excessive disciplinarianism." He kept "a whole class of little kids for six hours in the evening, because they had been noisy," and panicked their parents.[20] But in Emil's version, he was forced to look for a better job because of Julia's aspirations for respectability: she did not want him to be just "a teacher from The Flats."[21]

After failing as a teacher, Emil found plenty of work in Scranton, at least at first. World War I set off a boom in industrial production, and soon Emil was clerking at the Delaware, Lackawanna, and Western Rail Road and studying accounting at an English-language night school. He never finished the degree. In an interview given near the end of his life, Emil described himself as employed in respectable jobs, but said he never made a decent wage in his life. At one point, he and Julia had a small nonkosher meat market in the poor Dunmore district, but the business did not last long. He told one interviewer he clerked for the railroad until he lost his job after the crash. Actually, Emil's work was even less steady than this. City directories show him employed at an overall factory, working off and on as a meat cutter at various markets, and indeed clerking for the railroad.[22] In 1930 he was a timekeeper for a public works construction project.[23] In the worst years, he went house to house buying small amounts of gold for resale. And for several months, he worked unpaid in a freight rating office, hoping the company would decide he deserved a wage.[24]

Moving back and forth between clerical and manual labor, Emil strove to support his wife and growing family. Matilda followed Ruth in 1913, and another daughter died soon after birth. In 1917 the Legmans bought a modest but solid two-story brick house at 737 Harrison Avenue, a move up the hill, out of the flood-prone Flats, and into a multiethnic neighborhood. George Alexander, always called Gershon Eliezer, was born there in the front parlor, on November 2, 1917.[25] Daisy, the last child, was born in 1920.

The house on Harrison Avenue was an important family center and resource. Julia kept poultry and grew all the vegetables in a large backyard garden, which Gershon remembered digging up for her every spring. She was an excellent cook, known for her Hungarian pastries and for her ability to turn one chicken into two dinners for the family of six. Most of Julia's energy was devoted to raising the children, and she picked up extra money as a seamstress and embroiderer. She made everyone's clothes, and Gershon remembered they were always beautifully dressed in well-pressed, hand-sewn garments. When Emil was at work, he worked, but most of his energy went into prayer and activities at the temple. The children could walk to public school and temple, and everyone came home for lunch.[26]

Gershon remembered that they were "really a poor family trying to pretend to be middle-class."[27] The bills, the groceries, and the "muggidge" were

Julia and Emil Legman with their three oldest children (*from left*), Ruth, Gershon, and Matilda, in 1920. Courtesy of the Legman Archive.

a constant worry. Emil and Julia responded with what was, in many ways, a first-generation immigrant arrangement. The family was an economic unit, working together and using a shifting, flexible pattern of outside employment, work at home, rents, and part-time jobs for the children to survive.[28] The second floor was converted into an apartment that covered the house payment, and when the children were older, they worked after school.

With the move up the hill and both parents' efforts, the Legman family had risen to the upper edge of Scranton's working class, or the unsteady lower fringes of the middle class. Similarly, they shifted from the "Big Shul" congregation in the Flats to the new and classier Temple Israel, of which Emil was a charter member and first secretary.[29] They had migrated from an Orthodox congregation to a more consciously Americanizing, activist, and educationally adept congregation, served by a well-trained rabbi, cantor, and teachers. Temple Israel was Conservative, part of a successful movement to adapt Eastern European Jewish traditions and teachings to America.[30] One aim of the founders was to build a Hebrew school "more appropriate for a progressive community" like Scranton and replace the "very haphazard" Jewish teaching of the past. Now that the immigrants had settled, some sought "a middle ground between immigrant orthodoxy and German Reform," trying to be at once traditional and modern. They wanted to "break with what they perceived as the ways of Europe" and also keep their children from joining the Reform movement. They hoped to keep children who were tempted to leave Judaism within the fold.[31]

Temple Israel was a large, beautiful synagogue, built in a modern temple-revival style and large enough to seat a thousand in the sanctuary. It was located in a non-Jewish part of the city. In 1924 the congregation hired a new energetic rabbi, Max Arzt. A prominent activist in the Conservative movement, Rabbi Arzt would become a well-known theologian, "a scholar of Jewish liturgy," and professor at and "vice chancellor of the Jewish Theological Seminary" in New York. He made Temple Israel a center of progressive religious education in the eastern United States and "an upscale community center for the Jews of Scranton." It offered junior and teenage congregations, scout troops, and a choir. As the most important congregation in Scranton, over fifty years Temple Israel "produced a crop of rabbis . . . as well as highly committed lay people." Rabbi Arzt early recognized Gershon's prodigious scholarly talents and guided the formal part of the boy's Hebrew education. Yet there were difficulties fitting Hebrew school into the American scene. "Many children continued to rebel against added hours of school; and many of the teachers were less than skilled." As at many *hadarim*, the teachers could be sadistic toward the pupils.[32]

Emil enthusiastically supported the development of the new heder and new community services to keep the new generation (especially his only son) close to religious obligation. By everyone's account except his children's, he succeeded. At his death, he was hailed and praised for all he had done for the synagogue.[33] But Gershon had a different interpretation of the move to Temple Israel: Emil was a "Sabbath-breaker." His jobs obliged him to work Saturdays, and he sometimes even took a streetcar to work, so he was "no longer acceptable . . . to the Orthodox Jewish synagogue."[34] The family's striving and its precarious position had made it impossible to remain with the old faith, at least in formal synagogue membership.

Gershon remembered clearly how his early family life defined his intellectual interests and personality. He adored Julia and was close to her. At best he was oppressed by Emil, at worst threatened by him. In Gershon's account, Julia was a wonderful mother, warmly devoted to her children, with a sweet temperament that nearly compensated for Emil's domineering. While Emil thought Gershon could do nothing well enough, in Julia's eyes everything her son did was wonderful. She was tolerant and sympathetic to him in ways that were bolstering, comforting, and redeeming to him throughout her life. In his memoir, he recalls (or imagines) his first year with his mother, some weeks of it spent alone with her in quarantine during the "Spanish flu" epidemic of 1918. He floated, delirious, on a tide of her breast milk—while Emil was locked out and sleeping at the Elks Club.[35]

The Legman family seems to have been founded on a psychic split between accepting love and domineering hostility. This in some ways paralleled a typical Jewish immigrant pattern: the father's important life was at the temple and at work, and the mother's temple and workplace was the home. Perhaps the emotional pattern had a generational dimension as well as a specifically personal one. Emil seems like a negative version of the novelist Philip Roth's beloved father, Herman, whose death Roth described in *Patrimony: A True Story*. Roth writes that his father was "peremptory," obsessively stubborn, "overbearing," "anxious," and "bossy." His admonitory style was cruel, and he could, he would have insisted, "lead a horse to water *and* make it drink." But what others called "hocking" (from the Yiddish for "nagging"), Herman Roth called caring. Bessie Roth was a kind of opposite of her husband; father and son viewed her as the epitome of "modesty, humility, loyalty, efficiency, dependability," and for her children, she was "adroit" in a "nurturing domesticity."[36] For decades, she ran her efficient household entirely separately from Herman. The stark difference between Roth's family and Legman's was that Herman Roth was a mostly successful businessman, while Emil Legman struggled to stay employed. It wasn't just the disaster of the Depression, although that was bad enough. Julia's island of love and warmth was perpetually undermined by Emil's eccentricities and perversities.

The parents' different temperaments meant the children walked a treacherous line. The Legmans did not believe in physical punishment for the children, and Gershon recalled that when she was angry or exasperated, his mother would chase the kids around waving a wooden spoon. It was understood that she would never catch them. She would talk with them sympathetically about their questions and troubles. But any defiance of Emil's edicts, or even his opinions about anything, but especially about religious matters, would result in a kind of verbal and psychological punishment that was, without qualification, abusive.

The harsh discipline and nitpicking scholasticism that got Emil fired from the heder in the Flats was an expression of something basic, beyond his obsession with religious study. He needed to control and dominate others—but he lacked the sound judgment that might have led this authoritarian streak in a more benign direction. No matter how many times things went wrong, and they always did, he had an odd sense of entitlement to his own correctness. He was right, he was totally and compulsively right, and he nagged and berated his children, brooking no opposition. On top of this, he was a compulsive liar. Julia was usually indifferent to Emil's rantings and religious strictures. She would light the Sabbath candles and follow the halakha (religious law) formalities for a household—no cooking or housework or even electric light on the Sabbath. She kept a kosher kitchen. But Julia was not devout or even particularly interested. Her husband's obsessions must have been hard on her.

It would be an understatement to say that Emil Legman was troubled, and so Gershon's relationship with him was troubled also. There are hints in family folklore that Emil brought his craziness with him to the United States, but it is also possible that the stress of life in a new country affected him in ways that made his perversities much worse. Emil did not leave a testimony on this subject, and we have only his son's version.

Gershon writes that shortly after the time of his birth in 1917, his father became a compulsive gambler, given to violent and irrational outbursts. He may have experienced psychotic breaks. When Emil's compulsive gambling flared, it threatened to destroy the household. In Gershon's memoir, his first recollection of his father is of Emil in a delusional state, threatening to slit his children's throats with a piece of a broken milk bottle.[37] Only Julia's screaming to the neighbors saved the children, and Emil may have done a stint in jail or a sanitarium. Always, from Gershon's point of view, his family life and growing up would be punctuated by Emil's irrationality. Without a doubt, there was pressure to keep up appearances, especially at temple, to make the family seem solid and happy, but it was not.

Family redemption rested on Gershon as the only son. Scranton offered good public schooling and mobility for the second generation, but in Emil's view the road to prosperity and community respect would be through religious scholarship. Like the patriarch in Anzia Yezierska's *The Bread Givers,* Emil saw biblical study as his first calling, with wage earning a distant second. Gershon writes that his father and mother saw his path to becoming a rabbi and a "leader in Israel" as literally predestined. In part, his future was predicted because he was born on November 2, the "worst day of the year," arriving with the establishment of "a national home for the Jewish people" in Palestine, in the Balfour Declaration. "Born on so auspicious a day for

Judaism . . . I didn't stand a chance." (He also noted his birthday fell on the Day of the Dead and marked the start of the Bolshevik Revolution.)[38]

Gershon was smart, adventurous, and curious. Childhood pictures of him show that he resembled Julia, with a full mouth, a strong straight nose, smooth skin, and large firmly browed eyes. He learned to read early and loved to read immediately. So it was inevitable that conflicts with his father emerged early, too, because as soon as Emil realized his son could read, he placed heavy responsibility upon him. In Gershon's words, "I would now have to go to Hebrew School" as well as public school "all the rest of every weekday except Friday—and well into the evening, til long past seven o'clock—and Saturday mornings, too. . . . This was one of the special advantages of belonging to God's chosen people."[39]

Gershon was more than a capable student, just suited for the sort of biblical and Talmudic drilling (in Hebrew, Yiddish, and German) that Emil had endured and apparently even enjoyed. After American school let out, Gershon went to Hebrew school at Temple Israel—where he was taught the Bible and interpretation by the up-and-coming Hebrew teacher Mr. Wolf. At Hebrew school, Gershon was studying the Old Testament, "the rudiments of Hebrew grammar," and the kaddish, the mourner's prayer—"You never knew when the family might need it." The Old Testament they "read aloud in original Hebrew and [English] translation."[40] Then he went home for a third after-supper session, to be drilled by his father on the Hebrew school lessons, but with improvements or expansions of the teaching following Emil's own theories.

Gershon did not just have to go to Hebrew school. "I got a lot of extra training and glossing from my father." He could "teach me plenty of extra stuff they didn't even *know about* in American Hebrew School." Emil was the sort that would make the boy parse the Hebrew translation into English (which he didn't approve of) and compare it with the Aramaic, and then he would correct it. "What this meant was that there was one translation of God's unchangeable Word that I had to supply on demand" in Hebrew school and "quite another" translation to provide at home. Gershon remembered, "Nothing I ever learned in any school—Hebrew or English—was ever good enough for my father." After several hours of this, Gershon would do his public school homework and "topple into bed."[41]

The promise that Gershon would be "a leader in Israel" had "dominated" his "whole childhood and adolescence in a particularly crushing way." And as a child, he accepted this. Looking back, he thought, "The worst of it was that I agreed *completely* and was totally brainwashed on the subject. I worked, prayed, and studied like a maniac," in the ways prescribed by Moses Maimonides in the twelfth century.[42] He felt he had been robbed of his childhood, given no time to play or be a child. He would always see children as a particularly victimized social group, as "the little shut-up people."[43] And worse, "I have visibly borne the marks of this early training all my life," he admitted.[44]

But most problematic were the hypocrisies of the fundamentalist, absolutist religious teachings he endured. Emil and the Hebrew-school teachers were steeped in the commentaries on the sacred texts and practiced in interpretation of the commentaries. But when Gershon asked his own basic cosmological questions that boiled down to "Why?" the answer was always "Shut up!" Eventually, he would see his questioning as "inspired by the atrociously ridiculous and mendacious bullshit" he was asked to accept as religion, "especially in the primitive fantasies of the Bible."[45] But in the present of his childhood, it was painful and bewildering.

He had special difficulty, he wrote, with the frightening story of "the unachieved sacrifice of Isaac" (Gen. 22: 1–19). Was God "rewarding Abraham because he *didn't* sacrifice Isaac, which would have seemed more logical to me, or because he tried to, which I had a suspicion was the real idea. And I was right." Emil explained that the covenant with Israel was "because Abraham was willing to kill [Isaac] with a big knife in the first place. . . . And my father reread me and translated the Hebrew text, word by word." When Gershon wondered "what the whole idea of sacrifices and burnt offerings" was, and was God "going to *eat* Isaac?" he was told he "deserved a *slap* for such an impertinent question."[46]

Public school might have been a respite from Emil, but there were two problems. Gershon was one of only a few Jewish boys in his elementary school, and his intelligence stood out. There were teachers who hated and were suspicious of him because he was so bright and Gentile students who resented the Jewish kid as the teacher's pet. (There was one Jewish teacher, though, whose eyes shone when Gershon defended himself to a school assembly by reciting Shylock's speech from *The Merchant of Venice*.) It was a horrible thing, he later wrote, to be the smartest child in class. He sat in front, and the teachers either singled him out for special privileges or tormented him out of "love-hate" ambivalence. If it was important to be a good student, why did everyone hate him for it? When the Protestant and Catholic kids bullied him, he plotted revenge on his tormentors and one day brought his "Daisy" air rifle to school to defend himself. Gershon was suspended, and Emil confiscated the rifle and broke it over his knee. Later, a gang of his classmates pushed him down on the pavement and wrote "Kosher" in "horse-shit juice" on his forehead.[47] He won prizes and awards in elementary school, but when he scored among the very highest in a nationwide IQ test he was suspected of cheating.[48]

Gershon was in a difficult position as he came of age. As he began to feel his own stirrings of autonomy, things went badly wrong between the young

The Stranger 23

man and his father.[49] Gershon needed to identify with his father—but Emil had threatened to kill his own son. He had no other close male relatives from whom he might have drawn support. The manliness Gershon could absorb from his father took the form of a passion for the hard work of scholarship and textual study. But the uses to which he would later put these skills would be opposed to everything Emil held dear.

YESHIVA

At age twelve, in 1930, Gershon was sent to a rabbinical seminary, the Yeshiva Rabbi Jacob-Joseph, on Henry Street on New York's Lower East Side. It was the first of twelve planned years of intense study for which Rabbi Arzt had found him a $10,000 scholarship. He boarded in a house on lower Broadway and was supposed to go, on the Sabbath eve, to spend Saturdays with a relative in Brooklyn. At first Gershon was ferociously committed to his ideal of being "a perfect rabbi." But the curriculum was grueling, the principal beat the students, and he was bullied by the other boys.

Gershon and Emil traded letters discussing ideas, behavior, and goals, and a few letters survive from early 1931. In one he writes and diagrams his commitment: "This disciplining my soldiers will be an important part in my militant campaign against the bad habits." On the first page of this letter is a Star of David, with a circle around it, and the label "GOAL." In the center of the star is a crown labeled "not a pincushion" but the "crown of Jewish knowledge" in Hebrew. A later annotation by Legman says, "Bear in mind that I wrote this in the library while skipping school."[50]

Below the star, he writes to Emil, "I desire to be able to say two things on my death bed. One—I have reached my goal. Two—. . .—I have lived a good life and I have reached my chosen goal. I.e. I have become a perfect (in so far as is humanly possible) Rabbi."[51] Below this statement is a remarkable drawing of something like an exploded layer cake: the ten layers outline "my battlefield" with "*my forces*" arrayed on the left and the "*enemy forces*" on the right, including "the scuttlefish . . ., the atheists who muddy the water of the pure belief of good Jews like me." The oppositions continue down the page: "High school" versus "movies," "Obligations for scholarship" versus "what's the use," "optimism" versus "cussedness." In his battle for scholarship, he would instruct his men to "Fix bayonets! Charge!!!"

Clearly, thirteen-year-old Gershon was facing his own resistance to Emil's goals for him. He was confronting distractions all around him in New York City. In a description of this year in New York, he remembered that "the curriculum was so hard and hours so desperately long (from seven in the morning 'till nine at night, to cover both Rabbinical and secular studies, as

24 CHAPTER 1

required) that there was only one day, given us kids off each week—Saturday." When he was supposed to be in Brooklyn, he pretended to study in his room but stole "a whole glorious day of sinfully wandering around New York City each Saturday," sleeping rough on "bridges over the East River Friday night," especially the Brooklyn Bridge.[52]

These were the worst years of the Depression, and many homeless men gathered under the bridges at night. "More than a few of these would exploit sexually the boys and road-kids" sleeping out. The "homosexual demands and offers" upset him. He recalled, "I would run from one edge of the bridge to another to escape from the leering whispering men who approached me."[53]

Perhaps most distracting of all, he wrote to Emil at the time, were the "enemies which you counted that I did not," the "salacious writings" of the scuttle-fish. Emil had warned him against the secular publications and free-thought literature he would find in the city. Lower Manhattan was full of newsstands, candy stores, past-date magazine stores, and secondhand bookstores, which sold everything from erotic postcards and contraceptives to cheap copies of banned books. Gershon's letters give a glimpse into his other activities and the kinds of places he was haunting. He averred, "I do not consider that [reading to be] an enemy. Balzac, Maupassant, Boccaccio [sic], Daudet, Zola, Rabelais, etc. are not favorite authors of mine. There are books on the list Rabbi Artz gave me that are much more interesting than *The Decameron*, *Bad Girl*, or *True Story*. . . . Friday afternoon, time to go to Brooklyn."[54] In fact, exactly the opposite was true—all these authors were becoming fast favorites, and Gershon was not headed to Brooklyn. Emil wrote back demanding to know how his son knew so *much* about the "salacious literature" he was supposedly ignoring. Gershon had found the public library.

In late October, Gershon returned home for his bar mitzvah before the congregation. He did a more than creditable job but could not feel it was his own. Emil had insisted on writing Gershon's special speech (Dvar Torah) for him, taking away from the young man his first public intellectual accomplishment. In a photograph from that day, Emil Legman stands proudly next to his son, who is wearing knee pants, a yarmulke, and a prayer shawl. A close look at the photo card shows that with a pin or a pen, someone has punctured Emil's pupils and scratched out his mouth.

When he was back on Henry Street, things did not go well. Yeshivas were notoriously harsh and grim, and the teachers relied upon corporal punishment.[55] By May 1931, the principal had lodged a serious complaint about Gershon, and Emil had to travel to New York to straighten it out. Gershon had gotten into a fight with some other students who kept ruining the good felt hat that, following Orthodox custom, his teacher had declared he must wear in the street. If he wore his hat in yeshiva, the other boys would crush

The Stranger

Gershon and Emil at his bar mitzvah, Scranton, 1930. Courtesy of the Legman Archive.

it. He tried having the rabbi lock the hat in a closet, but two boys waited until the closet was opened and smashed his hat again. When he told the teacher, he, not the hat crusher, was punished.[56]

One day finding his hat smashed into "a solid mass of felt" while his antagonist laughed, Gershon lost his temper and threw the closet key at him, "hitting him on his neck." "Old Bow Wow" Abrahams exploded, called Gershon a murderer, and dealt Gershon a heavy whack with a ruler, cutting his hand.

The physical brutality of the yeshiva pushed Gershon's adolescent rebellion over the edge, and he went absent without leave. He continued to attend the attached English high school, because he loved his literature classes. He was ignoring the Sabbath, stealing from the landlady and his cousins, and sleeping on subway trains. In the bookstores on Fourth Avenue below Fourteenth Street and the public libraries, Gershon was learning that the freedoms of the city were intellectual, too. He was reading unsanctioned literature like Colonel Robert Ingersoll's *Mistakes of Moses* and "Mr. Heywood Broun's" excellent free-thought column.[57] He had become his own scuttlefish.[58] The scholarly task and Emil's expectations were impossible to meet in the face of these temptations.

Later, Gershon wrote that "Dad had to come to New York to plead with the principal not to send me home."[59] But things got worse when Emil found that Gershon had "skipped school for almost a whole month—spring fever—that I had spent all my money from the bank that month—and when it was all gone I had stolen $5 from the woman I boarded with and gone to the circus. After begging Old Bow Wow not to bounce me—learning all this nearly killed him."[60] Because he had violated the "obligations of the scholarship" arranged by Rabbi Artz, Gershon left yeshiva and was brought home in disgrace. He had lied to his parents, but as usual between father and son, there was another version of the story.

For public consumption at the temple, the story was that Gershon had ruined his own chances by skipping school. The reality was that Emil's gambling addiction had taken hold again. Foolishly, Rabbi Arzt had entrusted Emil with the whole scholarship, and, trying to double it, Emil gambled it all away at cards.[61] What Rabbi Arzt thought about this is not recorded. If the money had been there, perhaps Gershon might have been readmitted for the fall. But it stung to have failed out of yeshiva, and no one was angrier at Gershon than himself.

Looking back, he remembered feeling humiliated that he could not attain what he later saw as a life "of pietistic nonsense under the sexual, economic, and intellectual pressures of the 20th century." But Emil placed no such demands on himself because his entire plan was for Gershon "to live up to, not him." What infuriated the boy most was the hypocrisy: he had to take the blame for something his father could not own up to. Emil's compulsion, not Gershon's rebellion, disgraced the family, but this could never be admitted publicly.

HIGH SCHOOL

Once the weight of rabbinical study was lifted and the scandal calmed down, Gershon was freer to enjoy school life, and it seems as if he did. In the fall of 1931, he enrolled in Scranton's Central High School in the academic track, not the technical program his sisters attended. He remembered spending most of his time in the elegant Albright Memorial Library across the street, reading ceaselessly. Gershon did not have much good to say about his teachers: he sought their advice and support but did not find much. He remembered an elderly Latin teacher who was sympathetic—she told him from her reading of the classics that the world would break his heart. But his classmates were more interesting. Some high school friends would stay in touch for decades.

There was brilliant and rebellious Jane Butzner who, as Jane Jacobs, author of *The Life and Death of Great American Cities*, led a crusade to save Greenwich Village.[62] Joe Bernstein would go on to become an international journalist, later changing his name to "Joseph Amber Barry" and working for Time-Life. Cyril "Cy" Endfield, the son of a well-off furrier, later became a magician and film director; Gershon credited Cy with introducing him to paper folding and magic tricks.[63] Bob Sewall would become a New York journalist and collaborate with Gershon on erotica projects.[64]

In the spirit of the early 1930s, all the young men were interested in socialism. Gershon looked back on his emerging political orientation as very much a part of the scene of the industrial working-class city. He and some friends read Edward Bellamy's influential novel of future socialism, *Looking Backward, 2000–1887* (1888). Impressed, he shared Bellamy's teachings with his sister Ruth and then Emil, who absorbed them with his usual obsessiveness. The next thing Gershon and Ruth knew, their father was trying to "Bellamize" the railroad office, preaching socialism to the other clerks. Emil was summarily fired for radicalism, but he wasn't a socialist. Really, he was just being Emil, sure that everyone needed to hear from him, endlessly.[65]

By 1933 Gershon and his two best friends, Manny Grossman and Mel Cantor, had become committed leftists. They were, in Gershon's words, "the mainstays and almost the total membership of the kid communist faction" at Central High. "You said 'socialism' when you talked to grownups so as not to scare them. But we knew that what we believed in was Communism, and the Noble Experiment in Human Equality" unfolding in Russia. Manny, Mel, and Gershon had come to their "new Marxist beliefs entirely separately" through direct experience. The crash of 1929 "had practically dismantled the economy in both Europe and America," and their reaction was emotional, a "gut-thing," as they saw what happened to their families in the early years of the Depression.[66]

Manny Grossman's father was "a machine-shop steward and prime mover in the local Communist Party," and Manny and Gershon "were thick as inkle weavers there for a while and always deep in heated discussions of Russian Revolutionary tactics and history." Manny aspired to be a journalist on party papers. Gershon figured his own talents were mainly rhetorical and spent time

28   CHAPTER 1

copying out passages from revolutionary denunciation and oratory, especially *Left-Wing Communism, an Infantile Disorder*, by Lenin. As for Marx's *Capital*, he found the "sledding was too tough," so "I took it on faith."[67] As he saw the situation in 1932, "Everyone was flirting with Communism then. Even the very rich. But, of course, they weren't sincere. We were sincere. They were just scared."[68] Everyone was just "waiting to see which way the cat would jump." "The bigger millionaires" were hedging their bets with Hitler, he reflected, and their real idea was to get Hitler to annihilate Russia.

This was Gershon's analysis at the time, and not an inaccurate one. "The millionaires panicked knowing if everyone was unemployed, the entire system would collapse." And he remembered thinking the New Deal was part of the stabilization project: it was "a lot of fake optimistic hoorahing" and "worlds away" from real socialism. Even so, the real millionaires "hated it and they hated Roosevelt, too." Of course, Roosevelt was a straight upper-class man descended from a slave trader, perhaps, but the public loved him and his "Hahvahd accent." The New Deal, Gershon and his buddies thought, was just "priming the pump for monopoly capitalism" until the next war started.[69]

He reached an important understanding of the international economy very early: "The wars were geared to come every twenty years." "*Had* to." War spending was central to the way the world worked, and mass death was humanity's destination. "The new batch" of cannon fodder, Gershon and his friends suddenly saw, "was *us*." Antimilitarism was a practical necessity. Since "we were slated to die soon in puddles of our own guts," "we should do our damndest to prevent the coming war," whether that was in Manchuria, Spain, or Ethiopia. "By then most of us had woken up, of course, and had become solidly anti-fascist." Gershon and his friends were fiercely anti-Nazi and pro-Republican Spain, with strong leanings toward pacifism. Manny, Mel, and Gershon knew antiwar sentiments would get them in trouble at school, but they handed out antiwar leaflets in the hallways anyway and were suspended. This firmed Gershon's opinion that war was the only way for capitalism "to save its hide," and, inevitably, "our job was to die in it." As he reflected in the eighties, the logic of global antagonism remained the same. Now, "only the slogans and the enemy have changed."[70]

Gershon used to hang out with other "sincere young Socialist kids" at "Joey Wallach's house on Linden St. in the poor part of town." Here he encountered another doubting scuttlefish. Joey's father, a tailor, sewed dress suits in the old-fashioned way, "sitting cross-legged on a big padded kitchen table." Mr. Wallach "took a very dim view indeed of the [Soviet] Revolution" and "used to razz us," arguing revolutionary and postrevolutionary history with Gershon, "pooh-poohing all of our radical ideas." His main question was "Is it good for the Jews?" and his view was "I'm a Jew and you're a Jew and nobody is ever going to let us be anything else."[71] Gershon hated the tailor for his antirevolutionary politics, but over time he adopted Mr. Wallach's view on being a Jew. What was hard about being Jewish was dealing with the goyim.

As a high school student, he continued to be brilliant, and he read everything that crossed his path, including the dictionary for at least a half hour every night except Friday. He loved literature and wrote poetry "so bad it should have been in a cage." When the literary club adviser told Gershon he would do "more harm than good" to the high school magazine *Impressions*, he stalked off and produced *Suppressions*, a "four pager" parody version. *Suppressions* was run off at union offices; it was "smeary and stinking of stencil ink on yellow monograph paper."[72] It included pleas for free lunches for students by Mel, because they'd been told by a party organizer they "*had to have grievances!*" The cover featured a badly drawn portrait of Gershon, "a boy's face with a gag over his mouth." This got him kicked out of school again. His remaining years in Scranton were all like this. He was too smart to be docile, too cantankerous not to question, too angry at being bullied to cower. He loved being expelled because he could luxuriate in the library reading whatever he wanted. The upper mezzanine of the public library, it turned out, was a good place to dally with girls.

Another good hangout and meeting place was Stück's secondhand bookshop and magazine store. It had shelves to duck behind and a woodstove. One of his mother's uncles, Joel Friedman, was a washed-up radio comedian who minded the store and kept Gershon and his girlfriends entertained with his Low German dialect act. Stück's did not carry books of much interest to Gershon, and most kids came there to trade in stamps, but it was a good place to kiss and listen to jokes.[73]

SEX COLLECTOR

Gershon wrote that he had always been fascinated by sex, and he had been girl-crazy and sexually precocious before puberty.[74] As he remembered his adolescence, reading erotic literature and trying to make love to his girlfriends were the two major poles of his existence. The terrain of his battles with Emil now shifted from religion to sex, as all the Legman children's love lives became a source of open conflict with their father.

Gershon complained that his father was that rare thing, a Jewish prude. He was sexually repressed and intent on repressing everyone else. While Julia took a more relaxed attitude, Emil's response to any of his children's emerging erotic interests was ferocious censorship. He monitored their reading materials, controlled their language, and interfered in their romances. He was obsessed with filth and pollution and with keeping it out of his home.[75]

CHAPTER 1

From Gershon's childhood, Emil had needed to know the title of every book he touched, and he would burst into the boy's bedroom at night to see what he was reading under the covers. He seized and disposed of Gershon's "dirty" Robert Louis Stevenson adventures. (There was no respite from this: a public librarian refused to let Gershon sign out a copy of *The Sheik*, a torrid lady's romance, because it was a "bad book." If it was a bad book, Gershon wondered, what was it doing in a library?)[76]

Nothing that dealt with the body could be allowed in the house, not even mildly suggestive romance novels. Emil was always on guard. He read through Dreiser's *An American Tragedy* and pronounced that "it stinks." But he seems to have been defeated by his wife and daughters' passions for reading. Ruth was the family's first bibliophile, and she passed on the collecting passion to Gershon, who was reading about a book a day. Ruth had a shelf of Frank and Dick Merriwell novels, and she let Gershon read them—he found them so exciting that he ate all the corners and returned them to her in octagonal form. But now in her late teens, Ruth was rejecting boys' true adventure stories in favor of novels about prostitutes. When Ruth brought home *Susan Lennox: Her Fall and Rise*, a muckraking novel about a young woman's struggle with poverty and prostitution, Emil carried the book outside on a newspaper lest, like vermin, it contaminate him. He made a big deal about reading it outside, under a tree, all nine hundred pages. But it could not be inside his home.[77] Gershon remembered thinking this was crazy nonsense. Soon he was poring over the Gustave Doré illustrations in Ruth's copy of *Gargantua and Pantagruel*.

Ruth was collecting frankly erotic stories like Vina Delmar's best-selling *Bad Girl*, Balzac's *Droll Stories*, and Casanova's *Memoirs* and disguising them in the dust jackets of tamer books. Eventually, a secret library formed in Julia's clothes closet. Gershon remembered that visiting the hidden library underneath his mother's dresses was an erotic experience.[78]

At about this time, Gershon's folklore collecting took shape. He and Ruth were now amassing files of jokes, quips, and wisecracks. Gershon went through an intense joke-collecting and memorizing phase at age twelve: jokes were great because they were free, they made people laugh, and then people would listen to you. The jokes must have been very mild because they were clipped from the pages of the *Saturday Evening Post* and *Literary Digest*, which Ruth brought home from old Mr. Stück's bookshop. He carried a notebook everywhere and aimed to have a joke for any occasion: he was "now a menace to any conversation." But over time, Gershon's repertoire became more bawdy as he found other magazines like *College Humor*, *Captain Billy's Whiz Bang*, and the *Smokehouse Gazette*, a collection of off-color poems for men.[79] These retailed jokes dealing with sex and bodily functions, although they were still mild compared to what Gershon would dredge up in his later research. Copied and pasted into Gershon's notebook, the collection was also hidden in the back of Julia's closet where Emil would not think to look. When this collection came to light, Julia was mildly amused, but Emil was outraged by the vile corruption. Gershon does not tell us if Emil discovered his contemporaneous scrapbook of dirty postcards and nude photographs. But anything "unclean" had to be purged from his house.[80]

Yet, Gershon pondered, Emil was entirely familiar with the love, sex, blood, gore, murder, and revenge in the Bible. Gershon's own close reading of the Old Testament (with no parts left out) was an eye-opening, thrilling experience. He particularly liked the biblical bad girls Aholibah and Aholah in Ezekiel, who "doted upon their paramours, whose flesh *is as* the flesh of asses, and whose issue *is like* the issue of horses" (23:20).

And, he observed, the Song of Songs (Solomon) was still treated like erotic poetry, reserved for the men of the temple to chant on the Sabbath, preparatory to the Sabbath-night obligation to go home, be fruitful, and multiply.[81] There were two sides to the adult world—one that frankly acknowledged carnality and another that denied and condemned the urges of the body.

Even worse than Emil's literary prudery was his invasive, controlling nature. From a young age, Gershon always had girlfriends and was always looking to find the privacy for a tryst. The alleys, woods, basements, and chicken coops of Scranton offered some freedom, but soon Gershon was sneaking his girlfriends into the Harrison Street house—and getting caught. Julia treated Gershon's escapades tolerantly (though lecturing him to avoid pregnancies), but Emil's reaction was brutal. Gershon's first serious love affair with a young woman he called "Tia French" put father and son into irreconcilable conflict.[82]

When he found Gershon and Tia kissing on Julia's bed, Emil resolved that their romance was intolerable. He told Tia's parents that his fifteen-year-old son was a white slaver planning to sell their daughter into prostitution in Argentina. Tia's parents believed him and forbade the couple to see or talk to each other. Gershon never forgave Emil. And now he realized that his father was a compulsive liar and really crazy. He terrorized Ruth and Matilda, humiliating them when they came home from dates by demanding to inspect their underwear. Julia apparently did not intervene or remonstrate.[83]

Emil was a monster his children had to get away from. As a young man, Gershon was able to leave home after high school, and he rarely came back. His sisters, as women, stayed closer, although Gershon thought all three married as soon as possible to get out of the house. Ruth married first, in 1933, when Gershon was still in high school. Matilda horrified her parents and the community by becoming pregnant by her Catholic Lithuanian boyfriend, Joe

Malaken; their daughter, June, was born while Gershon was still at home. It was a double disgrace in Emil's eyes that she would have an illegitimate child with a non-Jew.[84] Daisy, the youngest, married within the faith. She ended up nursing both her parents and her disabled husband in their final years, in a superhuman, if all too common female effort.[85]

It was impossible for Gershon not to notice and make connections between his father's prudery and the hypocrisies of the larger world, and as he prepared to leave high school, he was unavoidably fascinated with what Emil could not tolerate. He saw that it was not just Emil: the larger American culture was also repressive and hypocritical about sex, and later, as he studied the history of censorship, Gershon thought it grew out of Puritanism, with plenty of help from the Catholic Church. The America of Gershon's childhood was terrified of the sin of masturbation, panicked about the sexual exploitation of women, and hypocritically punitive toward prostitutes. Public culture was repressive of women and fearful of interracial sex to the point of homicide. It viewed homosexuality as a religious sin, a moral perversion, an illness, and a crime.[86] Religious and political leaders ferociously opposed birth control and sexual health information; they determined to prevent the corruption of innocence through the enforcement of antiobscenity laws. None of this was unfamiliar to Gershon because he had learned it at his father's knee. Emil was his first censor.[87]

Gershon grew up keenly aware of censorship and sex controversies. Since the 1870s, under the Comstock Law, books, magazines, cheap print, and theater were overtly censored by an uneven and overlapping web of federal and local morals monitors. By enforcing standards of "mailability," the Department of the Post Office attempted to suppress the circulation of erotic material, birth control information, political sedition, and blasphemy. In the interest of cultural purity, the U.S. Customs inspectors kept close eyes on books and goods (often European-manufactured contraceptives) coming into the country, whether as a manufacturer's shipment or tourist souvenirs. Until the mid-1930s, the works of acclaimed modernist authors, like James Joyce and D. H. Lawrence, could be challenged and seized on any pretext, as could less artistic and cheaper erotica. The efforts of federal agencies were enhanced at the local level by surveillance groups (most famously the Society for the Suppression of Vice in New York and the Watch and Ward Society in Boston) that monitored the wares of bookstores and magazine shops and pressured major publishers to self-censor their literary offerings. While the Hollywood production code preemptively shaped what could be seen on-screen, city magistrates enforced local regulations on sexual content. As an example, Gershon noticed the ridiculous National Board of Review censorship at the movies, which allowed only the most chaste embraces to be seen.

The Stranger   **33**

This resulted in idiocies like Tom Mix, the cowboy hero, kissing his horse because he could not be shown kissing a woman.[88]

In Gershon's view, it was as if every city and town was run by a bunch of Elmer Gantries, Sinclair Lewis's personification of religious hypocrisy and political corruption. As Lincoln Steffens argued in *The Shame of the Cities*, moral corruption and political power went hand in hand. Upton Sinclair agreed. In *The Goose Step*, he described how every town's brothels were run by the city fathers and protected by the same policemen who were charged with enforcing moral codes and suppressing vice. This hypocritical repression was strengthened in immigrant areas by the Catholic Church.[89]

But at the same time, sex controversies were helping liberalize American culture. American journalists and artists, feminists and physicians, and lawyers and legislators pushed for a lifting of the repressive intellectual and sexual regime. From the 1920s onward, a broad coalition of political radicals and free-speech activists had begun to argue for a rethinking of attitudes toward sex and monogamy and toward better birth control and sexual health information for the young. The early twentieth century saw a decisive loosening up in the American discussion of sex, gender roles, and morality. Paradoxically, crusades for purity and moral reform had spurred a discussion of sexuality, gender roles, and morality.

Some of this debate was ignited by scandals in bohemia. Before the First World War, John Reed, Louise Bryant, Emma Goldman, Hutchins Hapgood, and Jack London mixed radical politics with unconventional sexual relationships and argued for rethinking marriage.[90] Lawyer Theodore Schroeder, founder of the Free Speech League, a forerunner of the American Civil Liberties Union (ACLU), argued that censorship damaged American political and intellectual life. He dedicated his life to the anticensorship cause and would become a sturdy correspondent of Gershon's. Literary critic V. F. Calverton proposed in the early 1930s that the Great War had decisively smashed an older religious moral consensus about sex and made marriage a bankrupt institution. Calverton shocked his readers by saying that this was a good thing.[91] Each effort for free thought and freer love met enormous public condemnation and legal sanction. When Gershon admitted reading Heywood Broun's column "avidly," he revealed that he joined this dissident intellectual tradition.[92]

As Gershon knew, free speechers and sex-information advocates were prosecuted and sometimes even ruined by the American censorship regime.[93] As he came of age, the American press was preoccupied with one of its successive sex controversies. In 1928 Mary Ware Dennett was indicted and tried for using the mail to circulate *The Sex Side of Life*, a basic sex-education pamphlet she had originally written for her young sons. Her case was reported around the country, and her victory on appeal in 1930, the year of Gershon's bar mitzvah, was a decisive victory against the Comstock Law.[94] In the early 1930s, Margaret Sanger's campaign for legal birth control was beginning to succeed. It was a moment of new thought and easing repression, and there was enormous demand for the small stream of medically sound sexual health information that was reaching the public.[95] Mary Dennett's campaign emphasized health, pleasure, and satisfaction in marriage; as a socialist, Margaret Sanger pressed the importance of birth control for the economic survival of poor women and their families.

It began to seem to Gershon that he might have something to say to the world about pleasure and sex. As he finished high school, Gershon dreamed of perhaps becoming a psychologist. Or a book collector or a writer. There was no respectable, Emil-approved path he could follow, nor could there ever be. As a twelve-year-old, he had been so constrained and abused that he struck out in New York for necessary freedom. Now, at the end of childhood, speaking and writing about the forbidden seemed to be the permanent and satisfying path for his own life. He would do a short stint as a birth control lecturer, combining his argumentative skills with his profound need to speak out. He even spent a night or two in jail for the American Birth Control League's cause.[96]

He had done the adolescent's job of defining himself: first, rejecting Emil, he would be for, not against, sex and love. Gershon now focused intensely on sex as a sphere of redemption, which he would approach in a scholarly way. From an early age, he tells us, he was absorbed in "a million dreamlike projects, connected with sex, sex technique, sexual folklore, its language, its literature and its immemorially practical and beautiful art."[97] He moved from the Tijuana Bibles and dirty postcards he could buy at the candy store to beautiful sex books, and at the same time he was scribbling folk sayings, beliefs, and practices in his notebook. By the time he graduated from high school, the predisposition to research sex as a human art was shaping his intellectual life.

This preoccupation made him a renegade, and his strong sense of himself as a social outsider bolstered him. He was an outsider in Scranton because he was Jewish, but he was an outsider to his faith because he had become profoundly antireligious. He had no tolerance for the "mendacious bullshit" that had smothered his childhood. He would always identify as a proletarian, interpreting the world through a working-class lens and refusing to work for a boss. Later he would call himself a Marxist, or a socialist, or a Marxian-socialist, and although he left political organizations behind after high school, he would always see big money and capitalists as the enemies of ordinary people.

The Stranger   **35**

In all this, we see Gershon's intense rejection of his father. What he could keep of Emil's was the profound respect for learning: he would remain a scholar with a deep love of words and language. But his learning would be for liberation. His fascination with books and bibliography (the poor man's book collecting) seems to have come from those moments when, in the back of his mother's closet, he could read, possess, and defend his beloved books from Emil. If collecting passions emerge from childhood injuries, Gershon's bibliophilia not only drew him closer to his mother and sister Ruth, but may also have soothed his vulnerability and calmed the real hate he felt toward Emil. And perhaps, collecting books, words, and jokes assuaged the absence of a loving father.[98]

Now might be a moment to ask how Gershon Legman came to think of himself as a folklorist. He does not tell us how he chose this emphasis. An awareness of oral traditions and the study in the Mishnah, the oral Torah, was a part of growing up Orthodox in the 1930s.[99] Emil was an excellent old-fashioned folktale teller, and Julia was skillful with Romanian jokes and proverbs. All those years of textual persecution could not destroy Gershon's fascination with words. For the rest of his life, he would hurl biblical wisdom effortlessly, as the occasion demanded, and often with startling effect.

He began the work of gathering and studying popular traditions (the notebook and the shoe-box joke collection) and decided what to call this work later. Interest in "the folk" and the working class was sweeping the country in the mid-1930s, as political organizing and cultural experiments from the grassroots began to shift dominant conceptions of what American culture could—and might—be.[100]

As someone who read everything, Gershon must have been aware of the enormous popularity of John A. Lomax's *Cowboy Songs* (1910) and (with Alan Lomax) *American Ballads and Folk Songs* (1934). Gershon's last turbulent year of high school (1933–34) saw intense awareness of America's popular traditions, at the American Writers Congress and in the beginnings of the Federal Writers' Project. Activist writers and artists pressed for an integration of working-class experience into American letters and visual arts and for "native" experience as an aesthetic resource.[101] Father and son John and Alan Lomax were promoting the remarkable singer and guitarist Leadbelly.[102] While radio companies made use of folk musicians in local programming, national broadcasts organized by the Lomaxes aimed to unify and revitalize the country through its diverse musics. This was an American folk revival.

Academic study in folklore was not an option Legman would have heard of in 1934. There was little formal training in folklore then, except in literature at Harvard with G. L. Kittredge or perhaps at Nebraska with Louise Pound. (He would later learn that his friend Vance Randolph had been rejected when he applied to study anthropology at Columbia University, because Franz Boas did not think rural white people were a proper anthropological subject.)[103] Like many people who would write on folklore at midcentury, Legman had an interest in a scholarly discipline that did not quite exist yet; his interest was very much "in the air."[104] He would teach himself folklore's emerging methods by reading, talking, and exchanging materials with other scholars, many of whom were also academic outsiders or pursued folklore as a sideline.

As for the folklore of sex, it was nearly unthought of, especially in the United States. But Gershon knew of an important exception in Vienna. Through his mother's family, he may have been related to a major European scholar, Friedrich Salomo Krauss, anthropologist, collector of folk erotica, and a member of Freud's psychoanalytic circle. Legman thought that Krauss was a great-uncle, married to a Friedman girl. It was a family story that Julia had been intended for one of the "Krauss boys" in Vienna. Whether Uncle Fritz was a real or fictional ancestor, he was very important to Gershon, who repeatedly cited him as a precedent.[105] Krauss had covertly published *Kryptadia* (1883–1911) and *Anthropophyteia* (1904–13), yearbooks of obscene and erotic material in multilingual scholarly formats, and if he was not close with Sigmund Freud, as Legman sometimes suggested, his work was noticed and even endorsed by the master.[106] Over the years when he wrote to other folklorists, he bolstered the legitimacy of his interest in erotic lore with references to Krauss.

With this substantial personal and intellectual equipment, Gershon Legman was ready to try to leave Scranton for a larger and, he hoped, more tolerant world.

2

SEX RESEARCHER

Sex is the central mystery and central reality of life.
—G. Legman, paraphrasing Havelock Ellis, in *Mooncalf*

Gershon was sixteen when he graduated from Scranton's Central High School in 1934, in the depths of the Great Depression. He had a plan to follow his ex-girlfriend "Tia" to Oberlin College, but he was not accepted, so he settled for the University of Michigan, which he could barely afford. With Emil in and out of work and the whole Legman family struggling financially, Gershon would have to live at home while he saved up his tuition.

His conflicts with his father continued. As the family tightened their belts, Emil demanded that Gershon take a job as a breaker boy in the mines. Adolescent boys worked sorting the coal as it tumbled down steep chutes; it was a dangerous, even life-threatening, job, and Gershon had seen boys injured and killed. He refused, and he would resent his father's disregard for his safety for the rest of his life. Instead, he worked off and on as a dry-goods clerk and as a dishwasher at a camp, and he sometimes hitchhiked to find work as he could.[1]

Family oral tradition has it that Gershon headed out on a folk song collecting trip, as he had heard folklorists did, but his foray was short. Predictably, he was more interested in the young women he met along the way than he was in music, and he was run out of the hamlets where he had hoped to collect songs. He tried riding boxcars and came close to being raped by a gang of hoboes. Eventually, he straggled back to Scranton to live with his parents and prepare for Michigan. It was discouraging to return home. His sister

Gershon at his graduation from Scranton Central High School, 1934. Courtesy of the Legman Archive.

Ruth had married and moved out, Matilda was working as a stenographer and caring for her baby, and everyone was under Emil's thumb.

His time in Ann Arbor was short and momentous. His freshman English professor read his first theme and told Gershon his time would be better spent reading independently. So Gershon had plenty of time to focus on his fascination with folklore. He connected with two instructors, young P. H. Erbes and Charles Walcutt, who were writing and editing a book of obscene limericks.[2] Walcutt and Erbes recognized a fellow enthusiast in Legman and turned him on to a dictionary that would change his life and give his scholarship its direction.[3]

John S. Farmer and W. E. Henley's *Slang and Its Analogues* (1859) was a rare, out-of-print nineteenth-century dictionary of slang; it was an attempt to put back in all the English words that had been expurgated from the first *Oxford English Dictionary*. As a synonymy, it provided a list of synonyms for words, rather than a glossary or dictionary, and was thus useful for an etymologist and lexicographer. Many of the words in it were frankly obscene, others long forgotten.[4] Gershon was hooked: he was now envisioning his own master list of folk obscenities and spending all his time copying out sex synonyms in two leather-bound notebooks.

His dean at the University of Michigan asked Gershon to leave at the end of the first semester after he had a caffeine-fueled breakdown while cramming for his chemistry final. He was apprehended for stealing two typewriters in a crazy scheme that involved helping his friend Mel Goodman become a journalist. Julia arrived *en catastrophe* to bring him home. Whatever happened in Michigan, Legman never expressed any regrets about his lack of a college education. He had seen it up close, and he knew he could educate himself better. So, after more kicking around at various jobs in stultifying Scranton, he headed to New York City in the fall of 1936.

At first, he lived with George Freems, an uncle on the Friedman side of his family, sharing a laundry shack atop a house on the Upper West Side. The house belonged to the Gershwin family, and George Freems was a vaudeville actor, sometimes cast in a Gershwin show. Freems quickly got his nephew a short-term job rewriting scripts for a struggling production. When George and the show sailed for London, Gershon was out of work again. He rented a single room at Thirty-Ninth and Lexington Avenue, close to the New York Public Library, and determined to look for work as a writer.[5]

Somehow, Legman hoped, he would fit himself into the city's literary and intellectual life. Later, he would see that this was an impossibly naive ambition. He had landed at the literal bottom of a great heap: he had no formal higher education, no money, no patron or family connections, and no introductions to anyone powerful. Breaking in was difficult, verging on impossible, for a callow eighteen-year-old with no resources. Writers were always underemployed, and the Depression had made this much worse. And there was overt anti-Jewish prejudice in many industries.[6] But Walcutt and Erbes (and his reading of Farmer and Henley) had signaled that he was on the right path. He strategized that he would "create an opening by studying the subject which no one else wished to study," namely, sex. He would make his living involved with what Havelock Ellis called the central mystery of life.[7]

His economic situation was dire, and his chances slim, but he could not have been in a better place. Manhattan in the twentieth century was the center for book publishing in the United States, second only to women's garment making among the city's pre-Depression industries. Thousands of people were employed at many different points of production in printing, binding, and publishing. Manhattan had scores of bookstores and many more used, secondhand, and rare bookstores clustered on "Book Row" on Fourth Avenue below Fourteenth Street. Great libraries and great universities helped make New York the literary and cultural center of the world, a place of overlapping webs of creativity. The city also had a unique concentration of theaters and concert halls offering entertainment from opera to burlesque—and appealing to all kinds of audiences with different tastes, languages, and levels of

CHAPTER 2

sophistication.[8] It drew people from small towns in the American heartland, but also from the wider world.

And there was bohemia. From the early twentieth century, New York generated experimental racial and sexual communities—artistic and literary worlds with global intellectual and political connections. Feminists, free lovers, socialists, communists, antiracists, Industrial Workers of the World (IWW), and experimentalists of all kinds created networks of political expression and personal influence.[9]

Gershon could not know this yet, but New York was becoming an international center for sex research. New York's large poor and immigrant population, its emerging welfare bureaucracy, and its many hospitals and prominent doctors made the city the center of the national birth control movement pressed by Margaret Sanger. Free-love experiments, socialism, and the demand for safe and effective contraception meant that sex research in New York had a radical edge.

Gershon survived by piecing together ill-paid work, taking any available job crafting words for almost anyone. Legman would later say that his jobs included writing pulp fiction, magazine articles to order, medical texts, and, following George Freems's introduction, burlesque theater dialogue. Hanging out in the burlesque world allowed Legman to hear the old oral traditions of the lower-class theater, as well as observe the working lives of comedians, actresses, strippers, and dancers. He formed a habit of dropping into striptease joints to hear the comedians. By 1937 New York's old burlesque was being suffocated by the La Guardia administration's theater censorship. But the jokes and the situations stayed with him and would appear later in his folklore collections.[10]

When not spending time in theaters, Gershon picked up work from marginal publishers, reading manuscripts for crooked vanity publisher Fortuny House, for example. He wanted to be paid for writing about sex and had been trying to place "semi-erotic love stories" with "the various *Spicy Stories* and *Snappy Stories* magazines then being published for the masturbatory adolescent audience."[11] But he was having little luck. The world of erotica writing and publishing was illegal and so underground that it required vetting to break into. No one knew or trusted Legman. There were too many other underemployed people writing and drawing cheap sex lit, and no one knew who was a police department or Vice Society spy and who was not.

BOOKLEGGER

Gradually, Legman made connections through the semilegal publishers Samuel Roth, Jake Brussel, and Benjamin Rebhuhn, men who were involved in a two-sided trade—publishing art and science books for their store windows while producing illegal and erotic books for their back rooms.[12] He began editing and translating obscure "medical" and anatomical texts, which could sometimes border on pornography, for these men who would eventually teach him all the angles of the rare-book business. During these years, Legman developed close knowledge of the bookmen and their stocks, especially their back rooms and basements, and he often picked up work scouting books for booksellers and publishers. In the Depression, all the booksellers were on the ropes, struggling to make a living in used books and magazines, cheap print, textbooks, and erotica. An earlier market for popular books had been destroyed by the stock market crash, and writers, printers, and binders were pushed into risky businesses they might otherwise eschew. Some booksellers started erotica lending libraries, where a book wrapped in brown paper could be borrowed for a small sum and returned a few days or a week later. Others retailed cheap and secondhand porn.[13] As Legman scrounged the bins, he was straining to build his own library.

When need be, he was building and painting bookcases—anything to subsist. He remembered living on milk and spaghetti. Eventually, he found another part-time job in the trade as "literary factotum and book designer" for Jacob Brussel, "the quasi-medical erotica publisher."[14] Jake was a "veteran antiquarian bookseller and reprint publisher" who for many years had one shop and then another on Book Row. He specialized in what the 1930s bookmen called curiosa, pseudoscientific works on anthropology and curiosities of other cultures. Much of this was borderline erotica, treating the diversity of ways the human body had been shaped, used, and satisfied around the world over the centuries.[15] Jake sold these marginal materials through a mail-order catalog for medical men, as well as through his shop. Legman was soon scouting secondhand erotica, and he became one of Jake's suppliers of "the Stuff."[16]

Jake had gone into the used-book business with his brother Ike.[17] The Brussel brothers were global book scouts, nosing out the obscure and rare volumes, and they became famous for finding "sleepers," the one-of-a-kind publisher's oddity that no one suspects will be valuable to collectors. The brothers represented both faces of the book trade: working for the presentable end of the trade, Ike sold to school, research, and public libraries and was well known for his bibliographies "on English and American fiction in the nineteenth and early twentieth centuries." He wrote about the "importance of the book scout in bibliographical research and the immense value of the scout's knowledge in locating extremely rare books." Scouts formed a kind of connective tissue for the trade, carrying a book "useless to one dealer to another dealer who needs it. . . . The Scout may keep a bit of the nectar, but at the same time he has accomplished the feat of having produced two or more transactions in place of one. He has put profit into three pockets."[18]

While Jake Brussel was "no slouch as a big book hunter" either, in Legman's view he was dishonest to the core. He had gotten his start lifting rare books from the New York Public Library's cataloging desk and reselling them, amassing the capital to start his first store.[19] His sharp memory and deep book knowledge meant that he "could always buy right [well] and make money on his books and other finds such as the wonderful Japanese prints, some of them erotic," that he was able to buy in England after the war.[20]

Jake Brussel's shops often moved around the Eighth Street area. At his Ortelius Bookstore at 100 Fourth Avenue, his specialties were mathematics, philosophy, science, sexology, and "early and unusual books." With his wife, Minna, he had a side business in color prints, facsimile editions, and "offset reprints" of classics of all kinds.[21] Behind this marginal conventionality, they ran a sideline in "unexpurgated erotica," such as *The Kama Sutra*, and more. Book Row's historians describe Jake and Minna's attitudes toward the Comstock obscenity law as "blithely casual," and antiquarian Walter Goldwater remembered that "whenever there was anything illegal, [Jake] seemed to get into it."[22]

Gershon got along with Jake and "immediately began doing a certain amount of book-editing and designing for him" off and on for several years, until he became a staff editor. He explains that he was driven by book collecting: "I desperately wanted the extra money to buy books with, and the books I wanted most were the classic sex books and bibliographies mostly out of my reach."[23] But Legman also wanted to absorb Brussel's prodigious knowledge of book design, printing, and bibliography.

In his behind-the-scenes print shop, Jake also retained the extraordinary surrealist erotica illustrator Mahlon Blaine, paying him in housing, a grimy corner for an easel, and a cot. For several years, the three men made "an underground erotica publishing team." Legman remembered conducting a lot of business at lunch counters and being paid mostly in chili con carne and hot pastrami sandwiches.[24]

Jake put Gershon to work editing, excerpting, rewriting, and proofreading Brussel's sex books. This should have been more enjoyable than writing fake manuscript reports for Fortuny Press, but Legman recalled with bitterness the exploitation of these "miserable hack jobs." At one point, Jake assigned him to expurgate the nineteenth-century porn classic *Memoirs of a Woman of Pleasure* (*Fanny Hill*), "the one literary job I ever did in my life of which I was most ashamed."[25] He hated taking out the florid, overwritten Victorian descriptions of sex, which he thought had their own beauty. But it was the Depression, and everyone was desperate.

After Jake Brussel, the most important bookseller Legman worked with was Frances Steloff, whose Gotham Book Mart near the Theater District was at the center of Manhattan's avant-garde cultural and social life in the 1930s.[26] Anaïs Nin memorialized Miss Steloff as playing the same midwife role for her art that Sylvia Beach had for James Joyce in Paris. Nin wrote that Steloff "befriended our books. . . . She welcomes those who stand for hours browsing, she welcomes unknown magazines, unknown poets."[27] Miss Steloff, as everyone called her, hosted parties for authors in the shop to introduce them to New York. The walls of the Book Mart were decorated with photographs of Virginia Woolf, James Joyce, Theodore Dreiser, and many others.

Frances Steloff had grown up in a large poor immigrant family, and she had "a great hunger for books." Like Legman, she was mostly self-educated.[28] Although Gershon thought she seemed like a flibbertigibbet, he acknowledged that she was a successful and astute businesswoman, sharp about publishing and money. After the Book Mart opened in 1920, it became the best serious reader's bookshop in New York. The atmosphere, Nin observed, was "not slick, or organized, or impersonal. . . . It is almost like being in a private library with a familiar natural disorder."[29]

Miss Steloff had an underground reputation, too. The Gotham Book Mart was the main erotica outlet in New York in the 1920s and 1930s. As Nin put it, "She had many treasures in her cellar."[30] The shop's famous sign was a silhouette of the Three Wise Men of Gotham fishing from their tub, and it had a double meaning: it read "Wise Men Fish Here." As Legman noted, "wise" was a code word among gay men, meaning "in the know," and "fish" was a folk code term for sex.[31] To cognoscenti the sign read "Gay Sex Here." Miss Steloff didn't admit to this and kept what she called "the other" at a distance in a building across the courtyard. Literature was the front, and, like Samuel Roth and Jake Brussel, Miss Steloff used the "two-store trick" to stay afloat.

For several years, Gershon was Miss Steloff's errand boy, ferrying brown paper–wrapped deliveries around Radio City for her. She never paid him. He was compensated with the trade knowledge she imparted and by being allowed to hang around and look at the books. He wrote later that he absolutely was not interested in the "high falutin'" modernism she dealt over the counter. He hated Hemingway and thought James Joyce was full of hot air. He couldn't afford the elegant "other" she offered to Manhattan's business executives and stockbrokers, but he could absorb the bibliography of erotica.[32]

It was hard surviving on occasional bowls of chili, but Gershon found he could make it as a general ghostwriter, booklegger, and errand boy "perfectly nicely in five half days of work a week," freeing up the rest of his time for afternoons studying at the public library.[33] He spent many days in the reading room of the New York Public Library on Forty-Second Street, because it was warm and because it was exciting. He was thrilled to have access to one of the great collections of books, and he began to work his way through a world literature of poetry, plays, philosophy, history, anthropology, and folklore, always searching for examples of sexual expression and suppression. Telling the librarians he was a Michigan college student, Gershon gained access to the library's restricted Three Star Collection and began extracting examples of sexual speech and slang from three centuries of rare books. His card files expanded into a complex mesh of references and cross-references as he built up a history of how people thought and spoke about sex.[34]

Back in his furnished room, he set a pattern that would continue for the rest of his life. If he finished his quota of twenty pages of paid writing work before noon, he might spend the rest of the morning writing letters or polishing his own "lapidary prose." He was writing mostly to "established authors in the fields of lexicography, anthropology, and sexology" whose books he was poring over, "chiding them for the various deficiencies in their most recent work, and shamelessly plugging [his] own projected *Encyclopedic Dictionary of Sexual Speech and Slang*," at this stage mostly cribbed from Farmer and Henley. "As books were then my only friends, except for the rare women in my life," connecting to like-minded people through eloquent, obnoxious letters became the core of his intellectual work.[35]

In what would be enduring Legman style, he was brutally honest in his criticism, "analyzing their errors sadistically chapter by chapter, or even page by page." To his surprise, the authors liked hearing from serious critics (they probably did not suspect he was eighteen years old), and they replied. He heard back from H. L. Mencken, Havelock Ellis, and Adolph Niemoeller, "the sex lexicographer I was obviously planning to bump," among many others.[36]

The men he was joining mixed science with popular writing. Niemoeller, for example, was the author of many works of armchair anthropology of sex. These included *Gods of Generation: On Phallic Cults, Ancient and Modern* (1933) and *Sexual Slavery* (1935), but also booklets like *Superfluous Hair and Its Removal*.[37] Niemoeller responded patiently to Legman's pushy criticisms of his just-published *Encyclopedia of Sex*, encouraging him but cautioning that this was no way to make a living. Pulp fiction offered a better cash flow.[38]

A turning point came when Gershon heard back from anthropologist and novelist Robert Briffault, then living in the South of France. Legman considered Briffault "probably the greatest library researcher of modern times," and he reflected, "Briffault's letters to me changed my life completely, although I didn't realize it then." A decade earlier, Briffault had published *The Mothers*, "his magnificent three-volume vindication of pre-historical matriarchy."[39] Largely forgotten now, Briffault's work was widely read in the interwar years as part of a debate over the meaning and future of marriage. Briffault's was an evolutionary anthropological project. His speculative studies of prehistory concluded that very early Paleolithic and Mesolithic European cultures were female dominated and practiced a religion devoted to female fertility and regeneration. After about 1940, as ethnographic fieldwork became the disciplinary standard in cultural anthropology, Briffault's work was eclipsed and neglected.[40]

Legman found Briffault's theories of the history of the family and marriage compelling, and he celebrated the arguments for matriarchy. The anthropologist explored the possibility that a different form of social organization might have preceded the male-dominated or patriarchal nuclear family that American social science (and Americans in general) considered normal. Briffault's *Mothers* gave Legman a platform for speculating about the deep history of relations between men and women. The theme of a hidden history of gender organization and sexuality crops up often in Legman's later writings on folklore. What if oral tradition carries traces of a world dominated by women? What if the folklore of sex held the remnants of celebrations of female generative power? These were ideas that Legman would repeatedly take up over the years.

Briffault's response offered Gershon a career breakthrough. Briffault referred Legman to Dr. Robert Latou Dickinson, who "was once contemplating a work of similar scope [to yours], and even asked me for my collaboration. You should get in touch with him."[41] On his nineteenth birthday, Legman took a bus uptown to the New York Academy of Medicine at 103rd Street and 5th Avenue and entered the world of medical sex research.

DR. DICKINSON

Robert Latou Dickinson (1861–1950) was the country's leading gynecologist for most of the early twentieth century and the head of the National Committee on Maternal Health. When Legman met him in November 1936, he was seventy-five and nearing retirement from his elite private practice in Brooklyn Heights. But, as Legman noted, Dickinson was just getting started on his project of publishing the results of decades of semicovert research on women's sexuality.

Dr. Dickinson was the leading American organizer and director of scientific and social-scientific investigations into a wide range of "sex problems"— from lack of orgasm in married women to prostitution, venereal disease, and birth control. In his organization of funding and projects, Dickinson *was* the center of sex research in the United States between the wars. Through his connections to European scientists and intellectuals, he helped American researchers and reformers connect with the most important and diverse intellectual currents on sex. As the Austrian and German sex scholars and psychoanalysts were shut down and forced to flee before the Nazis, Dickinson's projects arguably kept modern Western sex research alive.

During much of Dickinson's career, sex could not be discussed in the public policy circles of the United States, and so it was not officially researchable. He quietly labored to get funding, mostly in the form of private grants from wealthy women, for the research committees he organized to work sub rosa. In many cases, his committees defined sexual problems as health and hygiene issues, so that projects like improved birth control, but also women's sexual happiness, were labeled issues of "maternal health." As an advocate for mothers, Dr. Dickinson hoped "to engage medical leaders in research to practical problems of contraception, abortion, infertility treatments, menstruation, and other topics" with implications beyond maternity.[42] Dickinson was interested in sex from all angles, but he understood how to shield his committees and his researchers with medical and moral probity.

For Dickinson and his colleagues, women's sexual satisfaction was central to an emerging twentieth-century ideal: the "New Woman," who was white, educated, and civically engaged and whose sexual life was not always constrained by marriage.[43] From his practice, Dickinson knew that many women suffered from sexual difficulties. He became especially interested in studying female orgasm and recruited subjects to allow him to observe its physiology, making notes while observing vaginal changes through a large glass tube. And he interviewed women in detail about their sex histories.[44]

With his colleagues Katherine Bement Davis and Lura Beam, Dickinson directed systematic research on female sexuality in marriage. The team found that many women were unable to have orgasms during intercourse with men but found sexual satisfaction in masturbation. The practice was much more common among women than public culture could admit; Dickinson came to think it was a normal part of most women's sexual lives.[45]

Beneath the public cover of research into marriage, Dr. Dickinson understood a much wider sexual life existed and that the normative ideal of heterosexual adjustment "was at variance with [many] people's actual behavior."[46] Behind the scenes at the academy, Dickinson also supported research on homosexuality, transvestism, and prostitution, topics on which it was difficult to publish books and pamphlets in the 1930s without a medical degree and institutional affiliation. Legman found these subjects and the suppression of knowledge about them of great interest, too.

Dickinson hired the bright young man, telling Gershon he "understood my project, liked it, and said he had planned something very similar ten years before. He would help me. And he did."[47] Although Legman always emphasized Dickinson's eccentricities, especially his stinginess, the doctor was foresighted. He knew that libraries were essential, and fascism was destroying the great sex research collections of Europe. Legman was widely read in the subjects of sex, a skilled book scout, and a natural bibliographer. He was in touch with useful but disreputable people like Jake Brussel, whom Dickinson wanted to keep at a distance, and he didn't want to do anything except read and write about sex.

They agreed Legman would write a research proposal. Immediately, he typed up a prospectus describing "*THE NEW KRYPTADIA, AN ENCYCLOPEDIC DICTIONARY OF SEXUAL, SCATALOGIC, AND RELATED TERMINOLOGY—SLANG AND OTHERWISE—IN THE ENGLISH, FRENCH, GERMAN, LATIN, GREEK, AND NUMEROUS LANGUAGES. . . . . . . COMPILED BY GERSHON LEGMAN.*" He optimistically forecast that it would be published in San Francisco in 1938.[48]

"The New Kryptadia" project was grandiose, its title borrowed (as Dickinson was aware) from Friedrich Krauss's sex-folklore yearbook. It aimed to lay down "a somewhat better foundation than has yet appeared, upon which the great mass of work yet to be done may be erected."[49] Legman proposed that his dictionary would cover "the language (proper, technical, colloquial, and slang) of sexology and erotology; or in short the language of love in its normal, medical, psychiatric, poetic, historical, curious, and vulgar aspects, plus . . . allied terms" useful "to the proper understanding of the subject." He would cover words for organs, "their affections and abnormalities," their "sexual and allied functions, and their disorders." He would document terms for "instincts and relations," for "perversions, perversities and aberrations," "excretions," and the language for the "instruments, devices, and procedures" of "love, lust or reproduction," as well as the vocabulary of "sentiments," "institutions, doctrines, theories, or legal measures."[50]

Where Adolph Niemoeller tried to be encyclopedic, Legman wanted to push even further. He would take up the lexicon having to do with any bodily function that was sometimes connected to sex, including even "the vocabulary of urination, defecation, and the *crepitus ventris* [the fart]." And, even more adventurously, he would work in more than one or two languages: in fact, a final edition should include glossaries of the "forty-odd most widely spoken languages." English was first, with each subsequent language arranged alphabetically. Each glossary would be alphabetical, followed by a reverse glossary that would serve as an index, and "at the end of the dictionary, a general index is appended of *all* the terms." The languages would be cross-referenced, too. There would follow a bibliography of all his sources and a bibliography of the "entire sexologic literature" to date. Following this, he planned a bibliography of works on erotica, "for in the erotic literature of the world the reader . . . will find a great wealth of material."[51]

48 CHAPTER 2

It was obsessive, sprawling, and out of control. But not to leave anything out, Legman planned an appendix of drawings of "copulatory positions," an "exhaustive collection of photographs, drawings, and diagrams," of acts, positions, organs ("internal and external") and their anomalies and variations, rites, symbols, and representations of all kinds. "I do not hope ever to finish it," he wrote. Collaborators would be essential to make even a fair start.[52]

Dr. Dickinson must have seen that this was over the top and possibly mad, but he was amenable to circulating Legman's proposal to try to get a private grant. "A wealthy private individual interested in erotica, is more promising than a foundation in a matter of this kind," he wrote tolerantly.[53] Gershon submitted an itemized list of expenses, estimating that he could live and conduct the writing and research work on approximately $140 a month, although he had certainly lived on less: $8 a week for a room with a bath and a bed, $9 for food, and a few more dollars a week for laundry, wear and tear on clothes, and incidentals, including the rent of a typewriter, a desk in the National Academy of Medicine Library, and transportation costs. He would need to visit libraries and book dealers in Philadelphia and Chicago, at least.

Dickinson circulated the proposal and forwarded the replies to Legman. Dr. Adolf Meyer, the head of psychiatry at Johns Hopkins Hospital and the leading psychiatrist in the United States at the time, wrote that the project was interesting but wondered if it would escape medical control: "The question is whether it will be used more for pornography." Still, Meyer was "strongly in favor of collecting the data. The problem shows the great need of a kind of sanctuary for work and material" for scholars who could use it "for, rather than against humanity."[54] Havelock Ellis thought the work would be most valuable, although his health kept him from participating.[55] Dr. Gaston Vorberg wrote from Munich that he himself had published a lexicon of Greek and Roman sexual terms, "a work of 20 years!" He admonished Dickinson, however, "You do not seem to be aware, that the sexual science no more exists in Germany. They have entirely done away with it." In 1933 Magnus Hirschfeld's laboratory had been shut down by the Nazis, his research files and library burned in the streets in front of newsreel cameras, and "for the same reason, such a dictionary could no more be published in Germany."[56]

A private donor never stepped forward, but Dickinson still found ways to subsidize Legman's work. He gave him a cubicle at the New York Academy of Medicine and part-time work helping with staff publications. He craftily suggested a bibliographic project as cover for Legman's hunt for erotic books. Librarians, Dickinson explained, would be more tolerant of someone researching bibliography than someone researching sex. He wrote letters recommending Legman to specialized libraries. By now, Gershon had been bounced from the New York Public Library for submitting false credentials,

Sex Researcher

but he was elated to have access to the J. P. Morgan, Fricke, and Columbia University Libraries.[57]

Gershon had landed at the center of modern sex research in the United States, and he reported to his parents that his career as a sex expert was under way. Now he set the pattern he would follow for the rest of his life. Multiple big projects would be in play at the same time, and as he developed them, they overlapped and fed into each other. After joining Dickinson, he had a further burst of ideas. He wanted to compile an encyclopedia of sex techniques, a plan he formed "thru considering the article on coitus in the dictionary."[58] He also realized that someone should compile a list of books suppressed in America on the model of the famous Vatican Index of forbidden books.[59]

Legman's collaboration with Dr. Dickinson's staff had lasting results, too. He was asked to help another young employee, Thomas Painter, with a manuscript on homosexual prostitutes. Painter aspired to be the chronicler of New York's gay underworld, combining his personal interests with a research life. He and Legman became friends.[60] Gershon later remembered that "Tom Painter inherited money and spent most of it on boys. I shamed him into paying me $18 a week . . . for 1½ years to create a bibliography of homosexuality so there would be something to show." Painter's long typescript "Male Homosexuals and Their Prostitutes" was bolstered by Legman's detailed work.[61] After several years, the manuscript draft became so unwieldy that Painter (or Dr. Dickinson) hired Legman to edit it.[62]

The Painter-Legman collaboration was part of a larger study by the Committee on Sex Variants, one of Dickinson's protective clearinghouses within the New York Academy of Medicine. The chair of the nineteen-person group, Dr. George Henry, was a psychiatrist concerned with understanding more about the lives of his gay and lesbian patients. Henry had been convinced by Jan Gay, a lesbian activist, to support her ongoing collection of queer life stories, an innovative example of community research "from below."[63] Dickinson and the committee took up Gay's idea, and she and Painter enlarged the study. Historian Henry Minton writes that "the participants' narratives offered 'a rare glimpse into the shared experiences, sensibilities, and struggles of an underground subculture whose voices were typically silenced in medical and scientific discourse.'"[64] Legman accompanied Painter to recruit subjects and conduct interviews for the report, which was published as *Sex Variants* in 1941.[65]

Homosexuality was a topic of prejudice and confusion in medicine and public policy in the 1930s and 1940s, and the *Sex Variants* research was a mixed bag of goals and strategies. Everyone on the committee agreed that homosexuality should be decriminalized, but the doctors and scientists who saw gays and lesbians as psychologically damaged people were working at

cross-purposes with the activists like Gay, Painter, and their interview participants. Jan Gay and Tom Painter had social change as their goal. They hoped
to increase tolerance and move society away from seeing gays and lesbians
as dangerous deviants. According to historian Henry Minton, the medical
men on the committee "wanted to establish homosexuality as a medical and
social problem, thereby expanding their own influence over it." Bringing
"sexual pathology" under psychiatry's purview gave medical experts their own
"authority to challenge the view that homosexuality was a criminal offense,"
for example, in the courts. But the doctors also viewed their "projects as a
means of reinforcing marriage and the family against the disruptive forces of
modern society," of which homosexuality might be a symptom. Ultimately,
the medical men shaped the *Sex Variants* project evidence to "fit their pre-
conceptions of homosexuality as individual pathology and social problem."[66]
This profamily, proheterosexual stance was shared by Dr. Dickinson and to a
large degree by Legman. The question of whether homosexuality was "deviant" or a normal human variation would come up often in Legman's work, as
he tried to be both a scientific folklorist and a humane interpreter of cultural
materials.

HOMOSEXUAL GLOSSARY

Legman's first published work as a folklorist and his first product for Dickinson was a glossary or lexicon of homosexual slang appended to the first
edition of *Sex Variants* in 1941.[67] Tom Painter had been keeping a word list as
part of his prostitution research, and Gershon immediately saw how it connected to Farmer and Henley's slang synonymies. He expanded Painter's list
into a detailed glossary, adding historical depth, analogues, and etymology.
As he indulged his fascination with word collecting, he exercised his now
considerable research and comparative skills. This was the first published
"dictionary" of American gay men's esoteric language, and, as we shall see,
it attracted some notice.[68]

Legman and Painter's immersion in the harassed demimonde of gay New
York gives the glossary depth and ethnographic detail, as they probed slang
and argot to reveal customs and attitudes. Legman's analysis of this esoteric
terminology was so thorough that many decades later, historians would use
it as a source on the gay world of the 1930s and 1940s.[69]

Legman organized the glossary to focus on specifically gay usage, omit-
ting overlapping words like "make," which were "a part of the slang sexual
vocabulary of heterosexuals, too."[70] He modeled the glossary on Farmer and
Henley's *Slang* and on *The Oxford English Dictionary*, with their careful dating
and comparison of terms.[71] He placed old and newer uses next to each other,

evoking a strong sense of the collective historical dimension of slang, as it developed in a self-aware community. For example, he discussed the term "come out" in terms of historical shifts:

> The meaning of coming out has changed several times over the course of the 20th century. In the 1920s it referred to initiation into the gay world, and even when "coming out" was used in a narrower sense, to refer to the process by which someone came to recognize his sexual interest in other men, it referred to something other than a solitary experience. Indeed, before the war this process was more commonly described by saying that someone was "brought out," which necessarily implied that he had been initiated into homosexual practices by someone else, than by saying he "came out," something he could, at least grammatically, have done on his own. . . . [This] locution is losing its original connotation of initiation by another person, and circumstance or fate is coming to be considered the initiatory agent.[72]

Legman tried to differentiate slang communities and words of self-description from terms applied by outsiders: "Terms used exclusively by homosexuals are marked with a single asterisk: *, while terms used only by 'outsiders' are marked by the double asterisk: **." Here Legman attended to an "exoteric/esoteric" phenomenon, the way "insiders" not only use language to create their own identity, but also use it to distinguish themselves from outsiders, while they acknowledge and sometimes adopt the often derogatory terms that outsiders apply to them. An example of a word bridging these categories is "**fairy."[73]

Many of the terms Legman included remain familiar in the twenty-first century:

> **Dirt:** gossip or criticism, especially concerning sexual or sex-social behavior.[74]

> ***Flaming:*** VERBAL ADJECTIVE: obviously homosexual; using cosmetics, wearing flamboyant clothes.[75]

> ***cruise:*** To walk or drive in an automobile through the streets. . . . The verb is often used transitively . . . "That blond sailor looks good: I think I'll cruise it."[76]

Many others are less familiar or are linked to older meanings and have faded:

> ***Abdicated:*** Ordered by the attendant to leave the public toilets, said of male homosexuals ("queens" therefore "abdicated") who frequent park, subway, theater, barroom, and other toilets. Compare *dethroned*.[77]

Legman's glossary is explicit for its time, even as it is sensitive and thoughtful. He spent a great deal of time in his introduction defining and selecting terms. Sexual acts were his main focus; most vocabulary was not recorded except "in the sphere of sexual practice where every effort has been made to supply a complete and exhaustive record." Forecasting a change in thinking about homosexuality, he distinguished between people and acts and separated acts from identities. He included words for heterosexual men who solicit homosexual acts and homosexual men who solicit not necessarily gay men. Some men prefer only certain acts, in certain ways, times, and places. His bias was toward activity.

Legman and Painter were heavily influenced by the young prostitutes of their acquaintance, and their basic thesis was that underground, illegal activity was most conducive to the emergence of argot and slang. Legman included, therefore, vocabulary that is derogatory about exclusive or long-term relationships between men and a lot of words that deal with the relationships between procurers, prostitutes, and customers. It was the street world he was describing, and he attended to the roles of public spaces and places, as in "abdicated" from the public washroom and "playing checkers" (moving from seat to seat) in the movie theater.[78]

Legman examined the movement of words and phrases between homosexual and heterosexual communities, writing that "to let one's hair down" or "let my back hair down" is an expression taken from the general habit of women speaking frankly with each other and adopted into male homosexual usage. He noticed the playful dimension of slang, the way the shifted use of a word can change a situation and redefine the meaning of interactions. For example, Legman writes, a "very common use in the speech of male homosexuals . . . is the substitution of feminine pronoun titles for properly masculine ones. Male homosexuals use the terms *she, her, hers, miss, mother*, and *girl* (almost never 'woman') in referring to themselves and each other. This usage is sometimes rather confusingly carried over to references to heterosexuals, though an overtone, in such cases, of jocularity or mild contempt usually serves to mark the heterosexual [as] the person referred to."[79]

Legman was also careful to distinguish between male homosexual and lesbian uses in slang, pointing out that this difference indicated a partial separation in worlds and manners. Spending time with Tom Painter, he probably frequented exclusively male settings. He wrote that he found very little lesbian slang: "Very noticeable, too, is the seeming absence of almost any but 'outsiders' slang in relation to female homosexuality. It is difficult to assign reason to this absence, but, if there really is such an absence and a concealed argot does not exist, [perhaps] the tradition of gentlemanly restraint among lesbians stifles the flamboyant and conversational cynicism on sexual matters that slang coinage requires; . . . what little direct mention of sexual practice there is among female homosexuals is usually either roughly brusque and vague or else romantically euphemistic."[80] This observation seems to stem from ignorance. Legman thought lesbianism was a passing fashion of the intelligentsia in the late 1930s and early 1940s, and he argued that the lesbian community in New York in this period was smaller and less noticeable than that of gay men, an assertion that flies in the face of ample documentation by historians. A rich lesbian social life, including nightclubs, was visible in New York by the 1930s, and lesbians were neither unknown nor underground but were visible enough to be criminalized. Their women-only meeting places were subject to police raids and investigations. Lesbians even had their own jail: "Women convicted of this 'perversion' were often sent to the Women's House of Detention, known among them as 'The Country Club,' in Greenwich Village."[81] Whether lesbians were less numerous, or at least less noticeable, in the city, or lacked a "feeling of criminal community" among them, Legman was on thin ice when he argued they had less propensity for slang. He was simply not hanging around many lesbians, nor does he mention Jan Gay in his memoirs.

The glossary's construction suggests that Legman and Painter were assembling materials for a history of gay life in the United States. The way community is created and examined in everyday speech was a part of this history—a sophisticated point of view for the time. Gay men had a culture—a history of practices, rituals, gathering places, and covert institutions—and, most important, their culture had its own evolving perspective upon itself and its place in the world. Despite the glossary's limitations, and Dr. Henry's severe cuts to the manuscript, "The Language of Homosexuality" was a remarkable start to an underground career in folklore study. No one had previously published a collection of homosexual language in English.

If Painter and Legman planned an expanded documentary project, the times were not propitious. The war would separate Painter, who enlisted despite being gay, and Legman, who got a 4F draft status partly because of his homosexual experiences. They stayed in touch through letters.[82] The mobilization for World War II would bring a larger population of unattached men and women into New York and other big cities, giving rise to a more politically self-conscious gay scene. But the forces of state repression would bear down on gay men and lesbians. The police and the FBI would gear up their surveillance and harassment of "sexual deviants," helping to make a panic about homosexuals in government part of a larger Red Scare that would explode in the late 1940s.[83] And this "lavender panic" would come back to haunt him.

Legman would continue his interest in the history of sexual slang throughout his life, corresponding with lexicographers and writing expert scholarly notes on the history of words. In 1950, for example, he published a short note on "poontang," a southern term "for sexual intercourse," "mistakenly believed to be a Negro word, perhaps of African origin." Legman plausibly argues that "poontang" is a "Creole pronunciation of the French word *putain* (whore), and undoubtedly spread through the South through French-speaking Louisiana."[84]

PERILOUS PUBLISHING

When not working for Dickinson, Legman was Jake Brussel's all-around man, editing, proofreading, and supervising printing. He remembered the late 1930s and early 1940s as satisfying years when he learned the art of designing a fine book.[85] Yet he had an unsatisfied itch to write what ought not to be written and to break the prudish barriers to publication. He really wanted to get into erotica publishing, and through Jake Brussel and Frances Steloff, he found a way.[86] Jake was always in need of "the Stuff" for his private customers, and Legman began to commission work. He had the idea of using Brussel's workshops to publish the first American edition of Henry Miller's *Tropic of Cancer*. Originally published in English in Paris in 1934, Miller's first *Tropic* was banned in the United States in the late 1930s. It could not be brought into the country, sold, or circulated, and not until the early 1960s was it legally published. The U.S. Post Office and the Customs Department made it dangerous to import "obscene" materials, including novels like *Lady Chatterley's Lover*, although tourists and travelers would smuggle volumes and other contraband in across the borders.[87] Miller's book trickled in this way. In some cases, after 1930, a work of "recognized value" could be brought in for sale, but this value had to be established through a lengthy court process, as in the case of James Joyce's *Ulysses* in 1933.[88] Miller hoped that such a decision might be possible, although timing and careful assessment of the cultural and the political climate were always key.[89]

Legman had been introduced to *Tropic of Cancer* by his teachers Walcutt and Erbes at Michigan, who loaned him a smuggled copy. They "assured me it was as great as Joyce's *Ulysses*, the underground sensation of the decade before." It was not as good as *Ulysses*, Legman considered later, but it was "a bombshell, and had a terrific impact in its violent sexual cynicism and bitter anti-Americanism to those of us who first read it then . . . on the eve of World War II, which was when the lights *really* went out all over the world."[90]

Although separated by a generation, Legman and Henry Miller shared a great deal. Miller had grown up on the lower margins of the working class. His father was a hapless alcoholic, and Henry was soon on his own, making his way through odd jobs and hard manual labor in the streets of Brooklyn. When he left the United States in his thirties to try to become a writer in Paris, Miller experienced real down-and-out poverty. Like Legman, he understood the effects of sleeping in train stations and on park benches, of scrounging for food, or worse. Each man in his own way saw the established American society—its history and ideas about itself, its letters, magazines, and literature—as sterile and poisonously false. Miller wrote *Tropic of Cancer* as a brick-in-the-face, "box-car between the eyes" attack on American "litter-a-chaw" and culture.[91] Legman thought it worked.

Legman wrote to Miller at Villa Seurat in Paris, inquiring about publication plans for *Tropic of Cancer*, asking about Miller's history as a writer, and requesting a first-edition copy. He proposed an illegal or sub rosa edition to help shatter the ridiculous American antiobscenity laws. Miller apologized: he had no copies himself of the first edition, and he was "damned sorry." The second printing had also run out, and the third, fourth, and fifth editions were printed in Hungary and unavailable. He suggested contacting James Laughlin IV of New Directions Press in Norfolk, Connecticut, who held the rights to American editions of Miller's books.[92] He did not see what the secret edition would accomplish but asked to be kept informed. He was earning nothing in royalties in France, but he was happy, writing, and with a roof over his head, pace Hitler.[93]

Legman asked James Laughlin, was he just sitting on *Tropic of Cancer*, or did he indeed plan to publish it in the United States? Legman explained his reason: he wanted to draw on *Tropic of Cancer* for his sex lexicography project and wanted "direct dated quotations" so he required the "earliest dated edition in which they occur." But there was another reason, and now Legman fabulated. He was a "professional dishwasher" expecting, maybe, "a windfall of $1,000," and if he got this, he would offset "2000 copies of *The Tropic of Cancer* from the best edition available." He had no intention of profiting but wanted only to perform "a maniacal act of literary appreciation." He accused Laughlin of aiming to expurgate Miller—and that would be a real literary crime. But seriously, Legman argued, Miller had to have money, and *Tropic of Cancer* needed to be published unaltered in America. Perhaps, he wrote, a plan could be worked out "whereby nobody has to go to jail."[94]

Legman's letter was rude, in part because he knew Laughlin was an extremely wealthy man, heir to Pittsburgh's Jones and Laughlin Steel fortune and a graduate of Choate and Harvard. Laughlin took offense and prevaricated, writing that he intended to publish *Cancer* but was waiting for the right time. "There will be a better case—if it comes to court—if Miller has been established as a serious artist," Laughlin argued. Legman would *not* be helping Miller, if underground publication set off a wave of piracies.[95]

By late 1939, though, James Laughlin's shaky resolve was getting shakier. The attorney general of New York had threatened prosecution against anyone who dared publish *Tropic of Cancer*. Legman was keeping up the pressure, vituperating Laughlin, threatening to come to Connecticut and "put hair-brushes in your bed . . . and stink bombs in your piano," while the publisher insisted that there might still be a better, safer time to bring out the book.[96] Meanwhile, Henry Miller decided he was interested in Legman's plan after all and mailed him a second edition of *Cancer* as well as Lawrence Durrell's *Black Book. Cancer* was on the Customs Department's banned list, but apparently the books reached Legman safely.

Legman's plan was to have *Cancer* offset, bind the sheets in Brooklyn, and distribute the books covertly. When it came to money, Legman never trusted Brussel "any farther than I could throw him," and so he arranged a way to pay Miller that would keep Jake's fingers out of the pot. Brussel could sell a few hundred copies to his mail-order list, and there would be only two other buyers: Legman arranged for Frances Steloff and Ben Abramson, owner of Argus Books in Chicago, to provide advance payment. Each would send Miller $1,000 cash on delivery of the books by Legman. Steloff and Abrahams would then sell the books by presale subscription or under the counter.[97]

In a letter to Legman, Miller acknowledged how dangerous the business was for everyone. He wanted Steloff to be careful, and he predicted *Tropic of Capricorn* would be banned as well.[98] Leaving Paris in May 1939, Miller wrote Legman that *Capricorn* was on sale in advanced orders, but he worried about the French censors. He was surprised and pleased that the New York Public Library had accessioned *Tropic of Cancer* into its Three Star Collection.[99]

So Legman and Jake Brussel pushed ahead. *Tropic of Cancer* went secretly to press, in an edition designed by Legman under the imprint "MEDVSA." This first American edition of *Cancer* is rare and distinctive, showing Legman's preference for a mythological reference, nonstandard spelling, and typographical play. The title for this edition was taken from a Pierre Louÿs poem that describes a woman's vulva as an undersea fruit. Using a *V* instead of a *U* in "Medusa" suggested female genitalia.[100]

ORAGENITALISM

Making the operation even more dangerous, Legman and Brussel put into production at the same time Legman's own first book, *Oragenitalism*, a catalog of techniques in oral sex. While working for Dr. Dickinson, Legman decided to take his skills as a vivid describer of heterosexual sex acts and combine them with his scientific and collecting inclinations. By 1940 Legman had delivered this original work to Jake. It was a very daring book for its time, and Legman claimed it was the first-ever scholarly treatment of its subject.[101]

Legman intended *Oragenitalism* to be part of a much longer encyclopedia of sexual techniques and part of a larger study of oral sex. His first volume would treat only the practice of *men* performing oral sex *upon* women, not vice versa, and certainly not homosexual oral sex. Legman announced that he would return to treat other styles and varieties of oral-genital contact later.[102] The book had its origins in the "Dictionary of Sexual Acts" project Legman had pitched to Dr. Dickinson when they met. As Legman recounted later, as he worked his way through the alphabet, the *C* entry gave him pause. This was no surprise, because "coitus" and all its vernacular, folk, and polite synonyms could easily take up an entire volume. As he thought about the potential entry for "coitus," he realized it could be expanded—no, it *must* be expanded—into its own encompassing volume. Farther down the *C* column was "cunnilingus." Legman's idea for a volume (or two) about oral sex hatched here. He later told collaborators and lovers it was his favorite sexual act.

A book like this had to be published under a pseudonym, so Legman made up a goofy disguise in fake French, "Roger-Maxe de La Glannege," an anagram of his name. In the introduction, "de La Glannege" insisted that his book was not a marriage manual, nor a treatise on how better to please women. This was a slam at Dr. Dickinson and the new field of marriage counseling that stressed sexual adjustment in monogamy. To the contrary, *Oragenitalism* was a celebration of a practice *men* enjoy, Legman wrote, and an exploration of why they enjoy it. He began: "The erotic use of the mouth in caressing and exciting the genitalia is, after the use of the hands and the sexual parts themselves, the most valuable erotic technique. . . . It is also the most misunderstood and the most maligned."[103] This was daring, because in some states any oral genital contact was defined as "sodomy," and in many places a partner's preference for such unnatural acts could be grounds for divorce.

Legman researched the book with his girlfriends. As opposed to Brussel's endless recycling of rewritten erotica, this was a first-person account of what Legman did or claimed to have done. He writes that he kept three-by-five-inch note cards describing every sexual encounter and partner and his reactions and reflections afterward. A few of these cards or slips of paper, sometimes with stick-figure diagrams, turn up interfiled with his papers, but the location of his sex-act index is now unclear.[104] It seems improbable that such a hectically busy young man would document his sex life so carefully, but that was Legman. He was collecting himself.[105]

Oragenitalism reads like a how-to manual, a manifesto, and a pillow book. It is explicit but sometimes distanced and dry, as if the author is describing his diagrams rather than acts and emotions. Yet it is also full of practical suggestions on how to seduce a woman who may be reluctant to try cunnilingus. Legman recommends soothing classical music over pop tunes. He gives advice on manners: never show up unshaven; never, ever choke or gag;

spermicides taste awful, so always use a condom; never be heard rinsing your mouth out; and so on. Legman promotes likely places—outdoors is great, but bring a blanket.

The book is not just about clitorises and vulvae and sometimes astounding yogic flexibility (although it is about these). It is a document of the variety of manual and oral activities that can be combined to create mutual pleasure. It has the feel of extensive personal testing, literally: there is advice about the application of orange juice and wine to the genitals (try these), and brandy (don't). It is also a statement of a deeply felt moral and erotic position, one that Legman would return to in all his sexology writings. Although sexual attitudes and practices were cultural, deeply shaped by mores and repression, sex could and should be natural. For Legman, "naturalness" was the key—it was all body on body, skin on skin, without a lot of accoutrements. When he mentions accessories, they are "natural," "normal," and human, by Legman's lights: there is no interest in getups, masks, shackles, and silk bonds. And his claim is that an act denigrated as "unnatural" is in fact the opposite. It is deeply human.[106]

To bring out the two books, Legman and Brussel worked nights in the old loft of an Armenian printer "on Lexington Avenue, just opposite the Old Armory." The printer, illiterate in English, Linotyped the books "without understanding a single line." The run was "just a couple of thousand copies [of *Tropic of Cancer*], set page-for-page after the Paris edition, and bound up in bright green cloth." Legman read the proofs himself, in his furnished room on West Thirty-Ninth Street. The copy was held for safety by Bob and Alice Sewall, friends from Scranton who lived in the same rooming house. "Alice felt that the *Tropic of Cancer* was horrible" and couldn't understand why Gershon liked "so much a book that hated and humiliated women so violently. I couldn't explain it to her: that it was like the Feast of Fools, shitting wildly one day a year on everything one really holds sacred." Bob Sewall understood it the way Gershon did and found *Tropic of Cancer* "hilarious."[107]

The copies were "stacked on the wooden skids in the loft, where they would be wrapped to mail out," when Jake Brussel's "little island of safety . . . suddenly went smash." The postal inspectors and police "landed one morning at the post box on Fourth Avenue near [Jake's] shop. . . . They forced Brussel to take them to the secret loft where the illegal editions were stored, and they found Mahlon [Blaine] there, calmly working in his own little studio corner."[108]

Blaine talked his way out of the mess and disappeared. "Even Brussel was let out on bail," Gershon wrote, and Jake came to find him at his furnished room "in the middle of the night to warn me to get out of town immediately, which I did." Gershon hid briefly with a girlfriend and caught a prompt train to Washington, D.C.[109]

Legman later realized that he had been meant to take the fall. The vice squad and postal inspectors were looking for Jake, but they had also come to recognize Gershon on his book-delivery errands around midtown. Because he was only nineteen when he began working for Brussel, he could safely run the illegal mail drop without fear of prosecution. But by early 1940, he was twenty-two. It was just a fluke that he had gone uptown to work at the Academy of Medicine that day and Jake had picked up the mail instead. Jake had been willing to put Legman and his career as a writer in jeopardy—but at least he was decent enough to wake him up and warn him to get out of town.[110]

Legman's *Oragenitalism* became a collector's item. It may have been that the police burned all of Jake Brussel's stock, including Legman's book, a common practice at the time. Or perhaps the press run was not destroyed but simply limited to begin with. Jake was known for stashing extra copies in another warehouse, which made sense in an underground trade. Later, some copies of the MEDVSA edition of *Cancer* surfaced in unbound sheets, confirming this suspicion.[111]

In any event, Legman escaped, and Jake Brussel was indicted for distributing obscene materials, tried, and imprisoned in 1941. He served several years at Lewisburg, Pennsylvania, in the same federal prison that twice housed Samuel Roth and would later be home to some of the Hollywood Ten and other suspected Reds. Legman did not attend the trial; he was justifiably afraid and stayed put in the District of Columbia. There he could continue his work for Dickinson and Painter, using the Surgeon General's Library, the National Medical Library, and the Library of Congress.[112]

There was a sequel, too. After Jake Brussel was sent to Lewisburg, Frances Steloff got a message to Legman, telling him that Ben Abramson was reneging on his promise to pay Miller a dollar a book, or $500, before sales of *Tropic of Cancer* would begin. Now, with much of the print run destroyed, Abramson refused to pay the promised advance—so Legman traveled to Chicago to twist his arm. Abramson rejected all Legman's arguments, including Gershon's insistence that writers live by their advances. Gershon demanded to know why publishers and booksellers have such wealth relative to artists. Nothing availed until Gershon threatened to go straight to the Chicago central post office, confess to retailing obscenity, and have them both arrested. Miller got his advance, though Legman had to walk Abramson from the bank to the American Express office to make sure the money order got written. He told Abramson he was the kind of Jew who gave Jews a bad name.[113]

By late 1942, Legman felt it was safe enough to return to New York to continue his multiple writing, collecting, and bibliographic projects. He occasionally took a bus to Lewisburg to visit Jake and bring him oranges. It was a long trip up the Susquehanna into the mountains of central Pennsylvania, and perhaps these visits were evidence of a not fully acknowledged friendship. Jake was a good soul, Legman wrote. He had Legman's back and would usually give him money. Yes, he was a pirate and bought low and sold high—so did all book dealers—and that was infuriating. If they were not exactly close friends, there was some respect and warmth.

After his release, Jake's family survived on Minna Brussel's silk-screen business because he was banned from any further work in publishing. He would be remembered warmly by his book-trade colleagues for having dared to print "the definitely banned *Tropic of Cancer*." But Legman would not be remembered for the work he did in arranging and designing the MEDVSA edition.[114]

It is difficult to know what would have become of *Oragenitalism* if it had not been halted by the postal raid. By 1930s and 1940s standards, it was a filthy book, even though its advocacy was covered with scientific language. (It was obscene but not sadistic, Legman would write: "Notice, no one was tied up or beaten!") Its existence, if linked to Legman, would surely have resulted in jail time for him, too. But by 1940, everyone was more interested in the notorious Henry Miller, now world famous for his suppressed novels, and no one had heard of Roger-Maxe de La Glannege. Apparently, Jake said nothing. By the time the obscenity laws were finally fully lifted in the 1960s, *Oragenitalism* seemed an oddity. It was quickly pirated by sex manual publishers, only to be outsold by illustrated books like Alex Comfort's *The Joy of Sex*, to Legman's great frustration and dismay. Illustrations were beyond Legman's and Jake's capabilities in 1939. In 1970, when French publisher Editions Truong brought out a translation featuring a graphic glossy cover photograph, it was still too much. *Oragenitalism* was quickly removed from Paris bookstores.

A DOLLAR A PAGE

Legman's connections with Miller and Steloff had another weird but felicitous offshoot. His goal from the beginning was to be a writer about sex, but as Dr. Niemoeller had advised, there was no money in sex science. But writing to titillate could pay, and Legman wanted to write about the emotional and personal side of sex. So, it is not surprising that Legman began to freelance in erotica as well.

Legman's adventures in frank pornography writing began with an Oklahoma oil millionaire and erotica collector who needed a fresh story every time he wanted to excite his "virility." The collector, Roy Melisander Johnson, was connected through his agent in New York, a bookseller named Bernard Ruder, to the semilegitimate publisher Samuel Roth. Legman's friend the artist

Sex Researcher **61**

Clara Tice was a member of an erotica-writing ring formed for Mr. Johnson, and she told Legman how to join. A creepy go-between connected Legman and Ruder, who in turn cued Legman to the customer's specific demands. Gershon began writing for Johnson at a dollar a page but was also in charge of the dangerous delivery end of the deal, shuttling back and forth between a complicated series of mid-Manhattan drop-off points. Meanwhile, Legman was supposed to stay strictly clear of Ruder, who did not want to acknowledge the customer's or the pornographer's existence. He cranked out typescript for good money, and when he grew weary of the writing, he recruited Bob Sewall to help. In the end, they received only fifty dollars per one hundred pages between them because, no surprise, Ruder was taking an unannounced 50 percent off the top.

One series of stories Legman and Sewall did together was called "The Oxford Discourse on Love." The adventures are presented by a mock-English, mock-academic Oxford professor, named "Mentullus Longus, PhD" (Dr. Long Prick, PhD), and they bear witty epigraphs typed in the shape of a female pubis (using the tab key) and fake Latin slogans like "UBI PENIS, UBI PATER" ("Where there's a penis, there's a father"). At least one of the "Oxford Discourses" is hand illustrated with a delicate watercolor of a lounging naked woman. Other volumes feature elegantly produced close-up photos of women's genitalia, tipped in between each chapter.[115]

Suddenly, and for the first time, Legman had some money. He was making fifty dollars a week for part-time work (though usually splitting it with Sewall) "when the going wage for office workers was twenty or twenty-five," and he writes that he "began buying books on a scale I had never approached before."[116] Although formerly a snappy dresser, in pearl-gray hats and silk scarves, his clothes had long since begun to wear out. But now instead of sprucing up, "I completely gave up buying clothes except for one pair of low work shoes and a woolen sweater-coat about once every two years." Friends who met him during these years noted his pants held up by a rope belt and his raveling mittens.[117] Building his library was more important.

Later, Legman said that the pornography writing gave him writer's block: it made him impotent intellectually (though not physically, he was quick to assert), and devoting himself to another man's arousal exhausted him emotionally. Over several months, he pushed more and more work onto Bob Sewall, who was an excellent stylist and parodist. As the writers scrounged for fresh ideas, they copied popular genre fiction and all kinds of well-read stories, inserting erotic situations in the style of the author Dashiell Hammett, for example. When Legman loaned Sewall his volume of *Tropic of Cancer*, Bob decided to try impersonating Miller. Soon they had convinced the subagent, the agent, and the customer that indeed Henry Miller himself was writing

62   CHAPTER 2

erotica to order. Just as the scheme was beginning to fray, the real Henry Miller arrived fleeing the war, and Legman realized that it might make sense to step out of the whole precarious operation.[118]

Legman sent Miller a message to meet him at Gotham Book Mart to discuss an interesting opportunity, but Miller sent a proxy, his erstwhile lover the elegant Spanish American Anaïs Nin.[119] It was now over between Nin and Miller, but she remained his patroness and friend.

Legman would remember Nin as a real *"poule de luxe,"* who gave him a penetrating gaze as they shook hands. She was "very elegantly dressed but in a refined and underplayed way," and her shoes were marvelous, high-heeled, wrap-around suede booties. Nin had had a very fine education and was married to a wealthy banker before 1938, but "Hitler changed all that." Many people she loved had been caught up in the Spanish Civil War and the defeat of the Republic, although she had weathered the 1930s in Paris.[120]

Nin was a sexual adventuress, and Legman thought she had come to the meeting prepared to have an affair with him, if he had turned out to be interesting. But, he recalled, he was "too young, not rich enough." Yet she phoned him later at the Book Mart and asked to meet, and they began a short, intense liaison, at her direction.

When they met privately, he explained to her why his edition of *Tropic of Cancer* was called MEDVSA. The idea of the imprint was drawn from Pierre Louÿs's erotic poem "Aphrodite," "where the slave girl . . . is describing and adoring the body of the Greek courtesan, in terms consciously modeled on the Song of Songs; but stops in awe unable to describe her cunt." The courtesan continues:

> It is like a flower of crimson, full of honey and of perfumes
> It is like a hydra of the sea, living and soft, open at night.
> It is the humid grotto, the shelter always warm,
> The Asylum where man rests from his march to death.
> It is terrifying. It is the face of Medusa.[121]

His recitation had the hoped-for effect on Anaïs Nin. They made love on her velvet couch. For a few weeks, he took her for long walks around Lower Manhattan. She liked the secondhand bookstores, the riverfronts, and the homeless camps on the Bowery, a street whose "grimy sordidness and ugly poverty under the overshadowing elevated structure seemed to fascinate her."[122] They ate in immigrant restaurants.

Legman was trying to convince Nin to pass along the erotica writing business to Henry Miller or take it over herself. He was no good at it, he explained—in fact, he was terrible. But if Miller could do it, he should. Legman urged that they should not agree to take less than $100 per hundred pages, and he explained how Bernard Ruder had been skimming. And they should keep carbon copies of everything they wrote.[123]

To have a woman write erotica, he thought, would be wonderful. It would be groundbreaking for men to know how women thought about sex "in a totally frank way." For her part, Anaïs was shocked to learn that the famous erotic books signed with women's names "have almost always been fabricated by men," and she was taken aback by Legman's knowledge of eighteenth- and nineteenth-century classical and cheap pornography. He explained that it was all he was interested in.[124]

Legman showed her a manuscript he was producing for the oil millionaire, and she "read a few pages here and there." She was not impressed. "'Do readers find this exciting?' she asked me. 'I suppose so,' I answered, very subdued. The situation was depressing because we both realized what I was doing was literary prostitution of the most literal kind, and that I had offered to Miller and to herself nothing but the opportunity to do the same."[125] When their affair ended, it just faded away. Legman "never recollected our affair with any pleasure," because they had not really liked each other. She looked down on Legman's folklore pursuits and disdained low culture in general. They argued about this and about literature and psychoanalysis.[126] Later, Legman realized she had never allowed him into her bedroom, and she never introduced him "to any of the French and British writers and artists who informed her expatriate group."[127]

Anaïs Nin and Henry Miller did take up writing for Roy M. Johnson, but Miller quickly lost interest, and in any case he was headed west to work on *The Air-Conditioned Nightmare*. Nin organized some friends into a kind of porn writers' atelier and described this adventure in fragments in *Delta of Venus*. In the story "Marianne," a young woman secretary is aroused by her typing assignments and "accidentally" leaves a typescript of her own around for her employer (Nin) to read. Thus begins another story of seduction.[128]

Like Legman, Nin found it difficult to produce arousing stories on a production schedule, and she and her friends quickly came to hate Johnson's demands. All the artists in her workshop wanted to discuss feelings, emotions, aesthetic responses, fantasies, and dreams, while Johnson only wanted direct descriptions. He kept sending letters saying the work was satisfactory, but he wanted "less poetry, more sex." "Dear Collector," Nin wrote back, "We hate you!"[129] But actually, she and her comrades pitied Johnson and began to worry about *his* erotic makeup, so solitary, so direct, and so dependent upon them. After a few years, Nin was able to set up her own handprinting atelier and shed the burden of writing erotica to order.

Years later, when Legman read *Delta of Venus*, he credited himself with kicking off Nin's erotica career, although he was unaware of it at the time.

She *had saved the carbons* just as he had advised. She never wrote about him in her memoirs at all, but that was all right. Women wrote the best erotica, he thought.[130]

The years between 1936 and 1940 were intense and defining for Legman. He had begun his working life. In a short period, he had found a way into the world of sex research and learned his way around it. He was learning the ins and outs of New York's great libraries, including their secret collections. And he was mastering the keys to bibliography, absorbing the techniques of printing and binding, and becoming fluent in the book trade. As bad as the Depression was, he was supporting himself and becoming an expert in the folklore of sex, a subject he defined himself. He had organized a career that was completely unacceptable to his father.

Yet Emil's influence was there. The textual and analytic skills drilled into Gershon in heder and yeshiva were a foundation Gershon could turn to his own uses, as he invented his own mode of scholarship and collected projects to obsess over for decades. He had produced an exacting glossary and published his own first book, although *Oragenitalism* could not appear in any bookstore window. Gershon was a success on his own terms and was somehow keeping his own integrity in a double-dealing world. He was twenty-two, and his work was just beginning.

3

KINSEY'S BIBLIOGRAPHER

If you want a sex library, put yourself in my hands. . . .
No one was ever sorry.

—G. Legman to Alfred Charles Kinsey, January 28, 1943

In the fall of 1940, a copy of Dr. George Henry's book *Sex Variants* landed on the desk of Indiana University zoology professor Alfred Charles Kinsey. Impressed with the volume (which he called "Sex Deviants"), Kinsey wrote to Dr. Dickinson that he found it "very important" and that the glossary section "by George Legman strikes me as unusually scholarly."[1] Kinsey sent a personal note to Legman congratulating him again on his accomplished work. This was the beginning of a contentious and revealing relationship.[2]

In descriptions of Legman's New York years, he is often described as Kinsey's first bibliographer. Legman was a bibliographer, but the word does not reveal the centrality of the work he did privately for Kinsey and officially for Indiana University. Legman helped lay down the foundation for the Kinsey Institute for Sex Research (later, the Kinsey Institute for Research in Sex and Gender) by assembling and cataloging the core of its unmatched library and rare-book collections.[3] Legman donated some of his own folklore of sex materials to the institute archives, and he encouraged other scholars to donate "unpublishable" materials also.[4] "The Kinsey" became a place where people could deposit their secret sex collections for preservation. Thus, the ground was prepared for a remarkable assemblage of cultural materials, including fugitive and ephemeral documents, sex paraphernalia, and erotic art.

It seems improbable that the two men would cross paths, but they had a great deal in common. Both were obsessed with fighting America's sexual repression. Although separated by a generation, Legman and Kinsey had quite similar childhood experiences.[5] Each grew up amid economic instability and hard times, and each man's father was a brute and an economic failure by American standards. Kinsey's father was a Methodist, sometime lay minister, and a rigid disciplinarian; as we have seen, Emil Legman was a poor but highly learned Jew with a nasty, obsessive piety. Kinsey worked his way to Bowdoin College and then to Harvard for a Ph.D. He knew evolutionary theory and zoology, yet his biology and taxonomic skills were almost entirely self-taught. And although Kinsey's urban field trips would become more frequent, he was mostly stuck in provincial Indiana. They shared an insatiable compulsion to collect: in Legman's case, the bibliography and material of erotica and folklore; in Kinsey's, first insects, then sexual histories.

By 1939, while Gershon was covertly printing *Oragenitalism* and *Tropic of Cancer*, Alfred Kinsey had his famous sex histories project under way. He was far along with the enormous statistical collection that he would unveil in 1948 as *Sexual Behavior in the Human Male*.[6] For years, Kinsey had been experimenting with interview methods for collecting evidence of the range and variety of men's sexual behavior, and by 1940 when he read the homosexual glossary, he was gathering histories on the Indiana University campus. With the help of carefully selected researchers, Kinsey quickly fanned out into a much larger data-gathering project—collecting detailed sex-life histories from men's clubs, women's associations, prisoners, Rotarians, academic departments, professional and occupational groups, church congregations, fraternities, and sororities.[7]

The more interviews Kinsey did, the more variation and variability he found in sexual behavior, in what people did, or admitted to doing. Kinsey was coming to think that most human beings were basically bisexual and that social and cultural repression usually kept this out of human awareness. This was a radically modern view for the time. After several years, he decided that behavioral variation was "so great and so extreme" that the concept of abnormal sexuality made no sense from a scientific point of view. The extent of sexual variation "made moral judgment impossible—or valueless," and "the invocation of disease or dysfunction is really 'nearly always' asserting the *mores* of society."[8] Only social definition explained "deviance."

In its contemporary setting, Kinsey's research was socially and politically reformist, although couched in a thorough scientism. He often wrote privately that he hoped he could help end cruel laws and increase tolerance.

It is worth examining Kinsey's methods in detail here, so that we can better understand Legman's eventual attacks on "The Human Male" study.

Kinsey faced several complicated scientific and practical problems once he realized his interviews would be the basis for large statistical studies. First, how would interviewees be located? How could they be interviewed, frankly and straightforwardly, about such personal and delicate matters? How could the researchers be sure, or even tentatively confident, that the information offered was truthful? On the one hand, Kinsey needed to probe and uncover, but on the other, he needed to guard against exaggeration, boasting, and the vagaries of memory.[9]

Then there were recruitment problems: interviewees needed to feel they had total anonymity for their interview data; the researchers needed to feel that they were getting a whole picture of a population and not just interviewing the lonely, the obsessive, or the sex-talk enthusiasts.

Kinsey developed a solution to this problem with biologist Robert Kroc (brother of Ray Kroc, the founder of McDonald's): they called it the 100 percent group strategy. Volunteers were not volunteers in the usual sense but were pulled in by other members of their group for the sake of science. Thus, Kinsey aimed for 100 percent of a woman's club, a fraternity, a professional organization, or an occupational group in a city, and in some cases, he got 100 percent of a small rural community. The problem here was the definition of "group," which was too flexible: taxi drivers, hikers, and gardeners in small numbers were sometimes cast as "groups." But the Kinsey team worked effectively through affiliations and the American propensity for civic associations. His recruitment method was, in effect, a massively inclusive snowball sample.[10]

He chose his interviewers for their ability to be friendly and interested but scrupulously nonjudgmental. Kinsey trained his men and a few women extensively, often for more than a year, in his interview method. They memorized a long list of questions and coded answers for strict anonymity on a small piece of paper. Interviewers asked about everything, and in positive terms: "When did you first . . . ?" rather than "Did you ever . . . ?" which could force the volunteer to deny stigmatized activities such as masturbation or bestiality.[11] Kinsey did "retakes" or reinterviews after several years with small samples as a test of accuracy, truthfulness, and memory. Not surprisingly, his findings show that memories of past sexual activities changed over time, because as people added new experiences and partners, their lives changed in retrospect.

Although there were challenges to Kinsey's sampling methods, his biographers and historians of sex research agree that his statistical techniques were, for the time, standard and accurate.[12] His survey methods were the best he could have devised at the time without anonymous mass data-gathering techniques.

LEGMAN AND "THE HUMAN MALE"

In August 1942, Kinsey wrote to Legman in care of Dr. Dickinson, again admiring his glossary. "I consider it the most scholarly thing which has been done in that field," he wrote, " . . . a more accurate portrayal of the homosexual than any treatise I know of." He admired Legman's detailed work: "[It] is not often that we find someone who has such an abundance of first hand data and who can handle it in the scholarly fashion that apparently you are." Perhaps, he hoped, there would be "mutual value in our separate research studies."[13] But war mobilization made it difficult to arrange a meeting. For several months, Legman and Kinsey assessed each other by mail. Each man laid out the problems of working in a field that had to reckon with legal and social repression. Over a year and a half, they fitfully argued about method, tried out important questions, and discussed their philosophical orientations. Each man expressed admiration for the other, and Legman managed to muster some deference while showing off his erudition. Not only was Kinsey a tenured professor, but he held out the possibility that he might employ Legman, who was, as usual, hard up for cash.

At first, Kinsey asked Dickinson and Legman to work over an enormous aggregation of hundreds of thousands of penis measurements. Legman suspected the measurements had been collected under perverse circumstances. Legman quickly showed Kinsey that he had difficulty with statistics, and the project foundered.[14] But if Legman was a poor quantitative analyst, he was working to persuade Kinsey that he knew the European literature on homosexuality and that this was knowledge Kinsey needed.[15] With a good knowledge of the literature, Kinsey could do a much more responsible job.

Legman wrote that he had been working on a seven-thousand-card bibliography of homosexuality "covering *belles lettres* of the last 500 years, and especially the medico-psychiatric literature of the last 75 years," and by comparison with Magnus Hirschfeld's work and that of others of the past twenty-five years, Dr. Henry's book was pathetic, "utterly de novo," from "utter ignorance."[16]

They discussed Kinsey's emerging findings and the "causes" of homosexuality: "I do not believe that HS [homosexuality] can be 'cured,'" Legman wrote, "unless heterosexuality can be 'cured' too, and I consider the attitude of mind that studies any extreme psychosexual state involving such enormous numbers of the world's population . . . (40 million to 60 million, 2–3% [being] the conservative estimate) with an eye to instituting a therapy, to be unscientific in the extreme. Why not 'cure' the similar number of redheaded people?" He commented on a paper by Kinsey's team on the possible hormonal basis of homosexuality: "I think it [homosexuality] is psychological/environmental as much as hormonal or chromosomal." Psychology could not be divorced from biochemistry, he thought. But it was also the case that homosexuality was not a uniform or stable identity: there are "'milder' and vacillating cases," he thought, following the work of Magnus Hirschfeld, using quotation marks to distance himself a bit from the language of disease. He added, "The trouble with all *biochemical* and *antiseptic* research is the gaucheness [meaning here the raw uneducatedness] with which the biochemists pick their specimens and label them thus and so, before measuring their penes and sampling their urine."[17] These were human beings, after all.

Kinsey thought Thomas Painter's manuscript on male prostitution was profoundly important. Dr. Dickinson had hired Legman to help Painter get it into shape for publication and to compile a comprehensive bibliography to go with it. But there was great difficulty in turning it into a book. According to Legman, one negotiation over publication "broke down when the publisher refused to consider a chapter appendix (40 pages) of toilet room inscriptions." He found this infuriating. "When they dig up Herculaneum after 2000 years, the most austere publishing houses in Europe print the outhouse and whore-house scribblings; but nobody will print those of Times and Trafalgar Squares," he fumed.[18] Even without the graffiti appendix, the Painter manuscript was impossible to bring out. The behavior it described was too troubling.

When Kinsey could finally get to New York in late 1942, he, Dickinson, and Legman met several times, talking sex research late into the night. All three sensed that sex research in America was entering a new and expansive phase and that perhaps some of its stigma could be shed. In January 1943, Kinsey wrote to thank Legman "for the many hours you gave me when I was in New York and for the considerable education which you gave me. . . . You and Dr. Dickinson contributed more to my education than I have ever gotten in such a limited time before."[19]

During this visit, they must have talked about the New York scene that gave rise to Legman's glossary. Kinsey was by now collecting histories from everyone he could, and he spent significant time exploring the public men's rooms of Times Square, the "tea-room trade" of anonymous encounters. Legman may have been his Virgil, because these were the same bathrooms where he was collecting graffiti for his "folk epigraphy" project.[20] Undoubt-edly, Kinsey interviewed Legman about his sex history and measured his genitals. Legman gave Kinsey a copy of *Oragenitalism*. On the flyleaf of the copy of the rare Brussel first edition, he wrote, " . . . from Gershon Legman, 1943, (posthumously)." He was joking that Kinsey's grueling interview had done him in.

By early 1943, their correspondence was mainly about books, book buying, and the need for an excellent psychological and humanistic approach to sex research to complement Kinsey's emphasis on empirical description. They began to generate "want lists" of projected purchases. Shortly after they met, Legman loaned Kinsey a personal manuscript of New York City bawdy folk songs, limericks, and rhymes he collected during the 1930s, which formed the nucleus of his later folklore books.[21]

Kinsey hoped to use Legman in his project: he planned to come again to New York for a month or two in the summer or fall of 1943, mainly "to work with Dickinson and the libraries available in the city." He continued, "I definitely want a better control of the literature and in this end, you can help me." He suggested that he would like to allocate some money in his next budget "to persuade you to give us some concentrated time in working on a bibliography." Perhaps it would be a full-time job for a half year or more. Full employment working on the bibliography of sex must have seemed a miracle, or something close to it, to Legman. He was amazed when Kinsey suggested that he step down to Miss Steloff's Gotham Book Mart and look there for "any item with which you are not thoroughly familiar." Kinsey would pay Legman to explore Frances Steloff's secret stash.[22]

Legman answered that "your letter made me happier than I have been in a very long time."[23] He had been broke and moping, and living on the very margins, shifting from borrowed room to borrowed room. And now Kinsey had expressed warm concern and empathy, stating, "I am disturbed by your lack of opportunity to do the things in which you can contribute most," which Legman very much appreciated.[24] "Your letter was like medicine," he answered. He added that Dr. Dickinson had been enormously impressed by Kinsey and was planning to send him copies of the illustrations Mahlon Blaine had made for Joseph Weckerle's *Das Goldene Buch de Liebe* (The golden book of love), a nineteenth-century German manual of sex techniques that Legman had worked on for Jake Brussel. Then Legman immediately added a list of "two or three-star books that come to my mind off hand," which he knew Kinsey would absolutely need as part of "a good nucleus of standard jam-packed informative books from which you can spiral out" when someone was paying him.[25]

Legman worked hard to convince Kinsey that scientific sex research demanded a good library, not just a small collection of biology texts and cheap "sex-sellers." After a long discussion of erotica prices and book-buying problems, Legman came to the point. Kinsey had sent Legman a list of his existing library, and he thought only about thirty of the titles were worth having. "I suppose you tried hard in collecting the books you have, . . . but really Doc that stuff is all just skirting the borderlines. . . . If you want a sex library, put yourself in my hands. You won't be the first guy that did. No one was ever sorry." Legman constructed himself as a library buyer: "I usually lead the current chump far afield, but after a while he begins to see the concentric relevance and strata-built mass of evidence he is getting. Be assured it will cost dough. In the end, twice what you might offhand expect to lay out. *With luck though you will have a collection with as good a set of basic sex tomes as any big medical library."* At any rate, Legman was interested in just seeing "the high-class stuff that floats around. That would be my kick." Maybe Kinsey could publish the sorts of things Legman could not: "Take it awaaaaay, Indiana!"[26]

The library-building project was under way. Now both men had to be circumspect about the materials Legman was mailing from New York, and he included cautions like "disregard strange return address."[27] Legman suspected that he was on a police or Post Office Department watch list during these years because of his association with Jake Brussel and Samuel Roth; Brussel was in prison at this time, and Roth was on probation after serving one sentence and would shortly face another. Kinsey, however, was a distinguished professor and a charming person. His friendly relationship with the Bloomington postmaster usually insulated him from the Comstock laws.[28]

By late 1943, Kinsey and Legman had worked out an arrangement. Legman was now formally a member of Kinsey's sprawling, ambitious research project "The Human Male." They agreed that Legman would select books, make recommendations, assess prices, and get the purchased materials safely to Bloomington. At first, he refused to take a commission for his book finding and booklegging, but then he asked for a small salary that Kinsey declined to provide. Eventually, Legman agreed to a 10 percent commission on the sale price of each book. This money came out of Kinsey's private funds in order to protect Indiana University from charges of dealing in obscenity. (The booksellers also took 10 percent, which created an incentive to drive the price of rare or illegal books higher.)

A bit later in 1944, with Rockefeller Foundation money flowing through the National Research Council (NRC) to Indiana University and into Kinsey's expanding research, Legman was put on the first payroll at forty dollars a week, solely for bibliographic work. He was to send his bibliographic work regularly, with an invoice. Legman knew that a good specialized library needed a comprehensive checklist of the literature in its subject area—as well as a catalog of its own holdings. He began to create this essential tool for Kinsey. The dual flow of payments made good sense from Kinsey's point of view. But Legman found the arrangement finicky and hard on his cash flow.

For the bibliography, Legman's assignment was to build a master list of the international literature on sex, as he had done for Dickinson and Painter on homosexuality. He combed through medical as well as public and private libraries on the East Coast, searching for references in scholarly journals to articles relating in any way to human sexuality. If his reading skills in German, French, Italian, Dutch, Latin, and Greek were not perfect, they were improving fast. It was a richly productive time because his own interests were so close to what Kinsey needed: as he wrote bibliographies, he made notes for his folklore and erotica collections. He cultivated librarians and collectors, although he was poor at getting along with people in authority. Somehow in his spare hours, he was able to keep up with his own writing and love affairs. He was laying the groundwork for the much later *Horn Book: Studies in Erotic Folklore* (1963). His introductions to Patrick Kearney's study of the British Museum's Private Case, the "inferno" of inadmissible, uncataloged books, and to the pornographic *My Secret Life* were grounded in these book lists.

Kinsey's name could open doors and provide Legman with legitimate access to otherwise restricted collections. Sometimes the rarities he sought were really rare. He asked Kinsey to help him to gain access to Columbia's copy of the famous Turin Papyrus, which he described as "the oldest known visual representation of heterosexual intercourse, with thirteen positions illustrated, one for each sign of the Zodiac." (Legman knew or hoped that it contained depictions of oral sex.) The university librarian was suspicious of Legman, who had been hanging around the copy's display case, but, Gershon wrote, maybe a person of Kinsey's stature could open the way with a letter of introduction.[29]

Most important to him, Legman got to chase after, handle, and enjoy rare erotic and sexological works. Since he could not afford them himself, he was happy knowing they were becoming part of a great, new library. He later wrote that bibliography was the poor man's rare-book collecting: a way of cherishing the books, however temporarily. He was helping create an authoritative universe of the literature on sex and love. He would underscore "love."

Kinsey also benefited from the relationship. In Legman he had a cheap, knowledgeable, and multilingual book buyer with experience skirting the law. But it was not a trusting relationship. Kinsey, usually in Indiana, could not supervise Legman's work, and he repeatedly urged Dr. Dickinson to keep an eye on "George." He was exacting. Having grown up poor, Kinsey was more than careful with money, and because sex research was so sensitive, he could have no embarrassments. It had to be a secret that he was forming a great sex and erotica library, and costs and expenses had to be diligently tracked.

But problems arose more basically, from the deeper orientation of each man toward the work of researching sex. Legman was in it for the love of it all: sex and bibliography. Kinsey was fundamentally a taxonomist and an empiricist, but he was also a university man making a transition to institution building.[30] While Legman romantically sought feeling and mystery in erotic life, Kinsey was absorbed by his scientific method's ability to record an unsuspected range of sexual expression.

BLOWUP

As much as he loved book lists, Legman was becoming bored with chasing down bibliographic entries in medical journals. He longed to return to his lexicography and etymology projects. On the vernal equinox of 1943, Legman wrote to Kinsey that he was typing the homosexuality bibliography for Dickinson—and had finished the letter *C* in his own bibliography of sex technique. He would like to do more "glossarial work"—the glossary in the Henry book was just a tiny part of what was possible. Perhaps Kinsey would support this? Kinsey did not reply, meaning that the answer was no.[31]

A rare volume called Clowes's *Bibliotheca Arcana*, a list of prohibited books in English, caused problems.[32] To Legman, the books he tracked down, especially the scarce ones, were part of a suppressed human heritage. It is no wonder that he could not refrain from holding on to a few of them, taking notes and enjoying them, before forwarding them to Bloomington, as was the case with the *Arcana*. To Kinsey, this was research material paid for by himself, and it had to be kept track of.

The fight came to a head in the spring of 1944, when Kinsey furiously demanded Legman send the *Arcana* immediately. In Legman's view, all his work, and his clinging on to Clowes's *Arcana*, was in the cause of scholarship. Kinsey ought to appreciate his contribution to the field. Why, he wrote, did Kinsey care if *Arcana* arrived this month or in eighteen months?[33]

Kinsey charged that Legman was dilatory about sending books in general, and he revealed that he suspected Legman was not honest. He was sending Legman book money, but the books arrived slowly and sometimes not at all. This aggravated Legman. He pointed out that the war had dried up the imports of rare books from Europe. The books arrived slowly because there was no market to speak of. He had been generous with his research materials, and he called Kinsey a rigid hypocrite: "Let's be clear: When you asked to borrow the ms [manuscript] on male prostitution (*my* ms as everyone seems to have forgotten), no time limit was put by me on its availability to you. I do not remember how long you had the [erotic] folk-verse [of New York City] ms, but it was several months, and I remember very clearly the bad grace with which you returned it."[34]

Legman also accused Kinsey of being small-minded. Money worried him too much, but the commissions he paid Legman weren't so great that they were worth the trouble, and, he pointed out, "the various possibilities of danger are something you never even thought of paying for."[35]

Kinsey, who is said to have fought with all his librarians, complained that Legman's bibliographic method was inefficient.[36] They disagreed about his way of searching. In the 1940s, all bibliography was still produced by hand, in a craft process. The scientific and medical libraries Legman was consulting created special subject bibliographies from their own collections, with a card for every book or journal and often one for every journal article. Legman was using these tools. Kinsey had asked Legman to review every journal he could access and make a card for each article entry, a massive waste of time to Legman, since librarians and journal indexers had already done this. Among rare books and fugitive publications, he followed his own snowballing or spiraling method, often copying from others' footnotes, and then correcting these against rare originals. Kinsey was outraged to find that Legman's necessarily redundant work process resulted in what looked like duplicate file cards, and these seemed to contain conflicting or erroneous entries. Legman replied that Kinsey misunderstood. A master bibliography was the result not just of gathering references but of a process of cross-checking for maximum accuracy. Because author, publisher, place, and date were thorny problems in the fugitive fields of erotica and sexual studies, there would be multiple entries and contradictions. Tracing errors was a part of correcting the errors (or deceptions) that had crept into the record through the librarians' multiple recopyings over the years. Kinsey should *always* trust his most recent card. But Kinsey, who would not be contradicted, became furious.

Kinsey was always painfully sensitive to the possibility that he or anyone else might be cheated. He accused Legman of recopying work he had already done for Dickinson and submitting invoices for more work than he had completed.[37] On his side, Legman was outraged at being ordered to produce a quota of cards according to a schedule. This was serious intellectual work, after all. "I don't sell my time," he snarled at Kinsey. "I sell a finished product."[38] When he discovered that Indiana University was deducting payroll taxes (a federally mandated procedure after 1941) from his paychecks, he became angrier. This was impossibly unfair in the middle of a war, with inflation soaring, when he was making so little. He didn't even work for Indiana University! He reminded Kinsey that he was supporting two (fictional) children and their mothers![39]

It seems a trivial dispute, but Kinsey was an exacting boss, and Legman found it nearly impossible to be anyone's employee. On the technical question, Legman was right. His method of careful cross-checking was the only way to produce a bibliography that reflected the messy history of a suppressed, ill-studied literature. It *was* counterproductive to treat someone with his skills as an hourly copyist. But if Kinsey was paying Legman "by the card," Legman did have every reason to try to expand the number he submitted. With no capital, Legman could not buy books and then bill Kinsey for reimbursement: he had to hold on to the cash while he hunted the desired volumes. And he did have a bad habit of holding on to rare books as he read and put them to his own use.

In early 1945, when Legman still had not sent along Clowes's *Arcana*, Kinsey boiled over. He demanded either his books or his money be returned immediately. Not only had Legman been impossible to work with, he dictated, but "you have mulcted Dr. Dickinson, and his colleagues, and despise them for it." Kinsey's secretary was unfamiliar with the old-fashioned verb "to mulct" (to defraud or cheat), and she typed, "You have mulched Dr. Dickinson and his colleagues . . ."[40]

Legman replied immediately, discussing the value of vegetable matter applied to the roots of plants. Did Kinsey think he was composting poor Robert Dickinson? But perhaps Kinsey meant that he'd cheated the doctor in some way? He denied he despised Dickinson: "I hold the old coot in high regard!"[41] He signed this letter: "G. Legman, ("Mulcher")."

The fight spilled over to Thomas Painter's "Homosexual Prostitute" manuscript. Now Kinsey accused Legman of trying to make off with it. Legman affirmed he had briefly used the Painter bibliography, checking it for a reference on sodomy in the British navy, but he had not stolen it. Now he demanded access to the full manuscript, which he regarded as his because of all the work he had done on it. (Painter had enlisted and was stationed in Texas and was not part of the dispute.) When Kinsey told Dickinson that Legman was up to no good, Dickinson locked the manuscript in a closet at the New York Academy of Medicine.[42] He later transferred it to Kinsey.

The end of the relationship was maddening to Legman. It was one of many reenactments of conflict with an authoritarian man who could help, could understand, but refused to do so. On paper Legman used all his wit and psychological acumen to strike back. He blasted Kinsey with a "You can't fire me, I quit!" letter. "Money again—why does it worry you so?" he prodded Kinsey. Well, no matter, the professor would get his book, or his money, whichever he preferred, just as soon as the government refunded the payroll taxes they had deducted from the payments for Legman's bibliographic work.[43]

Was Legman ripping off Kinsey? Years later, the folklore of the Kinsey Institute had it that he was. One colleague of Kinsey's recounted that Legman was making up nonexistent rare books and selling them to Kinsey, but there is no support for this in the letters.[44] Legman simply took Kinsey's money, which he needed to live on, as a kind of loan against the cards he would compile and the books he was sure he would deliver. Some stories imply he was selling his own books to Kinsey at inflated prices, but this seems unlikely, since Legman the bibliophile really did care more for books than money. It seems more likely that Kinsey's two-track payment method backfired because, to Legman, cash was cash. When Kinsey insulted him, Legman used this as an excuse to keep the few books *and* the money, less than fifty dollars. He probably rationalized it as fair payment for the aggravation.

Legman and Kinsey would hold on to their mutual antagonism and resentments. The conflict and Legman's later criticisms of Kinsey's research for "The Human Male" reveal their different orientations in the nascent field of sex research. Sexual behavior inquiry was becoming a part of social as well as medical science, and it was becoming professionalized. Legman wanted to participate, as a sex expert and humanist. But Kinsey's letters show suspicion toward the uncredentialed younger man. Kinsey had his own tangle of intellectual insecurities. He came up through the prestigious but narrow channel of biology study at Harvard and felt he lacked cultural refinement. Perhaps he felt threatened by the striving young expert in the literature of sex.

Legman had hit a mark with his jab about money. By the 1930s, Kinsey was doing well financially, receiving royalties from successful biology textbooks. From 1945 he was funded by large grants from the Rockefeller Foundation. He had no rational reason to begrudge Legman a smallish loan, as he loaned many of his graduate students small amounts of money. But Gershon Legman was not a graduate student, and he was not part of Kinsey's inner circle. Kinsey could not bear to see anyone cheated, and he made Dr. Dickinson the symbolically victimized person in the dispute.

The two men's different sexualities and sexual philosophies surely underlay the clash. Kinsey was discovering his bisexuality well before he met Legman, although this had to be kept a secret in conservative Bloomington and from his larger public. Legman suspected Kinsey was not heartily heterosexual, and he noted Kinsey's penchant for surrounding himself with handsome young men.[45] The "vibe" Legman got from Kinsey added to his antagonism.

More important, Legman and other observers saw that Kinsey's work was unfolding an empirical basis for tolerance of homosexuality and other behaviors still seen as deviant: Kinsey argued that same-sex sex acts, along with premarital sex and masturbation, were too common, too much part of "the range," to be criminalized. This would be a major implication of all his publications.[46] But Legman found this disturbing.

In his petition for Legman's draft deferral in 1941, Dickinson's colleague Dr. Robert Laidlaw attested that Gershon had had homosexual experiences.[47] In his memoirs, Gershon tells us that when he was a teenager, he experienced homosexual seductions in Scranton and near assaults on the streets of Manhattan. He witnessed the rape of a boy while hoboing.[48] Legman's attitudes toward homosexuality vacillated between conflicted and homophobic. He was drawn to young homosexual men and their folklore—thus his work with Tom Painter on the manuscript and glossary—and at the same time, he was repulsed and frightened by male homosexuality. Especially in his later writings—for example, in *Love & Death* and his letters in the late 1940s—he expressed intense hostility to the cultural influence of gay men, whom he suspected of a conspiracy to subvert a normal heterosexuality. He was viscerally hostile to lesbians, seeing them as a threat to his masculine prerogatives, as his later writings reveal.

Certainly, his prejudices were very much a part of the mainstream in those years. Sensing Kinsey's position, Legman expressed a tolerant attitude. He initially wrote to Kinsey that he did not believe in punishments, prohibitions, or cures for homosexuality. But a few years after this, he would draft an essay, "On the Cause of Homosexuality," attempting to modify and recast Freud's theories of an "origin" for homosexuality that suited his own uneasy perspective.

"MINORITY REPORT"

When Kinsey's *Human Male* was published in 1948, Legman let loose with stringent criticisms. They were published as "A Minority Report" in *The Sexual Conduct of Men and Women*, a book thrown together by "Norman Lockridge," a pseudonym of the renegade publisher Samuel Roth.[49] Legman and Roth were aiming to take advantage of the publicity surrounding all things Kinsey. It is clear from its style and content that *The Sexual Conduct of Men and Women* was written almost entirely by Gershon himself.[50]

Sexual Conduct combined descriptions of contemporary dating and sexual customs with Legman's own opinions about love and sex, gender, and relationships. Although written quickly, in places the book revealed Legman thinking like a folklorist. Documenting attitudes and describing patterns of behavior, he detailed traditions, beliefs, and customs he observed in Scranton and among the men and women he knew in New York. Roth wanted the book to be sold over the counter, so Legman drew a curtain across the overt description of sexual acts. He wrote instead about the contemporaneous culture of courting and dating, from a man's point of view. He grandiosely announced that the book's first half would be "What Men Expect from Women," with the second half turning the question around. But when he approached "What Women Expect from Men," the book trailed off, probably more for reasons of time and space than the author's interest.

Sexual Conduct follows male-female relations through the life course, from birth through school, work, dating, love and marriage, and divorce, commenting all the while on the social pressures shaping heterosexual relationships. Typical of Legman, it is both full of detail and polemical. On matrimony, he demands to know why the married push and shove everyone else to the altar and why bachelors must be seen as woebegone and unhappy, when "domestic love is not an exciting spectacle." Weddings themselves have "the essential dismal formality of a funeral," and he notes the vows are changing from "love, honor and obey" to "love, honor and cherish." Is "cherish" not an obvious, rhetorical "dehorning," a reduction of masculine importance? And is it not ridiculous, he wonders, "for a man and woman to swear away their emotions for a life-time in advance"?[51]

He takes up the modern stag party, contrasting it with the Jewish custom of the groom breaking the glass chalice with his foot, and all the annoying joking that surrounds it. Then there is all the female "mewling and puling and crying," "the Jerusalem wailing . . . and the noisy cowlike commiseration with the bride."[52] He finds a weird psychosexual reaction among married women who cry at weddings. Apparently, they experience "a combination of simple lascivious picturing of the first embrace and a woebegone reflection on how badly their own marriages have turned out," he writes. In any case, "eventually, the guests run out of bawdy jokes and posturings," and the poor, cringing couple can leave.

Legman skips over the honeymoon's "unmailable details" but argues that what a husband hopes for is "glamour," important on "any night of love." Her beauty, carefulness, a lovely bedroom with good sheets, and a good negligee that displays "the article but does not protect it" can help "her nakedness seem to be more so," he writes hopefully. (This does not sound like the many urgent trysts in rented rooms in midtown that Legman describes in his own memoir.) But here is Legman the microhistorian of sex: "Traditionally women keep their stockings on and nothing else." But, he notes, this habit has now come to be associated with prostitutes.[53]

In the role of opinionated adviser, Legman writes that women should be "all woman and no fraud." He decries too frequent hair dyeing, changes of makeup, and clothing style. A woman should be who she is, with no padding, lifting, tightening, bolstering, or fake nipples. Any act of "physical possession," he writes, is actually "the culmination of a chase, a hunt . . . as primitive as any ice age mating in a cave."[54] No man wants to feel tricked after so much effort.

Love and marriage were not the same things at all, Legman argues here, although sadly women are often taught so. When it develops, love is a matter of taste, geography, and proximity. As for marriage, beauty was a bad idea in a wife. A woman who was intelligent and not obsessed with her looks was preferable. He fell back on folk stereotypes: "Blondes demand more and know less. . . . Redheads are temptations to adultery, but paradoxically, they are loyal and make fine wives."

Only a few pages later, Legman discusses "divorce" as "another word for hope." Family law in New York was "rigged" so that one had to "almost literally confess to moral bankruptcy" to get a different bedmate. Originally, in the Levant, "divorce was the privilege of a man," who could simply say "I drive thee away" three times, "*And she was druv!*" He thought, sadly, that contemporary women were "brought up to be parasites," who work until they can marry. To be brought up to be a wife was useless, and when things didn't work out, the "evil industry" of divorce lawyers, with "perjured witnesses, crooked detectives," and spy cameras, took over. Men were forced to let their wives go to lives of "embittered bitchery thereafter."[55]

Sexual Conduct was a mishmash and far from what Legman really wanted to accomplish in his sex-act encyclopedia and glossaries. He wrote it for the money, but also as a vehicle for his critique of Kinsey's *Human Male* and to make the case for a humanistic, cultural approach to sex.

His "Minority Report" was more serious. In fact, it was a full-bore attack. Legman objected to *Human Male* as an advocacy document, claiming neutrality and objectivity when these were impossible on the fraught subject of sex. It mechanically measured what was not measurable, in Legman's view. Worse, it dismissed Freudian discoveries as fraudulent nonsense. (Anthropologist Geoffrey Gorer pointed this out, and contemporary American Freudians Lewis Terman and Ronald Kubie were antagonized by Kinsey's neglect of psychoanalysis.)[56]

In many places, Legman's critique is accurate and well founded, based on a careful reading of the eight-hundred-plus-page tome and a clear understanding of what Kinsey was trying to do. He had, after all, worked and discussed the project with Kinsey over years. First, he attacked the title and the representativeness of the sample. How, he demanded, could about fifty-three hundred American men represent "the human male," or the approximately one billion men on the planet?[57] He pointed out that the population on which the study was based was mostly white, American, "college-educated, city-bred, middle-class Protestants." But this was not even "a proper sampling from which to generalize, even for the white, male American." Worse, he pointed out, "every effort seems to have been made to obscure" this sampling mess, despite all the charts and tables, and "no table or chart appears stating succinctly or even directly" how many men participated by age, geography, social, and religious background. "Do figures lie?" Legman asked. At the least, they could cloud and deceive. Later statisticians agree with these critiques.[58]

The collection of data (it really was not a sample in the representative sense statisticians use now) was wildly at odds with the U.S. population, and 70 percent of the "strata" or groups Kinsey studied were smaller than his own minimum for interpretation. The large groups Kinsey generalized from were men in universities, fraternities, and correctional institutions, hardly representative of the male population. White college men skewed the description of the American male, because "no matter how grouped," Legman argued, they were not in proportion to the age distribution of the nation.[59] The unmarried and urban were overrepresented. Factory workers and men earning under $2,000 a year were least well represented. Jews were overrepresented by about 100 percent and Catholics almost ignored. The statistics were largely gathered in the population centers of the Northeast and the Midwest, with little attention paid to the South, West, and Southwest, with all their diversity of language, ethnicity, and history. The book's proper title should have been "Sexual Behavior in 5,300 Northeastern [White] American Males," but even the extension of the fifty-three hundred cases to thirty million white American Protestants Legman called "a statistical crime." This was about as representative as the United States Senate. Data from African Americans was not included in *Human Male* but was held separately for a segregated volume.[60]

Aside from this small group of young, educated, single white boys, where was "the whole rest of the population," including himself, Legman demanded to know. What were they up to? Kinsey found an "average weekly orgasm rate for all his males" of four. But then he stated that an average rate "in non-restrained human animals (e.g. not prisoners) would probably be nearer to 7 per week." Legman demanded how on earth—even if his statistics were based on well-gathered data—could Kinsey know this? And even if it was accurate, what could it possibly mean? What was an "average orgasm," and where, if not into "sublimations and perversions," were the rest of those orgasms going?

When it came to social class, Legman found Kinsey's use of levels a conceptual mess. Kinsey was exquisitely sensitive to people who were poor and powerless, but he refused to allow any notion of systematic inequality into his analysis. He had developed the concept of upper and lower levels to stand in for social class, but upper level signaled educated or professional men and lower level a catchall for everyone else.[61] Kinsey detected differences in sexual behavior between the lower and upper but was vague as to what might account for them. "Lower levels" had heterosexual intercourse earlier, masturbated less, and were less involved in an imaginative and fantasy dimension of sexuality, he thought. Upper levels had heterosexual sex later, were less promiscuous, and were more involved with visual and literary descriptions of sex. The differences in sexual behavior were possibly related to religion, community, and education. But Kinsey collapsed culture and history into the nearly biological notion of level, never saying how it made a difference. Legman objected harshly to sorting people this way and to describing them as having behaviors "suited to" their level. Legman called this sorting "sexual fascism."[62]

His tone was extreme, but he accurately noted that *Human Male* had normative uses. It was being used to define what could be discussed and done, and it was helping men understand how to feel about themselves. The result was a kind of fifty-page "Gypsy Dream Book," in chapter 23. Like an astrology column, it told the reader what he already knew. "Every buyer of the volume," Legman argued, "is told his sexual fortune sight-unseen and is 'put at ease' and reassured." For $6.50, readers could locate their sexual behavior and see what others of their level were doing. This was scientism, but was it science?[63]

Legman objected (as did many others) to Kinsey's mechanistic construction of sex acts. Searching for the simply countable, Kinsey was interested in "outlet," the discharge of energy in orgasm, and he was recording what men said they did "to procure orgasm." Legman joked that if the *Male* volume was so devoted to "outlet," perhaps the forthcoming *Female* volume would analyze "inlet"? He found it revolting that human sexuality was uncomplicated by emotions or relationships. There was no charting of imagination, perhaps because it could not be recorded on a coding sheet. *Human Male* was all about "incidences, frequencies, facts." At the same time, Legman pointed out, it was odd that there was no list of the actual questions the interviewers asked, even though each interview covered between three and five hundred topics. There was no definition of terms. The interviewees might just as well have been "gorillas or gall wasps."[64]

Legman detected Kinsey's bias for sexual abundance: in the interviews, pressure to avow activity was placed on the interviewee. Although Kinsey admitted that subjects "lie and lie and lie," in Gershon's words, and that 50 percent of his reinterviewees changed their answers, "by some subjective method" the researcher decided which answer was true. Kinsey was conflating the frequent with the "natural" and through the magic of numbers constructing social facts.[65]

Kinsey's useless and far too technical statistical charts showed that the volume had been stampeded through the NRC and rushed to publication so that the Rockefeller Foundation would continue to fund Kinsey's long-term plans (true enough, Kinsey's team thought, looking back). The professor had found something that desperately needed to be done and had gone about it in a tragically misguided way, accompanied by a "flamboyantly executed publicity campaign." Sadly, public relations techniques were substituted for scientific integrity. Legman discerned that the import of the Kinsey report was less in its findings than in its impact: that it had been published at all, and what people said about it, was more important than what the work itself contained in the way of so-called facts.

What antagonized Legman the most—at least so far as he was willing to commit antagonism to paper—were Kinsey's less overt intentions. The report claimed to be an objective, scientific document, but in fact it was also a social policy brief based upon what Legman branded "an impertinent farrago of inadequate sample and unjustified extrapolations." Kinsey was "very specific about the use he would like to see made of his findings" in legal reform and the reduction of antihomosexual prejudice in the United States, so that law and custom "shall be more in conformity with the picture he draws." Kinsey argued for reform of the sex-offender laws and a future tolerance of a wider range of sexual expression. He was proposing that all consenting relations between adults ought to be decriminalized.[66]

Perhaps Legman would have gone along with Kinsey this far, but the assertion that there was no abnormal, that all sexual behavior was natural, and that there was a biological record supporting the prevalence of homosexuality in other mammals antagonized Legman. Here was a well-educated, foundation-supported researcher reducing everything to biology, claiming that sex existed somehow prior to and outside culture. Surely, the whole litany of repression and censorship indicated otherwise? Legman argued from Freud that human beings had evolved with repression, and so however tragic that might be, there was no way to know what was natural. Human beings simply had no idea and would never have an idea what this meant without much deeper and more careful investigation.[67] Drawing conclusions by comparing men and women to porcupines or beef cattle was neither logically nor philosophically sound.

Legman suspected Kinsey's personal investment in a better understanding of bisexuality and homosexuality. He undoubtedly felt what Kinsey's biographer Jonathan Gathorne-Hardy calls the insistent personal sexual undercurrent of the book.[68] *Human Male* sparked Legman's at best ambivalent feelings about gay men. As he would shortly take up the homosexual threat in his writing for the magazine *Neurotica*, it is clear Kinsey had struck a very raw nerve or touched some deep injury.

Legman wanted less prudery, less punitive sexual attitudes. He, too, wanted the destruction of the Comstockery that kept information from people and even jailed them for "abnormal" acts. It was a scandal that a preference for oral sex could be grounds for divorce. It was a scandal, as Kinsey pointed out, that some druggists who sold condoms didn't even know how they were to be used. Ignorance was excruciatingly damaging to the souls of American young people.

But "soul" was a word Legman knew would never creep into Kinsey's scholarly writings. This was a central difference between the two enthusiasts—sex and love were not separable for Legman. In his view, men "naturally" tried to have sex without love, but Legman idealized the melding of something essentially male with something essentially female. In his view, to reduce desire to functions that could be counted, or to "outlet" and "inlet," was not liberating; it was obscene. As he put it, "The deepest and worst error in the

Kinsey Report is in its presuming to study human beings while scientifically rejecting every aspect of their life which is specifically human."[69]

What kind of sex study would Legman have conducted, could he have designed one? There are a few hints in his "Minority Report." He wrote that Kinsey has "one really good idea, luckily independent of the statistical hokum and mystical rubber hose questioning." The idea is simply that "a human being is prepared by the womb to live one kind of life, and is required by society to live another." He thought it could hardly be questioned that "some such [natural] life is vaguely discernible behind the hugger-muggered patterns of social behavior, and ought to be discovered and described as a point of departure."[70]

There *is* a "nature" there, but Legman argued that we have almost no idea what it is. Where did Kinsey get off throwing around poorly collected, distorted statistics and saying he had found it? We have "hardly more than a few scraps of systematic knowledge against which to assess any findings," Legman insisted.[71] But where would such knowledge come from, if not from empirical study in the present? He thought, as did his correspondent anthropologist Robert Briffault, that the answer lay in the prehistory of human organization: before patriarchy, before monotheism, before repression in the name of the father. Legman's golden age was a matriarchal, heterosexual one, freed from the impositions of tyrants like Emil.

Human Male added up "the human distortions wreaked by civilization, in sex and in everything else," Legman wrote. In his view, "What is needed is the discovery of that original womb—transmitted, Natural human life, against which—and against which alone—both the advantage of civilization on the one side, and its disasters on the other, can be measured." The notion of "womb-transmission"—a biological, physical, and hormonal process, precultural, in Legman's thought—refers directly to a mother, or perhaps a Mother. It recalls Legman's description of his early months as an infant, quarantined with Julia all to himself, floating on a tide of breast milk. Perhaps this—the total attention of a caring, maternal, and warm woman—was his ideal of a relationship and his ideal grounding for a civilization. What was needed was a long, careful, qualitative investigation of what human life might be without repression, cruelty, and exploitation. How would one afford such a study? The kind of money this would take, Legman wrote grimly, was the kind that was applied only to killing people in world wars.[72]

Legman's criticisms of the *Human Male* volume were almost entirely fair, if written in his usual biting and personal style. They align closely with more recent readings of Kinsey's report. Legman's might be the only nonglowing review written by someone who had worked with the Kinsey team and who had closely discussed the aims of sex research with Kinsey during the project's formative years. All the other former team members either stayed quiet about their disagreements while Kinsey was alive or wrote positive reviews. Of course, Legman's perspective was that of someone who had been shown the door. Personal slams about Kinsey's stinginess, prudery, and dishonesty are sprinkled through the "Minority Report." But Legman hadn't really been asked for his opinion, he had no standing without a university position, and "Minority Report" seems to have been lost in the tumult surrounding *Human Male*. There were no reviews of *Sexual Conduct* in the mainstream press of the day, perhaps because it was obviously published by Roth, a pariah in New York publishing.

In the spring of 1948, Legman alerted Kinsey that an "attack" was coming from anthropologist Geoffrey Gorer.[73] Legman warned that Gorer was not to be trifled with, and he would go straight to the weak spots in Kinsey's data and arguments. In turn, Legman wrote to Gorer that he had cribbed many of the criticisms in "Minority Report" from his forthcoming article "Justification by Numbers," which Legman had read in draft.[74] Gorer's critique of Kinsey was much more respectful. Whether Legman lifted ideas from Gorer, or whether the two exchanged notes, they produced similar conclusions in starkly different styles.

BLACKOUT

"Minority Report" was noted and taken seriously by Kinsey. Paul Gebhard, the team's anthropologist, described it later as disloyal.[75] Legman replied that his criticisms of Kinsey were well founded, had also been made by prominent statisticians, and had resulted in methodological changes that made for a much better, indeed brilliant, *Human Female* volume.[76] As to the personal nature of the attacks in "Minority Report," Legman said he wrote personally and angrily, because "that is who I am." But, he told Gebhard, he didn't say in print what he really thought, and that was that the effect of the *Male* volume was to make the world safe for homosexuality, a goal Legman absolutely could not countenance. He did not believe gay men should be punished, he told Gebhard, but they should be "cured," probably through psychoanalysis.

Over time, Kinsey's perspective slowly won the day, as homosexual civil rights groups mobilized for legal change. But their victory was a result of politics, not science narrowly construed. Kinsey's sex research methods, as Legman and others pointed out, didn't hold up very well, even if they have not been much improved upon by survey researchers since.[77] Through the magic of numbers, Kinsey succeeded in opening ground for desperately needed policy reforms. As Geoffrey Gorer also argued, *Human Male* was poor science and great propaganda.[78]

The kind of research anticipated by Legman, if he could barely gesture at what it would look like, has also flourished and has been important for advocates of sexual reform and civil liberties. It looks less like a Freudian and anthropological prehistory (although there is this as well) than a history of how civilization has produced postmedieval sexualities through law, medicine, religion, and literature. The writers of this new history rarely know about or acknowledge Gershon Legman, although as we will see in a later chapter, some of their most important work has been based on his. By 1948 he had laid out his implacable resistance to quantitative studies of human behavior. His antagonism to big conclusions drawn from data, and later to the computerization of cultural research, would come up again in his writings.

Kinsey stayed angry at Legman for the rest of his life, although when they corresponded, each saluted the other with respect for his professional accomplishments. Kinsey followed Legman's lead and became voraciously interested in all kinds of literary, visual, and sculptural depictions of sex and reproduction, from pre-Columbian figurines to B movies. He would begin to lay down an enormous collection of erotic art, including folk art, at the Kinsey Institute Archives. But Legman would not be acknowledged publicly until after his death in 1999.

Kinsey enforced a blackout on Legman in the aftermath of their dispute, and institute staff spread stories of his unscrupulousness. On several occasions in the early 1950s, Legman wrote to ask for help from the institute with his expanding folklore projects. Could Kinsey, he asked, loan him a copy of Vance Randolph's manuscript "Unprintable Songs from the Ozarks"? A loan was impossible, but Legman could come study it in person, Kinsey replied imperiously, knowing that he was now living in France and had no money to travel. Yet in the early 1940s, Legman had loaned Kinsey an early manuscript version of "The Limerick" and allowed Kinsey to keep it for as long as he pleased. He had also loaned Kinsey his collections of obscene folk songs from New York City. Legman would have a slight revenge in the 1950s: he warned Kinsey that he was about to pay far too much for a spurious copy of the missing last volume of Sir Richard Burton's *Arabian Nights*. Actually, "I knew he'd already bought it!" Legman noted on his copy of the sent letter. Every subsequent request to the Kinsey Institute for scholarly exchange or research help was denied.[79]

When Kinsey died in August 1956, Legman sent a letter of condolence. A few years later, he wrote to Kinsey's successor, Paul Gebhard, to complain bitterly that he had heard from Indiana folklore graduate students that he had a reputation for being dishonest, and he demanded to know who was circulating this canard.[80] Gebhard replied that it was Kinsey himself who had told everyone that Legman was a mulcter, and as to bad-mouthing among the living, he wasn't going to name any names. Painstakingly, Legman told his side of the story all over again. The book money advances. The low salary. The collapse of the rare-book trade. The careful bibliographic cross-checking. "Where is the mulcting?" he roared across the Atlantic.[81]

Gebhard wrote back blandly that he was sure that "there are two sides to every story." He indicated that he appreciated Legman's folklore interests and assured him that plans were under way for the new Folklore Institute at Indiana University to work closely with the Kinsey Institute. Indeed, they might begin using Professor Stith Thompson's international folktale-motif index to categorize some of the erotic materials Legman had gathered. Legman must have groaned in despair. He had been analyzing his own folklore collections for years, and he knew well that the Aarne-Thompson international folktale-index system had no place for erotic and scatological folklore. It was another idiotic case of starting de novo.

Kinsey and his close senior associates took care that Legman was for many years cut off from all credit for the institute's beginnings. For example, in the first history of the Kinsey Institute, *Dr. Kinsey and the Institute for Sex Research* (1972), by Wardell B. Pomeroy, there is no mention of Legman. Neither his nor Tom Painter's name appears in the index. Nor are there index entries in Pomeroy for pornography, male prostitution, or folklore. Even more suspiciously, Pomeroy's account of Kinsey's visit to the British Museum to see the secret book collection known as the Private Case is written as if Kinsey knew about this erotica trove through his own erudition.[82] But before meeting Legman, Kinsey knew nothing about the centuries-long history of publishing and collecting erotica. It was Legman who introduced him to the world of secret books and insisted on the importance of literature and folklore to the study of sex.

4

LOVE & DEATH

We bravely say kill. Rob. Betray. But that other we dare pronounce only between clenched teeth?

—Michel de Montaigne, *Notes on Virgil* (1588)

After his break with Kinsey and Dickinson in 1946, Legman threw himself into his own ambitious projects. In an attempt to break into the New York critical scene, he was writing a series of essays assessing the effects of sexual censorship on American literature and culture and trying to place them in New York's intellectual magazines. As he aimed to become a public spokesman on matters of sexual freedom, he wrote opinionated letters to all kinds of thinkers. And he was actively collecting limericks, folk songs, and jokes, following a plan he had worked out for a multivolume series of studies of sexual folklore. All this effort would come to a head seven years later in a confrontation with the forces of literary and political repression.[1]

BEVERLEY

His personal life was transformed when he met Beverley Keith, who would be his wife and intellectual partner for the next two decades. In about 1945, as the war was winding down, they turned up at the same party on Grove Street in the Village. Beverley came from a wealthy and aristocratic Canadian family, but she had no desire for anything material.[2] She had just returned from Mexico, where she had taken a bus to Oaxaca with only a cigar box full of belongings. After two years there, she somehow got back home the same way.[3]

Beverley Keith about 1945. Courtesy of the Legman Archive.

He was twenty-eight and she was thirty-two, although she gave the impression that she was much younger. As Gershon got to know Beverley, she materialized as a complete nonconformist, one even he could be surprised by. Beverley was sweet and honest and "innocent about all practical things." He could not recall "ever hearing her tell a lie or catching her in one."[4] She was quiet, "small and slight, with dark brown hair, and a strange soulful face . . . with enormous starving eyes, very hungry." Later, his friends called Beverley "the original hippie," but she struck Legman as "rather like Melville's Bartelby the Scrivener . . . who was withdrawn internally from life and whose mild-mannered answer to every offer and suggestion is: 'I'd rather not.'"[5]

She was used to living on nothing: her wardrobe was two simple denim jumpers she had made herself, which she wore in turns and washed by hand. She cut her own hair and wore no makeup, nor did she pluck her eyebrows, shave her legs, or wear stockings. She spoke slowly, in a "rather low voice," as he remembered. "And even my untrained eye had already noticed she was

Beverley and Gershon Legman-Keith on the steps of the cottage at 858 Hornaday Place, the Bronx, 1950. Courtesy of the Legman Archive.

deeply depressed." They were, in fact, "as different as night and day," garrulous Gershon and silent Beverley, "except that we were both somehow total outcasts and non-partakers at the world's feast."[6]

Beverley had been supported by her mother but wanted to get free because she rejected her family's prestige and their expectations for her. Gershon found her family nightmarish, especially her mother, Kathleen, "a decayed, would-be society woman flapping around on the edges of the fashionable world and wishing and pretending she was rich." He observed, "It was obvious Beverley did not love her mother and didn't even approve of her." Gershon soon discovered the feeling was mutual: Kathleen found Beverley an embarrassment. Her father had remarried and wanted to hear no more about his ex-wife or daughter, ever.[7]

Legman's friends remembered Beverley as a well-trained intellectual who projected great seriousness. She had a degree from Barnard College, where she studied preclassical and classical civilizations. Judith Legman, Gershon's third wife, met Beverley during her final struggle with lung cancer in 1965–66 and remembers her as deeply read, and as Gershon noted, "She observed everything and said nothing. And she smoked cigarettes incessantly."[8]

Gershon and Beverley spent a lot of time listening to classical music together at her brother's apartment. At first, they were not lovers, since he "found her childlike and unattractive sexually." But after a while, Beverley became pregnant, and although she was only one of his many girlfriends, out of guilt and responsibility Gershon felt he should take her "under his wing, such as it was."[9] "Beverley's unwillingness to live according to the white WASP world's rules was very consternating, even to an outcast like me. . . . I wondered how long she could survive in New York." They declared themselves married in late October 1947.[10]

Julia Legman wrote she was surprised to hear the news but was glad they changed their minds "about certain rules in life."[11] She offered traditional wishes and a gift of ten dollars. They had told everyone that their last name would be "Legman-Keith." Julia poked Gershon about the name change. "That's nothing new to me. You've been changing it ever since you've been nine years old but this time it sounds very silly to me." She was eager to visit them and was coming to New York City for her thirty-eighth wedding anniversary: "The Question is, do you want Daddy?"[12]

Gershon wanted "to come and see you, and walk over the places where I used to walk when I was a little boy, because Beverley says this is what she wants." But "We love you and want to see you—but only you." He would not allow Emil to "shit all over" Beverley. In the end, Julia had only a brief meeting with her daughter-in-law in the Scranton train station.[13] In another indication of how separate he wanted to keep himself from his Scranton family, when his favorite sister, Ruth, died of breast cancer that same spring, Gershon refused to attend her funeral.[14]

They set up housekeeping in a tiny apartment on Bedford Street in Greenwich Village, while Gershon kept a room at West Seventy-Sixth Street for an office. Apparently, Beverley was not too depressed to help support this arrangement. She was a welder's helper in a New Jersey shipyard, hard, high-paying work, where she took note of the dirty jokes told by other welders. Later, she took in work as a typist. Gershon relied on her heavily throughout their marriage for skillful typing of his bibliographies.

As it turned out, there was no baby. According to Gershon, Kathleen Keith interfered, concluding that if Beverley had a child, she would be unable to work, and then she, Kathleen, would be on the hook to help all three of them. So, Kathleen pressured her daughter to have an abortion performed by a boyfriend of hers who was a doctor. Following the procedure, Kathleen suggested Beverley really ought to marry the doctor. After this, Gershon always regarded his mother-in-law as "an entomological specimen."[15]

Beverley would have liked to have children, but possibly because of complications from the illegal abortion, she never did. Gershon claimed always to have a horror of abortion, and he wrote later that he felt horrible about allowing it to happen: "I know I did wrong." But Gershon and Beverley remained married.

Many years later, Gershon described the marriage as a terrible mistake, the worst in his life since it precluded all kinds of other happiness. Beverley held the world away from herself, he thought. She "wanted nothing from it," but in a sense, she also wanted everything. In a passive way, she hoped all she needed would be provided. Gershon saw that "she was too badly hurt from too long before." Whether she had experienced sexual abuse or emotional hostility, the same thing had happened to both, he wrote—leaving them painfully detached and vulnerable.[16] They both understood how badly they had been damaged by their parents—and this kept them together.

Sexual happiness was lost to the couple. Using the terms widely used to describe women's sexuality in the 1940s, he wrote that Beverley was "frigid," unable to have an orgasm during intercourse. No matter what he did or tried, she was unresponsive and uninvolved. Legman leaves the reader baffled as to why this might be, especially coming from a man who thought he knew a great deal about female sexuality and claimed to have fully understood the possibilities of the vibrator. At the time, the theories of sex and marriage firmly held that frigidity existed—it was a part of some women's psychic makeup—and it was an expression of hostility toward men. A "normal" woman should respond to penetration with pleasure and orgasmic climax. Legman begged the wealthy Keiths for money to pay for psychoanalysis for Beverley, but her parents flatly refused, nor would they help them in any other way.[17]

This irony of Gershon's assessment of Beverley's difficulty would be funny if it were not so sad: a young man who aimed to be a sex researcher and expert on sex techniques married to a woman who is (apparently) unable to enjoy sex with him and to whom he applies the pejorative label "frigid." Gershon was convinced that sex was, ideally and normatively, penetrative, involving a man and a woman. In his writings, it goes without saying that pleasure for women depends upon men. For a sexual revolutionary, this seems an oddly conservative (and tiresome) position. It was an article of faith for Legman that women needed men absolutely, whether they knew it or not.

In the years between 1946 and 1953, Beverley and Gershon lived, ate, read, entertained friends, and went to the movies together. And they wrote, collaborating on Gershon's editorial projects. The most memorable of their joint works was an English translation (probably the first) of Alfred Jarry's surreal "pataphysical" trilogy, *Ubu Roi*, brought out by Samuel Roth's Boar's Head Press as *King Turd*.[18] Jarry's Père Ubu is a monstrosity, a stupid, greedy brute who seizes his kingdom in a senseless coup and designs to conquer Poland through murder and treachery with the help of Mère Ubu, his disgusting wife, and some faithless underlings. Ubu himself is a walking obscenity—his first word spoken to the audience is "merdre!" (merde!) or in Legman's translation, "Pschitt!" This utterance, and all the blasphemies that followed in the play, scandalized the Parisian intelligentsia. The opening of *Ubu Roi* set off riots, with the theater audience yelling, applauding, and throwing things, the critics storming out. The play folded after its second Paris performance, satisfying Jarry's intent to destroy theater as it had existed.[19] Père Ubu himself was an allegory for Europe on the brink of World War I: a cruel, hypocritical, and obscenely violent world. This was Legman's view of the world emerging from World War II. It was a view he would seek to find more ways to express.

ST. JEROME OF THE BRONX

In 1948 Gershon and Beverley moved to the Bronx, to 858 Hornaday Place, near the zoo and Grand Concourse. The tiny cottage they had rented was a minor landmark—it had been built by Charles Fort, the early-twentieth-century naturalist, journalist, and investigator of "anomalous phenomena."[20] Legman was now at work on his studies of sex censorship, and he started a small weekly gathering. Over stew and cheap wine, he would hold forth. The Thursday evenings became, briefly, a scene to make in bohemia, the visitors and the evenings contributing to the legend of Legman. Novelist John Clellon Holmes and his friend hipster Jay Landesman took Allen Ginsberg and Jack Kerouac there.[21] Lionel and Diana Trilling, among other New York intellectuals, braved the long subway ride to the Bronx.

The evenings were modest and outrageous. Beverley and Gershon were famous for scraping by. Clellon Holmes noted, "Legman could fill a shopping bag for forty cents. . . . [H]is soul took some of its sustenance from the very ingenuity of feeding the two of them."[22]

Legman's friend Osmond Beckwith, a poet and novelist, remembered how cramped the cottage was, with everyone sitting on a bed in the front room. The whole place was "very dusty" and full of Beverley's cats, "which were not to be picked up or held." He noticed Beverley's remoteness, that she "seemed to keep herself under great restraint; spoke and acted without much feeling." Legman was volcanic, speaking "with the pent up energy of someone who hadn't met anyone in weeks." He talked so fast and "made so many references" to his research that Beckwith felt dazed by "the most non-stop talker I'd ever known."[23]

The library was Legman's real work. Beckwith eyed Freud's *Collected Works* and several important dictionaries with envy. He later told Gershon, "My impression was you had the best, the original references, those I'd heard of but never bought, lacking the money." When Legman showed him *Oragenitalism*, Beckwith was taken aback. He had never heard people speak of oral sex positively or even "recommend it." Legman displayed posters he had had made from comic book covers; he "brought out a book with some homosexual illustrations" that surprised Beckwith more.[24]

John Clellon Holmes was stunned by the contents of Legman's tiny house. Past the weedy yard and the unpainted fence, he recalled, "the first thing you noticed were books. Books everywhere, books overflowing the shelves on every available wall, books tucked under the desk." The cottage contained the "carefully assembled literature of a scholar and bibliographer . . . [of] sex and language," with "dictionaries and lexicons, rare and expensive books," and editions of Freud running to many volumes, which had been "liberated one book at a time for hard-earned cash." Hornaday Place was a command post, Clellon Holmes wrote, "and from that overflowing desk a species of war was being carried on with the world that lay just beyond the hand sewn drapes."[25]

At the back of the cottage, an original bedroom was now the "Filing Cabinet," Legman's research warren. Clellon Holmes noted how carefully Legman guarded it: "The precious files that represented over a decade of effort to preserve every evidence of contemporary sex life, and its debasement, had to have a safe, dry room and a door with a lock. This was Legman's *sanctum sanctorum,* you were not allowed to linger there." There were "packing crates where hundreds of comic books were arranged according to degree of atrocity." "Reams of erotic photos going back to the camera's earliest years were motif indexed under such headings as 'Intercourse—Oral—Homosexual' and 'Bondage—Masochistic—Female.'" Letters were meticulously filed. Partitions separated the tiny rooms, but finally Clellon Homes saw that "the Work and the Life were indistinguishable."[26]

The supper conversation was uninhibited and confrontational. Legman would tell about his miserable childhood in Scranton, about the prudery and anti-Semitism, and having had "Kosher" written on his face in horse-shit juice. He described his projects: his encyclopedia of sex techniques, his lexicon to supplement *The Oxford English Dictionary,* which would contain all the suppressed words. He described his "massive collection of erotic limericks and their variations."[27]

Legman had a habit of attacking his visitors, and Clellon Holmes got the impression that a lot of people came for just this. In his words, "Legman had a curious effect on people. Frankly, an evening with him could be an ordeal. If you had a secret layer of apathy, compromise or dishonesty, he would instantly sniff out and subject it to a barrage of sarcasms." Although he treated most women with old-fashioned gallantry, "he nevertheless insisted upon talking about the most intimate matters, in the most pointed obscenities, to all of them."[28]

Clellon Holmes summarized Legman's sexual politics: "I have seen him say to a girl he had just met that evening, 'Anything that fouls up the relations between men and women, I'm against. Starting with your panty girdle, honey. . . . When are you going to give this guy,' indicating her delighted swain, 'a chance to prove he's a man, instead of a god damn tennis player?'" These shocks felt stimulating and liberating, at least to the male dinner guests, because, as Clellon Holmes reflected, "There was an aura of total freedom about him, of honesty without mercy, of having nothing to lose, that made you realize your usual social armor was unnecessary . . . even as he hacked away at it like some psychiatric Genghis Khan."[29]

The one-sided conversation usually turned to the theory behind the work in progress. Legman told Clellon Holmes (and everyone else) he had discovered that the "increasing violence and sadism of American culture was the direct result of our society's relentless suppression of sex." The stand Legman took was unique in those days, summed up in the title of the book he was working on, *Love & Death*. His book had been rejected "by an entire alphabet of over thirty publishers in America," before Jay Landesman began to publish parts of it in *Neurotica*. The loneliness of Legman and his ideas put Clellon Holmes in mind of "St. Jerome of the Bronx,"[30] but his persistence was remarkable. He had sent out the usual avalanche of correspondence to publishers and people who might know publishers and to well-known writers who might help his campaign to uncensor sex. A surprising number replied: he heard back from Upton Sinclair, Wilhelm Reich, and Edmund Wilson. Dwight Macdonald thought the chapter he considered for *Politics* was interesting but was not quite sure what the point was.[31]

Love & Death: A Study in Censorship was a series of essays on popular culture. Looking back on it, Legman would call his "little hundred-page indictment" his favorite work, a cri de coeur. In fact, it *was* him "down to the marrow" of his bones, he wrote when he sent a copy to Ewing Baskette, a fellow collector of banned books.[32] *Love & Death* was an early salvo in what would later be called the mass-culture debates. From the mid-1940s, Legman was increasingly preoccupied with cheap print culture, particularly in the crime novels and comic books that would draw the attention of critical cultural analysts of a later generation. He was not alone in this, but it was an outsider's enterprise. Caribbean Marxist historian C. L. R. James was at almost the same moment writing about Dick Tracy, albeit in a much different vein.[33] Leo Lowenthal, the Frankfurt School literary scholar, was working on a study of iconic patterns in popular magazines and novels.[34] In Great Britain, first F. R. and Q. D. Leavis, and later Raymond Williams and Richard Hoggart, would develop modes of criticism to take popular reading seriously.[35]

But in the late 1940s, this was an outsider's job. In the context of the early twenty-first century, after decades of academic and critical attention to the cultures of reading and television viewing, it is hard to re-create the shock that an analysis of cheap print could cause in intellectual circles. Engaging with inexpensive and unsanctioned images and texts, and by extension with the lives of people who created and enjoyed them, was almost unspeakable in the serious literary circles where popular reading was viewed as a subintellectual waste product.[36] There were no university programs, no granting agencies, no journals interested in studying such trash. So Legman invented his own method, collecting comics and pulps from kids in his neighborhood. Osmond Beckwith remembered asking Legman how he did all the research for *Love & Death*. Gershon replied, "I did it all at the corner candy store."[37] In a little social welfare project, he sometimes traded less harmful comics to kids for their grotesquely violent ones, but there is no evidence that he interviewed children about their reading habits.

COMIC BOOKS AND THEIR CRITICS

Legman's letters from 1946 to 1949 show him thinking about commercial print culture, including reading material and advertising, in a direct reaction to the catastrophes of World War II and the country's psychic state as the war ended. In his approach to what was now being called "mass culture," he was intensely aware that American life was becoming dominated by expanded consumption at home and an aggressive and domineering military stance abroad. Legman registered the newspapers' triumphal celebration of the American way as the alpha and omega of history with disgust.[38] He berated one correspondent, publisher E. Haldeman-Julius (creator of the "Little Blue Books"), for not taking advertising seriously and for his old-fashioned, free-thinking views about religion.[39] As a Marxist, Legman understood the world in terms of exploitation of the poor and weak by the rich and powerful, and he agreed that religion was a gigantic diversion from class struggle. But now capitalism was the new religion, and Haldeman-Julius needed to reckon with this reality. Legman prodded him:

> You keep beefing about religion and capitalism in different columns—why can't you get the idea that they're one and the same thing? Time was when religion tore the paper when the Rich sat on the toilet over the heads of the working class, but now . . . in the papers the attitude [is] that capitalism is sacred and not to be attacked by logic or satire or anything like that, . . . it is beyond criticism, that nothing is expected of it, that it just is THE THING, and that since the alternative is the outer darkness and Anti-Christ of communism we must clutch capitalism to our bosom no matter how gruesomely (like the Spartan boy's wolf) it feed on our innards.[40]

An even larger, more sophisticated commercial and ideological system of exploitation was emerging, and the exploitation of ordinary and working people was becoming even more complete via the mass media. As for the relief felt at the end of the war, it was undercut by people's completely justified fear of a future dominated by atomic mass murder. But Legman wanted to push this critical perspective further: "As to the atom [bomb] the real danger is missed by everyone—it isn't that they will blow us all to subatomic smithereens without warning it's that they won't do it soon enough and we will have to live with this here now world of the future they are preparing!"[41]

"They" were preparing for the citizenry a planet intellectually as well as physically laid waste, all in the name of the glorious American way. Legman saw this manifested in an aggressive postwar rush of new advertising. He was fastidiously collecting the pushy new ads for consumer goods, and he argued from his evidence. "Get hold of a copy of *Scientific American*—man, it's appalling. Sky writing that can be lit at night and will burn for 30 minutes, blotting out Cassiopeia with DRINK GREPSI-COLA, ITS THE CRAP FOR YOU!! Broadway science which will belch the odor of cooking coffee, frying bacon, last month's Kotex pads and Secaucus stock farms over the harmless pedestrian! Etc. and omigod."[42] Here we see Legman's concrete and vivid polemic style, and while he was being satirical, like many Americans he was really frightened. What appalled Legman was not only that the United States failed to prevent catastrophe in Europe, but also that it celebrated the nuclear murder of hundreds of thousands of people in Japan. And even worse, this horrific violence was becoming seamless with the violence of advertising, a manipulation of minds that in Legman's view permeated everything.

As he wrote in *Love & Death*, America, like fascist Germany, seemed to be moving deathward; people took pleasure in mass killing, and this pleasure was efficiently distributed by commercial entertainment. He was writing as the United States heated up the Cold War abroad and laid plans for an open conflict with China in Korea that would devastate and divide that country. At home, dissent was repressed ferociously with political witch hunts and purges. Legman called out that this was the absolute last moment to avoid a planetary descent into sadism. Because popular culture permeated the intellectual life of the nation, Legman made it his ground zero.

Love & Death was made up of linked essays on popular fiction. Legman unpacked detective and crime fiction in "The Institutionalized Lynch" and assailed misogynist depictions of women in mass culture in "Avatars of the Bitch." A central piece of the book, the chapter people admired the most, was "Not for Children," a sustained attack on comic books. Here his perspective on kiddie reading was delivered with characteristic heat and force, and he used the psychoanalytic concepts of repression and displacement, albeit in an entirely negative, antimodern critique. Legman's main argument was that because of the dominant American pattern of sexual repression, cheap fictions offered a kind of distorted expression of human desire. America's censors allowed stories that dealt in woman hating, racism, violence, and sadism, and they trained a generation of young Americans to enjoy murders, corpses, and the torture of "bitch-goddesses," at the same time forbidding practical knowledge and the open enjoyment of sexual desire. The result was a perverse national culture dominated by men (most likely homosexual) who hated women. Women sensed that they were hated and thus became "frigid," and normal men lost their masculinity and became too confused to do anything about it.

"Not for Children" was part of a long American tradition, expressed in a new way. The comic books had evolved from newspaper comic strips, and like their ancestors the dime novels, they attracted concern from the guardians of youth and public morality. As comics historian Bradford Wright points out, America's respectable tastemakers had been perturbed and discomforted by cheap cultural novelties for a full century and a half. Since the early nineteenth century, religious and moral reform leaders had been attacking and attempting to regulate the theaters, dance halls, penny press, burlesque, jazz cabarets, movies, and, of course, the erotica that appealed to the urban working class. What was unsettlingly new about comic books was that they spoke directly to children and adolescents and were easily available at the local newsstand and candy store. The little booklets were cheap, trashy, and from the wrong side of the cultural tracks. They were also a blazing commercial success, and they posed a problem of parental and educational control.[43]

Bradford Wright points out that the comic book industry was "controlled [and made] by urban young men," many of immigrant backgrounds, "with worldviews far removed from Victorian middle-class ideals, and guided, above all, by the pursuit of quick profits." Comics performed an unsettling exchange of culture across class and ethnic boundaries, and this exchange "took place in the language of violence, crudeness and absurdity." Often poorly produced, the little comic stories catered to offbeat, even weird sensibilities.[44]

Early attacks on the comics had come from children's librarians, specialists in reading, and children's book writers, who immediately attacked them as poorly written and taking the place of more wholesome reading for young people. While criticism had coalesced in the library journals from the 1930s, in 1940 Sterling North, an accomplished children's author, sounded a new alarm in the *Chicago Tribune*. North criticized comic books for their cheapness and their violent content; his arguments were widely reprinted. Yet another campaign to clean up children's reading was under way.[45] Elite journalists and writers for the better magazines climbed into the ring, including in 1941 James Vlamos in the *American Mercury*. Vlamos was critical of the view of society comic books presented, and he noted a potential connection between cheap reading and attitudes toward order: he found that in comic books, "lawful

CHAPTER 4

processes have disappeared" and "only superheroes keep us safe." In Vlamos's view, this was a totalitarian ideology, paralleling the rise of Hitler.[46]

But the Second World War intervened, and the moral panic eased as comic book publishers found new strategies. Anxious to avoid paper and ink rationing, they adapted defensively by printing "patriotic" comics and taking government contracts. The comic book industry produced educational and instructional materials for the troops and urged their customers to buy war bonds in a "rare convergence of interests" with the U.S. government. Comics became an intimate part of G.I. culture, along with the soft erotica of photoplay magazines.[47] Some comics featuring violent crime were banned from the military postal exchanges, but surveys discovered that comic books were the main reading material of young servicemen. They were so popular among G.I.s that after 1945, the content of comics became a concern of some European governments, which saw them as American agents of cultural infiltration and degradation.[48]

Eventually, rising incomes during wartime led the comic book industry into a boom. In 1943 25 million were published each year, with 125 titles on the stands monthly. By early 1945, *Publishers Weekly* cited sales of 15 million comic books each month; each comic was estimated to have five readers, as they passed from hand to hand. After World War II, the industry reoriented to follow its now older dedicated G.I. audience. Detective, "true crime," and sex comics expanded.[49] After 1945 the anti–comic book panic surged again, articulated now by even more powerful and vocal cultural authorities who found the violent "crime comic" titles especially problematic.

Among these critics were judges, district attorneys, and doctors, their voices amplified by prominent journalists. By 1946 legal authorities were alarmed about what seemed to be a spike in violent crime by teenagers. Police departments and bar associations worried about disrespect for law and order and reported that crime comics were fueling disorder. The traditional guardians of reading matter, the Catholic Church and its civilian decency leagues, played a leading part in the renewed anticomics campaign, along with the local and state-level vice suppression and purity societies.

Although it is unclear if there was such a crime wave, the social category "juvenile delinquent" was salient and preoccupying.[50] And there was awareness, born of the urban concentration of young workers during the Depression and the war, of the "problem" of homosexuals, especially young men. A "lavender scare" unfolded as city authorities cracked down on gay men and lesbians, passing ordinances to criminalize their public presence as "disorderly" and dangerous.[51] Delinquents and perverts were new labels for traditionally stigmatized people, and these messy categories merged into a moral panic over reading, violence, and sexuality.[52]

The debate was only overtly about the relationship between delinquency and comic book content—cultural power was the underlying issue.[53] The mainstream and conservative critics felt that an unfamiliar, overwhelming mass culture was coming between children and parents and educators. The child guidance and psychiatric professionals worried about delinquency and added their voices to the comics debate. By 1947–48, the arguments were sharp and urgent. Meanwhile, the press, magazines, and entertainment media took up the theme of out-of-control youth, with fervid reporting on spectacular bouts of youth crime and teenage gang violence. All of this was inseparable from the surging Red Scare and the calculated public perception that America was being subverted from within.[54]

At the war's end, a powerful intellectual spokesman emerged for the anti-comics chorus, and Gershon Legman surely noticed him immediately. Fredric Wertham (1895–1981) was a psychiatrist educated in Germany, Vienna, London, and Paris. His mentor, Emil Kraepelin (a psychopathologist expert on schizophrenia), rejected the Freudian orthodoxy that "made diagnosis based on symptomatic readings and theoretical assumptions" to emphasize family history in interaction with social and economic factors, arguing that all this had to be brought to bear in the treatment of a patient.[55] Wertham extended this sociohistorical approach in his clinical work and many popular writings.[56]

After moving to the United States in 1922, Wertham became deeply involved in problems of child behavior and mental health and juvenile delinquency. He sought to put the insights of his divergent version of psychoanalysis at the center of public debates over the causes and prevention of crime and delinquency, and this is where Legman noticed his writings and determined to cross his path. As a public psychiatrist, Wertham was especially interested in the problems of "juvenile delinquents," a category that included young homosexuals. Here his interests crossed Legman's. In his years hanging out with Thomas Painter and his male prostitute friends, Legman would have been labeled a delinquent himself.[57] In the 1940s, homosexuality was defined in mainstream medical thought as a psychosexual disorder, although Dr. Wertham, who saw these young men clinically, was more sympathetic.[58]

By delinquency Wertham meant truancy, gang membership, and even serious crime. In conflict with most delinquency experts, he saw these problems as not inherent in the child, but as expressions of the adult community's dysfunction. His central concern was violence, and he saw the United States as a deeply violent society in its traditions of racism and unequal justice. Wertham thought that the use of force against the vulnerable, especially in imprisonment and capital punishment, helped create and spread mental pathology.[59] Legman would later say of Dr. Fredric Wertham, "He got all of his best ideas from me!" But given Wertham's own history and efforts, it is more accurate to say that the two seem to have developed parallel lines of thought.

By the late 1940s, Wertham was head of psychiatry at Bellevue Hospital. He also served as chief clinician to the Court of General Sessions (later the state supreme court), "which gave examinations to every convicted felon in the city."[60] Here Wertham helped shape forensic psychiatry, defined as the effort to explain what led a person to criminal behavior. He strove to direct legal thought away from theories of biologically determined depravity and toward an understanding of the interaction of social factors and psychic structures, helping reform sentencing practices and understandings of culpability. But he was up against enormous resistance. As he documented in *The Circle of Guilt,* New York's social workers and educators were often racist and indifferent toward the children they were supposed to help.

Wertham was deeply antagonistic to the mainstream of psychoanalysis as it had developed in the United States. Legman shared this view. Wertham argued that American psychiatry ignored the part played by culture, class, and poverty in creating social problems and focused exclusively on the individual and his or her drives. American psychiatrists acted as a kind of "praetorian guard," an elite class of enforcers who contained social unhappiness by defining problems as solely individual.[61]

In Wertham's view, the most telling evidence of American psychiatry's failure was its racism. At the time, most psychiatrists and psychiatric clinics refused to treat African Americans and had nothing to say about the social and psychological effects of segregation on blacks and whites. At the same time, Wertham pointed out, psychiatrists were perfectly willing to offer opinions in court that affected the fates of black and Puerto Rican youth.[62] In 1945–46 he took the bold step of organizing a free community psychiatric clinic in Harlem—with the financial support of prominent black intellectuals such as Paul Robeson, Ralph Ellison, and Richard Wright. An interracial staff offered treatment to the children of Harlem. The Lafargue Clinic (named after Karl Marx's Creole Cuban son-in-law) was a practical expression of Wertham's belief that psychiatry needed to do away with its own color line and that African American children and their families were entitled to community-based help with emotional or behavioral problems.

Wertham's attack on comics came out of this broader orientation toward racism and violence. In 1948–49 his critical articles on comics in the *Saturday Review of Literature* were widely read, but he was also criticizing housing segregation and the atom bomb. Later, in 1954, he would offer crucial testimony on the psychological effects of school segregation in the *Brown v. Board of Education* case; this testimony was his most important contribution to American history.[63]

Violence, in Wertham's view, was Western society's central social problem, and it was the root of many individual mental and emotional problems. By violence he meant interpersonal and familial violence, but, significantly, he also meant social and economic violence. In *Dark Legend: A Study of Murder*, Wertham's first volume for popular readers, he tried to show the connections between an individual's mental illness—resulting in matricide—with the social illnesses of poverty and communal neglect.[64] Wertham found that mediating the social realm and individual pathology were powerful mythologies—violent conceptions of how to be human—that gave rise to disturbed behavior.

Wertham believed that American society had to take some responsibility for the profound distress it created. War and capital punishment, he thought, were contributing factors in mental illness, and he humanely expressed this position in *The Show of Violence* (1949), which Legman read and admired, and *The Circle of Guilt* (1956).[65]

Legman and Wertham had arrived in New York City at about the same time, and they may have met in Dr. Dickinson's offices at the New York Academy of Medicine.[66] Legman remembered "hanging around" the Lafargue Clinic in Harlem, but why he was he hanging around, he does not say. His clip files show that Legman read Wertham's frequent magazine and newspaper columns on public mental health. He was assaulted, as all Americans were, by the panicky discussions of the late 1940s, as the atomic bomb, Red Scares, and beginnings of a new war dominated the news and public talk.

For example, Legman saved a 1949 report from the *Daily Worker* that gives a feel for Wertham's radical public stance. Wertham had participated in a radio panel discussion on the social responsibility of the religions.[67] *Worker* columnist Bob Lauter reported that he "made the most notable contribution of the evening in a forthright speech which raised a number of very specific questions. He said that in our society the poor man who does wrong goes to the cooler, while the rich man who does wrong gets a deep freezer."[68]

Lauter detailed Wertham's attack on "the use of the atom bomb at Hiroshima as a totally wanton use of a terrible weapon." Wertham dressed down religious leaders for their irresponsibility: he demanded to know "if there had ever been a military weapon in the world's history not blessed by religion." He discussed racial and religious intolerance, which he saw as at its height, and called the explicitly segregated Stuyvesant Town public housing development "a monument to race hatred." As Lauter summed up, Wertham's was a full-frontal attack on all religions for failing the poor.

In his concern for the mental health of young people, by the mid-1940s Dr. Wertham had become the most prominent medical critic of the effects of mass-mediated culture. He viewed comic books, movies, and later television as contributing to the violence of American life by normalizing race hatred and the legitimacy of physical force. He thought that mass media, like comics and movies, stepped in where family and community failed and gave potentially disturbed children unhealthy ways of seeing themselves and the world. From the testimonies of some of his young patients, he drew the conclusion that fantasizing over comic books had edged them toward violence. In his popular writings, he tended to cite these conclusions as hard facts, and from a small number of children he extended his conclusion that the rising brutality of American youth (an increase that was assumed, but unproven statistically) was due in part to the flood of comics.[69] Although Wertham did not think comic books or movies per se determined delinquency, he was beyond impatient with apologists who reasoned that they therefore had no effect on children's minds. He thought they were a factor in a public health emergency. Legman heartily agreed with this position.

Bart Beaty writes that Wertham was perhaps the first major public intellectual to take comic books seriously; his work is an important though unacknowledged foundation of American media effects theories, particularly "cultivation" theory,[70] which considers mass media as an influential part of the experiential world of the viewer. In this view, the effects of media upon people are not single measurable items that can be isolated for study. Rather, media must be considered as part of an entire mental and interactional world. In *Love & Death*, Legman was developing a similar approach: he was also a proponent of taking "mass culture" seriously, and he saw mass-produced popular culture as creating a whole influential mental environment through which people understood (and tragically misperceived) the world.

In January 1948, Legman wrote to Wertham to enlist in the battle against comics. He had been influenced by Wertham's articles in the *New Republic*, which appeared as the doctor was involved in crafting a proposal restricting violent comics' sales to young children.[71] Legman wrote that he felt very uncomfortable with the whole debate. "I distrust the entire literature of violence, pro or con, not so much because bad faith may be suspected in the writer. . . . But because even in covering this topic, the mass media were speaking to and cultivating sick tastes." He thought any reader's "interest in reading about death, madness, violence, &c.&c., is extremely suspect, pictures of murdered children in newspapers may serve as a deterrent to Medean murder, but I have a feeling they are printed for no such worthy purpose."[72]

He continued that he and Beverley were forced to agree with Wertham when he was "unwilling to say that 'obscenity' is good." Although they approved of it, to say so flew too much in the face of current mores. "For the same reason you are unwilling even to say that . . . 'obscenity' is preferable to the sadism [in comics], although we do feel you could say this without the slightest prejudice. . . . Basically you feel that comics are bad, and, if they cannot be destroyed must at least [be] attacked with whatever weapon comes to hand." Targeting comics as "obscenity" might work.[73]

Where they disagreed, Legman wrote, was on the use of prohibitions or suppression. Censorship itself was part of the problem: "10 years ago there were no sadistic comic books, and 'obscenity' was a crime. . . . 10 years from now there will again be no sadistic comic books, but 'obscenity' will still be a crime. . . . Since, as Freud shows, [we] censor dreams, we surely will not be free of waking censorship soon. It will be good enough if we are free of sadism."[74]

Legman was coming to think censorship of violence might be necessary, while an uncensoring of "normal" sexuality was called for. One of his favorite points was that the most horrific attacks on women could be depicted in comics—so long as no naked breasts were shown. Wertham, as a German immigrant, was deeply uneasy about legal restraints on any expression. He wanted to press his objections to fictional violence as part of a multifaceted public mental health program, but he would go no further than recommending age-grading comics, with violent comics prohibited for children under fifteen.[75]

Legman showed Wertham his comics chapter, and Wertham invited him to present it a few months later at a panel on psychoanalysis and the comics at the New York Academy of Medicine. Wertham introduced the symposium, which also included presentations by medical doctors and one of the first exhibits of a collection of comic books.[76] Covered in the press, this forum became one of the defining moments in the postwar anticomics movement. Legman read a version of "Not for Children" ("The Psychopathology of the Comics"), and afterward he wrote to Julia that it was "a very great personal triumph. I was interrupted three times by applause—something unheard of in the dignified Academy of Medicine—and the editor of 'CRIME—Does Not Pay' wanted to fight me. Whether it will have any effect practical results, though, remains to be seen."[77] Julia was disappointed that she had missed it: she would have taken the first train from Scranton had she known. She hoped to hear him lecture someday.[78]

Wertham had arranged for the symposium to be covered in the press, and it got a lot of attention. The papers were abstracted in the *Saturday Review of Literature*, *Reader's Digest*, the *New York Herald Tribune*, and *Collier's* (these last two by Judith Crist). Julia wrote to say that people in Scranton were asking if that was indeed her son who got "a big write up" in *Time*.[79] Comic book historians see the New York Academy gathering as Dr. Wertham's first big salvo in the comic books wars, and Legman was central to the event.

In his lecture, Legman alternated between heartfelt cries for honesty over censorship and rage at the hypocrisies of the world. To set up his analysis, he first outlined a history of the genre, tracing the flood of noxious stuff. He distinguished between the old comic strips in the newspapers, aimed at adult [*sic*] readers and full of "pranks, jeers, and naughtinesses." He gave some background: "In 1933 there was not one comic book published openly"; only the newspaper strips flourished. But the Depression had hatched a new form. By 1936, he thought, the forty-eight-page books were everywhere, although their larger history had not yet been properly traced.[80]

He introduced his nascent Freudian perspective: literature and folklore were a form of dreaming—a condensed but distorted way of dealing with the world. "Like all other forms of dreaming, literature operates under a censorship," and, viewing this negatively, "it allows for no direct attack on frustration."[81] Comic books were a form of fantasy life too, but a more dangerous one.

He fused his Freudian perspective with political economic analysis: the excitement of killing was offered to let people slough off "sexual and economic frustration." In fact, this was the nature of mass culture in general, including radio and television just coming into wide availability: tabloids, weeklies, murder movies, horror, violent sports—they all told the same bloody story while accommodating people to exploitation. Death was everywhere, but comic books were the special "kiddies' korner." The fist, the hood, the disguise were children's entertainment. The graphic dimension was important, too. Along with other comic book critics, Legman thought the colorful visual nature of comics made them especially seductive, and he asserted that soon pictorial murder would replace printed murder.[82]

Legman's brief against the comics was that they celebrated violence. The volume of violence in print was astounding. He figured that every American child could (and did) read ten to twelve comics a month and that there was "one violent picture on every page." He counted thousands of "beatings, shootings, stranglings, blood puddles and torturing to death." Children were getting an enormous supply. Other mass media fortified this surrounding with similar "violence over the radio daily and both together in the movies on Saturday."[83] Here Legman, like Wertham, considered the comics as a part of a whole mass media–dominated environment.

Legman proceeded to pile up the evidence: he noted comic books fell into age-graded market segments: from Walt Disney's perversion of little children by the violence of the Three Little Pigs, to the superhero comics aimed at kids and teens, to murder and "squinky" (weird or sick) comics for older boys and men. Little boys move up to crime "classics" at age nine or ten, where "all the most violent children's books of the last two centuries are condensed into forty-eight-page sequences." Now, with the help of experts in children's literature, history comics were being produced that followed the Teddy Roosevelt line, with "buffalo-killing and boxing gloves."[84]

If media and their stories provide a kind of model for identification, then the child was being asked to identify with the doer of violence as hero. And "with repetition like that you can teach a kid anything," with dangerous collective results in the present.[85] The child's natural job in life, he thought, is not to go along, but to resist parents and educators who would break his spirit by civilizing him. Resistance (and perhaps self-knowledge) is paralyzed by overwhelming "fantasy violence"—it is "siphoned off" while adults are busy "abnormalizing" the child to fit in. Comic books were a kind of "Universal Military Training of the Mind."[86]

He denounced psychiatry's promise that "the civilization we have now is preferable, and normal." Why should people adjust to a society that had more jails than high schools?[87] Legman's anticomics argument here parallels the Frankfurt School's attempts to combine Marxism with psychoanalysis: the dreams of mass culture are offered in place of the possibility of working-class revolt, and in Legman's view, violence was the essential ingredient in the bread-and-circuses formula, because it felt better than passivity.[88]

Superheroes, Legman thought, "teach the right of the individual to take the law into their own hands," "a philosophy of Klan justice." Superman expressed a kind of eroticism by flying, but, more important, he was a projection of the reader's "paranoid hostility," as the stories showed "every city in America . . . in the grip of fiends."[89] Clearly, this was Cold War paranoia in fictional form: having first obliterated Native Americans, and bombed hundreds of thousands of Japanese into oblivion at Hiroshima and Nagasaki, the guilt of the atom attacks had stunned Americans into "the daily conviction that we are menaced in our innocence." "Every country in the world" was "about to attack us," and only the vigilantes can save us, Legman declared.[90]

There was both elitism and a populist critique of authoritarianism in Legman's argument. For his whole adult life, he was a *passéiste* in his tastes—he looked backward to the literature of the past as superior to what the twentieth century was throwing off. To the extent that comics and pulps displaced other reading, they degraded a literate culture. Legman shared much of the perspective of other intellectuals when he argued that the very massness of comic books, with their factory production, poor paper, and bad inks, debauched readership wholesale. But he seems also to have been viscerally horrified by the comic book depictions of violence, especially against women, and by the overt racism of many of the story lines and depictions.

But Legman probably recognized how much of the anticomics sentiment was fueled by the sense that the books came out of a "lower" social stratum, a world of working-class, second-generation immigrant kids, like him. Comics' lack of respectability and tone came, in large part, from the world of the writers and artists, who did not fit in at all. Legman focused his blame not so much on these people, but on the organizers and distributors, "the combines," who supplied newsstand owners and candy-store keepers for profits. Combined with the censorship of sex, the wholesaling of comics would waste the minds of the already ill-prepared.[91] That these stories saturated the world of children, Legman saw as "prima facie an immoral act."[92]

Children had a special place in Legman's argument, as they did for many of the mass-culture critics, although he acknowledged that many comics readers were adults. Recalling his own childhood, he called children the "poor shut-up little people" who had cramped avenues of escape and only minor chances to resist. They were more vulnerable, and the 1930s had made things worse. "In the Depression, it was not difficult to peddle the cult of death." Children had few other outlets; they needed the excitement of violence in increasing doses. It was addicting. In Legman's view, industrial culture like comic books not only took up space but also victimized the weakest. And the helping professions were just another part of the repressive equation. It was they who were squashing grade schoolers into the horrible mold of modern civilization, with bad history, bad morals, no sex education, and rotten patriotism. As he put it, "We train children . . . by breaking their spirit."[93] Here Legman was at odds with Wertham and mainstream child-guidance experts who were urging parents and educators to step back into their proper roles, get control of the mass media, and prevent juvenile delinquency by limiting what children could consume. Legman did not trust parents and doubted American culture had a positive place for children at all.

Legman's critique of the comic books was inseparable from his prejudice against homosexuals, and his idea that they were predominantly sadists was not unusual, although it was becoming less polite to express it publicly. His argument that comic book publishers were turning young people into "perverts at 10 cents apiece" channeled the antigay anxieties of the time. He was reworking a draft of his article "On the Cause of Homosexuality" into a pamphlet (it kept getting refused at magazines); eventually, it too became part of another chapter in *Love & Death*, under the title "Open Season on Women."

It is possible that the public preoccupation with homosexuality was personally distressing to Legman. On the back of a 1950 lecture program of the Auxiliary Council to the Association for the Advancement of Psychoanalysis, Legman drafted a note to Dr. Wertham. He wrote that he had been thinking over "disturbing things" and felt uneasy when he found his book listed in a catalog as "Psychiatrica" and saw himself "rubbing elbows with Freud, Roheim, Ranke." He squirmed with feelings of unworthiness and presumption.

His article addressed problems of "homosexual masochism as expressions of castration anxieties," and he wondered how he had the right, "with no training at all and probably no motive but the need to control this area of my own problems and fears, to put his ideas into print." Would Wertham recommend a Freudian psychoanalyst? It is unlikely that he mailed the letter, but the draft suggests he felt anxiety over his own compulsion to write about homosexuality.[94] Why *was* he so interested in the topic?

Love & Death survived endless tribulations on its shaky way to publication. By late 1948, Legman was serializing it in Jay Landesman's magazine *Neurotica* (this story is taken up in the next chapter). Several publishers finally accepted the book, only to back out when they read the text. James Laughlin of New Directions Press even had it printed, but canceled publication when he saw the galleys. At the very last moment, Legman picked up the unbound sheets from the printer, substituted his own title page and the imprint "Breaking Point," and had them bound himself.[95] By the late summer of 1949, *Love & Death* was beginning to reach its audience with a very respectable print run. Legman sold two thousand copies in advance and then printed and sold an impressive five thousand more, with almost no advertising. He promoted the book through *Neurotica*'s mailings, and this would shortly get him into serious trouble.

The response to *Love & Death*, and especially the comics piece, was enthusiastic. Jay Landesman thought "Not for Children" was excellent, and Clellon Holmes wrote several times to say that it was "heady stuff," clarifying the muddled issues. Felix Giovanelli at the Vanguard Press liked it, although Vanguard passed on the book. Giovanelli picked up on Legman's antihomosexual arguments: he wanted to discuss a Donald Duck movie he and his wife had seen recently. "Talk about homos on the job behind the scenes!"[96] Stanley Edgar Hyman, the literary historian and critic, saw Legman's name turning up all over. He read several chapters and thought Legman was going "from strength to strength." Philosopher Robert Gorham Davis thought "Not for Children" was an admirable analysis.[97] As the chapter circulated, more correspondents and friends wrote to praise it.[98] Poet Conrad Aiken liked it and asked Giovanelli, "Where or what is 'Breaking Point'?" (Breaking Point was not a place, Giovanelli told him, unless it was all of New York City.)[99]

Architecture critic Jane Jacobs, whom he had known from high school in Scranton, found *Love & Death* bracing. "You did a wonderful job," she wrote, "witty, readable clear, full of apt and telling examples . . . [and] a great many important truths."[100] He was fulfilling the promise their early friends had noticed. Joe Bernstein, another high school friend who was now a journalist in Paris, reported that UNESCO had added *Love & Death* to its library.[101] His girlfriend, Louise "Beka" Doherty, wrote that it had a "terrific impact" in her offices at Time-Life.[102] And of course, his mother was thrilled.

A new acquaintance, Marshall McLuhan, got the book and found it exhilarating.[103] Poet and novelist William Carlos Williams wrote to Legman that the book was a "brilliant study of a sordid theme . . . the death that thrives so well in all our thoughts."[104] Clellon Holmes praised *Love & Death* as brave, "an affirmation of life . . . in many ways a wild and cleansing celebration of it" for all its "moral indignation and verbal violence." Holmes had heard Legman was hungry, and, typically, he sent money. "For Christ's sake, grub money can always be scrounged for, Gershon."[105]

The praise was not unqualified. One problem readers found with "Not for Children" was its style: Legman began with the collection of textual evidence and analysis and launched into polemical denunciation, but he did not return from this to analysis. R. G. Davis agreed with much of what Legman had to say, but thought his tone was a problem, as was "the flat and final phrase."[106] Similarly, Alex Comfort was impressed at Legman's tackling of sadism, but hoped he could be "more dispassionate."[107] Weston LaBarre, anthropologist, fellow Freudian, and limerick collector, thought it was wordy and repetitious: "Concision, pal! Why don't you try it?"[108]

Of course, as Bart Beaty points out, most of the other critics' arguments about comics were blasts of opinion and prejudice, too. Almost no one argued from carefully collected evidence.[109] Wertham's attacks were based in his clinical evidence and experience, but patient confidentiality limited how much detail he could present.

Another limerick collector, Thomas Keller, liked *Love & Death* but found the language too subjective, too obnoxiously Gershon's own.[110] Legman answered that "objectivity" was bad faith under the circumstances of half the world preparing the other half for death. To a Dr. Lipson who wondered whether Legman's analysis might be stronger if he used case histories, Gershon admitted he *was* a case. But this was "the first serious attempt to explain where all the frigid women are coming from."[111]

Not everyone was in full agreement with Legman's theory of effects. A longtime correspondent, W. L. McAtee of Chicago, thought Gershon was right that the world was a mess, but he recalled his own dime-novel reading in childhood and wondered if there was so much cause for alarm. All his military heroizing of Napoléon had left him a "mild and inoffensive oldster."[112] Legman sent a copy of *Love & Death* to Maria Leach, the editor of Funk and Wagnall's *Dictionary of Folklore*, telling her that the dictionary's article on comics was "disgraceful" and proposing himself as an expert who could do better in handling "sub-literary expressions." He received no reply.[113]

A CANTANKEROUS BUT BRILLIANT BOOK

Love & Death got only a few published reviews, but they appeared in notable places. William Carlos Williams cited it in his list of the "Best Books I Read

This Year" in the *New York Times Book Review*.[114] *Harper's Magazine* featured it in its list of new books, including it in the category of social history as a study of the cultural moment of mass production. In his review, Richard Rovere described it as a "cantankerous but nevertheless brilliant essay," "arrogant and cocksure." If Legman was right, the United States was on its way to becoming a "nation of lynchers and flagellants."[115] Censorship of sex did not seem to be a strong-enough cause for the effect, Rovere thought, but Legman's reasoning had its points. While Legman missed how prevalent sexual violence and death were in respectable literature, his analyses of the content of the popular forms were "the best studies of their kind" he had ever seen. Rovere read *Love & Death* as a feminist defense of women and called it a "stout hearted humanistic essay."

The most influential reviewer was Malcolm Cowley, literary critic and editor of the *New Republic*. He met with Legman to discuss the book, and Gershon took a lot of joshing when Cowley described him in his review as "small, round and excitable." Recounting the book's tortured publication history, Cowley gave an evenhanded review.[116] He found Legman the sort of critic "who likes to ride his argument over the fences and into the ground," and he seemed to imply that "sex, and its substitute, death, are the only valid themes for literature."[117]

Cowley thought the importance of Legman's little book did not rest on its central argument. "He is best in his incidental observations. . . . I was impressed by a group of statements he makes about the detective story as a standard form." Legman argued that in detective fiction, the mystery was unimportant, because "the murderer is the real victim. . . . [T]he function of the crime . . . is to put the murderer outside the pale" and confirm the detective as "an extra legal avenger. . . . [T]he usual end of the story is a kind of lynching." Legman had uncovered a pattern of meaning in the detective story that connected it to America's growing authoritarianism.

Like others, Cowley found the comics chapter the strongest. When Legman argued that comics asked children to identify "with the heroic beater, shooter, strangler, blood-letter and/or torturer," Cowley felt real-world connections: "He is saying . . . that the paranoia of the Superman comics helps to explain the paranoia of the present [anticommunist] loyalty crusade. He is also saying—and long before the two Peekskill riots—that the teenagers who stoned automobiles leaving the [Paul] Robeson concerts were picturing themselves as the heroic incarnations of Blackhawk and Captain Marvel, crusading against, beating, maiming and lynching the inhuman foes of America in peril."[118] Cowley remained uncertain that sex censorship was responsible for all the violence and paranoia, but it could not be wrong to look at popular culture for part of an answer.

Not all literary men thought fictional violence was bad. A young Leslie Fiedler, with whom Legman was conducting a typically combative correspondence, wondered if the "literature of violence and aggression, even on its most vulgar level (e.g. Captain Marvel and your own book) [should] be placed under ban as being psychologically harmful, or can it be understood as cathartic and emotionally true?" Fiedler identified Legman's logical problem: he assumed one kind of reader, "a unitary child." Like "a Manichean goy," Legman was seeing the world in a black-and-white, good-versus-evil way. But did the comics not have a "frankness and self-knowledge" in them that a Jew could recognize? Legman was already feeling antagonistic to Fiedler for positing, in an article in *Partisan Review*, a normal homoerotic stage through which all children passed on the way to heterosexuality.[119] For Legman, this made Fiedler part of the problem. What, he retorted, did Fiedler know about Judaism anyway? He had been translating the Torah when little Leslie was still "dreaming over his foreskin on Delancey St." As he often did, he cited a biblical denunciation: "Your hands are defiled with blood and your fingers with iniquity, your lips have spoken lies, your tongue hath muttered perverseness" (Isa. 59:3–12).[120]

If Legman's voice was one of the harshest and earliest in the mass-culture debates, the uproar over comics had some effect. The late 1940s saw a flood of alarmed editorials, conferences, reports, and even comic book burnings around the United States. As urban authorities cracked down on the gay social world, homosexuality, crime, and mental illness blurred with comics in the public mind. After the 1950–53 Kefauver Committee hearings on the juvenile delinquency named comics as part of the problem, the industry preempted governmental restraint with the Comics Code, a form of self-regulation.[121] Subsequent comics fans have blamed Wertham and Legman for the code and its effects on the industry, although they were part of a much wider moral panic.

The publication of *Love & Death* in 1949 marked Legman's moment to become a writer on the New York scene, an independent, uncensored critic who would influence American culture. It could, perhaps, help him break into the tight, Ivy League–dominated circles of the *Partisan Review*, *Politics*, and *Commentary*. Unlike many aspiring writers, Legman did not hope to join these men or manage their editorial offices. Having gotten their attention, he wanted to persuade them—he demanded, in fact, that they join his war on sexual censorship. Would they be convinced and sign up, or would they regard him as a blot on the literary landscape?

It was a compelling question, but the literary leftists were moving quickly rightward, under pressure from the American loyalty crusade in full force by 1949. Legman's mass-culture critiques sat uneasily next to the anticommunist politics of the intellectuals, since criticism of American consumer culture could seem like an attack on the American way. The comics panic blended weirdly into these politics, too. Postwar New York and Washington, D.C., were seeing a brutal bout of civic intolerance to the visibility of homosexual citizens, as legislators enacted regulations on public spaces and social gathering places and put in place harsher legal sanctions for "degeneracy" and disorderly behavior. The federal government and State Department led the antihomosexual terror, as hundreds of gays and lesbians lost their jobs in an upsurge of anxiety about "security risks." But was it gays, communists, or Senate committees that Americans should fear?[122]

Humanity more or less survived the early fifties. There was no nuclear holocaust, although the Korean War was a catastrophe, with saturation bombing of the North followed by famine and no peace. At home there were witch hunts, purges, and public executions. Legman and his fellows assessed the world's advertising-swamped and military-dominated future with black and bitter urgency. In Legman's writings on mass culture, the sense of emergency sometimes blended into paranoia, a feeling that a conspiracy was being put together to destroy people's minds. This was amplified by an awareness of what could not be said, or at least not printed: that the anti-Soviet panic was manipulated, a new and terrifying war was being ginned up, and the American government *did* spy upon and imprison its own people. For Legman, it was all of a piece: existential threat and political suppression were inseparable from repression in the sphere of the intimate and personal. As he saw it, the real world of the sexual body and its knowledge were viciously suppressed by the same forces that threatened all human life. The question remained: Would Love prove stronger than Death? He was not optimistic.

5

NEUROTICA

What a mealy-mouthed world it has become.
—Marshall McLuhan to Gershon Legman, July 11, 1949

Despite the praise for Legman's polemics in *Love & Death*, the manuscript was rejected all over town. So it was very good luck for the stalled book when Louise "Beka" Doherty, one of Legman's girlfriends, connected him with *Neurotica*, an upstart little magazine out of St. Louis. *Neurotica* is forgotten today except by devotees of the Beat movement, and the intentions in its assemblage of poetry, story, and social analysis can seem nearly impossible to decipher. But in the four short years of *Neurotica*'s hectic run (1947–51), it made a mark on American literary and popular culture. It was a touch point for the early Beats, but it is pre-Beat, channeling an anticipation of what was to come.[1]

Allen Ginsberg, Jack Kerouac, Carl Solomon, Chandler Brossard, and Tuli Kupferberg made their first appearances in print in *Neurotica*; Anatole Broyard and John Clellon Holmes contributed as well, as did some of the other writers who went on to be known beyond the Beat movement.[2]

According to *Neurotica*'s publisher, Irving N. Landesman (known as Jay), the magazine was a joking experiment, almost an accident. Jay was a college dropout from a family of antique dealers, unhappily married and frustrated selling chandeliers.[3] He was also a jazz and blues lover who kept up a vigorous nightlife in the St. Louis bars and theaters, with a wide circle of artist friends. He seems to have had an ability to pull odd performances together and eventually became a theater producer.

St. Louis, with its old wealth, staid brick town houses, and heavily Catholic working class, might seem an unlikely place for a bohemian scene. But the city had just gone through a boom as wartime production brought young workers from all over the South and Midwest to its factories. St. Louis's location at the confluence of the Mississippi and Missouri Rivers made it a venerable crossroads of intercontinental rivers, railroads, and highways. And there was a brilliant music scene, rooted in the Great Black migration from the Deep South and the city's long-standing orchestral and marching band traditions. By the war's end, St. Louis was a blues and jazz seedbed, primed for a musical explosion: in the 1950s, Miles Davis would become the city's coolest son, and Chuck Berry and Ike Turner were preparing to upend American popular music. The G.I.s were returning to school at several large universities. It was not Manhattan or Chicago, but it was happening in a mid-American way.

With haphazard flair, Landesman made his way running open houses where the hospitality "attracted the best collection of rejects St. Louis literary, artistic and musical life had to offer." As he described the scene, "The only price of admission was a healthy maladjustment to society. . . . 'Square' was the dreaded word. To be 'serious' was to leave yourself open to attack without chance of survival."[4]

Jay and his friends were antimilitarist, or at least against the hyperpatriotism saturating America in the postwar years. He describes a telling party scene, probably in 1945: "When someone brought ex-paratrooper-turned-artist Stanley Radulovich around for the first time, he was wearing his veterans discharge button in his lapel." Poet Richard Rubenstein accosted him. "Take that corny medal off, soldier. You'll never get laid with that on." "Radulovich was about to punch Rubenstein," but he "took the button and flushed it down the toilet to tumultuous applause." So much for patriotism and sincerity, Jay observed. They had had their war, and they were done.[5]

Landesman, Radulovich, and Rubenstein started an art gallery and bar called Little Bohemia in an old downtown storefront. They invented a weirdly atmospheric environment. Thomas Hart Benton exhibited his paintings there, but "the real attraction was the people." As Jay described it, "The poet, writer, radical, non-conformist were no longer threatening outsiders in Little Bohemia, they were the star attraction." Poets read, writers wrote and made passes at artists, and students argued. Strangers wandered in and out, and Radulovich ran the bar. He had too little time to paint, but Little Bohemia was booming.[6]

One day in 1947, Rubenstein showed up with a copy of W. H. Auden's *Age of Anxiety*. Auden, he thought, was describing something real and new. Rubenstein demanded: "Let's cure the ills of America by starting a poetry magazine." He reasoned that "all of the poetry rags are so goddamn academic, it's time for something radical." What was needed, they agreed, was a magazine "for and about neurotics, written by neurotics" because "the poet is the first to recognize the rot, the first to celebrate the glory, and the last to be appreciated." W. H. Auden had put his finger on it in the *Age of Anxiety*: the new look was going to be the anxious look in "the club of the New, Forgotten Men."[7]

Typically, Jay thought of publicity first: he began by ordering stationery headed:

NEUROTICA, A Quarterly Journal
Publisher and Editor, JAY IRVING LANDESMAN

Later, he wrote that the word "neurotic" characterized all his friends: "Adding the 'a' was an afterthought." With no publishing experience, Landesman placed a small ad in the *Saturday Review of Literature*, asking for submissions. To his surprise, he got a strong response. "Manuscripts, poetry, and subscriptions from professionals and amateur writers began flowing in at a brisk pace. Even from psychiatrists!" He got letters from Karl Menninger and Dr. Gregory Zilboorg (a noted New York analyst), who joked, "I doubt if any analysts would be interested in writing for *Neurotica*. They are much too neurotic to be associated with anything so neurotic."[8]

Landesman was not much of an editor, so he worked on distribution. Interest was surprisingly strong. Quickly, there were five hundred subscriptions and five hundred copies ordered for newsstands in St. Louis: "With confidence I ordered a first printing of 3000 copies." "You would have thought the magazine's name was Erotica," he joked. The first issue appeared in bookstores around the United States, especially on college campuses. At the suggestion of Beka Doherty, who worked at *Time* and *Life* in Manhattan, Landesman made trips to cultivate bookstore owners in the Village and uptown. Her personal contacts made sure that the newly fledged *Neurotica* was visible around town on counters and in store windows.[9] Newsstands and bookstores demanded second and third printings. Soon Landesman and friends had enough material and money for new numbers, although the submissions were very uneven. Rubenstein wrote filler poetry and edited articles.

Neurotica was a mix of ostensible social science essays and literary experiments. Reflecting the interest of Landesman's St. Louis friends, the first numbers emphasized poetry. The first issue had a poem by Kenneth Patchen; another by Ellis Foote, a Utah experimental poet; and one by Leonard Bernstein, already well known as a composer and conductor. *Neurotica* also reprinted, usually with permission, poets like Henri Michaux, the Belgian surrealist.[10]

NEUROTICS, INCORPORATED

The first volume of *Neurotica* gives off a feeling of diffuse but intense alienation. There is almost never mention of specific social problems or catastrophes in the magazine. In his article "Neurotics, Incorporated," Gerald W. Lawlor describes and speaks for the contributing authors. Lawlor had listened to a talk by the executive secretary of Alcoholics Anonymous and thought that "there are thousands perhaps millions of people who would like to join such a group . . . but they don't happen to be alcoholic. . . . [T]here are other people . . . who are suffering equally as much and have been suffering longer, usually from childhood. . . . They are people with strong urges, many of them with creative abilities and keen sensitivities, but they dare not express these to a world that they believe is hostile to them."[11] Neurotics have feelings they "can't understand, and impulses they can't cope with . . . nor can they understand themselves." All this maladjustment could be eased, if not cured, if like-minded people would at least listen and understand when the neurotic "feels himself sinking under the waves of societal oppression." Where "societal oppression" originated, Lawlor did not say.[12]

Although the sources of distress remained vague in *Neurotica*, the late 1940s offered no shortage of reasons for anxiety. Panic and paranoia filled the newspapers. It is worth remembering that some of the men who later called themselves "Beat" were World War II veterans like Stan Radulovich. Jack Kerouac had been in the army, and novelist John Clellon Holmes was deeply affected by his work with injured veterans in a naval hospital. Allen Ginsberg had been involuntarily committed to a mental institution for "disruptive behavior" (homosexuality) at Columbia University; his friend Carl Solomon had endured commitment and electroshock therapy.

The G.I.s, if anyone, had a right to be anxious, or worse. Some had liberated European concentration camps; some had survived Japanese prison camps. The whole country had registered the mass death at Hiroshima and Nagasaki. Like the war, demobilization was traumatic. As the hundreds of thousands of veterans came home, they were met by a sharp recession and a severe housing shortage. And as the returning veterans tried to find their feet, a new war threatened in Korea. Many were placed on reserve and pressured to reenlist.[13]

At home, there was an anti-Russian Cold War. By 1949 a serious panic about the subversion of the U.S. government was being spread by congressional investigating committees, and a "lavender scare" erupted about homosexual infiltration of the State Department. Senator Joseph McCarthy created uproar by claiming that the army was riddled with communist spies. Anticommunists were publishing "Red Channels," a list of supposed traitors in the mass media.[14]

CHAPTER 5

As its title suggests, *Neurotica* registered these uneasy, panicky feelings in the language of psychoanalysis. Landesman and his friends drew on a growing middle-class awareness of psychoanalytic theory, cultivated by American mass-readership magazines. The concept of neurosis was becoming a way of talking about the effects of combat and trauma on the returning troops.[15] Psychoanalytic treatment was being widely used in the military to treat "war neuroses," what is now called "post-traumatic stress disorder." A bit later, popular fiction and film would spread the notion that returned soldiers had fractured psyches and terrifying pasts they could not face, most famously in Sloan Wilson's 1955 novel, *The Man in the Gray Flannel Suit.*[16]

Despite its oblique style, many of *Neurotica*'s readers felt it was describing something new and real, that it was "hot stuff!" as Jay wrote. Although the magazine did not focus on overt politics, it is impossible that the escalating Cold War and scorching repression of the new Red Scare were not felt in the magazine's pages. What *Neurotica* writers did take up was depressing conformism and a numb alienation. Psychological pain is clearly the topic, but today's reader must stumble toward an understanding of what the cause might be. There is an awareness of hypermilitarism and excessive patriotism. Fear of a nuclear war is there, present but unnamed. What is clearly articulated are feelings of meaninglessness.[17]

Neurotica was barely off the ground when, again with help from Beka Doherty at *Time* and *Life*, the magazine was being covered in the press. Landesman recalled that he was staggered when it was profiled in *Time* (March 1948), mentioned in *Life*, covered in the *St. Louis Post-Dispatch* and *Writer's Journal*, noted in *Harper's*, and slammed in the *Partisan Review*.[18] All this attention made the little magazine seem significant when, really, he had no idea what to do next. Still, all the publicity sold out the first issues, and Jay had to order several thousand reprints to take care of the daily reorders from all over the country.[19]

When Landesman made a promotional trip to New York, he met with twenty-two-year-old John Clellon Holmes, who had just published a short story that used "the language of the hipster" in the second issue. Clellon Holmes told Landesman that the magazine was "going over big in the colleges; people are talking about it—some love it and the establishment hates it. . . . I see it everywhere. How you do it, man?"[20]

Landesman was not sure *how* he did it, but his problem was content. He was still looking for writers who could express this new sensibility and not having too much luck. Now Beka Doherty put him in touch with Legman: "the perfect man to write for *Neurotica*." She described Legman as so good, he was "unprintable," and told Jay, "Try having an affair with him sometime!"[21]

DYNAMITE

So, the cranky demimondaine and the St. Louis hipster connected. Legman pitched his article analyzing the violent content of comic books and then turned to abusing *Neurotica*: Jay recalled that Gershon said it could be something, "if you got rid of all that poetry and fake psychiatric prose. You've got a good idea there. . . . [I]t shouldn't be trusted to a dilettante like you." Landesman reflected that this was true and was suddenly convinced Legman was his man. How was it, he wondered, that all the earlier critics of mass culture, "the H. L. Menckens and the George Jean Nathans, the Gilbert Seldes and Lewis Mumfords never tied up the connection between sex and violence in popular culture in the 30s and 40s?" Working alone, Legman had put his finger on the problem.[22]

Legman declared there should be no more poetry. "I'm going to get you writers who clearly see that America is on the brink of a nervous breakdown." Jay briefly wondered if they would save the country "or push it over the edge."[23] But for now, he was under Legman's sway.

On this same July weekend, Clellon Holmes had taken Landesman to a party in Spanish Harlem, where they met Kerouac, Ginsberg, and Solomon, who had just been released from a mental hospital. Afterward, Clellon Holmes and Jay remembered this as the first time they were aware of a sensibility they would call "Beat." Ginsberg whispered to Landesman that Solomon was a great poet. Solomon confided that Ginsberg was a great poet. But, Jay recalled, "I was up to my neck in poets already. It was writers just out of nut houses that I was interested in."[24]

After this stoned but bracing interlude, Landesman returned to St. Louis, read Legman's comics piece, and thought that it was superb.[25] Clearly, Legman was the man to pull *Neurotica* into focus. Not only was he the editor Landesman needed, but his New York networks also gave him the content. And there was *Love & Death*. Legman had run out of potential publishers, and *Neurotica* looked like a promising outlet. Testy discussions followed, but Landesman and Legman ended up striking a deal. *Neurotica* would publish some of Legman's stuff, serializing *Love & Death* in four installments, beginning with "The Psychopathology of the Comics." When all four installments of the book were published, the same type would be used to print the complete volume. (The same unreliable James Laughlin of New Directions Press who had stalled Miller's *Tropic of Cancer* expressed an interest.)[26] Legman would get a bit of cash for overseeing the magazine's production.

This initially turned out to be a fine arrangement. Legman's expertise at printing and design made *Neurotica* look much better, and he knew how to get the magazine produced through New York's intricate small-batch printing industry. Landesman kept soliciting articles and less than mediocre poetry from St. Louis. But in under a year, by mid-1948, the magazine's center of gravity had shifted to New York, and Landesman decided it made sense for Legman to take over more of the editorial and production work. In August of that year, he wrote, "I give you full rein." He asked only to be kept informed of any radical changes.[27]

The two men wrote each other constantly about production, distribution, and editorial problems. From Gershon's standpoint, finding good material was the big problem. "Critical material, psychiatrically oriented . . . does not seem to be getting produced in much profusion," Gershon wrote. But he always had a line in the water. For example, there was "this Herbert M. McLuhan, . . . who did that remarkable job on Time-Life-Fortune (in *View*, Spring 1947) [and he] ought to have something."[28] Legman's writing and editing, and his network of correspondents, would sharpen *Neurotica*'s attack on alienation by focusing on mass-mediated culture, the connective tissue that ostensibly held a frightened and fractious country together.

The first blast appeared in *Neurotica*, no. 3, as "The Psychopathology of the Comics," the latest version of Legman's critique of the comic book industry. In late October 1948, Gershon wrote to Jay nervously, asking, "Please understand that the reaction to my stuff will not be favorable. . . . You will be told that I am looney &c. Try not to let it shake your faith in me. It has not shaken mine."[29] For the moment, Landesman's confidence held. In November he told Legman that *Neurotica* was selling out, and more copies were at the printer. There were nothing but rave reviews for *Neurotica*, no. 3.

John Clellon Holmes was very enthusiastic about the number, especially the comics piece. It was "one of the finest examples of polemical argument I have ever seen."[30] More correspondents and friends wrote with praise. Felix Giovanelli at Vanguard Press liked it; Stanley Edgar Hyman, the literary historian and critic, thought Legman was going from strength to strength; philosopher Robert Gorham Davis wrote from Smith College that he thought it was an admirable analysis.[31]

Issue 3 was strong. It had come out on time, in a better format. Gershon's comics piece took up half of the sixty-four pages, Jay wrote, "but it was dynamite: [it] gave a tone to the magazine that was not only contemporary, but investigative journalism at its very best, something that was to be a model for the kind of reporting that became popular years later." *Neurotica*'s readers thought Legman was doing something new: he was moving beyond alienation to address the psychological effects of popular culture on everyday life.[32]

Legman was improving the journal's content. It was more scholarly, more serious. There was another poem by Patchen and a piece by Lawrence Durrell, as well as a review of recent books on psychoanalysis by Lila Rosenblum.

Judith Malina, founder of the Living Theater, contributed a dreamlike "Voyage," and Clellon Holmes wrote a pre-Beat statement of Beat sensibility—"All the Good Rôles Have Already Been Taken."[33]

Despite Legman's and Landesman's promotional efforts, the New York intellectuals and other literati looked down on the little magazine, perhaps because it resisted the national slide into the Cold War anticommunist panic. Landesman was snubbed by Dwight Macdonald at a cocktail party, but he secured larger orders for *Neurotica* at bookstores and received an encouraging pat on the back from Frances Steloff at the Gotham Book Mart.[34] There was praise from "the most unexpected places." Beka engineered a positive notice in *Newsweek*.[35]

MARSHALL McLUHAN

In *Neurotica*, no. 4, Legman tried out another piece of *Love & Death*: "Institutionalized Lynch: The Anatomy of a Murder-Mystery."[36] Again, he and his cultural critique were in the foreground, and the journal was becoming more intellectual when it was serious, more caustic when it was playful. There were portraits of a gentleman and a housewife in a "psychodrama" fictionalized by poet and novelist Osmond Beckwith, a "story of pain" by Norma MacLaine, and an essay titled "The Decadent Superman" by Louis Triefenbach. Beverley Keith reviewed a book on art and the unconscious, and Lila Rosenblum summarized *Listen, Little Man!* by Wilhelm Reich. There was still too much "green armpits" poetry about alienation coming in, but Legman was trying to squelch it.

In the spring of 1949, more mass-culture criticism was in the works. An unknown academic named Herbert Marshall McLuhan had written to Legman after reading his comics piece. McLuhan was trying to get a sprawling manuscript called "The Folklore of Industrial Man" published with Felix Giovanelli at Vanguard Press. Giovanelli thought McLuhan would enjoy Legman and described him as a "walking encyclopedia of anecdotes, scandals, inside stuff." Legman was too Freudian for Giovanelli's taste, but he thought he "redeemed himself with his general disdain for North American psychiatrists and psychoanalysts and his criticism of the baneful influence of homosexuals." He later recalled Legman showing him and McLuhan "a rare two-volume dictionary of slang," the foundational Farmer and Henley.[37]

McLuhan admired Legman's article on comics a great deal, but he thought they were both suffering at the hands of clueless publishers: he had had a similar experience of rejection for more than sixteen years. He wrote Legman that editors just did not get the big change that had happened "in perception and thought." "The 'serious' mags are also out of touch, being run by those who got their intellectual set in the 20s and a big dose of illusions in the 30s."[38]

Legman was being rejected because he was too plain-spoken, McLuhan told him. "Your article is unpalatable . . . because it isn't about Kafka or Sartre. . . . You don't provide any outs for the intellectual floozies. . . . You are angry, and you aren't stupid. Therefore, you are the guy who stole the last sleeping pill." McLuhan thought this was not a time, nor was America a country, for honesty. American intellectuals thought culture trickled down, he wrote, and they had no interest in how popular culture really functioned: "They nourish a vague conviction that the zeitgeist flows only in esoteric channels. . . . But times have changed. There are now a multitude of allies for your kind of activity. . . . I for one would like to assist in a new mag which would find its audience on the American campus." Only on campus was there any space free from commercial pressure, any room for "mental detachment."[39]

Legman praised McLuhan's devastating critique of Henry Luce's Time-Life empire in Giovanelli's little magazine, *View*. Here was another man thinking about the wildly proliferating American popular culture (McLuhan was using this term) and about the implications of the mass media in general. Legman and McLuhan agreed that the study of commercial culture was pressing and that most of the intellectuals with access to a wide readership were too snobbish to study stuff they were appalled by.

Legman advised McLuhan, "I wrote the comics article practically on the pattern of your inside man at the skunkworks analysis of TLF [Time-Life-Fortune]. Outside of yourself I know only one critic (Alex Comfort, as in his article on literary sadism in *NOW* 7) who really handles what the million are reading. . . . I wish I could believe with you that the critical function is coming out of its atrophy, handing back the upstairs money that subverts it . . . but I don't see any signs." He wanted for *Neurotica* "all kinds of needle nose psychoanalysis of a country that's plainly going nuts (and is going to Americanize Europe in the bargain)." Would McLuhan write for them? Legman urged, "I'm desperate to raise the tone of the mag since it's the only one that will take my stuff, and I'll go to daggers ends for anything you'd be willing to send."[40]

They discovered they were running on parallel tracks. In February 1949, Legman read McLuhan's "Footprints in the Sands of Crime" on the genealogy of the detective story. Now he was excited to hear that McLuhan had an article under way on the Blondie and Dagwood comics.[41] Legman was revising "Avatars of the Bitch," his chapter on misogynistic stereotypes of women, so perhaps McLuhan would send him "Blondie"? He was still fending off lousy stories and bad poetry.[42]

Although the two men appeared to have little in common besides manic personalities and bulky archives of clippings, Legman and McLuhan undertook a vigorous private correspondence about how to approach the critical analysis of contemporary culture. While Legman was feeling his way into mass-cultural analysis, McLuhan had a more formal background. He had studied literature at Cambridge, where he absorbed F. R. Leavis's advocacy of studying the "cultural environment," the idea that literature scholars ought to study the mental world people lived in every day. This included magazines, radio, pulp novels, and newspapers.

McLuhan's "Folklore of Industrial Man" manuscript presented his own way of looking at commercial media, and it would become, after much cutting, his first book. It had its origins in lectures McLuhan gave to students and other interested people while he taught at St. Louis University—he seems to have given these talks to anybody who would sit still for them—featuring slides of newspaper and popular magazine advertisements.[43] On much the same trail as Legman, McLuhan was immersing himself in the strangeness of postwar advertising. A new kind of critical "reading" unfolded as McLuhan presented his audiences with unexpected commercial images and text, adding his own commentary. The public examination of media texts is familiar now, but it was at the time a daring, even peculiar, thing coming from a college professor. McLuhan would take, for example, an ad that promoted Lysol as a vaginal douche and talk it through with the audience, treating it as a significant piece of culture that needed close interpretation. What did it mean to sell something called "feminine hygiene"? Who wanted to think of women as needing disinfection, and why? McLuhan was intrigued by the problem of the mechanization of human bodies and experience.[44] He was coming to view the new forms of industrially produced culture—especially ads—as a means by which human experience was standardized.

At this time, Legman was also fanatically clipping and compiling, building files for his erotica projects. In the files dealing with analyses of advertising, movie posters, magazine covers, comics, and greeting cards (especially "cruel Valentines" and hostile greeting cards, a fad at the time), he was assembling evidence for a new kind of censorship. His developing theory was that after the war, advertisers were firing up mass consumption with a semihidden sexual symbolism that spoke to repressed desires, directing them toward consumer products. He was interested in phallic images of umbrellas and hats, cigarettes and lipsticks, protuberant noses, and handbags and fur coats that suggested women's crotches. Like McLuhan, he was saving examples of ads that played on people's distorted views of their own bodies. Because sex sold products, but could not be openly shown, advertisers were pushing subliminal, contorted imagery. Legman compared brassiered breasts to missiles and bombs, arguing that sex was being used to sell death.[45]

For a few issues, *Neurotica* featured powerful statements by Legman and McLuhan on the subversive and disturbing qualities of mass-produced popular culture. This cheap, commercial stuff was not validated by intellectuals, nor was it approved by high school teachers or librarians; it was middlebrow at best, although it sometimes strained to be improving and enlightening. They both thought it was the core of American culture.

McLuhan's "Folklore of Industrial Man" article for *Neurotica*, no. 8, summarized his book, and in it he laid out his own position on the relationship between cheap culture and human consciousness. He examined the Charlie McCarthy show, *Time* magazine and its stance toward its readers, *Life, Fortune* ("paeans of praise to machine production interspersed with numerous scenes of luxurious and exclusive playgrounds for the *gauleiters* of big business"), *The New Yorker, Reader's Digest,* and *Harper's.*[46] McLuhan scrutinized the Book of the Month Club and best sellers, Gallup polls, Blondie and Dagwood, the "cult of hygiene," bathrooms and bathroom cleansers, and the way popular novelists described human beings as machinelike.

By "folklore" McLuhan meant a collective dream life, and the paradox he pointed to was expressed in the book's title: human mental life today is quite literally an industrial product. By extension, those collective dreams that offer us a promise of tender sensuality, even sexuality, are in fact parts of an enormous machine.

McLuhan argued that "industrial man lives amid a great flowering of technical and mechanical imagery of whose rich human symbolism he is mainly unconscious . . . not unlike the turtle that is quite blind to the beauty of the shell which has grown on its back." Even the workers (reporters at a newspaper, for example) producing the imagery are unaware that they are part of a larger whole—they would rather stay immersed than "have any aesthetic or intellectual grasp of its character and meaning."[47] McLuhan offered his audience an aesthetic and critical guide to the larger sea of imagery.

As an example, he gave a startling headline from a Chicago paper reporting on an execution:

SEE SELVES ON "VIDEO"

THEN TWO DIE IN CHAIR

April 21, 1950—(A P.)—2 condemned murderers saw themselves on television last night and a few hours later died in the electric chair. . . . [T]he doomed men . . . were filmed in death row yesterday afternoon. The film was then put on a 7 p.m. newsreel show and viewed by the men on a set loaned them by the warden.[48]

In a typical aphorism, McLuhan wrote, "What a thrill these men must have got from being on the inside of a big inside story. Participating in their own audience participation, they were able to share the thrill of the audience that was being thrilled by their imminent death."[49] While McLuhan's metaphorical tortoise shell is exquisitely beautiful, the account of two men participating in the spectacle of their own killing is hideous.

The early McLuhan had put his finger on the endlessly reflective, house-of-mirrors quality of the modern visual media. The execution example was "an illustration of the situation of those in the modern world who contribute mindlessly and automatically to the huge technical panorama which they never raise their eyes to examine."[50] Perhaps all humans could do was raise their eyes and try to appreciate the spectacle. McLuhan's biographer Philip Marchand writes that when McLuhan's book finally appeared (now titled *The Mechanical Bride*), it presented "a critique of an entire culture, an exhilarating tour of the illusions behind John Wayne westerns, deodorants, and Buick ads." Its chapters can be read in any order, and classified ads, snippets of reporting, and especially consumer advertisements are juxtaposed with probing questions and sardonic commentary. As Marchand notes, *Bride* is "not without an occasional hint of admiration for the skill of advertisers in capturing the anxieties and appetites of that culture." His tone was considerably more playful than that of his teacher Leavis and less horrified than Legman's.[51]

In a spate of letters, Legman and McLuhan discussed the postwar media, especially advertising. They registered the aggressive explosion of advertising in the years following the war, as the American consumer economy struggled to get back on its feet after years of rationing, dislocation, and austerity. Both men heard advertising as an impressively loud voice inside people's heads, as admen used wartime propaganda techniques to instruct Americans what to want, feel, and think.[52]

The voice inside the public cranium addressed its audience with a penetrating, authoritarian hectoring that McLuhan and Legman found unnerving. It was not just that advertising and public relations guided consumers, as the industry leaders described their work. In Legman's view, advertising and mass culture spoke to destructive impulses already lurking in the American psyche. For every adorable new appliance or fashion, there was a lethal spurt of violence. The power of mass images could distort aggressive urges and lead a disturbed country further down the path to complete destruction. In what now seems a bizarre twist, Legman and McLuhan connected their critique of mass-produced consumer desires to the baneful influence of homosexuals.

In mid-1949, Legman was writing "On the Cause of Homosexuality," a retort to Freud's argument about how familial patterns shape sexual orientation. Legman posited a unitary cause for homosexuality. Nasty, overbearing fathers, like Emil, made men afraid of their natural desire for women. The homosexual began as a child who wanted to be close to his mother but "was frightened away from the Oedipus conflict by his father's . . . strength. His subsequent detestation of women is simply a defense against the Oedipus situation . . . [an] overcompensation."[53] At the same time, and separate from paternal influence, Legman thought that men could be deluded by culture into thinking they were gay.

McLuhan argued back that the entire modern world was emasculating, and homosexuals were men feminized by industrialization. When the heterosexual family was subverted by mechanical production and the dissolution of organic communities, "natural" relations between women and men went badly awry. This was the source of the collapse of the masculine ego. In McLuhan's view, modern society and industrial production left no paths to "order or prestige" except war, and Western society was sliding toward female domination, whether "of will and character" or simply "sentimental smothering." His evidence for this was that homosexuality had "increased enormously in the last 40 years."[54] This touched on the cool reception of McLuhan's own work: "The homo *necessarily* sabotages art, letters, intellectual and social life."

Legman offered that one of the biggest problems in literature was the "invariable and disgusting" "maniacal denigration and detestation of women," created by "the motion out from under [men] of an entire culture."[55] The negative view of women as the problem came from the homosexuals themselves, who did not like women. But Legman made a distinction: the real "son of a bitch" was not a homosexual but a pseudohomosexual, an unvirile male masochist, who was "weak and fearful" but in other ways did not "conform to any possible definition of homosexual." McLuhan jumped on this notion. It should be developed. Legman could "have a terrific time showing that pseudo-homos" were "barking up the wrong arsehole."[56]

Whatever the cause of homosexuality, Legman and McLuhan agreed on a central issue: men with no virility were sabotaging the culture industries. Gay men dominated art and publishing, as well as fashion, where Legman thought they were busy "putting over ugly styles for women," including short hair, neckties, and pants. And, he underlined, they were very active as spies in "Departments of State, I believe is the euphemism—a well-known industry."[57]

Maybe, McLuhan speculated, the world was just too exhausting. Perhaps homosexuality was a way of "trying to simplify a too complex situation?" And this was destructive because just as homosexuals "hate sex," they hate "all vital art and thought." Since they "require endless thrills" to feel alive, they gravitate toward art and writing and the exciting fields of opposition to society. "Every publisher's office is loaded with them." "Needless to say," McLuhan went on, "Vanguard won't let me say any of this."[58]

As they hashed out their radical perspectives on popular culture, Legman and McLuhan frankly expressed utterly conventional and self-serving prejudices. They were preoccupied with masculinity (including their own), convinced they were having difficulty getting published because they were virile, and they had no critical distance on the "lavender scare" being drummed up by the FBI and surging in the mass media. The purging of "known homosexuals" from the State Department and other government agencies would soon be under way, but it seemed to escape Legman, McLuhan, and most of the rest of America that homosexuals were not the problem. In the pervasive silence around the gay experience, the American right wing was sowing discrimination, fear, and intolerance.

The McLuhan-Legman correspondence shadows the uneasiness of the late 1940s: well-known definitions of masculinity and femininity were in question and unstable, and the new visibility of homosexuality made this clear.[59] Legman thought Kinsey was confusing people by claiming homosexuality was normal, extending a phony tolerance to the less than virile. "Milque toasts need to know they are only that," he wrote, but by convincing men they could be homosexual, Kinsey was widening a circle of perversion.[60] Their mutual friends were obsessed with these same questions; Jay Landesman and Felix Giovanelli often joined them in homophobic denigration.

Some of the uneasiness came from the disruptions of the war years. After 1945, as supposedly "traditional" relations between the sexes were being reestablished, women like Beverley were forced out their well-paying wartime jobs. There was a marriage boom and a baby boom, as couples started delayed families. But while we think of the late 1940s and early 1950s as a period of stifling gender conformity, with men and women squeezed into rigidly defined roles, in fact new patterns of ideas about gender and sexuality were also forming. The reorganization of home and family, footholds in education, and political activity made for new opportunities for women, even as they caused confusion. Gershon's high school classmate Jane Jacobs started out as a reporter covering mining and metal industries. Now a full-time journalist and a working mother, Jacobs was on her way to becoming a leading architecture writer and urban critic.[61] She was a talented woman, but not an anomaly.

Political movements stirred opposition to sexual and racial discrimination. As the war had made same-sex life and relationships more visible, in the postwar years it began to be possible, and necessary, for gays and lesbians to follow the lead of civil rights organizers and refuse to be invisible.[62] And arguably women were sharply aware of their limited roles because they had seen opportunities open during the war. At the same time Betty Friedan was diagnosing "the problem that has no name" for housewives, she was working as a left-wing political organizer.[63]

The late-1940s conversations between Legman and McLuhan underline that many men, even some who styled themselves cultural radicals, found midcentury gender arrangements frighteningly unstable rather than reassuringly old-fashioned. As a sex radical, Legman wanted a root-and-branch change, a lifting of sexual repression but only for heterosexuals. McLuhan wanted to change perceptions, to make people aware of the mechanization of feeling. And both longed to go back to a safer time and place where men were men, women acted like women, and no one was queer.

That they met in discussions of mass culture and mass consumption was not surprising, since this was the arena now confusingly promoting new gender models for Americans to absorb. While McLuhan worried that men were being "Dagwood-ized," or emasculated in the bosom of a consumerist modern family, Legman found the emergence of career women, as displayed in fashion periodicals, downright scary. For Legman, pantsuits were evidence of a sadistic, dominatrix culture that was communicated through the offices of corporate capitalism—and it was all being promoted by "the homos." He seems to have found it deeply unsettling that women could work effectively in the arts, business, and media and still adhere to commercial stereotypes of femininity. Yet in real life, he met many such women in the theater and printing and publishing industries. Beka Doherty was one: a tall, beautiful redhead and a professional researcher and writer. That there was distance between the images of women Legman found fearful and the actual women he encountered does not seem to have eased his mind.[64]

After months of correspondence, McLuhan got his copy of *Love & Death* and was invigorated by it.[65] He wondered if Legman ever considered that the reason *Partisan Review* and other New York magazines had "never done any *serious* work on popular culture is perhaps this:—that for them culture is a consumer activity. As highbrows they must consume, as publicly as possible, goods that are labeled 'highbrow.'"[66] Legman was more interested in the authoritarianism he saw emerging in America. He recommended Wilhelm Reich's analysis to McLuhan, pointing out that the first 174 pages of the latest edition of *The Mass Psychology of Fascism* were the important part of the book and the rest "some current garbage."[67] On Reich, Legman wrote, "It is enough that he throws down this incisively worded challenge between mysticism-cum-fascism on one hand and sexual freedom-cum-socialism on the other."[68] He knew he was on the right track with *Neurotica* because of the "anti-reactions" he kept getting. He cataloged the stupidities: "V. W. O'Connor in *Poetry* says I am a sex maniac and that all the reading of murder mysteries is not sadism after all." Vardis Fisher "says that people are not aggressive because they are frustrated and that millionaires are the frustratedest of all." He thought he would be "like the speck of dirt that makes the oyster create a pearl, but I seem to be getting results closer to that of a quick- acting enema. *No pasaran.*"[69]

Meanwhile, Legman was readying McLuhan's attack on the Luce Time-Life-Fortune empire for *Neurotica*. It had been rejected at many other journals, and McLuhan was relieved and grateful that it might see print. He told Gershon, "*Partisan Review* held it for three months. *Commentary* dallied with it. *View* didn't pay a nickel for it."[70] McLuhan expressed respect for Legman's kind of work, "*and* your uncompromising tone. What a mealy-mouthed world it has become." But he thought that Legman should not waste himself studying only sexual censorship; his mind was too good to not to range widely. McLuhan advised him to try for "a cubistic not a monolinear perspective."[71] (It is not clear how Legman, who loathed cubism and abstract art, received this suggestion.) But in *Neurotica*'s later numbers, published between 1949 and 1951 when Legman was the editor, the magazine became provocatively collage-like. The same kinds of juxtapositions that McLuhan worked with created a useful perplexity that suited Legman: *Neurotica* produced many side-by-sides that asked, "What is going on here?"[72]

In June 1950, McLuhan announced that he had finished his "folklore book." It was a relief to be done. "I yearn to crawl back into the womb of scholarship," he wrote. "Any old womb would do after a bout with the maelstrom that is the world of ads."[73] Legman was hoping for more pieces of the clippings-based "Folklore of Industrial Man," but McLuhan had signed a contract with Vanguard Press, and there would be no more spin-offs. When the book appeared, Legman was angry: there he was struggling with his little magazine and a self-published book. He sent McLuhan a postcard saying he was "profoundly shocked" to read an announcement of the folklore book "under the hot-jazz retitling of *The Mechanical Bride*."[74] It seemed McLuhan was taking the cheap route.

The Mechanical Bride, McLuhan told him, was the name of an early section of the book, and Vanguard had suggested it as the title. Now Legman sensed that the English professor was selling out to sell books. Still, the two kept up their correspondence. McLuhan republished several of Legman's articles in *Explorations*, a journal he edited at the University of Toronto, and the next summer he wrote to suggest an article on the influence of research-granting agencies in shaping culture and consciousness. "The Guggs and Rockfs &c" sounded like a great idea, Gershon replied, and he hoped that McLuhan would follow up. McLuhan, meanwhile, was not happy with his book's reception. Vanguard had had to reduce the size of *The Mechanical Bride* severely (something Legman would never have tolerated). As Philip Marchand puts it, "McLuhan complained of some vague homosexual influence in the publishing world that was horrified by the masculine vigor of his prose and was trying to castrate his text." He'd been subverted, he felt, by the Vanguard staff.[75] Perhaps no one fully understood *The Mechanical Bride*, or perhaps its timing was bad: McLuhan felt he published "just under the wire," "just when the mechanical bride was being replaced by the electronic bride." Perhaps the book "appeared just as television was making all its major points irrelevant."[76] Or perhaps television so amplified what McLuhan was describing that it became impossible to absorb its effects, except to conceive the cultural change as rupture rather than extension. In Marchand's words, "Many of McLuhan's favorite themes—the Dagwoodian American male, the origins of the contemporary sleuths, the desiccated rationalism of the great books program, the delinquent adults behind the comic strips, the crudity and cynicism behind the Dale Carnegie type of self-improvement—these are all gathered in a final, mordant farewell to machine age civilization. It is also a farewell to McLuhan's own long efforts to oppose that civilization." After 1950 McLuhan turned sharply away from political criticism of the content of mass culture and toward a celebration of the potentialities of media technologies. As Marchand writes, in his own work he "was soon to discover that the automatism portrayed in *The Mechanical Bride* was yielding to a new tribalism. The study of this new tribalism would strip the last traces of moral earnestness from his prose."[77]

McLuhan decided that Legman was too morally earnest, too ferociously negative toward the mass media. This was not a hard conclusion to come to. Legman, as he watched McLuhan become first celebrated and then exalted as a media guru, decided the professor was a hopeless phony, and he would ever after view McLuhan as an opportunist.[78] But for a brief few years, their ideas jostled interestingly in *Neurotica*.

Just as *Neurotica* was becoming a success, it began to fall apart. Some of its problems were interpersonal. By 1949 Landesman had moved to New York to be closer to the art and film scene. He was so dissatisfied with his life in St. Louis that he split from his wife, Pat, and got out of the family antique business. He jokingly blamed "the new man" in his life, Legman, for the breakups. He entered psychoanalysis and eventually moved to midtown to be near the jazz cabarets and the Museum of Modern Art film series. He began to hang around with Clellon Holmes and Kerouac and the intellectuals in Greenwich Village. More friends accompanied Jay to Hornaday Place, including Chandler Brossard, who thought Legman was obsessive and "too romantic." Anatole Broyard liked Legman even less, and the feeling was mutual. But Landesman wrote later he felt the magazine needed to keep the other writers involved to save *Neurotica* from "going over the cliff."[79]

Now that Landesman was in New York, Legman was much less affable. He considered *Neurotica* his project now, and he was not interested in swanning around with trust-fund hipsters. Jay recalled Gershon saying, "We've got a big job to do"—even if Landesman thought the magazine was a toy, Legman did not. "He considered himself a Goliath in a den of thieves and perverts," Landesman thought. "He had all the facts, and faith, he'd print them."[80]

DEGENERATE'S CORNER

But other problems were caused by Legman's relentless provocations. He kept daring Jay to joust with the censors. The biggest fight the two men had was over a feature Landesman dreamed up, a serious joke called "Degenerate's Corner." It was a parody of the personal columns in the *Saturday Review of Literature*, which ran thinly veiled advertisements "for sexual contacts, the main reason that many people bought the magazine." A *Neurotica* contributor with an interest in fetishism (Landesman remembered suspecting it was poet Louis Triefenbach) "wrote many of the fictitious ads that livened up the column." Some of the ads explicitly solicited sadism and masochism, and they were all taken aback when serious responses rolled in. Jay remembered the letters "became quite specific. . . . In fact, I was overwhelmed with the intensity of their fantasy life."[81]

One William Fischer was pleased overall with *Neurotica* and breathless about the personal ad from "a strapping young woman." He found "a great imagination is revealed in the requests and answers, specifically Miss Box 124 and her ardent applicants, including the young photographer's assistant, the New York writer on page 46, Mr. Bronx of page 47, Miss Quebec of same page, and above all Mr. Orange, N.J." He asked to be in touch with any and all of these writers, "of course entirely at your discretion."[82]

Landesman showed the letters to Legman, only to find out that Gershon himself had written the ad from "Miss Box 124" and was now going to publish the replies. These were important documents "of the extent of perversion among my subscribers," Legman argued to Jay, saying they confirmed his theory that the American mass media were creating a thriving death cult of sadomasochistic practitioners. They were just barely being kept under wraps, and "they must be exposed," Legman declared.[83] Just at this fraught moment, Henry Luce's representatives declared they would like to purchase *Neurotica* to make it part of the Time-Life-Fortune conglomerate. Jay could make some serious money, and *Neurotica* would have an unparalleled promotional machine behind it.

Legman had often warned Landesman that the commercial media world would try to suck *Neurotica* in and destroy it. Now it turned out to be true. ("Didn't I tell you Legman was just right for you?" Beka Doherty twitted Jay.)[84] Not only was "Degenerate's Corner" scheduled, but Legman was giving space to Marshall McLuhan for his slashing attack on Henry Luce's empire.

130 CHAPTER 5

What unfolded next Landesman and Legman would later call the Noel Busch Affair. The events were easy to satirize even as, looking back, neither man was quite sure what had really taken place. A journalist for *Life* magazine, Busch was drafted to serve as Henry Luce's agent in purchase negotiations, and a dinner meeting was arranged at the Legman-Keith cottage. Legman was now furious at Landesman, because he was treating *Neurotica*'s exposure of American hypocrisy as just another salable commodity. He did not believe for a minute that he would retain editorial control if the magazine were sold to Luce. Busch had made the mistake of wearing lace-up espadrilles and cropped pants to Legman's house, and Legman immediately discerned a homosexual *and* a phony. He mocked him to his face.

Over the next few weeks, while Landesman tried to stall issue 5 of *Neurotica* and arrange the sale over cocktails with Henry and Clare Luce in Westchester County, Legman worked behind the scenes to subvert him. When the issue with "Answers to an Ad," Legman's riff on "Degenerate's Corner," and McLuhan's Time-Life piece, was published, Noel Busch got the message. There would be no deal, but he told Landesman there were no hard feelings. When Jay protested, Gershon replied that of course the mass media were trying to crush *Neurotica*. But it was better to be a "footnote in history" than be swallowed by the machine and disappear. As Landesman reflected, he knew this was right, even though he was starting to think Legman was completely crazy.[85]

But when Landesman tried to mail the copies of *Neurotica*, no. 5, from the Stamford, Connecticut, post office, he wrapped them incorrectly and dropped them off at the wrong time. The postmaster was there and held the suspicious package for investigation. Since issue 5 contained Legman's sado-masochistic prank, they were now really in trouble. Panicked, Landesman consulted around but was surprised at how feeble the response of prominent civil libertarians was. Even Morris Ernst of the American Civil Liberties Union thought the issue was not worth fighting in court.[86] After behind-the-scenes negotiations, and with a healthy payment, Landesman and his lawyer were able to make the problem go away, and no postal complaint was filed against *Neurotica*.[87]

Legman, meanwhile, continued to urge Landesman to make a strike in the courts against the censorship regime. Exasperated, Landesman briefly put Legman completely in charge and announced the editorial change. But just as quickly, Landesman found out that Legman was planning to produce an entire issue on the "castration complex," and this would have been "too much," perhaps placing them all in legal jeopardy. Another screaming fight erupted. Somehow, Landesman reflected, he always lost his editorial fights with Legman. He sent *Neurotica*'s readers a questionnaire asking what they wanted to see the magazine run.[88] The answers were predictably all over the map, asking for less Legman, more Legman, even demands they stop publishing altogether. Weary of battling, Landesman began to make sure the legal responsibility for *Neurotica* was no longer on his shoulders.[89]

Legman used *Neurotica* to continue his critique of sex and repression in mass culture, often emphasizing the threat of perversion, especially homosexuality. Landesman and Clellon Holmes had been trying their hands at popular culture criticism together under the pseudonym "Alfred Towne." In "Sexual Gentlemen's Agreement," published in *Neurotica*, no. 6, in the spring of 1950, "Towne" explored their idea that much of commercial culture was thinly veiled gay propaganda. In number 7, they examined the fixation on the gun in pulp and movie westerns. "Alfred Towne" went on to propose a series, "The Culture Speaks," to other magazines, including the *American Mercury*, with some success. Apparently, Landesman and Clellon Holmes felt they needed the alias as protection from the homosexual mafia.[90]

The last two issues of *Neurotica*, nos. 8 and 9, were impressive and bore Legman's coherent stamp. Despite Jay's objections, these issues were structured around a single idea or theme; the whole of issue 8 took up the problem of the machine. In addition to debuting McLuhan's "Folklore of Industrial Man," there was a discussion of the paranoid concept of the influencing machine by a German psychoanalyst, Victor Tausk, abstracted "from the literature" and accompanied by commentary and clippings on the mechanization of feeling and the use of electric-shock machinery in psychotherapy.[91] Legman's friend John Del Torto submitted (and perhaps cowrote with Gershon) an examination of the human machine in American folk verse and song, in fiction and sociology, especially a "sex machine" or "screwing machine." Del Torto signed it with his Social Security number. The writing shows the strong hand of Legman, as it moves to criticize cybernetics and computerization, themes he would return to in the 1960s. Artist William Steig (then just beginning his career) submitted a brilliant cartoon of a person in a gas mask, being hooked up to pipes at every junction and orifice, titled *Every Contingency Taken Care Of.*[92]

As Legman had threatened, he brought out the castration issue. *Neurotica*, no. 9, dealt with Struwelpeter, the German children's book character who is a giant scissors and cuts children's thumbs off. A piece by Otto Fenichel, again abstracted from a journal article, treated the castration complex and its development in children. F. Scott Fitzgerald's "Boy Who Killed His Mother" and a selection from Melville's *Pierre* illustrated Legman's contention that fear of homosexuality and fear of castration ran together as a strong current in American letters. Legman inserted news clippings about how Nevada cowboys castrated sheep with their teeth and followed up with his analysis of anxiety in penis jokes. This he juxtaposed with a text lifted from the Christian American Tract Society urging that dirty jokes were unworthy of the teller and degraded all interaction. Legman's collages pointed to an inescapable conclusion: America's public and private culture were convoluted and weird. The only way to make sense of it was to lay out publicly the things that could not be admitted. His technique of placing disjunctive, unexpected ideas parallel to each other (children's books and sheep castrations?) strengthened his argument, as McLuhan had suggested, and it did create weird vibrations. *Neurotica* may have been failing, but it was going out with a bang.

UNMAILABLE

It was not the machinations of the Luce empire, or Jay's exit, that brought *Neurotica* to an end. After the successes of 1948 and 1949, catastrophe struck. As it turned out, and unbeknownst to Landesman, the New York Post Office, the city police, and the FBI had been surveilling Legman and his publishing projects. It was not the content of the journal that drew the authorities' interest, but the fact that Legman had been using the magazine's mailings to advertise *Love & Death*, now about to be published from the *Neurotica* plates. Quickly, Legman was in serious legal trouble with the New York Post Office, when one of its inspectors found *Love & Death* obscene and unmailable.[93]

People born before 1960 may still remember the Post Office rubber stamp "Report Obscene Mail to Your Postmaster" on letters. But for everyone else, some background may be needed to explain why the Post Office would be concerned with Legman and his tiny publishing operation. Until nearly 1970, the Comstock Act of 1873 shaped the practical and imaginative universe of Americans. At the urging of the self-appointed cultural purifier Anthony Comstock, Congress had granted the Post Office Department near-absolute power to regulate material sent through the mails. The act authorized the postmaster general to ban any book, picture, letter, or any other material he found to be "obscene, lewd, or lascivious," but notoriously it failed to define obscenity, thus leaving applications of the charge to local postmasters and inspectors. For many years, this made the Post Office Department, along with the Customs Department and Hollywood's Hays Office of film review (run by a former postmaster general), a powerful arbiter of what Americans could see, read, and buy. Well into the 1960s, as Eisenhower's postmaster general, Arthur Summerfield, boasted, the Post Office was "an apparatus that reached[d] into every home and business in America." Postmasters also wielded the power to root out political materials they deemed seditious or radical.[94]

Although the law was being weakened by legal challenge and by custom, in 1950 "unmailable" was still a capacious category. The definition of "obscene, lewd, or lascivious" was expansive and variable, in large part because it was locally enforced. It could encompass information about reproduction, contraceptives, and birth control; it ranged from marriage manuals and nude picture postcards to overt pornography.

Book dealers and publishers of all kinds, not just pornographers, were vulnerable to Comstockery because they depended on the mail for advertising and distribution of their materials. From the 1930s, the Post Office had been going after the mail-order business of big-time pornographers, notably Samuel Roth, and smaller ones like Jake Brussel and Benjamin Rebhuhn, all of whom went to federal prison for publishing obscenity and all of whom would be hailed later as courageous pioneers in the publication of experimental literature. Samuel Roth, with whom Legman sometimes worked, was responsible for publishing the first excerpts of James Joyce's *Ulysses* in the United States. Using police raids, pretrial gossip in the press and scandal sheets, highly publicized prosecutions, and long prison sentences, postmasters and attorneys general sought to put the fear of God into the smutmongers.[95] The general effect was less to stamp out smut than to keep moral and political pressure on the whole publishing industry.[96] Small book dealers and publishers who could not afford lawyers or bribes were especially vulnerable. As Legman often complained, censorship's major result was an atmosphere of stifling timidity in American letters.

As Legman well knew, the Post Office did not wait for complaints. It used entrapment. The advertisement card for his book read:

Published Sept. 12 [1949]

Love & Death by G. Legman, A Study in Censorship:
Murder-Mysteries. Comic Books. Bitch-heroines. Attacks on Women.
95 pp. paper bound.
Retail price $1, Breaking Point, 858
Hornaday Pl. New York 60

Around the card's border trailed a tantalizing quote from Montaigne's "Notes on Virgil":

We Bravely Say Kill. Rob. Betray.
But That Other We
Dare Pronounce Only Between Clenched Teeth?

A postal spy had gotten hold of the ad card and requested a copy, sending a money order for one dollar. This practice, known as a "test letter," was used to prove that Legman was advertising and selling the book through the mail. He received this kind of correspondence from many parts of the country, and he claimed to be extrasensitive to techniques of entrapment: they set his nose twitching. On one postcard, he scrawled, "Smells like a Post Office rat to me, but fill anyway." In this instance, when he answered "George Barnett," Legman knew where it would lead, but he took the offensive, sending several copies of *Love & Death* to postmasters in New York and Washington, D.C., to make it clear he was not hiding anything.

When "Barnett" got his copy of *Love & Death*, he sent it to Washington for an opinion. A small group of Post Office Department lawyers judged it obscene, and Legman received an official letter accusing him of retailing "indecent, vulgar and obscene materials" in the mails under the Fraud, Fictitious Business, and Lotteries Statute, the main tool the Post Office used against what it deemed obscenity. The order banned Legman from using the mails to sell *Love & Death* and threatened prosecution if he persisted. This was a serious threat to Legman's tiny operation and his book. While Landesman had paid to make his problem with the Stamford postmaster go away, Legman had no money and no lawyer to help. He could dodge the Post Office, shifting the name and place of his business and keep publishing until he was caught again, as many marginal publishers did. He could give up and go out of business. Or he could confront his accusers and hope to prevail by convincing them of his sincerity and innocence.

Confrontation was the most courageous and the most Legman-like path, since he believed so firmly in the power of words. So in June 1950, wearing a borrowed suit and limping on a pair of broken crutches (he had fallen off his roof while rescuing one of Beverley's cats), he took a train to Washington, D.C., to argue his case.

His hearing was before J. C. Haynes, senior trial examiner, in the Office of the Solicitor, U.S. Post Office Department. Also present were Mr. Melaugh, a lawyer for the department, and the government's main witness, Chester Battles, the postal inspector for the New York District. The hearing was part of an imbalanced, uncontested process that took place "ex parte," meaning it was essentially off the public record. The cases could be argued by one party only, the Post Office, and the hearings were held in house.[97] And because this was an administrative hearing, the same person who had already decided his work was obscene would be holding the hearing on whether Legman's work was obscene. The outcome was ensured.

Further, there was no oversight or review, and no formal counterallegation or defense could be made. Legman did not have to be tried or convicted of a crime to lose his mailing privileges. It took a fair amount of courage to represent oneself, without a lawyer or other resources, in such a one-sided and biased proceeding.

The hearing minutes reveal that the postal officials brought a range of fraud charges against Legman, probably to intimidate him maximally. He was accused of running a fraudulent business ("Breaking Point") under a fictitious name ("G. Legman") and under this cover using the U.S. Mail to distribute an obscene book. Clearly, they desired to put him out of business.

The postmaster's accusation of using a fictitious name and running a fake business would have been familiar to Legman. Many mail-order dealers in erotica were forced to use false names and addresses, and, indeed, Legman knew from his own research that centuries of bibliographic tangles in pornography were created by this necessity. As he would later write, authors of erotica rarely published from a traceable place, and the names of presses and dates of publication were completely unreliable. No one was whom they seemed, whether in the world of pulp or among the stylists of high-class erotica. Successful pornographers were always on the move.

But Legman had been straightforward—he had registered his business, "Breaking Point," with Bronx County and paid the fee. He was not using a fictitious name: G. Legman was his well-established pen name, and Legman-Keith was the "Lucy Stone" name he shared with Beverley. The books, magazines, and pamphlets he was advertising were real items, and he could show them the positive published reviews. He was proud of his work. He submitted the list of more than fifty publishers who had rejected *Love & Death*, mostly because he refused to expurgate a single word, establishing that the work was real.

The Post Office lawyer testified at the hearing that for all his odd social views, Legman did appear to be an orderly and efficient businessman. People who wrote for information about *Love & Death* received it promptly; when they sent money orders, they got their books. Legman affirmed that he answered all letters, including the entrapment letters, and cashed the money orders: "I did mail the books. I was glad to mail them their books. I wish to get the greatest publicity to my work!"

But Senior Examiner Haynes did want to explore the obscenity question. Several people in the room said they deemed *Love & Death* obscene, but they would not say why. Eventually, Legman got a turn to ask his own questions. "I would like to know who complained about me," he demanded of Chester Battles, the New York detective, who refused to answer. "Does the Examiner know," Legman asked, "that I myself mailed copies of *Love & Death* to several postal officials?"

Battles claimed that he had no idea who had been sending him copies of *Love & Death* or why. When Legman demanded to know whether Battles had read the book, the inspector asserted that he'd never opened the covers of *Love & Death* and implied he never wished to. But Legman pointed out that at that moment, he could see a copy lying on Haynes's desk with passages underlined. He demanded to know if they had any idea what the book was about; somebody ought to have looked at the contents of the book to decide

CHAPTER 5

if it was obscene. Chester Battles allowed that he "brought certain parts of the book to the attention" of his superiors.

Legman's argument was that the postal inspectors used no criteria at all to make their obscenity finding. The complaint was impossibly vague. Yet "the complaint, as I received a copy of it, states that 'this book is obscene and of an indecent character' containing 'vulgar, obscene, indecent and morally offensive words and phrases.'" They had not specified any words or phrases as obscene, so how could he defend himself?

Postal Examiner Haynes dismissed the problem of words and phrases as irrelevant: recent legal decisions meant that words and phrases in isolation could no longer be used to define obscenity. It was the total effect that had to be considered. At any rate, he declared, "I am capable of reading the book myself, and I will." Legman asserted that Morris Ernst and the ACLU were taking an interest in this case, but Haynes was unimpressed.

To show that they were deadly serious, the examiners extended the hearing into a probe of Legman's activities and associations and suggested that he had a tendency to publish obscene works. Examiner Haynes asked Inspector Battles, "Do you know whether he ever published any article entitled 'Sex Variants'"? Legman interrupted to point out that *Sex Variants* was the title of Dr. Henry's 1941 book, and his article in it was a bold glossary of homosexual slang. And "I have contributed many other lists of books and bibliographies . . . as an expert on certain subjects related to sex and censorship."

Legman offered his credentials as a scholar, including his work for Drs. Kinsey and Dickinson. He spoke of researching *Love & Death*, a process of nearly ten years or more of thought and discussion. All his work was on the same theme of sexual censorship; he was preparing a history of censorship in English language, not political or religious censorship, which had been well covered, but sex censorship, a very difficult topic. Censorship, in fact, had been there from the beginning. The gentlemen should know that William Caxton's *Dictes* (*The Sayings*), the first dated book printed in England (1477), was also "the first expurgated book printed in England."

Mr. Melaugh, the Post Office lawyer, wondered if Legman's character led him to publish obscenity. He asked if Legman had not been arrested for draft evasion in 1944. Legman allowed that he was picked up in a police sweep and arrested for not carrying his draft card. Melaugh then accused him of consorting with known homosexuals. This was true. Gershon and Tom Painter's research into New York's gay scenes had brought him homosexual friends and consultants. But this was a frightening question in 1950, when any taint of homosexuality could cast doubt upon one's political loyalty.

Just a few months earlier, Joseph McCarthy had begun an investigation of subversion in the State Department, one witness testifying that it was a nest of disloyal homosexuals. Now, at almost the same moment as Legman's Post Office hearing, the Senate was holding a formal inquiry into the employment of "homosexuals and other moral perverts" in government. The country was seized by the "lavender scare," and people were losing their jobs.[98]

Legman explained that homosexuals sought him out for information, sympathy, and psychological advice. Then did Legman present himself as a psychologist or psychiatrist, Melaugh demanded? Legman answered that as he had written an article, "On the Cause of Homosexuality," he thought he could offer some expertise during the recent scare. The inspectors were uninterested.

Combing through his police file, the lawyers noted that Legman had also been arrested for waving a loaded pistol in a restaurant. Legman said he was not waving the pistol, which was not loaded, but that he had been trying to prevent a suicide attempt. Then, alarmingly, the Post Office lawyer referred to Legman's FBI file and case number. These numbers were a centralized means of tracking people who had been arrested, a tool that let state and federal authorities coordinate surveillance of potential subversives. Legman may not have known that the FBI had started a dossier on him, and in fact the file had probably been initiated at the request of Postal Inspector Battles.[99] When the inspector wrote to the FBI, its agents had responded that they had no independent information on Legman, but they opened a file on him anyway, to be on the safe side.

The hearing concluded, and Legman was told he could file a written defense of *Love & Death* in two weeks' time. Throughout the hearing, to judge from the transcript, Legman was frightened and defiant. Certainly, it was a terrifying affair. He had not been charged with a crime, and he could not confront an accuser, but his small mail-order business depended on proving his innocence. He was worried that a federal indictment might follow. Just as scary, when he asked the officials to explain what they found obscene about his book, they refused—and accused him of hanging around with political subversives and perverts. Then they disclosed they'd given his name to the FBI. The message from the authorities was not subtle: the Post Office was not kidding around.

Legman's friend Osmond Beckwith remembered seeing him after he got back from Washington and observing that he was shaken but thought "it could have been worse." He was, Beckwith thought, "considerably more light-hearted than the seriousness your writing would have indicated." He remembered Legman had "infinite patience," although he was surrounded with infinite idiocies. Beckwith took one hundred copies of *Love & Death* for safekeeping and later brought them to Eli Wilentz's Eighth Street Bookstore, where they sold well.[100]

Finally, a few months later, Legman got word that the mail block was upheld on the grounds of obscenity, but no charges were sent up. (It is unclear, since they provided no analysis, what the postal officials found obscene about *Love & Death*. Since the book took up a variety of topics having to do with sex and popular culture, this apparently was enough to characterize it as obscene as a whole work.) The Post Office stopped delivering mail to 858 Hornaday Place. Now Legman could not receive answers to his advertisements for *Love & Death*, and he could not legally mail the book out. He urged the ACLU to keep following the case, but apparently got little response.[101]

In retrospect, Legman felt that the situation had been impossible. He was not surprised that the Post Office had decided to harass the book. *Love & Death* had been attended by a chain of difficulties through its whole history. This was just a small part of the censorship that went on every day in the United States. The Post Office did have the right to suppress mail fraud, but it used this power illegitimately against books "it does not like, but *which are not obscene* as that term is generally understood." It had been doing this for decades. His hearing showed that the Post Office worked by "shuttling back and forth between 'obscene' and 'fraudulent,' not to mention 'fictitious,' depending on which they think will be the easiest to make stick." The point was to intimidate writers. This was a method of preventing the free communication of ideas: it was a kind of prepublication censorship and "certainly a refusal of due process."[102]

He got no help at all from the New York free-speech advocates, he remembered. He wrote to legal scholar John C. N. Paul, "I have had a lot to do with liberals and I have found their attitudes toward 'free speech' to be delusory and, in the end, tending to support things just as they are." He summed up, "In the end most of them really do believe in censorship, but they also believe they shouldn't and their confusion is the measure of their inevitable failure." He did believe in censorship, and could not imagine a society without it, but the question was censorship of *what*?[103]

From that day in June 1950, he and Beverley began planning to leave the United States. They could not know how much worse things would get, but the McCarthy hearings and the new Red Scares were well under way, and Gershon saw that his life and work would only get harder. Jake Brussel's and Samuel Roth's prison sentences, the civil service purges of deviants and radicals, and the public spy trials all added up to a nasty intimation of the future. Legman had expressed the core of his being in *Love & Death*, and if his own self was illegal, his situation as a writer was untenable. If he was going to be dogged by the FBI, the police, and the Post Office, he could not continue. Many other dissidents were coming to the same conclusion.[104]

The three-year improvisation that was *Neurotica* crumpled to an end. After the mail block went into effect, more issues came out, but it was impossible for Legman to promote them. Landesman had decided he was sick of New York, and he and his new wife, Fran "Peaches" Deitch, moved back to St. Louis, where they started the Crystal Palace, a smash-hit cabaret in the Old Gaslamp Quarter. Clellon Holmes's novel *Go* was a hit; Chandler Brossard was doing well at the *American Mercury* and had sold a novel, too. Ginsberg and Kerouac were headed west. If *Neurotica* ever had a core group, everyone in it was moving on.[105]

In a brief memoir, Eli Wilentz, owner of the essential Eighth Street Bookstore, remembered *Neurotica* as a touchstone for the early 1950s.[106] But the magazine's sensibility is hard to grasp today. Perhaps this is because the language of psychological discomfort has changed so much and because *Neurotica* writers were making up their terms for dissatisfaction as they went along. But it is also hard to grasp because political repression meant they could not always be explicit about what they meant. Ways of expressing opposition and dissent would become broader and more general in the 1960s. In the 1950s, the ideological weight of the "American century" was stifling. There were immediate material consequences to seeming "un-American," as Legman found out.

Neurotica flickered as an early, unauthorized postwar attempt to take popular culture seriously. Its writers emerged not from the city's serious magazines but from the edges of the heartland and bohemia. Its readers found it refreshing because it was a space to say what could not be said elsewhere in a vocabulary that seemed new. Using the language of maladjustment and refusal, its themes were anticonformity and antipatriotism, at a moment when conformity and Cold War Americanism dominated the commercial mass media. Without ever mentioning politicians like Eisenhower or Truman, *Neurotica* was anti-Republican, anti-Democrat, and suspicious of left parties: to a twenty-first-century reader, it is oddly apolitical in its antibomb and antiwar stance. And it attacked, through the proxy of the comic books, the popular reading of young people. Whereas now we tend to think of mass-produced popular culture itself as antiestablishment and nonconformist in the resistant pleasures it is supposed to offer, in the late 1940s and early 1950s, commercial culture was felt by these writers to be authoritarian.

The *Neurotica* writers were unnerved by the existential threats that gathered in an overwhelming wave. The atomic bomb and the Red Scare were the foremost of these. These events were headline news daily; union members, college professors, and teachers across the country lost their jobs, but politics in its explicit form never made it into *Neurotica* and rarely appears in the writers' private correspondence. The Peekskill Riot, the Rosenberg convictions, the derailed Henry Wallace presidential campaign, and the threats of a new war, followed by a devastating famine and stalemate in Korea, as well as the allegations of a communist conspiracy—none of these is ever mentioned directly. By implication, in *Neurotica*, mass culture was moving America in a rightward, authoritarian direction—but ironically, and following a Freudian logic, actual political events could not be spoken of when Legman and McLuhan criticized the uses of mass entertainment and cheap reading. Going against the grain, the *Neurotica* group argued that it was society that was neurotic, not the individual, and that adjusting to such a sick world threatened human life. But the only response to the impending catastrophe was refusal. (This was Stanley Radulovich's answer: flush your war medals down the toilet and begin painting.)

Much later in the 1970s, when Gershon and Jay were working on their memoirs, they discussed their publishing adventure. Gershon thought they had registered something, made some brief difference. "*Neurotica* . . . shook the American university—(and C.I.A. [Central Intelligence Agency])—funded lit mags & rags to their fundament," he wrote. It was the introduction of psychoanalytic thought that was so subversive, in his view. "They have been trying to form a pearl around Freud ever since."[107]

But by 1950, Legman was beginning to think that the real psychoanalytic investigation into the world's insanity should take place elsewhere. He had been absorbed for years with collecting limericks, jokes, and songs. These were, he thought, the real record of ordinary people's lives, loves, worries, and obsessions. Maybe in Europe, where publishing about sex was easier, he could bring out his collections of sexual folklore and give them the place they deserved in the world's libraries.

6
ADVANCED STUDIES IN FOLKLORE

Get it all at once and never miss a chance . . . there is never any going back.

—G. Legman to Roger D. Abrahams, July 7, 1959

Gershon sailed for France in mid-August 1953, leaving Beverley at Hornaday Place while he tried to settle in Paris. He would now organize, research, and write the series of advanced studies in erotic folklore he had conceived when he started work with Dr. Dickinson in 1939.[1] *Les Hautes Études*, as he now called the plan, was patterned on the folklore compendia of his real or imagined great-uncle F. S. Krauss, published in the *Kryptadia* and *Anthropophyteia* yearbooks from the 1880s to 1913.[2] It would cover every kind of folklore no one had dared to publish since: there would be volumes covering rhymes, songs, jests, and jokes as well as, he hoped, at least one of gestural and material forms of obscenity. By now Legman had given up the idea of working in languages other than English, but otherwise his plan hewed to his early outline. The job was to put back into the record everything the censors had excised. Paris, with its bookstores and Bibliothèque Nationale, and its proximity to libraries in England and Scotland, would prove an excellent place to push ahead on the ambitious project. These envisioned studies would occupy Legman for most of the rest of his life; the years dedicated to library research in erotic folklore would be some of his most productive as he laid the groundwork for future books and essays. Some parts of the works that made up the series would be published to acclaim over the decades, and some would remain unfinished at his death.

THE LIMERICK

Legman had been working for nearly a decade on a definitive collection of obscene limericks, and upon arriving in Paris he put this first volume into production. In 1953 his friend Seymour Hacker, a bookseller, was willing to print and distribute *The Limerick*, but he could not bring it out in the United States, so he and Legman worked out a swap. Legman agreed to keep an eye on Hacker's various publishing projects in Paris, and Hacker picked up Gershon's room and board and paid him a small salary. Legman used the type, printers, and binders he lined up for Hacker to print his *Limerick*.

Legman began a small sideline in buying and selling hard-to-find books. Paris was a bibliophile's dream, he wrote to his friend Harry P. Johnson, a collector of literary references to the penis: "Paris is *it*. In every way, cultural, human and all other opportunities. See Paris and Live!"[3] To John Benson, a New York book dealer, he celebrated the uncensored attitude he found. "All of the impossible items are available here with hardly more than a faint refusal. . . . Miller's two *Tropics*, *Sexus* and *Plexus*, the Stockholm edition of Lawrence's *Lady Chatterley's* in English, Genet's *Our Lady*" could all be purchased. "Customs are lax, especially through the mail and prices are half what one would see in New York City," he wrote to Benson. His only problem was money.[4]

His years learning the rare-book trade and his work with Dickinson, Kinsey, and Brussel had taught him how to price and buy sexological works. According to Judith Legman, for a time he went "berserk," buying books unavailable in the United States. Not only was Paris the intellectual center of postwar Europe, but the war and the economic crisis that followed had also forced the sale of many private libraries. Legman began buying books, magazines, and other print works on commission for American dealers and collectors. It was difficult breaking into the business without stock or backing, since one had to have books to sell or trade books. But by early 1954, he was finding items for Frances Steloff and Archer Taylor, a bibliographer, proverb expert, and eminent professor of German at Berkeley.[5]

Through this long-distance book scouting, Legman began to build his reputation as a folklore expert and bibliographer among American academics. He traded notes on custom and oral tradition with Taylor, as he did with many others. In a typical exchange, the two men discussed the history of rude gestures. Taylor was writing an article on nose thumbing, the "Shanghai gesture."[6] They discussed the possible genealogy of hand signals and conversing in signs. Taylor recalled that when he was growing up in Pennsylvania, nose thumbing meant "an invitation to kiss the buttocks." Legman did too, but he wanted to know why Taylor left this out of his article and wondered why Taylor "completely omitted the clearly related gesture of the *fica*, thumb-biting (as in the opening scene of *Romeo and Juliet*) and similar gestures," including "the movement of the hand away from the nose or teeth." How, he asked, could Taylor "overlook the Rabelais story of . . . the *fica* as arising from the plucking of a fig from an ass's fundament by a vanquished people." Legman argued that leaving out the *fica* distorted the record.[7]

While booklegging for Americans, he was hassling over *The Limerick*'s paper, type, book design, and bindings. Legman was a perfectionist about book production, and there was endless trouble with printers and binders. He wrote to his friend Jan Kindler in New York, "They have half-sabotaged my book. . . . It has been AGONY." He was broke and had no money to buy books for himself, and it was "*killing* me" to be around all these amazing collectible things, even as Beverley had no money for coal. He had been sending Kindler antique tarot cards, and in return Jan had been sending him a few dollars and helping Beverley, who was still by herself in the Bronx.[8]

Gershon urged his friends to look in on Beverley and help her. He wrote Morty Kogut that she was "terribly lonely and easy to scare. . . . Somebody has got to be there for her to count on."[9] He was also worried about a piece of his manuscript on dirty jokes that he had left with Beverley and publisher Henry Schuman. Schuman wrote several times to press him toward publication, but Legman turned him away. He could not give the work on jokes his attention, he wrote, because "I am trying to bring my home here and have no money to do so."[10] The joke book would be written and published, but for now it seemed far away.

When *The Limerick* came out in the spring of 1954, it was beautiful, a "splendid volume, on pure rag paper," he boasted to friends.[11] Legman had published it anonymously and planned to sell it by subscription as a collector's item at 5,000 Fr (about $15), but he knew it would never get past U.S. Customs. Tourists would have to smuggle it into America and England.

After *The Limerick* was finished, he told Stanley Edgar Hyman he felt deflated. "Lonesome. Have been struggling getting this first volume of this folklore series off the press here. . . . [I]t has turned my hair half gray." But, he told Hyman, he was looking forward. "I am not sure I will ever be able to go it again, but just in case I can, I am putting together the ballads."[12] Despite the difficulty, *The Limerick* was the only book that would provide him with income over the years, even though it was extensively pirated. A worldwide dirty-limerick fandom would keep buying it.

The Limerick put the depth of Legman's knowledge of international sources on full display and showed his tireless tracking down of rare published, unpublished, and privately circulating collections. He drew on famous

144   CHAPTER 6

obscene collections such as Norman Douglas's 1928 *Some Limericks*, published in Florence. He cited *The Pearl* (1879–80) and *The Cremorne* (1882), English magazines of "facetiae and voluptuous reading" that collated songs, nursery rhymes, and peculiar items. He extracted from Krauss's *Anthropophyteia* and from unpublished manuscripts such as "Lapses in Limerick," written by his friends Walcutt and Erbes in Ann Arbor.[13] Privately printed books, such as *Immortalia*, an anthology of songs and ballads published in 1927 by a "Gentleman About Town," debuted as his important sources. He included rhymes he had collected in New York between 1934 and 1952.

The *Limerick* is a tour de force. Distinguished folklorist Roger Abrahams thought it was brilliant. "It found its audience right away," he reflected, and "became a very noted book," in fact a cult book in the United States.[14] In *The Limerick*, Legman presented his staggering collection of seventeen hundred verses but offered no history of the genre and no explicit analysis. He was holding back his ideas about what the short rhyme was and where it came from for another volume, *The Horn Book* (1964), a clutch of essays on erotic bibliography. In it he would show that the limerick emerged from men's colleges and clubs in the nineteenth century, possibly before about 1852, and was circulated orally, in manuscripts, and in fugitive print. Because making a good limerick was a challenge, competitive new rhymes were recorded and circulated further. Working against the grain of most folklore thought, Legman presented a tradition that belonged mostly to the well educated and depended in part on writing for its continuity. He would argue that the earliest limericks were obscene, and the clean, nonsense ones were later bowdlerized productions.[15]

Although this first volume appears to be just a collection, an analysis of the limerick emerges from the way Legman arranged his examples. His categories showed the way he was thinking about the folklore of sex. Legman sketched a concept of folk mind at work, a shared way of perceiving the world and the erotic body. He grouped limericks according to sexual topic and then according to a division between normal and abnormal, as he saw Anglo-American sexual and scatological preoccupations taking shape.

The chapters are arranged with the mildest sexual adventures first, moving to present more peculiar encounters and events. "Little romances" are heterosexual "good screws" that feature innocents like "a young lady in Twickenham,"

> Who thought men had not enough prick in 'em
> On her knees she would pray
> To her God everyday
> To lengthen and strengthen and thicken 'em.[16]

After straightforward heterosexual encounters, Legman began to trace folk preoccupations with virginity, virginity's loss, pregnancy, birth control, birth control's failures, and maternity. To take one subject category, among virgins there are the eager, ignorant, and resistant, young women who preserve or give up their virginity by natural or other means. Here is a mild example:

> No one can tell about Myrtle
> Whether she's sterile or fertile.
> If anyone tries
> To tickle her thighs
> She closes them tight like a turtle.[17]

Once virginity is relinquished, the problems of contraception and its failures become a major preoccupation:

> There was a young lady named Myrtle,
> Whose womb was exceedingly fertile
> Her pa got contortions
> At her frequent abortions
> And bought her a chastity girdle.[18]

From the mild sexual irregularity, Legman turned to distortions of the body. Limericks describe sex organs of fantastic dimensions and abilities. There are enormous penises, micropenises, penises that are large and thin, and wart-size ones. Men have enormous brass balls that play pop songs "when they jangle. ('Stormy Weather!')." In limerick world, women have "twats" that are large, small, singular, and plural. Some have bottoms or vaginas that can whistle and sing, and some have no vagina at all. Breasts grow, shrink, and also ring like bells. There is invisible pubic hair and forests of pubic hair; there are flat, lumpy, curly, and "backshooting" organs.[19]

Limericks document outright perversions like zoophilia and coprophilia. In a section called "Strange Intercourse," verses propose eccentric behavior and nonstandard partners. There are bisexuality, excessive intercourse, and fantasies about rare excitements. Occasionally, there is dated social satire:

> The Reverend Henry Ward Beecher
> Called a girl a most elegant creature
> So she laid on her back
> And, exposing her crack
> Said, "Fuck *that*, you old Sunday School Teacher!"[20]

In a problem that Legman would return to in all his advanced studies, he took up the idea of displacement, the substitution of "natural" sexuality for something else, whether masturbation or substitute genitalia. Vagina substitutes include holes in walls; eels, candles, and broom handles take the place of penises. In the extreme, substitution becomes mechanization in the idea of a sex machine. A mild version is the vibrator:

> There once was a horny old bitch
> With a motorized self-fucker which
> She would use with delight
> All day long and all night
> "Twenty bucks: Abercrombie and Fitch!"[21]

Limericks even predict what sex will be in the future:

> The geneticist living in Delft
> scientifically played with himself
> and when he was done
> he labelled it: SON,
> and filed him away on a shelf.[22]

In a large category of limericks dealing with "diseases," Legman documented sexual worries. Most common were venereal diseases of the "gooseberries" and the "coosie." Not so serious problems like pubic lice ("pants-pigeons" and "bugs in my hay") crop up alongside "pox," "leuco," and "the drip." The limericks capture jocular cures and folk remedies for sexual problems from satyriasis to warts.

There is anxiety about injury and loss. The verses describe accidents to the genitals and athletic mishaps. Organs are frozen off, medical cures go wrong, and men wear out their genitals with too much sex. There are battle wounds and fireworks accidents.

> . . . Young Henry Lockett
> was blown down the street by a rocket
> The force of the blast
> Blew his balls up his ass
> And his pecker was found in his pocket.[23]

Toward the end of *The Limerick*, Legman shows bodies stretched beyond contortion. A "Chamber of Horrors" features horrific expulsions of gas, excrement, and semen. But these monstrosities are peripheral to the collection. Legman put what preoccupied him in the center of the work—the more ordinary sex acts that society considered "immoral" and treated as illegal, like oral sex. Although on the surface *The Limerick* appeared to be only a collection, Legman was concerned to delineate the tight boundaries of Anglo-American normality and to show what lay, in imagination, beyond.

"COME, SING ME A BAWDY SONG..."

As he promoted *The Limerick* to correspondents, Legman immediately turned to what he hoped would be the second volume of his series, a study of folk songs he called "The Ballad Unexpurgated."[24] This would prove to be a much more vexing and complicated project. Legman's "Ballad" was modeled on F. J. Child's *English and Scottish Popular Ballads*, but following the approach Farmer and Henley had taken in *Slang and Its Analogues*, Legman's book would gather up everything that had been cut out and left out of the great published song collections in English.[25] He tried a first run at the topic in an article for Marshall McLuhan's journal *Explorations*. Predictably, the editor was forced to delete thirty-six lines of obscene examples.[26]

Since at least 1950, Legman had been writing to well-known folk song scholars, asking to work with their unprintable collections. He was at pains to win the confidence of the Ozark folklorist Vance Randolph. Between 1946 and 1950, Randolph had published his four-volume *Ozark Folksongs*, a life's work, but due to the usual prudery, a full manuscript of unprintable songs was held back.[27] Copies of Randolph's erotic songs and folklore were held at the Kinsey Institute Archive, the Library of Congress, and the Western Historical Society of Missouri, under restriction by Randolph. Throughout the 1950s and 1960s, Randolph's collections were the subject of much dispute between Legman and the archivists. It took Legman decades, but in the 1970s Randolph finally granted him the rights to edit and publish many of his X-rated files.[28]

In 1951 he had written to Duncan Emrich at the Archive of Folk Song at the Library of Congress to ask for copies of the unprintable Ozarks songs, but Emrich would make them available only in the archive. Before leaving for Paris, Legman had been to Washington to try to work with the files, but, he complained to Emrich, "Mr. Randolph air mailed his express prohibition to me to make any other use of his manuscript than to look at it."[29] He was not even allowed to take notes. Randolph seems to have thought Legman was an eccentric millionaire out to steal his collections. Now Legman sent him *The Limerick*, hoping Randolph would believe he was a true scholar.

He wrote to Emrich again, describing his plan for his advanced studies. For the ballad volume, Legman had the choice of publishing his own collection, which was "extremely uneven and ... poor," or convincing Randolph that this was a chance to see his own collection "printed and printed well."[30] As he regularly did now, he enclosed his *Neurotica* article on dirty jokes to show he was serious about bringing "some order into the chaos left by more formal folklorists."[31]

Emrich was unimpressed. Legman persisted in more long letters, outlining the attitudinal and practical obstacles he was meeting. The well-known folk song scholar Herbert Halpert at Murray State College had told him he had relevant tapes, but they were not transcribed. Halpert was no prude, Legman related, but he did not type and could not assign the tapes to undergraduate students because of the content.[32]

This kind of stonewalling irritated Legman, but he redoubled his efforts. From Paris, he sent circulars to all the major folk song scholars he could find, asking "folklorists with hair on their chests" to share their improper songs.[33] All the scholars knew that practically every (male) folklorist had a hell drawer. Legman used this word of mouth to track down other bawdy song collections. He was on the trail of Robert Winslow Gordon's "inferno." Gordon had separated out vulgar songs and cataloged them by date, but none of Legman's correspondents were sure where Gordon had left his files.[34]

He wrote several times to Richard M. Dorson, the ambitious leader of the new folklore graduate program at Indiana University, asking for uncensored song texts. He had heard of famous obscene songs and poems like "The One-Eyed Riley" and "While Strolling through Norfolk," but he lacked full texts.[35] Legman had heard about many such songs, but scholars had been assiduously ignoring them for centuries. He launched an argument he would repeat over the years: erotic song was living folk song. But folklore scholarship was "like the Mad Hatter's party. . . . They sit at an empty table, printing sixty page articles on 'motifs' and 'traits' in a single Child ballad, but hollering 'No room, no room, go away' when I come diffidently into view with what represents half of all jokelore, and the best third of folksong."[36] Folklorists claimed to be documenting a dying tradition, while ignoring its most vibrant living part.[37]

To advance his cause with the archivists, Legman collected statements of support from prominent academics and collectors and attached these to his next volley of letters. In 1956 Alan Lomax, now working in England, wrote to Dorson endorsing Legman's project. He thought *The Limerick* was "extremely important and beautifully edited," and "The Ballad" would be even better, an "extraordinary collection of material of very great importance to folksong collecting in the west." "I am going to give everything out of mine and my father's collections which will be useful to him," Lomax wrote, "and I will help him to round up all the British material from my friends here." (Apparently, this first promise was not fulfilled.) Lomax wanted Dorson to help Legman "overcome the resistance of our colleagues in parting with their material, material which of course they will never be able to use so well themselves."[38] As Lomax knew, Dorson himself complained about folklorists who expurgated and watered down living materials to produce popular treasuries. Dorson and Legman should be on the same side.

The long wrangle between Legman and Duncan Emrich that began over the Vance Randolph songs carried over to Raye Korson, Emrich's successor, and Harold Spivacke, head of the Music Division. Going over Korson's head, Legman wrote Spivacke that Pete Seeger had told him to get in touch and that his project had been endorsed by "some of the most prominent and austere people in the folksong field," including Louise Pound, George Herzog, R. D. Jameson, Alan Lomax, and Archer Taylor.[39] He was not being frivolous: "This is a long awaited opportunity for serious publication in the one last area of folksong that has not yet been responsibly dealt with."[40] Legman asked Spivacke to supply songs and help him contact singers and song collectors.

Spivacke replied primly that he did not think he could help. The materials were only partly cataloged, and the lists they had were not organized "in accordance with your viewpoint."[41] This was not entirely true. Although the Music Division had never collected sexual folklore per se, the Archive of Folk Song did classify some materials with a "delta" (Δ) indicating obscenity.[42] Anything with a delta would be important, Legman persisted, and tunes were of great interest, too. He pleaded for the Lomax delta materials, the Randolph materials, the R. W. Gordon collection, and some unissued Jelly Roll Morton recordings.[43]

Raye Korson advised Spivacke that the Jelly Roll Morton materials were controlled by the estate's executor. Randolph had already refused Legman, and she would need Austin Fife's consent to copy the soldier's songs he had donated. As for the Lomax items, why didn't Alan just share them directly with Legman? "Frankly, all the collectors have been giving Legman the runaround," Korson groused.[44]

Spivacke sent Legman a no on the Morton materials and left his other requests unanswered.[45] At this point, Legman seems to have given up on the Library of Congress. He had acquired the reputation of being a crank among the older, more cautious scholars, and it was not until Joseph Hickerson became the head of the Archive of Folk Song in 1963 that Legman had a cooperative research partner there.[46]

"WHO OWNS FOLKLORE?"

Legman carried his dispute with the Archive of Folk Song into print, using his letters as the basis for "Who Owns Folklore?" an important article he first published in 1962.[47] The core of the conflict was the ownership and copyright asserted by folklorists of the field recordings they had deposited. "Who Owns Folklore?" was an early salvo in a broader heated argument among folklorists over whether oral traditions should be considered the creative work of singers, the intellectual property of collectors, or a part of the public domain.[48] Legman was often told he could not use songs he had not collected or that the archive did not have permission to make copies for him. His argument

150 CHAPTER 6

with the archivists was not just about proprietary rights, but also about ethics. From their perspective as archivists, Emrich and Korson could not violate promises they had made to collectors about restrictions on their donations. But the archivists also seem to have viewed Legman as a crazy amateur. All this was a hardship on a scholar with no funds for travel, but in Legman's view it was also unethical. If the songs belonged to anyone, they belonged to the singers who had performed them, not to the folklorist with the tape recorder. As he and the Lomaxes understood it, the notion of national heritage implied that folk songs were part of a public cultural domain. If folk songs were the property of ordinary people, what were they doing locked up in the publicly funded Library of Congress where no one could use them? Worse, Legman demanded to know, what were folklorists doing copyrighting to themselves materials from the oral tradition? Certainly, some were profiting from the copyrights they had taken out on other people's music.[49] As usual, Legman's critique was fundamentally moral.

The erotic songs Legman sought were not only tangled in an ethical thicket, but also being held back by the same toxic mix of politics and prudery that had made Legman's work impossible in the United States. The Archive of Folk Song was moving away from its New Deal and Works Progress Administration origins, and Harold Spivacke was facing congressional hostility to the folklore projects John and Alan Lomax had created. Alan had fled the United States after being identified in *Red Channels*, an anticommunist watch list.[50] Whether Congress thought the folk song archive was Soviet subversion or useless make-work, or both, in the early 1950s the archive could not risk drawing attention to the fact that it preserved obscene folk songs.

The resistance of American archivists was a major obstacle for Legman's work on "The Ballad." But if file cabinets were still locked in the United States, he was finding openings in Britain. In early 1954, with great excitement, he planned his first trip to London to work in the British Museum's library and to approach its storied Private Case, a room of books so indecent that they were not cataloged by the museum.[51] The core of the Private Case was the library of Henry Spencer Ashbee, known as "Pisanus Fraxi," author of the *Index Libros Prohibitorum et Tacendarum* (list of forbidden and suppressed books), at the time the only sound bibliography of English-language erotica. Legman would develop a special interest in Ashbee.[52]

Seeking entrée to the Private Case, he had shipped about 120 books to the British Museum before leaving New York.[53] From Paris, he followed up on the gift with Eric Dingwall, the assistant keeper responsible for the collection.[54] The gift strategy worked. He spent most of a six-week visit luxuriating in the British Library's remarkable assemblage of seventeenth- and eighteenth-century broadsides, pamphlets, ballad books, and anthologies

Advanced Studies in Folklore

and examining Ashbee's erotica. He was tracing the history of the limerick and trying to understand the life of oral tradition in print. Over the next ten years, he made several more extended research visits.

He made friends, as he did everywhere—connecting with psychiatrist Alex Comfort (later author of *The Joy of Sex*) and members of the English Folk Dance and Song Society. He met Margaret Dean-Smith, the librarian of the Cecil Sharp House who had just published a checklist of English folk song collections.[55] Peter and Iona Opie, the pioneering children's folklorists, had him to their house for supper. Through these English folklore scholars, he began to meet influential English and Scottish song collectors and folk song–revival performers. By 1954 the new British folk song movement was in full swing, and he frequented folk clubs and pubs. Around this time, he met Alan Lomax, who was working in London as a broadcaster, and Lomax put him in touch with Scottish nationalist poet and folklorist Hamish Henderson. Lomax also gave him introductions to Ewan MacColl and his partner, Peggy Seeger, and it is likely he met folk song scholar A. L. "Bert" Lloyd on this first trip.[56] These and other prominent British singers and collectors would help "The Ballad" over many years.

When he returned to Paris, he wrote immediately to Morty Kogut that despite all the new friendships, "London was *ghastly*" and the English the "most unrepressedly impolite bunch of barstards on earth."[57] He didn't want to live anywhere but Paris, he wrote Kindler. "Even an old sour puss like me feels happy here. Dead broke of course. But living, and I do call this living."[58] He was out and about in the cafés some evenings, drinking sociably and even gambling a bit. He met up with his high school friend Joe Bernstein (now journalist Joseph A. Barry) and was able to place several pieces of *Love & Death* in Sartre and de Beauvoir's *Les Temps Modernes*. He later claimed to have discussed racist jokes with Richard Wright.

Beverley arrived in Paris in late 1954, along with crates of his books and papers. They moved out of the Left Bank to tiny rue Victor Letalle, close to Père Lachaise Cemetery. The neighborhood was quieter, which suited Beverley. Not too long after this, a magazine publisher was unable to write Gershon a check and paid him for an article in one-way railroad tickets. He and Beverley took a train to the Mediterranean coast, got off at Cagnes-sur-Mer near Nice (where Henry Miller and Robert Briffault had lived in the late 1930s), and decided they liked the South. It offered very cheap living. They began a period of renting small rooms in different towns along the coast: at Cagnes and Auribeau-sur-Siagne, until they finally settled into an old barn in an olive grove at Valbonne in the backcountry of the Pays de Grasse.[59]

Somehow, without electric light or running water, Gershon plugged away on his advanced studies. The rural South was isolated (it could be a day's round-trip by bus to buy a typewriter ribbon), and he relied heavily on letter writing for his projects and for his sense of the larger world. The friends he made in Britain were central to Legman's labors. By as early as 1955, he and Hamish Henderson were conducting a warm and fruitful correspondence.[60] In the early 1950s, Henderson was immersed in collecting songs, stories, and language from the poor and working people of Scotland, especially from the stigmatized migratory laborers known as "the Travellers." Because Henderson camped with Traveller families and helped them with their legal and political problems, they gave him their oral traditions generously and without embarrassment.[61] Hamish was an antirespectable, antiauthoritarian radical who celebrated the erotica he collected. Gershon was staggered by the frankness and fullness of what Hamish was willing to send.

OBSCENE DISCOVERIES

Henderson was already famous in Britain for his collections of obscene soldier songs, some of which he wrote himself. The most notorious of these was "The Ballad of King Faruk and Queen Farida" (or "Fuck Faruk"), made up in 1942 by the Australian and Scottish troops who would fight the battle of El Alamein in Egypt. King Farouk collaborated with Rommel, and in the great tradition of political pornography the soldiers abused him to the tune of the Egyptian national anthem (which was borrowed from a march by Verdi). Henderson pieced together fragments of songs he heard in the movie theaters of Cairo and presented his version at a military musicale, and immediately the British troops were singing it everywhere. It was Egypt's counteranthem.

> O we're all black bastards, but we do love our King
> Every night at the flicks you can hear us fuckin' sing
> *Quais ketir, King Faruk*
> *Quais ketir, King Faruk*
> *O you can't fuck Farida if you don't pay Faruk.*[62]

"The Ballad of King Faruk" was a modern folk song par excellence. Picked up from popular rhyming by a skilled satirist and launched into a charged political context, "Faruk" accumulated scores of new verses as it moved with English-speaking troops around the world. Soldiers who broke the German line at El Alamein remembered later that songs like "King Faruk" got them through the hell of siege and bombardment.[63]

Henderson took field notes in a private shorthand, and as their friendship grew Legman nagged him to get all his songs written out in full. Henderson began to do this, often sending copies to Legman. Legman urged Henderson to write out a full text of the elusive "Ball o' Kirriemuir" for him, noting that it was "the prize modern piece everywhere" and "the main Modern Scottish folksong in English."[64] "The Ball" fascinated Legman because it described a rural wedding party that turned into a no-holds-barred orgy. Because "The Ball" was "everywhere sung and nowhere recorded," he argued, it was just as crucial for the study of obscene song as "The Bastard King of England."[65]

From the mid-1950s through the 1960s, Legman followed Alan Lomax's advice to stay in touch with Henderson. Hamish directed him to unpublished song collections in Britain and America, and Legman began the arduous process of visiting them when he could scrape up travel money or sending friends in his stead when he could not.[66]

In the late 1950s, Henderson pointed him to Sidney Goodsir-Smith, an important Scottish poet and dramatist with an interest in vernacular song. Trading song lyrics with "Goojer," as his friends called him, led Legman to rediscover and republish a significant lost part of Robert Burns's bawdy song book *The Merry Muses of Caledonia*.[67] As Legman told it, he had sent Goojer a "jocular offprint or preprint" of a clutch of texts of "The Ball o' Kirriemuir" as a kind of teaser for "The Ballad Unexpurgated." Goojer wrote back to Gershon that the oldest text anyone had yet found of the "The Ball o' Kirriemuir" was in a little late-nineteenth-century bawdy collection called "Forbidden Fruit," which reproduced and added to *The Merry Muses*. "Forbidden Fruit" was so rare that only one copy survived in a Burns collection in the public library at Dumferline, "the ancient seat of the kings of Scotland."[68]

Upon learning this, Gershon rushed from Cagnes-sur-Mer to Scotland by express train, not even stopping to buy books in Paris or London. The Dumferline librarian was "extremely nervous about the whole matter of Burns' *Merry Muses*" and refused to make a photocopy. But she did allow Legman to retype the manuscript "for several days in the bright library. . . . It was fascinating bawdy folksong stuff, all right." The material was just what he had hoped for, and half of it was new to him.[69]

On the way home from Scotland, he stopped in London to work again for a few weeks in the Private Case at the British Museum. Here he uncovered a singular reproduction of the Cunningham Manuscript, a hand copy of another lost Burns song collection. Together with "Forbidden Fruit," this would allow Legman to conduct expert bibliographic detective work on the history of the *Merry Muses*.[70] He also took time to meet Ewan MacColl and Peggy Seeger and to hear them perform.[71] Legman hated the new folk song boom, but he was impressed with Seeger. She was "honest and real, right to the bone, and the perfect revival folksinger," he thought. MacColl he judged a natural "concert-singer working with folksongs." Legman didn't expect to like the performance, but he found it superb.[72]

Legman admired MacColl's and Seeger's work in part because they refused to clean up the Travellers' and sailors' songs in performance. Along with Stanley Hugill, a former sailor who sent Legman an entire uncensored manuscript of sea shanties, MacColl, Seeger, and Henderson emphasized the songs of working people.[73] MacColl, Lloyd, and Henderson (though not Peggy Seeger) shared working-class backgrounds and politics; as revivalists, the singers were committed to using folk song to present the hardships faced by workers and the poor in postwar England. MacColl had grown up very poor in Salford, a slum of Manchester, and was entirely self-educated. Ewan's father was a union man, blacklisted for radicalism, and a wonderful performer of poetry and songs who gave his son a strong sense of the importance of singing in people's lives. Ewan remembered his father comforting a dying friend with Burns's songs.[74] Henderson was an illegitimate orphan who had received a fine charity education and gone on to a brilliant military career. While MacColl, Henderson, and Legman differed on the question of Soviet communism, they shared an intense opposition to American imperialism and Cold War nuclear politics. Along with many in the folk song revival, they thought the brave new atomic world was mad.[75] Unlike his experience with American folklorists, Legman felt encouragement from these British song collectors.

Legman returned to France to conduct his detection process on "Forbidden Fruit," and eventually it was added to another scholarly republication of *The Merry Muses*. The story he told—of the loss, expurgation, rewriting, and forgetting of Burns's drinking song collection—would appear in *The Horn Book*, and it was one of his major pieces of work on song.

OPENING UP FOLKLORE

In the United States, things *were* moving forward in the academic folklore field: Legman was astounded when Richard Dorson invited him to speak on erotic folk song at the 1960 American Folklore Society (AFS) annual meetings in Philadelphia. He could not afford to travel to the United States, so he had his friend Jan Kindler deliver "Misconceptions in Erotic Folksong" to a packed audience. Kindler reported that the two and a half hours of discussion that followed centered on Legman's paper and ignored the other two speakers. According to Jan, when a "miserable fink" named Moritz Jagendorf denounced Gershon as a phony, he grabbed the microphone and defended his friend's sacrifices for folk song, to great applause. Kenneth Goldstein got up to extol Legman as "the one man who was doing anything worthwhile in the field," and Alan Lomax followed, "punching hard and accurately" with perceptive remarks on the censorship of folk song.[76] Much of the legend of Gershon Legman was propagated that afternoon.

Under Dorson's editorship, the staid *Journal of American Folklore* began to take a new approach to publishing impolite materials. After Dorson published the papers and discussion from the Philadelphia panel in 1962 as a symposium, Legman wrote to congratulate him on the publication of "Hair of the Dog," an article on folk remedies for hangovers that prominently featured sex acts among the cures. While it had been unpublishable in an academic journal a few years earlier, it was now in print, "full, frank, fearless." Besides, Legman wrote to Dorson, "what is there to fear?"[77]

Legman's correspondence was expanding to include a younger generation of folklore scholars. Dorson called these men and women the "Young Turks." Many of them were Jewish, and they set themselves in opposition to the tone and methods of the older Protestant folklorists. In contrast to their elders, who focused mainly on texts from the deep past and took pains to keep folklore respectable, the "Young Turks" were more interested in living cultures, and they even ventured into cities in search of the folk. They emphasized the careful observation and documentation of practices and performances, and they were not resistant to obscenity. The Turks looked up to Legman, who was now in his middle forties, and they tried to keep him up to date on changes in the academic discipline in the United States. One important contact was Kenneth Goldstein, who had been dazzled by *The Limerick*. Goldstein was a specialist in British and American folk song and blues and an influential record producer for Stinson, Riverside, Folkways, and Prestige.[78] He began to send Legman ballad texts and recordings.

Goldstein's small publishing business, Folklore Associates, specialized in books and monographs on folklore and folk song. For most of the 1960s, Folklore Associates would publish dissertations, bring back out-of-print twentieth-century folklore collections, and republish lost, suppressed, or prohibited song books from the eighteenth and nineteenth centuries. In several cases, Goldstein arranged for Legman to contribute annotations and introductions to reproductions of works like D'Urfey's song and tune collection *Pills to Purge Melancholy*. Legman was surely pleased at the uncensored publication of so many lost and lonely classics. In the mid-1960s, Goldstein and Roger Abrahams would also work seriously with him on his "New Kryptadia" yearbook of erotic folklore.[79]

In 1959, at Goldstein's suggestion, Legman wrote to Roger Abrahams in Philadelphia.[80] He had heard Abrahams was working on "Negro folk songs" and asked him, "What can we do for each other?"[81] In the 1950s and early 1960s, few white folklorists were working on modern African American folklore, and Legman admitted he had little African American material for his book because, he explained, he never separated his materials by race. He wrote that Alan Lomax had looked over his files, "huddled all one frozen morning in a storage loft in Paris," and said that one song, "Brother Joe Hardy," was of black American origin. And he had "a strange half-chanted brag . . . called 'Signifying Monkey' of which I have never been able to learn what the title means. This is not a song, but more like a dozens playing." He added that Guy B. Johnson of the University of North Carolina had once offered the "sexually forthright" part of his and Howard Odum's Negro songs collection, but after a long delay Odum wrote to say that the obscene part was lost. Could Abrahams go see Johnson in person, "for me, for folksong?"[82]

Abrahams was collecting songs, rhymes, and sayings from his South Philadelphia neighborhood for a Ph.D. in English at the University of Pennsylvania. He had started out recording children's games in the small street, but he hit upon the strategy of loaning his tape recorder to some young men who were practicing doo-wop and wanted to hear themselves sing. He was astounded when they returned it to him with the tape full of traditional African American toasts, boasts, rhymes, and chants. They were "actually doing the collecting for me," Abrahams recalled. He began opening his living room to his neighbors for boasting-toasting sessions. In Abrahams's words, "I took one of these tapes in to play for Mac [MacEdward Leach] and Tris [Tristram Coffin] and they said, 'that's what you're going to do your dissertation on.' It was just everything I recorded from the streets there. One chapter was on the toasts and one was playing the dozens. The rest is on children's games, holy talk, anything that I found."[83]

Most of the material the young men performed, such as "The Signifying Monkey," the boasting songs about "Stack-o-Lee and Billy," and the long story of Shine's escape from the *Titanic*, was well known. But the toasts, especially, had not been previously studied by the almost entirely white academy. He remembered that he didn't know how to approach the wildly obscene stuff. "I was corresponding with [Legman] and with Mel[ville] Herskovits and Dick Dorson and three or four others, and just asking 'what the hell do I have here?'"[84]

Abrahams sent transcripts of some songs and rhymes to Valbonne. Legman wrote back immediately. He thought what Abrahams had come across was remarkable, and he advised him to "collect like mad and spread out as far as you can." He argued for a holistic approach, telling Abrahams not to make "the mistake of collecting only the bawdy stuff in spite of its apparent uniqueness."[85] He should scoop up everything.

Legman advised Abrahams to take down

> turns of phrase ("went through Pittsburgh like shit through a goose"), similes, Wellerisms ("they're off! as the monkey said when he backed into the lawnmower"), proverbs ("a woman kissed is a woman half-fucked"), hypostases ("that woman is cunt *all over*"), and purely vocabulary elements ("boy in the

boat" for clitoris) etc. . . . . There are riddles: there are chalk items that go on the walls repetitively, on both fences and toilets; also "catches" for fools. YOU HAVE GOT TO GET IT ALL AT ONCE AND NEVER MISS A CHANCE. . . . THERE IS NEVER ANY GOING BACK.[86]

Legman was intrigued by the vocabulary Abrahams reported, and he peppered him with requests for information. "Please gloss for me 'raunchy,' 'booty,' 'collard,' 'Bulldagging.' . . . I know *what* all these mean but want to know why." The "why" would be found in the historical trail of the words. He thought Abrahams was right to look for versions and variants of the songs and toasts he was recording. "Their significance is in the variation," he insisted, and the essential cultural history was to be found in "the stuff that keeps changing." And he stoutly encouraged Abrahams: "Stay with it. You are the man."[87]

In October 1961, when Abrahams sent a completed draft titled "Negro Folklore from South Philadelphia," Legman was astounded.[88] He wrote, "You have made history . . . particularly in that you are not a Negro." Roger had the "plain, ornery bucknaked COURAGE at the highest point that has yet been seen in the annals of Anglo-American Phudnickery." He saluted: "Abrahams I dips me lid!"[89]

In his dissertation, Abrahams interpreted the songs and toasts as expressions of social conflict within the neighborhood and gender conflict within the family structure. Young black men were constrained by underemployment and a matriarchy. Unable to head families, they found their masculinity in a symbolic sphere of verbal contest and in sexual boasting and toasting, much of it overtly hostile toward women. Legman did not have much to say about this theory. He wrote, "I don't even know what the hell that jive is about. I am now of the Kittredge school: 'THE TEXT IS THE THING' so don't ask me about matrilocal elements, etc." His interest was "four square in the Negro Art involved."[90]

Legman predicted that Abrahams's dissertation committee would not accept the work as it stood. He admitted that he had no idea how dissertation committees worked. Would Pennsylvania withhold his degree because of obscenity? Did Abrahams really believe it might be published as a book?[91]

A bit later, when Abrahams wrote to say that indeed his dissertation was accepted, Legman declared that Abrahams had accomplished something that he in his time could not. He had been "kept out of teaching," but now Abrahams would present obscene materials in the classroom. "You are there, basically ahead of me now, and so is Ken Goldstein."[92]

It was time to get to work. Legman gave the dissertation a bibliographic going over, helping make literary-historical connections in preparation for the book Abrahams would soon publish. Legman offered citations to antecedents and his own psychoanalytic interpretations. As usual, he was interested in cultural connections through time and in patterns of sexual symbolism. The work was difficult because his own library was in storage, and all he had at hand were his books on songs and ballads, but still he commented at length.

The result was a virtuoso performance, a forty-nine-page single-spaced letter, densely packed with references to the Anglo, Scottish, and French connections to the African American songs, toasts, and vocabulary. Legman concentrated on drawing out the toasts' ties to old European folktales and jests and admonished Abrahams, "You have to cite tale texts if you know about them." He urged him to make connections across genres, noting that Stagolee and Billy's epic fight was over a hat and "curiously paralleled by many references to brags and fights engaged in over *hats* in early 17th Century French jest books." What was it about hats?[93]

He was not surprised to find French connections in African American folklore. A lot of it, especially sexual folklore, came from France to the United States through New Orleans. He cited the French "*putain*" (whore) as the background of "poontang" and told Abrahams he had been working for years on the connections between "*coquille*," French for scallop shell, and "cock" as a southern usage for female genitals.[94] He showed he was fully conversant with eighteenth- and nineteenth-century French and English jest books and almanacs. For example, the story of the "Sleeve Job" (the impossible quest for the ultimate sexual act) was a "shaggy dog story, on a pretty ancient formula." It could be traced back to Henri Monnier, the French Mark Twain, he thought.[95]

He connected the Philadelphia children's lore to rhymes and suggestive songs in his own collections. He was interested in "teases," or kids' songs that imply dirty words they don't say ("Ass/ask me no more questions"). He argued that white adolescents play "the dozens" too: "Your mother is an artichoke heart—everybody takes a piece." He related the Philadelphia toasts to sea shanties he had gotten from Stan Hugill, adding, "Shantying is originally and always was, basically, a Negro art."[96]

Finally, as he approached page 50, he complained, "I sort of wish *you* would glossarize." But he glossed anyway. He found the survival of the verb "ball" and its use to refer to secret orgiastic sexual intercourse "almost unparalleled in its philological history." It had first appeared in Samuel Pepys.[97]

Legman emphasized the European background of much of modern African American oral tradition and neglected African origins and analogues, largely because he did not know about them. He was correct that from the seventeenth century, Africans and Europeans had lived, worked, and sung together in the Americas, creating hybrid oral traditions. But like most

Americans of his era, Legman had read almost nothing about the African roots of African American culture, and he overlooked the enduring creativity of black communities. Although he claimed to have hung around Harlem and collected insults from shoeshine "boys" on West Forty-Second Street, his folklore and sex research were as segregated as the academy. At the same time, his isolation in France kept him unaware of the extent to which everyday African Americanisms influenced general American English, now through the civil rights movement and popular music.[98] Abrahams must have smiled when Legman asked him what TCB (taking care of business) meant—"Does it mean going to the toilet?" "Greens" was a euphemism for sex in nineteenth-century England, but, he wondered, what were collards?[99]

As always, he offered his psychoanalytic view of the men and women. If Abrahams was correct that the matrifocal Negro family put enormous pressures on young men, Legman thought this could be distorting people's gender roles. He worried that dominant women could confuse everyone about their sexualities. Certainly, he thought, there was male homosexuality in Abrahams's neighborhood, and there might be covert lesbianism. Legman was usually a fan of what he called "matriarchy," but now he found the possibility troubling. Sexual abnormality would not abate until men in the black community were economically secure enough to reassert themselves. He referred Abrahams to his "Avatars of the Bitch" chapter in *Love & Death*.[100]

Roger Abrahams was staggered by Legman's display of erudition. To trace all the connections Legman suggested would mean researching at least another dissertation. Instead, Abrahams took apart Legman's dense letters and copied many of his suggestions and interpretations into the footnotes of the book manuscript, citing and quoting him directly.[101]

By late 1962, Goldstein's Folklore Associates was bringing out *Deep Down in the Jungle: Negro Narrative Folklore from the Streets of Philadelphia*. Goldstein and Abrahams even offered to share royalties with Legman, but he declined. It was enough that Roger was doing long-distance mimeographing for him and arranging to have copies of songs from Mack McCormick's blues collections sent from Texas and that Goldstein was sending him folk songs on tape.

When the first edition of *Deep Down in the Jungle* appeared in 1964, Legman's detailed annotations were an important part of the book. *Deep Down* attracted some scholarly notice, not all of it positive. One reviewer doubted the book should have been published at all, since more than half of it was "gutter talk of south Philadelphia." What Abrahams called jokes were "indistinguishable from barrack-room boasting or Pullman car smut."[102] But Richard Dorson called *Deep Down* one of the most important folklore collections yet published, in large part because of the "hitherto unreported" toasts in "powerfully obscene and highly charged vocabulary."[103]

The first edition of Abrahams's *Deep Down* became an underground sensation, and it kicked off a brilliant career. Between 1966 and 1970, he revised the book heavily, refocusing it on verbal art as performance and de-emphasizing the psychological functions of obscenity.[104] He cut out Legman's speculations about the dangerous psychic effects of female power, and he dropped *Love & Death* from the bibliography. Legman found these cuts profoundly discouraging. But the significantly changed book was adopted and praised by leading African Americanists as a classic. Anthropologist John Szwed wrote, "It was striking simply for documenting the existence of a rich tradition of oral folktales and poetry among urban African Americans." Before this, in Szwed's view, the prevailing orthodoxy of race-relations sociology had made "any discussion of the culture of lower-class African-Americans appear gratuitous, if not racist." Abrahams had shown the Philadelphians as verbal artists of real accomplishment.[105]

Although it stung Legman to be excised from *Deep Down*, he and Abrahams continued to trade manuscripts and advice for a few more years. As Abrahams shifted his focus to Afro-Caribbean verbal art, he continued to send Legman songs, rhymes, and jokes collected by his students at the University of Texas at Austin. Legman went on pestering him about obscene songs that might be rescued from oblivion. What about Guy Johnson's missing files? What about John Lomax's erotic songs? He demanded to know if there was a good, full text of the chanted insults, the dozens.[106] Abrahams was a rising academic star, and, over time, he became less interested in psychological patterns in folklore and more focused on aesthetics. The friendship dwindled as he recalled his discomfort with Legman's insistence on sharing the details of his own sex life, "the joys of young love and all that." As Abrahams put it, "He was too weird for me."[107]

7

"THE BALLAD" AND *THE HORN BOOK*

The prudes be damned.

—Ed Cray to Gershon Legman, January 19, 1960

Through the early 1960s, Legman persisted with his research on "The Ballad Unexpurgated." He struck up a correspondence with Ed Cray, a young journalist and friend of Wayland Hand, who was studying anthropology at the University of California, Los Angeles (UCLA). Cray was enthusiastically involved in the California folk music scene, and he aspired to publish a comprehensive, uncensored index of American folk songs. Legman wrote to Cray that perhaps they could help each other. He now had more than two thousand texts of about seven hundred British and American erotic songs that he had gathered from archives and others' fieldwork. He was tracing these to rare specimens of seventeenth- and eighteenth-century English street literature, the obscene "broadsides and drolleries" no one else knew much about.[1]

Cray answered that he shared Legman's goal of creating "a realistic view" of folk song, and he planned to include erotic songs in his index. He agreed that erotic material was central, "probably the oldest in oral tradition." Cray sent Legman a sheaf of more than forty songs that one of his undergraduate students had gathered from his fraternity brothers. He flattered Legman, writing that "everyone" was on tenterhooks waiting for the big folk song book.[2]

When the UCLA songs arrived, Legman was stunned. He had never heard of a lot of them, he wrote Cray. "Even the two I already had (under other titles) are utterly different in *tone*" than what he had gathered before the war. He thought they were more hostile than erotic and full of strange fantasies. He urged Cray to send more.[3]

CHAPTER 7

The two undertook a long discussion of the thorny problems of identifying and indexing folk songs. Legman's files were full of overlapping versions, variants, and parodies. He wanted to trace the erotic songs back to their first appearance in print, but the lyrics had usually been suppressed. The melodies posed additional complex problems. Legman hoped the association of tune and text could be used to establish a song's antiquity, but he was stumped. For all his love of music, he did not have the technical skills to conduct tune analysis.[4]

Legman was on firmer ground when he laid out the history of song censorship. Three periods made up a complicated picture, he wrote Cray. "Essentially, before 1800, materials were freely published," as in D'Urfey's *Pills to Purge Melancholy*. Under the harsh Victorian censorship, Burns's *Merry Muses* became "the principal erotic songster in England." But for most of the nineteenth century, what appeared in print was mostly "music-hall stuff."[5] After the late nineteenth century, in the still-dying Victorianism of the present, there was more erotica but in fugitive forms, such as mimeographed songsters.

The English folk song collectors of the early twentieth century had created chaos, he wrote. Sometimes they noted the tunes and ignored the words. Or they stuffed the lyrics in a hell drawer and pretended they didn't exist. Francis James Child himself had recommended the erotic ballads he came across be burned, and Cecil Sharp had refused to take down the coarse lyrics of songs about lovemaking.[6] There were uncounted, unstudied erotic ballads in manuscripts and broadsides, scattered all over, in the libraries of prestigious universities like Harvard and Brown. Thousands of ballads lay unindexed and unstudied in libraries all over Britain. These needed to be assessed to help construct the narrative—if Cray and others could find the courage.[7]

Like many of the early-twentieth-century scholars working on folk song, Legman was fixed on continuity with the past. Of course, a song was most desirable if it could be dated to Shakespeare's time, but, he wrote Cray, he was always in search of the oldest text still "in *authentic* folk transmission."[8] He hoped to show that the obscene songs were the oldest and that cleaner songs had come later, and he wanted to uncover an older sexuality persisting in folk song. For example, he spent a good deal of ink trying to show that "Three Old Whores from Winnipeg" was related to a much older poem about old women discussing their own genitals and their husbands' prowess. "Three Old Whores" suggested that the unrepressed sexuality Legman glimpsed in Burns's *Merry Muses* was still alive. He and Cray searched for evidence that someone had recently sung it.[9]

As Legman and Cray discussed the prospects for publishing "The Ballad," Legman was not optimistic. He was up to his nose in texts, and he ranted bitterly to Cray, as he did to all his correspondents, about his eye problems, the costs of bringing out such a big book, and how other folklorists assumed he was wealthy.[10] He was concluding that he would have to bring out "The Ballad" as he had *The Limerick*, privately and at his own expense.[11]

Cray argued that the American folk song revival, now in its second bloom, was creating openings for Legman's work. On the other hand, they were both disgusted that the popular folk singer Oscar Brand was issuing LPs of "bawdy songs and backroom ballads."[12] What Brand was selling was simpering fakelore, as Legman put it, "pure shite."[13] Everyone in the revival was cashing in on folklore, he wrote Cray, and he urged him to circulate the still unpublished "Who Owns Folklore?" his attack on fakelorists, folk singers, and copyrighters. Legman asserted that "the damn copyright law" ought to be repealed altogether so that people couldn't use it to steal folk artists' materials.[14]

Cray noted that Grove Press was bringing out D. H. Lawrence's *Lady Chatterley's Lover* in the United States.[15] Perhaps if someone could smuggle "The Ballad" into Los Angeles, he could shop it to publishers. "Do not hesitate to send everything," Cray urged. He counseled Legman to face reality. Instead of selling his library to keep going, he should try writing for U.S. men's magazines. The trick was to be ribald without using dirty words and to pitch the lowest common denominator: "Limericks, god help us, make excellent fillers."[16]

As they became more serious about publishing a book of songs in the United States, Legman wrote that he foresaw two volumes of at least six hundred pages each. He advised that Cray should work on the tune transcriptions and musical headnotes, which he was capable of doing, while Legman would round up missing, rare items.[17] Legman did not send the manuscript but mailed Cray an outline: his opening section in volume 1 presented songs he could trace to the sixteenth century, including "Brinzi O'Flynn," a ballad that contained a rare mention of oral sex. He moved on through songs of the seventeenth and eighteenth centuries, then to military, college student, and children's songs. Volume 2 dealt with occupations with singing traditions. He emphasized that he would not make a separate category for "Negro songs," but he had few of these and asked Cray, "Are there bawdy blues?"[18]

When they began to consider contemporary erotic song, they were stumped. Legman was covered head to toe with the tapes Abrahams, Goldstein, and others had been sending him. But since he had neither electricity nor a tape player, he had not been able to assess them. In early 1963, Legman was able to send laboriously copied duplicates to Los Angeles by freighter. When Cray listened, he thought that Legman's collected recordings were at best a hodgepodge.[19] There were recordings of Marines and college students singing. But the tapes also included copies of commercial LPs, including "party records."[20] There were some good versions of bawdy songs—Cray especially liked "My God, How the Money Rolls In," about a family bootlegging and prostitution enterprise. But a tape from Goldstein included the art

164 CHAPTER 7

tenor Richard Dyer-Bennett and activist folk singer Josh White. These singers were not "folk," according to Cray's and Legman's standard. Even worse, Cray informed Legman, there was commercial interference. People were singing songs they had learned from Oscar Brand's LPs.[21]

Legman instructed Cray to drop "all concern with Brand materials . . . &c. This is nobody's folklore, god knows."[22] Although his tapes were a fair sample of the dirty songs people were singing, Legman disliked them. He was getting bales of undergraduate songs from academics like Bess Lomax Hawes, Richard Reuss, and Edith Fowke, showing that the folk music revival had resuscitated college singing traditions, but the material was crude and not what he hoped for, he wrote to Fowke. On the other hand, it was obscene, and "I never expected to get it." College material would represent modern erotic folk song.[23]

Legman was looking backward in a search for a more organic, sexual dimension of folk song. As he saw it, old preindustrial erotic song had been suppressed by censors and remade by the working classes in the industrial cities, but there might have been a purer bawdy tradition lurking somewhere in the past.[24] His desired erotic folk song was heartily masculine and frankly sexual, but also poetic and tied to an earthy, rural past. And folk song should have no truck with commerce. Presented with the mixed bag of what people were singing in the present day, so far from his ideal type, he turned away.

THE HORN BOOK

Although "The Ballad" was moving slowly, by early 1963 Legman's years of archival digging and song tracing had proved productive. As he often did when at an impasse with one project, Legman turned to another. The result of his expeditions to great archives were *beiwerke*—expansive, supplemental works of history, analysis, and commentary he developed as deep background to the texts and the analysis he hoped would follow. Legman organized his bye-essays into *The Horn Book: Studies in Erotic Bibliography*, published in the United States in 1964.[25] Years later, his friend Osmond Beckwith would call *The Horn Book* one of Legman's finest pieces of writing and scholarship. Beckwith reread it in the late 1990s and found it "full-flavored midlife Legman" and as fresh as ever. He also found it "essentially impossible to summarize."[26]

A decade of work had let Legman develop his own style of scholarly argument as he galloped across a broad landscape of folklore problems. *The Horn Book* studies were grouped into three parts. A first segment presented studies in erotic bibliography, including his attempt to identify the author of *My Secret Life*. Legman tried to show that "Anonymous" was book collector and bibliographer Henry Spencer Ashbee (Pisanus Fraxi). A second was centered

"The Ballad" and The Horn Book show the historical connections between on the rediscovery of Burns's *Merry Muses* and considered manuscript and published versions as folklore. A final section of 250 pages grouped together essays on conceptual problems of erotic folklore, including a look at science fiction, and the history of the publication and suppression of bawdy songs and poems. Now he presented a full history of the limerick as a folk rhyme and unfolded a longer version of "Who Owns Folklore?"

All the essays in *The Horn Book* show the historical connections between old and new texts, based on the careful examination of obscure, often unique sources. Legman used the techniques of the literary historian on his fragmentary print and manuscript sources; he found the texts tangled in a mare's nest of prudery and hypocrisy extending at least from the English Reformation. He traced recondite publications across place and time; he compared imprints and texts and made well-read allusions to literary history, but he also drew on popular cultural forms like broadsides and cheap underground magazines. This mosaic of evidence revealed oral tradition's interaction with the world of print.

In one group of studies, "The Rediscovery of *The Merry Muses of Caledonia*," Legman worked out a history of the posthumously published collection of the lost bawdy songs of Robert Burns (and, probably, several people pretending to be Robert Burns), working from his finds in the British Museum and Scotland. The "Forbidden Fruit" manuscript he had copied in Dumferline originated as a pocket-size songbook, circulated among gentlemen. The little books were a clubman's fashion from the sixteenth into the nineteenth centuries, brought out for singing and toasting at festivities, in Burns's case at a backstreet bar in Edinburgh. Burns had collected verse from others, but he also rewrote, expanded, and composed songs, so that his pocket book was a mix of old and new. Its impolite verses described and joked about heterosexual intercourse, praising, damning, and hypostasizing genitalia. Whether it could be termed folklore was a question Legman went on to investigate.

Legman compared the circa 1800 Cunningham manuscript, now the earliest exemplar, with existing published versions of *The Merry Muses*, and "Forbidden Fruit," constructing a story of bricolage and bastardy. Robert Burns's own songs and his added collections "made up only the core of the printed work appearing as [his own] for a century," he argued.[27] Onto this was grafted at least as much material by others, which Legman called falsification, impersonation, and imposture. His evidence was difficult: this was not just a story of censorship, but one of collation, plagiarism, and marketing, in the production of an iconic text.

Legman was ahead of his time in taking the entire one-hundred-year hodgepodge of *The Merry Muses* on its own terms. He did not disallow the songs as subject matter because they had come from such impure sources

166   CHAPTER 7

and been published under false pretenses. This was the ground condition of working with material produced under censorship. It was not possible in the world of erotic folklore to find purity of descent, and if one wanted to know what had happened, unprejudiced bibliography was essential.

Legman developed a picture of *The Merry Muses* as popular print, part of a world of cheap books with close relationships to oral performances and private manuscripts like Burns's pocket book. Chapbooks and broadsides were popular in the crowded English cities of the seventeenth and eighteenth centuries. As a resource for singers, they were mainly enjoyed in commercial settings, in tiny drinking spots like coal holes and cider holes, in public houses and music halls, and at public executions, markets, and festivals. There was no one folk in this city, but there were many singing "folks," from the market crowd to the tippling gentlemen.[28]

Muses came out of this context. Considered as folklore in print, after it was first published the song collection became a nucleus to which more mixed material then adhered. As it was republished, in snowball fashion *Muses* accumulated all kinds of additional songs, toasts, and rhymes, most of it frankly obscene.

For all his historical realism, there was a romanticism in Legman's study of *The Merry Muses*. Amid the detritus of popular print, he was searching for something else: "the thread of the older folksong" that Burns might have preserved, not, as Legman worded it, "the sugary string of poetizing, of the pastoral and wayside seduction type" of the eighteenth century but "the far older roistering humor concerning full bodied men and full-fleshed women, with large sexual appetites and larger buttocks of the kind Chaucer and Dunbar had already handled centuries before." He thought *Muses* was heavily Irish in origin, but he preferred the older "Highlands evocation of sexual passion, with the accents on the humorous anatomy and the accidents of that passion" to the "crank turned" unpleasantness that had been attributed to Burns when he was no longer around to defend himself.[29] Burns could be a link to a purer, realer bawdry lurking somewhere in the past.

Legman's studies of *The Merry Muses* appeared long before the flourishing of scholarship on early modern popular culture, much of which he would have appreciated. In *The Horn Book*, he foresaw many of the conclusions later historians would draw about the relationship between print and oral traditions.[30] He knew printing made possible the study of the songs he cherished, but he suspected print of distorting the emotional essence of oral tradition. The "printed revision" of folk song, he wrote, does not bear the mark of "folk acceptance. It is overwhelmed by the newer personality of its reviser." The part of folklore that can be commodified is the part that dies "or is long since dead and decayed." A mysterious part that "does not easily unveil itself" is the part that lives.[31] This was a romantic and aesthetic position, difficult to sustain with the evidence in his careful historical reconstructions.

Reviews of *The Horn Book* were limited to scholarly and library journals, but they were generous. Alan Dundes, a young faculty member at the University of California at Berkeley, loved the book. Praising Legman's "unmatched mastery of his subject matter" and "superbly creative command of English prose," he called Legman "the James Joyce of folklore." The bibliographic studies were "fascinating examples of the high order of sleuthing required to illuminate the incredibly complex publishing histories of erotica" and provided "valuable descriptions of manuscripts and where they might be found." Especially important to Dundes, *The Horn Book* was "a clarion call for honest folklore collection" and a plea for study "rather than just more collection and retention" of folklore.[32]

Alex Comfort, the physician and psychiatrist, wrote a thorough review for the English journal *Folklore*. He lauded *The Horn Book* as "a vast improvement on recent and catchpenny books which purport to explore erotica but contain no independent research." Legman was right to call for museums to "stop being coy about their hidden books" and for scholars to seriously study "sexual-social ephemera." Comfort found Legman cranky, but his energy made him a wonderful companion in research. He predicted the book would be useful long after censorship ended.[33]

The Horn Book made Legman's scholarly name, and it was well timed. It brought him to the attention of editors and publishers just at a moment when it was becoming easier for them to reprint the rare and fascinating expurgated books he knew well. Folklore Associates brought out a facsimile edition of the original *Merry Muses of Caledonia* (1965) and reissued volume 1 of Farmer and Henley's *Slang and Its Analogues*. A. N. Afanasev's *Russian Secret Tales: Bawdy Folktales of Old Russia* and the anonymous *My Secret Life* made their way back into print in the midsixties. In each case, Legman contributed a learned introduction, although the publishers were not academic presses (in the case of the *Secret Tales*, the publisher was Jake Brussel). Writing introductions became a significant sideline that allowed Legman to frame collections of erotic folklore with serious discussions of the history of publishing and censorship. Thus, he ensured that these books found a place in university libraries and a clear location in the murky history of erotica. As a part of the process of opening folklore and publishing in the United States to materials that dealt with sex and the body, Legman helped make possible the modern consideration of the history of pornography. He arranged to have Patrick Kearney's expert bibliography of the Private Case published by Jay Landesman (now in London), and he wrote a thorough introduction for it.[34]

168 CHAPTER 7

Heartened by the reviews of *The Horn Book*, Legman thought that perhaps now was the time to return to the United States, and he began pushing out letters of inquiry. He wanted "a temporary lecture seminar . . ., on erotic literature and erotic folklore," and he hoped for an offer from Berkeley. Maybe Alan Dundes could help. "I'm actually thinking of doing six months stands in more than one place," he specified. Most of all, he wanted to place his "thinking and experience in this difficult field" before as many students as he could reach.[35]

Dundes had suggested Legman to Richard Dorson a few years before and been disappointed that nothing had come of it. At Berkeley, he reported, the prospects were "only fair." He had been trying to launch a folklore program, and he had been talking to Henry Nash Smith about inviting Legman. However, Bertrand Bronson in the Music Department was opposed to any change in the way folk song and folklore were studied. Dundes suggested contacting Marjorie Fiske (the wife of Leo Lowenthal and drafter of the American Library Association's statement on the freedom to read) about a position at the Langley Porter Psychiatric Center. He felt Legman "definitely should be training some students. It's just too big a field for one person."[36] It was difficult: an advanced degree, or at least a college degree, was becoming required for university teaching. Combined with Legman's persistent interest in obscenity, this was a major obstacle.

LA JOLLA

As it turned out, through Roy Harvey Pearce, Legman was offered a one-year position in 1964–65 as a writer-in-residence in literature at the University of California's new San Diego campus in La Jolla. From a perch on the West Coast, he could now meet all the men he had been cultivating since 1953 and, he hoped, get a good look into their hell drawers. He claimed to have proposed two courses, Orgasm I and Orgasm II, and was disappointed to be given a nonteaching assignment.

At the same moment, Gershon and Beverley's marriage had become rocky, perhaps because he formed liaisons with other women when the couple was apart. During 1955, when he visited Amsterdam to teach at an important exhibit of paper folding, he met and had an affair with Sima Colcher, a young Jewish woman who was the daughter of Eastern European refugees.[37]

Shortly after the exhibition was packed up, Gershon and Sima left for Paris, where they lived for a half year. Then they moved to Auribeau-sur-Siagne on the coast, where they lived until the early spring of 1957. As their daughter relates, "All that time Gershon didn't tell her he was married to Beverley, and Sima didn't ask." When Beverley, who had been away for a long visit to Canada, announced she was returning, "Gershon gave Sima the

Gershon teaching paper folding in Amsterdam, 1955. Courtesy of the Legman Archive.

excuse that he had to go to the US on 'family matters' and put her on a train back to Amsterdam.... It was only in Amsterdam that Sima found out she was pregnant."[38] Ariëla Legman was born in September 1957. Gershon was proud to be recognized as a father: on a 1958 New Year's card to banned-book collector Ewing Baskette, under a photo of a rosy, WASP-y family, he wrote, "You Ain't the Only One!"[39]

The liaison with Sima and Ariëla's birth set off a crisis with Beverley. By 1963 Legman was telling his correspondents, "I asked my wife what she'd like for our twentieth anniversary and she said simply 'a divorce.'"[40] When he and Beverley ended their marriage in early 1964, Legman decamped to New York and she remained at Valbonne. In Greenwich Village, he met and married Christine Conrad, "a red-headed banjo player" and expert on English Renaissance poetry. Photos of Christine show a glamorously made-up woman with a beehive mound of red hair. She looked very like a Playboy Bunny and most unlike Beverley. When they came back to Valbonne to try country living, Christine hated it, and they retreated to Manhattan in 1964. Gershon wrote to Frank Hoffman that after Labor Day, he planned to hit the lecture circuit.[41] And then suddenly, the couple sought an annulment. According to Judith Legman, when Christine bought an expensive raincoat, Gershon realized she had no plans to move to La Jolla with him.[42]

CHAPTER 7

In August 1964, he wrote to Ed Cray that "coming back from France definitively, and almost on mad erotic impulse" was a shattering experience. His life was broken in half. He was heading west to "a little suburban backwash, or I don't know wut . . . determined to work it all out in the end: be Reborn and All." He asked Cray to "Write me and Pray for me."[43]

By September 1964, he was renting a house overlooking La Jolla Shores, without his manuscripts and books, and walking up the hill to the campus to use the library. (He recalled being stopped by police officers who were suspicious of pedestrians.) The faculty, he claimed, gave him the cold shoulder and disinvited him from meetings. All his teaching was informal, conversations on the grass with students, and the faculty disapproved.

Looking for further work as a visiting lecturer, he went north to Los Angeles, dropping in to folk clubs and chanting vile limericks at a party given by D. K. Wilgus.[44] He tried to meet up with Cray, but could not find him. He went on to Berkeley to meet Dundes and Peter Tamony, a lexicographer and longtime correspondent. Dundes remembered a restaurant supper during which Legman propositioned two different women.[45]

In San Francisco, Tamony arranged for Legman to lecture on the erupting free-speech movement, which he denounced as phony. He later claimed to have spent a good deal of time observing LSD-addled behavior at orgies in Berkeley, but he left no direct accounts of these events. He later rewrote these speeches into *The Fake Revolt*, a small book denouncing the counterculture as a CIA-directed fraud.[46] Legman had been out of the United States for more than a decade, remote from its political turmoil. Whatever sex and drugs parties he participated in, he did not have much feel for the current American scene. He missed the connections between the civil rights and antiwar movements and free speech at Berkeley, and he reviled the drug culture and the hippie ethos of cool, so he denounced it all as dangerous fakery.[47]

At some point during this American sojourn, he may have given a guest lecture at the Ohio State University where, a persistent legend has it, he told a gathering of antiwar students that their slogan should be "Fuck, Don't Kill." This caught on as "Make Love, Not War." It has proved impossible to document this visit or show that the slogan, which began appearing in antiwar demonstrations about 1965, originated with Legman. Whether he said it first or only heard it and then claimed it as his own, it was a summary of the points he had made so ferociously in *Love & Death*.[48]

In the spring of 1965, Legman received a letter from Beverley telling him that she had been diagnosed with lung cancer and needed his help. He hurried back from La Jolla to care for her. The end of Beverley's life was a tragedy and an enormous strain. Her cancer was terminal, and surgery was not contemplated, although expensive and debilitating radiation treatments could slow the disease. As a foreigner, Beverley had no right to the French national health insurance, so Legman began to sell parts of his library to universities in the United States to help pay the medical bills. Finally, medievalist Francis Lee Utley helped arrange a major purchase by the Ohio State University library, although payment was slow to arrive.

To maintain his sanity, Legman continued to work intensely. He complained to correspondents of the huge trouble he had getting folklore materials, especially the Randolph manuscripts, from the Kinsey Archive. He kept up an intense back-and-forth, first with Grove Press and then with Goldstein, about "The New Kryptadia," his prospective yearbook of erotic folklore. He actively solicited articles for this project from folklorists Dundes, Roderick Roberts, and Richard Reuss, among others.

In late 1965, he wrote to Frank Hoffman, "My wife is dying now." The cancer research hospital in Nice was demanding cash in advance. He described the scene: "When the payment was stopped on my shit-ass publisher's check . . . they put my wife out in a chair in the hallway downstairs (*unable to walk*)." At the last moment, his luck turned: "Jake Brussel,—the old pirate with the heart of gold," sent an advance for his introduction to *Russian Secret Tales*. (This was not how he later described the events. In desperation, he robbed a friend's cash drawer and was arrested, but not before rescuing Beverley from the hospital.) He wrote Hoffman that the doctors told him, "'Allez! [Get lost!]' . . . This, my friend, is how a woman dies of cancer."[49]

By January 1966, the outlook was very grim, and he was asking Hoffman and others for money. Practical help arrived in the form of a young woman, Judith Evans, the daughter of one of Legman's San Francisco folklore correspondents. Judith stayed for several months, aiding Gershon and Beverley. When she and Gershon fell in love, Judith left Valbonne and returned to California. She and Gershon wrote to each other and planned to marry in the near future.[50]

In the summer of 1966, Gershon took a final photograph of Beverley and recorded in a burst of letters that she died in his arms in the early hours of July 15, listening to a Beethoven symphony, "another victim of the American tobacco industry." He buried her in the Opio cemetery, in an unmarked plot where he planned to join her.[51]

There followed a period of exhaustion and grief. He had been hard-pressed caring for Beverley, and his hopes for an academic position in the United States were defeated. He now inherited the farm he called La Clé des Champs, as well as responsibility for Beverley's elderly mother, in a nursing home near Cannes. He threw himself into his work, launching again into his advanced study of dirty jokes.

SCOOPED

In August 1965, Ed Cray announced the publication of an anthology of American bawdy songs. Legman was shocked and wrote to ask for a review copy, and when he did not receive a reply, he exploded, accusing Cray of conning him out of his song tapes.[52] Cray wrote that his volume was under contract but nowhere near publication; his work had been disrupted by the Watts Riots. He pointed out that he had sent Legman more than a hundred song texts collected by his students, and it was odd for the same Legman who had authored "Who Owns Folklore?" to assert proprietary rights over oral tradition and tapes he had not even made himself.[53] Each man threatened the other with denial of permission to reprint shared materials. Finally, Legman huffed that he had too many songs to print anyway, and "The Ballad" would only benefit if Cray published his book first.[54] In fact, if Cray was going to seize their joint project, there was little Legman could do about it from rural France.

In 1969 Cray brought out *The Erotic Muse*, presenting many of the materials he and Legman had worked on together. It became the definitive collection of North American bawdy songs, but it was written as if Legman and Cray's extensive consultation had never happened. In his introduction, Cray cited his students' collecting and "a quartet of colleagues generous to the point of collaboration." He recognized Bess Lomax Hawes, Barre Toelken, D. K. Wilgus, and Roger Abrahams for contributions from their own files. Pointedly, Cray did not mention Legman in the acknowledgments, although he cited *The Horn Book* in footnotes.[55]

Cray's *Erotic Muse* was closely modeled upon the plan Legman had laid out. It moved from songs with traceable old English pedigrees (including some with connections to Child ballads) to the United States, to focus on occupations, soldiers, and students. Cray shared Legman's goal of showing that even some very old songs could be shown to have been sung recently. Bawdy folk song was a living tradition.

Legman was left with the material Cray had not published. There were rhymes he had collected in 1930s Manhattan, songs sent by Henderson, Hugill, MacColl, and Goldstein, among others, and potentially texts from Randolph's "Unprintable Songs of the Ozarks" manuscript. Although Cray's book was big, there was still an ocean of obscene song out there.[56] But Cray had produced a scholarly offering that folk singers could use, and Legman correctly assessed that now no publisher would be interested in a similar book of erotic folk songs. He turned his attention to copying his rare and ephemeral materials and mailing them to archives he hoped would accession and preserve them.[57] For the time being, he put the daunting manuscript aside.

Legman's "Ballad" had been hampered by distance and technical problems, but mainly by his theory of folk song. His backward-looking passion for folk song was shared by most writers on English-language oral traditions up until the 1960s. Like other folk song scholars, Legman loved the songs as poetry and cherished the way they unfolded on the page.[58] The difference between Legman and the other ballad scholars was that he saw the old songs as an archive of bodily practices and sexual dilemmas, rather than as pieces of the history of poetry. He hoped folk songs could be used to write a history of sexual feelings, from tenderness to lust.[59]

For Legman, the most important force shaping the song legacy was censorship. While the survival of folk song on paper was a story of bad collecting and textual purging, hatred of sex had the biggest impact. Despite all the problems of evidence this posed, his urge to reconstruct a past sexuality was overriding. Legman had certainly collected enough material to publish an anthology of contemporary obscene song had he wanted to, but he was more concerned with the preservation and presentation of older songs.

The scholarly field was changing, as students of folk music were turning their attention to living traditions in contemporary communities. In the United States, they were led by Alan Lomax and singer-scholars like Edward Ives, Bess Lomax Hawes, and Michael Seeger.[60] In their research with the Travellers in Scotland, Ewan MacColl and Peggy Seeger were interested in folk singing as the art of marginal groups. These fieldworkers turned their attention from folk songs as poetry to the place of music and song in everyday life. They proposed that one way to find out where the songs had come from and what they meant was to interview living singers. When it came to folk songs about sex, collectors were finding they had to negotiate a singer's sense of propriety and her community's standards. Legman was correct when he wrote that erotic folk songs were mixed in with the rest of a singer's repertoire, sometimes acknowledged, sometimes held back. It was a question not just of asking for the dirty songs, as one could in an archive, but also of the song's meaning for the singer, a living person.[61] In turn, this dictated a different way of writing about folk song.

The kind of songs under study were changing, too. Francis James Child's romantic cultural framework had dictated a prejudice against broadsides, based on the conviction that print and orality were fundamentally different and separate. Legman and Cray had dismissed folk songs tainted by commerce. But from the early twentieth century, much of traditional musical culture was intimately involved with recordings and radio broadcasting. Scholar-collectors like Archie Green and Harry Smith, for example, were interested in popular and folk music on 78rpm disks, in the hybrid roots of country, jazz, rock, and pop. Old ideas of purity and authenticity were becoming less compelling, and when closely scrutinized they crumbled. A wide, new audience did not want to be told their favorite music was tawdry and fake.[62] These shifting ideas made Legman's preferred old bawdy song seem like a rusty antique. And as for modern erotic song—to his horror, there was rock and roll.

8

THE KEY TO THE FIELDS

Where the barbed wire ends . . .

—G. Legman to Jay Landesman, May 4, 1970, giving directions to his home

Legman lived and wrote in France from 1953 until his death in 1999. The libraries and bookstores of Paris had provided a grounding for his *Hautes Études* series and his book-buying adventures, but by the spring of 1956, Gershon and Beverley were seeking cheaper arrangements. The couple took a train to France's southern coast and decided to stay.

Legman would settle down in Les Alpes-Maritimes to build a new rural home, a refuge from the noise and expense of the city. Eventually, he was able to turn a rude encampment into a modest but comfortable homestead. Here, with his third wife, Judith, he would simply sit and work for almost four decades with few interruptions, conducting research in his private library and by mail, producing still more big books, articles, and polemics. Judith supported him practically and grounded him emotionally, making his life possible again after Beverley's death. Their partnership enabled him to concentrate for years at a time on each huge project. But his work demanded enormous sacrifices from his wife, and, later, his children. The costs of his dedication, isolation, and poverty were high.

In later years, as his advanced studies were published, younger writers came to Legman's farmstead in the impressively beautiful countryside made famous by the postimpressionist painters. These pilgrims were sometimes shocked by the difference between the writer's life they romantically imagined and his hard-pressed reality. Visitors observed the daily pattern of the second half of Legman's working life, pondered the household's economy and gender relations, and queried him about his ideas. Their testimonies, along with his voluminous letters and his family's recollections, show Legman trying to reckon with American culture from afar. He pounded out his unstinting critique and unfolded his folklore collections, making sure he got it all down on paper for posterity.

ESTABLISHING LA CLÉ DES CHAMPS

For several years, Gershon and Beverley had moved around the little coastal towns west of Nice, always seeking the cheapest lodgings. They lived simply and were often disrupted by the summer tourist season, when their landladies would ask them to move on. A snapshot of one Legman dwelling shows a single-room hut with a blanket covering the entrance. But it was a productive time. If Gershon had a working typewriter and a supply of ribbons and paper, he was content, although in these first years most of his library was in storage. Another photograph shows him typing energetically on a balcony at Auribeau-sur-Siagne, vineyards and the sea below him.

He kept a lively social life. In the 1950s, the coastal towns housed a floating crowd of artists, musicians, novelists, and filmmakers, and some displaced royalty, and they adopted Gershon as their raconteur.[1] He became friends with a small colony of American leftist filmmakers in exile from the Red Scare, including Paul Jarrico and Ben and Norma Barzman.[2]

Gershon writing on his balcony at Auribeau-sur-Siagne, France, about 1956. Courtesy of the Legman Archive.

CHAPTER 8

Eventually, they sought a permanent home. A few miles in from the coast, the agricultural areas were severely depressed, and farmland could be bought for as little as one franc a square meter. In 1960, using a small inheritance from Beverley's family, they were able to buy the remnants of an old farm between the walled seventeenth-century town of Valbonne and the much older hilltop village of Opio. The property they assembled eventually became two hectares (a bit over four acres), with two small neglected buildings and an old grove of olive trees.[3]

The farm, as Gershon called it, was really a disused olive grove and had not been tended in a long time. On a rise above the River Brague, their *oliveraie* was surrounded by a remnant of one of the largest live oak forests near the coast. To the east, the River Loup rackets down through narrow gorges to the coastal plain, and one can sight *les baous* (the steep headlands) above it. To the north and west, the *pics*, the first balconies of the Alps, rise abruptly. Gershon immediately felt a special love for massive Le Cheiron, visible on clear days from the grove. Named for the centaur who taught Achilles, it became "his Fujiama."[4]

The land purchase was a complex legal and social process. Gershon and Beverley bought separate parcels to piece together the four acres. Their original house, with two rooms down and one up, was purchased from two different families, who may have been distantly related, although no one was certain. The floors had no internal communication, and the upstairs was accessed only by an external stone stair. In fact, the original was less a house than two joined outbuildings—a centuries-old *cabanon,* or sleeping place for people working in the olive groves—and a little trapezoidal goat barn attached to it in the 1920s.

Appropriately for a folklorist, the property transfer involved concessions to local tradition. There were lingering memories of the farm's particularities, and people had to defer to them. One of the two families Legman bought property from included an elderly woman, without whose permission the family could not sell. She likely had a usufruct, the right to everything produced by the property, whether olives or rent. This woman demanded Legman agree to treat a very large boxwood tree with respect and never cut it with any metal instrument. Whether this would have been bad luck for her family or Gershon's, for as long as the tree lived he was careful to keep that promise. There was another boxwood story. On the walk to the well where Gershon got water in the early years, there was a pair of tall boxwood trees, which, he had been told by one of the locals, could take the troubles off a person if they just slipped through the branches backward.[5]

The *cabanon* was remote and extremely basic. It had no running water, electricity, telephone, or indoor plumbing for many years. In the early days,

Gershon at La Clé des Champs, Valbonne, France, about 1967. Courtesy of the Legman Archive.

Gershon and Beverley lived inside and outside at the same time, cooking over a butane flame and heating with a woodstove. They climbed the exterior stones to their sleeping quarters, carried water from a cistern, and used buckets for an outdoor bathroom. They awoke when the sun rose and went to sleep when it set. In the beginning, they had about 250 olive trees, some of them two hundred years old by their size. They grew herbs and a few tomatoes, and Beverley planted roses.[6]

In 1960 Legman wrote to Ed Cray on "the proof sheet of the first letterhead of the first home I've had since I left home (in 1935) and started as a 'folklorist,' or bum, as my family plainly put it."[7] It was imperative he unpack his library after seven years in storage. Somehow, the materials he had crated in 1953 were slowly shipped from New York and Paris and over the years (mostly) got unpacked. Legman's astonishing collection of rare books and papers would grow as people around the world sent him letters and manuscripts. Beverley bought herself a grand piano, and they acquired a battery-powered phonograph and a kerosene lantern. With no car, they walked to Valbonne for services and the all-important post office and used the rural bus for trips to the paper stores and printing shops in Cannes and Nice. Gershon got occasional jobs reviewing films and reporting from the new film festival at Cannes. Eventually, he purchased a small prefabricated house nearby to hold his office and library.

Life was quiet and barely affordable. Sometimes they were short of food, but having grown up in a poor family, Legman knew about making ends meet. As Clellon Holmes remembered, he could fill a grocery sack with a nickel. He was competent at house painting, basic carpentry, and tree trimming, and he exchanged labor with their few neighbors. He really did not care about money except insofar as it was necessary to survival. What was important was his work, and he had made a place to do it.

It is not clear when Gershon named the homestead La Clé des Champs, but he soon began having announcements and stationery printed up with that name and the simple address "Valbonne," giving some correspondents the impression that he lived on an estate. It was an old French turn of phrase: *prendre la clé des champs*, "to take the key to the fields," which means to take one's freedom, to walk out and away from the town. This was "where the barbed wire ends," as he often wrote, where he had taken his personal, intellectual freedom. A friend painted a rough sign with Old French lettering: for many years, this hung from a big oak and marked the house.

There were plenty of other romantic ideas. The old road they lived on was named after a Roman camp remembered to have been there, perhaps in the fourth century CE, and there are remnants of Roman aqueducts in the Brague Valley. La Clé itself stood on the rubble of some older walls. Gershon liked to tell correspondents he lived in the ruins of a fort of the Knights Templar, which was not impossible, as a sect of templars had had an installation a few miles away and the entire region was crisscrossed by Saracen and Christian invaders in the ninth and tenth centuries. But perhaps the ruins were just those of an older farmhouse.

The hills around Opio have ancient forts and lookout posts, and the name "Opio" is likely derived from *oppidum*, Latin for "fort." From this perspective, seventeenth-century Valbonne is new construction, although it sits near an ancient *abbaye*. Built by a bishop to wall out the plague, Valbonne is now a perfect and picturesque tourist town, with pricey inns and well-planted window boxes. When Gershon and Beverley arrived in 1960, Valbonne was much more modest, housing people whose families had farmed sheep and goats, pressed olive oil, and run small shops there for many years. Outside the town walls, there were a few neighbors in scattered houses who got by in an informal economy, exchanging goods and labor. Beyond La Clé, the road to Opio was almost unpopulated.[8]

In 1966 Gershon's life changed radically. Beverley died that July, and in the fall he married Judith Evans, the young Californian who had visited with them the previous year. At twenty-six, she was twenty-three years his junior, but well prepared to become his lover, wife, and formidable partner in the production of his books. Judith had grown up in an artistic and book-loving family. Her father, Henry H. Evans, was a secondhand bookseller, and her mother, Patricia, sometimes helped him in their store.[9] Henry Evans was also a reputable bibliographer and a knowledgeable appraiser of antiquarian books and private libraries. He had a handpress that he used to print pamphlets by San Francisco poets and local historians. He also printed artwork, including his own portfolios of block prints and etchings. As a girl, Judith was "the printer's devil," taught to distribute and set type. Her father encouraged her to set up her own press, and he took her around to other print shops as he was perfecting his craft.[10] The family hung out with poets and other bookshop owners, including Lawrence Ferlinghetti. Judith was a great reader. There were always books in the house, and, she emphasizes, she was never forbidden to read anything.[11]

Patricia Healey Evans was also interested in folklore. She and Judith participated in California Folklore Society meetings, and at one point Patricia was elected an officer.[12] Besides this, her real folkloristic activity was collecting children's folklore, which she did when Judith was at playgrounds. Judith recalls, "I would be playing with other children and she would be asking them their jump rope rhymes, and how did they play jacks. Jacks, jump rope rhymes, hopscotches, and insults were things she collected enough of to make little books of them, and my father printed them up in tiny pamphlets."[13] He sold these along with the booklets he wrote about Chinatown "and what he called 'Bohemian San Francisco,' for twenty-five cents each."[14]

With a folklorist mother, a printer and book-dealer father, and her own expertise in librarianship, Judith found much in common with Gershon. But Legman and the Evanses had another connection: Henry had caught Gershon's attention when, in about 1950, he was arrested at his store at 555 Sutter Street for selling a book by Henry Miller through the mails. It was national news. Judith remembers that there was "a great deal of publicity, and he almost went to jail." Henry's lawyers defended him successfully, and he was given only three years of probation.[15]

In about 1957, Patricia struck up a long-distance correspondence with Legman about children's folklore. It came about, oddly, through the same origami exhibit at the Stedelijk Museum in Amsterdam where he had met Sima Colcher, mother of his daughter Ariëla. When Gershon taught paper folding there, class leaders gave him one of Patricia's folklore pamphlets. Judith remembered that "Gershon immediately wrote to my mother and said 'Hey! This is great! Who are you, and what else do you do?' And so began a correspondence which they carried on for quite a while." In Judith's words, Patricia "in her heyday was an extremely outgoing and fascinating person," and Legman was charmed. In any case, he was already a character in the Evans household: when Judith was fifteen, she read *Love & Death*. She was deeply impressed.[16]

Judith had studied at Stanford between 1957 and 1959, but after an unhappy sophomore year she left college, then reenrolled at Berkeley to study French and library science. She graduated in 1962 with a bachelor's degree in French and a master's in library science. She was recruited by the New York Public Library and went to live in Manhattan. After three years working as children's librarian in the Bronx, she felt a little stale. She had always wanted to go to Europe and had saved some money, so she quit the job. She remembers, "I went off to Europe in September [1965] and didn't come back until after the middle of February." As she planned her European trip, she had written to Gershon to introduce herself as Patricia Evans's daughter and was invited to visit. They met on December 10, 1965.[17]

As Judith assessed the situation at La Clé des Champs, she felt that Beverley, who was now critically ill, might need a companion and that Gershon certainly needed help with her care. "Otherwise everything fell on him," she saw. What began as an effort to help an admired friend of her parents became an emotionally fraught situation. Things went very well for a while,

Judith Evans at the time of her marriage to Gershon, 1966. Photograph by John Waggaman.

Judith tells, until she and Gershon "got very interested in one another, and then that was not good. And I had to go." It was a difficult situation in which Gershon loved both women, and, as Judith put it, "neither of us could bear having him be in love with someone else."[18]

She went back to Berkeley and got an apartment and a job at the public library. By letter the couple made plans to marry after Gershon had begun to recover from Beverley's long death. Judith received her parents' blessings, assembled a small trousseau, and in September returned to France.

They had a small wedding at the *mairie* in Opio, on October 29, 1966. "My mother had made me a wedding dress," she remembered, a friend ordered a cake, "and Gershon bought a little butane-fueled refrigerator so that we could put the Champagne in to cool." Only a few friends attended, including the typewriter sales and repair man from Nice and his wife. Art photographer John Waggaman stopped through and made prewedding portraits of them.[19]

In Judith's recollection, "At the civil ceremony, the mayor's clerk who was also the primary school teacher left his students giggling and chanting their alphabetic syllables 'Ay Aa Ay, Bay Ba Bey' while he helped marry us. That was our music. . . . And then we signed the register and came back and ate our cake, and that was the wedding."[20] A photograph shows Judith in her handmade white dress, nearly as tall as Gershon, leaning into him with a large bunch of red and white flowers.

Gershon at the time of his marriage to Judith, 1966. Photograph by John Waggaman.

Judith and Gershon on their wedding day, October 29, 1966, Opio, France. Courtesy of the Legman Archive.

The couple were careful about their symbolic statements. Before the wedding, a friend had taken them to Italy, a short drive over the border, to buy a wedding ring. The French jewelers stamp gold jewelry with an imperial eagle, and Judith did not want that mark on her ring. She emphasizes that "Gershon asked the mayor to please take out the word 'obey' because I wasn't having any of that."[21]

Gershon had a wedding announcement printed to send to his many correspondents. It read:

> Judith Evans and Gershon Legman,
> October 29, 1966
> For Love.

Patricia Evans made sure the news was out in the United States: they even had congratulations in the California Folklore Society Newsletter.[22]

Now Judith found her life utterly changed. It was revolutionary "being married to someone I was absolutely crazy about and who was crazy about me, and whom I admired enormously morally, intellectually, in every way." And the living was primitive, "far more rustic than anything I had ever encountered except camping on an old fishing boat ... a more pioneering type of life, which didn't displease me at all." She compared her life to a fantasy book she had read; she was like the wife of the "wise man who lived in the woods, who other people would come and consult."[23]

Older ways of living persisted in Valbonne. Judith remembered seeing "*la transhumance*, the herds of sheep being taken to and from the mountain summer pastures," at the beginning and end of grazing. Farmers still pressed olives at a cooperative mill, and laborers picked roses and violets in the fields for the old *parfumeries* in Grasse. Out of town, it was nearly wild. *Les sangliers*, or wild boar, sometimes came out of the low oak forest to forage near her kitchen. The woods were full of wildflowers, hedgehogs, and toads, even the occasional venomous snake. At night she heard frog and bird noises. Judith remembers Gershon taking her to look at trees in the dark and teaching her that one saw a tree's structure only by looking at it in silhouette.[24]

In 1966 there were only a few houses along the forested road to Opio. "It was a very isolated life," she remembers. "If we hadn't been so crazy about each other I might have felt that it was a bit unsettled. As it was, it took quite a bit of adjusting." Her French studies at Berkeley had focused on literature, so she found, even with a bachelor's degree from Berkeley, "I could not speak French!" It took her several years to become fluent in the language.[25]

Judith had made an almost total break with the United States and urban life at a time when many other young people were trying to do the same. But La Clé des Champs was not a commune. She was alone with a husband who already had a well-developed working life. Judith did the shopping, the cooking, and some sewing and knitting. She found it "very challenging, keeping house with no electricity and one water faucet, which was already a great improvement over the cistern system Gershon had used when Beverley was alive." They did not have electricity until 1971.[26]

She was "willing to go to quite a bit of trouble cooking" to please Gershon, especially in the early years. Judith was an early natural foods enthusiast, following Adele Davis's high-calorie, high-protein nutritional program, which was very popular during the 1960s. They also wrote to Julia Legman for favorite Hungarian recipes and kitchen advice. Gershon made her a fake folk art plaque for the kitchen wall, which read, "Cookin' wears out / Kissin' don't."[27]

She felt their life was well set up and strongly defined by the complementary male and female roles Gershon insisted upon. He had strong feelings about the overt expression of gender: women should wear their hair long, with a little jewelry, makeup, and perfume. They should never wear pants. She regarded this as a minor inconvenience. Judith's traveling blue jeans went by the wayside, and she converted a pair of fashionable velveteen trousers into a sitting pillow.

Their workdays were partially separate. Gershon usually got up around four or five every morning, went to the study to work for a few hours with classical music blaring, and then came back for breakfast. Then, she remembered, he would go back and work some more and come back for lunch at one o'clock, often declaiming what he had written. With ferocious and disciplined energy, he put in a full eight-hour day. His maxim was "Always give the hind part of the day to the boss, and keep the best for yourself," or, as he put it less politely, "Sweets to the sweet, and piss on the boss's shit."[28]

Over the years, Judith would become indispensable to Gershon's work. Eventually, she had a small office in his study where she helped him with bibliographic projects, cataloging, proofreading, filing, annotating, and often typing and retyping. When his eye problems flared, she took dictation. They also started fun projects together: one was a collection of customarily paired words: "salt and pepper," "rack and ruin," "time and tide." And occasionally, it was tripled words: "rag, tag, and bobtail" and "Tinker to Evers to Chance."[29]

Gershon's mornings were devoted to work on his advanced studies. With *The Limerick* and *The Horn Book* completed, he alternated work on "The Ballad" and with his two volumes of *The Rationale of the Dirty Joke*, as well as many other articles and books. The folklore books were all one big project, with "lots going on at all times," in Judith's words, and "only when one work was published would that manuscript retreat and another one come forward." There were many intermittent projects: "There was more starting than stopping: extra ideas would evolve and absorb time without always coming to completion."[30] When she arrived, he was busy finishing a study of the Knights Templar.[31] Then, "shortly after we married, there was a project to bring out an anthology of erotic literature, which was never finished."[32]

A bit later, "Gershon had agreed to write a collective biography of great composers for Karl-Ludwig Leonhardt, a remarkable collector of books and a prosperous publisher in Germany."[33] This book was never completed, either, but it occupied several years of intense reading about composers and long bouts of listening to their work. This was an important part of the liberty of La Clé des Champs. Legman had the freedom to take up projects just to see where they led. There were enough hours in the day that he could explore a topic, sometimes for years, and then decide to drop it and head in another direction, whether back to ballads and jokes or on to something else.

By now, he suffered from serious intermittent eye troubles from years of intense reading, aggravated by an untreated eye infection endemic to the eastern Mediterranean. Sometimes he had to take full optical rest for many months, as he had since adolescence, allowing himself no reading, no typing, and no bright light. During these long periods, he dictated letters begging his friends to send more recorded music. Many did.

When he could work, he worked. After his intense first hours of writing, Legman usually turned to letters. Judith recounts that "all the years I knew him until he lost his health in 1991, he had a very voluminous correspondence going. He would write three and four and five very long letters sometimes in one day, and he would get as many answers which would send him back to the typewriter."[34] He could type faster than he could think, and this was how he stayed in touch with the world, very much on his own terms. He had no newspaper subscription and "no radio, thank God!" He depended on his friends in New York and California to send clippings and the occasional magazine or journal.

Because he was isolated in a way he had not been in New York or Paris, Legman depended heavily upon letter writing to keep him updated on folklore and bibliographic matters. In his letters, he did not discuss theoretical issues in folklore with his correspondents, although folklore study was experiencing a theory boom.[35] His own ideas were worked out and the structure of his books arranged. The thing was to get them exactly the way he wanted them—and into print. Larded with precise bibliographic detail, Gershon's letters endure as vastly entertaining writing: wordy, vigorous, sometimes sarcastic, and at other times warm. Arguably, they rival his library and his manuscripts as his main work product.

His correspondence was critical for his research. Travel was almost impossible now that he had Judith, and soon a family, to support. His digging had to be done in his library and through long-distance item swaps across a web of scholarly connections. How elaborate his research network became is shown by his correspondents file, housed in a tall, wooden cabinet holding thousands of cards.[36] On these he recorded the names, addresses, and pertinent facts about thousands of friends and acquaintances, going back at least to the 1940s. There are anthropologists, nuclear physicists, magicians, origami practitioners, folk song collectors, housewives, sex researchers, and semioticians. There is a card for Paul Krassner and a card for L.L. Bean, his favorite supplier of canvas trousers. There are girlfriends, spouses, and alleged spouses, along with some alleged children. Circumstances of meeting or anything remarkable were often noted in a personal mnemonic he was developing for use in his memoirs. For example, he met Alan Lomax and admired his wife:

Lomax, Alan Columbia University.
Met future Mrs. Lomax (Italian!)
And followed! his high yaller sec'y! 1962.[37]

This notation indicates that he met the musicologist and broadcaster Alan Lomax along with the future Mrs. Lomax in 1962 and that perhaps Legman had pursued Lomax's attractive African American secretary through the streets.

Topics of shared interest, such as "BALLADS," "PF" for paper folding, "Limerick nut," and notes of gifts ("sent phonograph records") are carefully recorded.

On the cards of people he felt close to or thought fascinating, he often commented on their sexual predilections or jotted remarks they had made about sex that he found witty or stupid. He diagnosed: "masochist!" "Sicko," "closet case." Years later, he marked deaths with the year and a Star of David or a small Christian cross. Some entries are crossed out and marked "FBI stooge."

For all the happiness of his new life with Judith, there was also a sense of time passing. In 1966 Clellon Holmes sent a draft of his *Evergreen Review* profile. Holmes thought that the once uncomprehending world now seemed to have "grown up" to Legman's ideas, until anticensorship had become a kind of common sense.[38] But it was weird to be an object of retrospection. And the folklore old-boys network was falling away, too, being replaced by a group of younger scholars who were excited by Legman's daring. But there was also a critique of library research, the textual tracing that Legman admired. Judith was inspired to embroider a turquoise velvet banner, with lettering in gold and red thread, to hang above Gershon's desk. It read, "The Text is the Thing," the quote from Harvard ballad scholar G. L. Kittredge that Legman took up in defiance of the new ethnographic emphasis in the study of folklore.[39]

Judith and Gershon began to think about children right away. They had agreed she would come to live with him and make his life possible again, and he would give her a family. Their first child, David, was born in the suspended time of the French general strikes of May 1968. Judith recalled the strange days when "the grocery stores in town were down to pots of mustard in the window and nothing else, the post office stopped functioning, the banks had closed up, there was no transportation. There was no mail in and no mail out, which was very traumatic for Gershon."[40]

David was delivered easily in hospital, and Judith was ecstatic. So began a period of intense family happiness. Gershon wrote to his friend Walter Toscanini, book collector and son of the composer, enclosing a picture of Judith and David, "who is really so big we should have named him Goliath. . . . Judy is as beautiful in her heart as the picture shows and spends all her time nursing the baby at her breast—and planning more babies—when she is not making homemade bread . . . so life is very quiet and beautiful here. . . . It is like a miracle, at a moment when I felt my life was going down the drain."[41] A second child, Rafael Amadeus, was born in January of 1971 and the third, a daughter, in June 1973. So now there were three children at La Clé and one in Amsterdam.

The years of child rearing were a challenge. At one point, Judith was caring for three children under six years. When Rafael was born, she says, "Gershon decided that handwashing the laundry of two babies really was an awful lot to ask," so he had electricity put in, and Judith's father gave her a washing machine, a dryer, and an electric refrigerator.[42]

Judith Legman with her children at La Clé des Champs, 1973. Courtesy of the Legman Archive.

Money was a serious concern. In the 1960s, their taxes were not high, and there were only a few bills. They were living outside the boss's system, and that was a point of pride. But in general, the Legman household could not count on royalties for Gershon's work. He wrote appreciations, scholarly articles, and introductions to folklore books, and these were usually unpaid. Occasionally, he ghostwrote medical articles.[43]

He worked extensively on Patrick Kearney's book on the British Museum's Private Case and arranged for it to be published by Jay Landesman, but according to Judith, there was no payment for Gershon. It was worse than annoying when in the 1980s Landesman published *The Compleat Neurotica*, a reproduction reprint, with no payment to Legman, who owned the rights to the magazine. With no money for lawyers, American contracts were unenforceable.[44]

The issue of money was always treated as secondary, and Judith emphasized that "Gershon was somebody who couldn't be bothered spending his time on making money. He had to have some, and he did only what was essential to make sure there wasn't a big problem. Otherwise he did his Work with a capital 'W'." Judith viewed the book that brought in cash as perhaps his least important—*The Limerick,* which "he did not even entirely write" but rather anthologized. In her words, "Enough of them were sold by people who agreed that they owed us something" that they were able to get along "without any grave worries most of the time." She thought *The Limerick* was the least significant in a scholarly sense, "but it was the most useful" to the family. They scrimped every possible way, typing on onionskin paper and weighing letters carefully to save postage. In Judith's view, "It would be hard to say there was nothing superfluous, but we were very careful."[45]

VISITORS

The Limerick and *The Horn Book* brought a number of scholarly visitors in the early 1960s. Wayland Hand visited when Beverley was still alive and took the author's portrait for *The Horn Book.* When visitors made the detour from Paris or Marseille to visit, many camped in the grove, the olives crunching under foot. Utah folklorists Austin and Alta Fife came, as did folklorist and filmmaker Bill Ferris. Canadian folk song scholar Edith Fowke came over while in Nice. It was a bit easier for people from England: Hamish Henderson came to camp (although his wife, Kaetzel, was too heavily pregnant to join him), as did Ewan MacColl with Peggy Seeger and their sons. Peggy remembered feeling she had entered "an entirely different world." Jay and Peaches Landesman came from London for a *dejeuner sur l'herbe*: Peaches took off all her clothes to sunbathe in the meadow, and Legman planted a daisy between her buttocks.[46]

The publication of the *Rationale of the Dirty Joke* in 1968 and *No Laughing Matter* in 1975 brought attention from the American media. Legman's family remembers that when someone made the trek to do a press interview, they were treated coolly. Gershon always suspected that these were not journalists but CIA or FBI agents justifying their plum assignment on the Côte d'Azur.[47]

Articles in mass-circulation magazines helped keep Legman's writerly reputation alive and his books selling in countercultural circles. But the Legmans did not always like the write-ups. The one in the *Village Voice* by Helen Dudar was friendly. But Jon Vinocur, a stringer for *Oui,* insulted Legman's belly, his worn-out T-shirt, and his tendency to hold forth on his opinions. Still, a journalist from *Time* praised Legman's work "in all its pocked dignity, authenticity and embattled romanticism," which pleased him.[48]

Not everyone wanted to visit. Patrick Kearney, the bibliographer who worked on *The Private Case,* could discern his difficult personality. *The Horn Book* inspired Kearney, and Legman helped him enormously, answering endless questions and helping arrange a contract with Landesman as publisher.

The Key to the Fields

189

But Kearney never met Legman. He knew a get-together would be a bad idea, and he preferred to limit the relationship to the mails.[49] Similarly, many of Legman's American colleagues and admirers never met him.

Visiting friends and relatives were sometimes delighted by La Clé des Champs, sometimes taken aback and confused. Martha Cornog thought it was wonderful. When she was in high school near Philadelphia, Martha had corresponded briefly with Legman about origami. They were in touch again when she was in college and read *The Horn Book* and the 1962 *Journal of American Folklore* symposium on obscenity in folklore. In 1967 she and her husband took a postwedding trip to Europe and arranged to visit. The place was hard to find: Martha remembered an almost endless bus trip on winding roads. Judith impressed her as "serene and lovely," and Martha thought she had done a beautiful job setting up the goat barn for housekeeping. Gershon she found "large, and avuncular and penetrating and genial." She and Gershon got right into talking origami and had a fine time.[50]

Martha thought La Clé was lovely. When she asked to use the bathroom, Gershon waved his hand to the woods and said, "*C'est la!*" "Although," she remembered, "as it turned out, the serious bathroom facilities were a blue crock. . . . And it was wonderful. . . . [T]here was a little row of trees where you could sit, and birds chirping."[51]

But at some point, Gershon, who never hesitated to assess people's romantic choices, told Martha that he disapproved of her husband and that she should divorce him. "He thought I had married beneath me," Martha said. "And in fact, we divorced three years later." Her letter-writing friendship with Legman eventually foundered because, according to Martha, "his pronatalist attitude really started getting in my way. He wasn't really prescriptive, but he thought marriage and motherhood were enormously fulfilling for women, and he couldn't see why anyone wouldn't take the opportunity."[52]

Legman could be a difficult host, especially for those who wanted to draw near. When his sister Daisy Birnbaum came for a visit, they got into a shouting fight, and Daisy left almost as soon as she had arrived. No other American relative ever visited, perhaps because the family pain persisted down the years. Gershon underscored this by refusing to answer Emil's final letter to him.[53]

In 1974 Ariëla Legman came from Amsterdam to meet her father and his young family for the first time. From her point of view, the visit was hardly planned. In fact, her mother had almost never spoken of Gershon, and "it's quite a story how she managed to keep her mouth shut" for all those years. Her family was vacationing a few hours away when her mother put her on a bus to Grasse.[54]

Ariëla remembered a bewildering meeting. She had been told Gershon would be waiting for her at the bus stop. But she did not know whom to look for. She had never knowingly seen a picture of him. There were more people waiting at the bus stop for other bus passengers, so she decided to get out last. She remembers "there was one man already looking at me from outside the bus. But that could not be him, I thought, too old, too fat." But there seemed to be no doubt that he was waiting for her. Later, he showed her a portrait of himself as a fifteen-year-old and told her, "You see, that was who I saw through the bus window."[55] He bought her an ice cream and folded her an origami bird from the wrapper.

Her next memory is of walking from Valbonne, along little goat paths, to La Clé des Champs. Gershon showed her how to stamp on a thistle with one foot and uproot it with the other. He told her that way he destroyed the evil in the world. They were met by the boys, three and five years old, who were waiting impatiently for them at the boundary of the farm. Unlike Ariëla, they had been anticipating the meeting for months in advance.[56]

Ariëla was shocked by how uncomfortable it was. Away from the sea, it was brutally hot and dry. The family spent most of the day inside out of the sun, Gershon in the studio and Judith and the children in the barn—with its thick walls and few windows. She noted the house's rudimentary arrangement, a sink and stove, a table, a twin bed, and a crib for the baby. The two boys slept in a half room attached.[57]

Ariëla stayed in the room above, "which could only be reached by going outside and climbing the stairs carved in the rock around the barn. There was no bathroom, no shower, no toilet."[58] As an urban girl, she found the rural isolation and her new family intimidating. She was especially frightened by the dark rural night and its strange noises.

But during the day, she was just as scared. She remembered, "From very early in the morning on the boys would wait outside my bedroom door and as soon as I moved in bed they would bounce at it. And as I opened the door, they jumped on me and would follow me everywhere." Unless Judith locked them in, she had "not a minute of privacy."[59]

Gershon would leave at the crack of dawn for his studio, and he would stay there for most of the day. Unlike Judith and the kids, Ariëla was invited to spend many hours there. Her father seemed anxious to explain himself. He talked endlessly. Ariëla remembers, "I learned most of what I know about my mother and him during that summer. And he talked a lot about himself, about his ideas about the world. What it was like, and what it SHOULD be like." Sometimes the little boys were literally howling outside the door, demanding to be let in or to persuade them to come over to the house for lunch or dinner.[60]

Ariëla absorbed a lot that summer, but she recalls she also had to "say no to many things: food, attention, too much information." Her defense against

Gershon's continuous *apologia pro vita sua* was to fall asleep on the studio couch, accompanied by Mozart's clarinet concerto in A major.[61]

After a few days she was very homesick, which was confusing because she had always wanted to meet her father, and now she wanted to leave. "So back we went," she remembers, "Gershon and me, leaving everybody else in tears because he had very nastily told them they could not come to the bus stop." They traced the same paths downhill to Valbonne and took the bus to Grasse where they had met a few days earlier.[62]

But a letter followed Ariëla back to her mother. In her words, "It was all about how much he already loved me, and Judith and the children [loved me] too. And how we had to get to know each other better. 'Now, not later.'" Gershon sent several more letters, insisting she return as soon as possible. And then he telephoned. Ariëla went back to Valbonne three more times that summer. She was able to visit him just once more after that, in 1979.[63]

A few years later, in 1976, Bruce Jackson and his wife, Diane Christian, stopped on their way from Paris to Rome. Jackson was a folklorist who had corresponded with Legman about his work on African American toasts.[64] He and Christian were professors at the State University of New York (SUNY) at Buffalo, and together they made documentary films focusing on prison life and the death penalty. Jackson remembered that, like everyone else, he and Christian had trouble finding the place "in the back-woods boondocks of the South of France." They were taken aback by the distance between the image of La Clé des Champs that Legman implied in letters and its reality. As Bruce remembered, "Because of Legman's baroque prose, we expected some baroque barn. . . . And we get there and it's this real ugly barn . . . just flat out, uninspiring ugly. It wasn't even so decrepit as to be interesting for its decrepitude." Bruce said he was stunned, "because I had heard for years that Legman was living in this abandoned Knights Templar place." Legman sometimes styled himself "the Count of Valbonne," so Jackson expected a tower and perhaps a staircase. But the bathroom was still the bucket in the woods, and the little house was crowded. The bedroom had niches in the wall. Bruce "couldn't tell if they were niches to put clothes in or put children in. And there was a kitchen. And that was it."[65]

Legman separated Diane and Bruce, saying the women would want to have "girl talk." (Bruce objected that with a Ph.D. from Johns Hopkins, Diane "doesn't do girl-talk!" but Legman brushed him off.) The men went back to the studio, "and *it* had a bathroom. And a grand piano. And phonograph records." Bruce wondered where Legman got the money for all the books. The studio was off-limits to the children, and Bruce and Diane thought Judith was paying a price for Gershon's work. As Bruce recalled, "Mostly what we talked about that day was his health . . . and how hard it was getting by. I

192   CHAPTER 8

asked him how he lived, and he told me he did ghostwriting for doctors. He was very vague about it."[66]

In the kitchen, Diane was surprised that Gershon and Judith were speaking French to the children, although neither was a native speaker. She chatted in English with Judith and told six-year-old David, "You should try it!" When he fiercely forbade Diane to speak English, she told him, "But it's your mother tongue. You would get it in a moment." David threatened to bite her, and Diane offered to bite him back. "He said, 'Stop it!' and he came over and he bit me!" And to her surprise, she bit him back. When the men returned from the studio, David was in tears and the women were sitting in stony silence. After an explanation and an explosion, everyone became friends. Later, Diane sent English-language children's books.[67]

Jackson took excellent photographs during the visit. For Legman, "The picture of Judith and the kids is just the masterpiece I've been waiting to see of them for years. . . . And also that of Diane arm-wrestling me." He approved of one of himself walking in front of the studio. He was shocked to see himself as a portly, elderly figure, but "I look like what I look like."[68]

Not long after this, Bruce Jackson wrote "The King of X700," an appreciative and expansive profile for a Legman festschrift in Reinhold Aman's new journal, *Maledicta: The International Journal of Verbal Aggression*. It featured photographs of Gershon working in his studio and walking under the oaks. Jackson appropriately grouped Legman with the admired independent folklorists Vance Randolph and Benjamin Botkin, and he called out the academic establishment for ignoring Legman's contributions. On erotic folklore, he argued, "No one knows as much about this stuff as Legman." If he had simply published his collections innocent of analysis, he would be renowned as one of the greats. He described the Legmans' circumstances and pointed out that the scholar lived off no grants, no salary, no tenured position.[69] Later, Gershon would thank Bruce: "I guess everyone should get a festschrift for their 60th!" He groused that Bruce's article shamed him into having indoor plumbing installed in the main house.[70]

If short-term visitors were sometimes perplexed by life at La Clé, so too were the Legman children. David, the eldest son, remembers a difficult childhood and a confounding father.[71] As with Gershon's parents, David's mother and father were foreigners and very different; they were attached neither to France nor to America. The little boys did not at first attend *école maternelle* (preschool) or elementary school. Judith and Gershon disapproved of the authoritarianism and nationalism of the French schools, but after a while they found homeschooling impossibly hard. As Diane Christian had noticed, they aimed to raise the children with French as their first language and spoke only French to them, although neither parent was a native speaker. Eventually, they decided reluctantly that the children would be better off in the local schools.[72]

The children quite naturally needed to be out and about, exploring and making themselves part of the world of Valbonne. Although Gershon doted on his children intensely when they were small, Judith remembered that "as soon as they began to have their own ideas about things," relations with their father became worse than strained.[73] Gershon reproduced the troubles he had had with his own father: he could be overbearing, nasty, and unrelenting, especially when the children put up resistance. Perhaps the separateness Ariëla observed in Gershon was also a protective distancing. The little boys were noisy and rambunctious: they wanted to be around their father, but their father found himself most comfortable immersed in his work.

From about 1975, when he was seven or eight years old, David remembers his father writing intensely. (He had finished *No Laughing Matter* and was now at work again on "The Ballad" and on Vance Randolph's "Unprintable Songs of the Ozarks" manuscript, to which he'd recently acquired the rights.) More clearly, from about 1980, David has memories of Gershon keeping himself busy with letters and locking himself in, spending days writing. "This of course, was a lifelong pattern: 'working' was a big word with him," David said. "He'd walk 200 yards to the other house, where he'd brood." David felt that Gershon didn't really know how to be a father, and so he withdrew into his work and "walled himself off from the world." When he was not writing, he kept himself busy with the house, managing building renovations to make the *cabanon* more livable.[74] But perhaps he was also trying to avoid the resurfacing of traits he'd developed under Emil—the rage at any opposition and the granite certainty that he was right.

When David was a bit older, Gershon tried to interest him in his intellectual projects, especially in questions of censorship and suppression, but David could not see what all the fuss was about. Perhaps Clellon Holmes was right and the world had fully grown up to Legman's ideas. Or maybe a less prudish upbringing made it hard for David to feel the urgency of the question. He thought the important censorship battles were over, and his father was obsessed with something that was no longer pressing or important. He remembers Gershon receiving and opening boxes from Breaking Point, taking out and holding a book with a yellow and brown cover: *No Laughing Matter: Rationale of the Dirty Joke, Second Series*.[75] To David, it seemed like a communication from another planet. Gershon did not see it this way. Even after forty years, his absorption in the problems of sexual repression, folklore, and censorship remained intense.

9

THE HELL DRAWER

... as often in tears as in laughter.

—G. Legman, *Rationale of the Dirty Joke: An Analysis of Sexual Humor*

Of the big projects that occupied Legman throughout the late 1950s and early 1960s, the most central was the two-volume *Rationale of the Dirty Joke.*[1] His studies of jokes were conceived before his move to France and first tried in the article Legman had published in the "castration issue" of *Neurotica* in 1952.[2] The publication of *Rationale (Series I)* in 1968 and *No Laughing Matter (Series II)* in 1975 would reintroduce Legman to an intrigued reading public and to skeptical folklorists. His best-known books opened sexual humor as a field of study and brought him popular attention as well as scholarly criticism, some of it harsh.

From the beginning, Legman thought of his joke studies as part of the *Hautes Études* series he had begun with *The Limerick* and "The Ballad" and was modeling on Friedrich Krauss's *Kryptadia* and *Anthropophyteia* collections. He was proud of *The Limerick*'s design, and he envisioned the joke volumes as similarly beautiful books. He hoped they would further establish his mastery of folk erotica and perhaps even bring in some money.

His joke collection was the result of decades of research begun as early as 1925–26, when he and his sister Ruth started their shoe-box collection of magazine and newspaper clippings. Some of the jokes in *Rationale* are cited as collected during this period. About this time, Gershon was writing down and memorizing jokes he heard from other people—his mother, his father, his sisters, friends, and strangers, in an ever-widening circle. A famous joke registers marital unhappiness: "A man goes to the village rabbi and says he wants to divorce his wife 'because she has such filthy habits.' 'What are these habits?' the rabbi asks. "Oh, I can't tell you,' says the man, 'it's too filthy to describe.' The rabbi refuses under those circumstances, to grant him the divorce. 'Well, if I must,' says the man, 'I'll tell you. Every time I go to piss in the sink, it's always full of dirty dishes."[3]

In 1936, upon his move to New York, he expanded from men's magazines and cheap dirty joke books (available from under drugstore counters and in bookstore bins) to systematic searches for rare published books of uncensored humor. At the New York Public Library, Legman began to trace contemporary jokes back through time into an older literature of humor. Over years of research, Legman worked through nineteenth-century Americana, to eighteenth- and seventeenth-century English literature and jest books, and then into earlier French and Italian jest collections. Here his bibliographic skills served him well, and he seems to have begun compiling his joke-book bibliographies at this time.

He was also always working on the present. Most obscene contemporary material had to be collected face-to-face, so he wrote down jokes he overheard on trains and buses, in the burlesque theaters, and in the print shops and binderies. The boxes of slips of paper grew until eventually he had amassed more than thirty thousand separate cards.[4]

He also followed the older method of the folklorist as literary historian. As with ballads and limericks, Legman pulled texts from manuscripts in archives and traded them with other joke-obsessed collectors. He wrote to editors, scholars, and college teachers, asking them for their hell drawers, their files of unpublishable materials.

One significant correspondent was E. Haldeman-Julius, publisher of the popular Little Blue Books. Legman was struck by a description in Haldeman-Julius's autobiography. The publisher wrote, "The bottom left-hand drawer of the main desk I call my Hell Box. In it I throw all unprintable obscenities that come from readers—off-color jokes, wicked gags, lascivious novelties, erotic poems, and anything else that's amusing but unmailable. That long, deep drawer is almost jammed. . . . It's an odd collection, and downright unfortunate that the Good People won't allow it to be circulated legally." Haldeman-Julius thought a lot of cleverness was going to waste and that his hell drawer would appeal to "Mark Twain, Jonathan Swift, Voltaire," and many other "lost and damned souls."[5] He wondered what would become of it when he was gone.

Legman wrote to Haldeman-Julius to say he was very interested in the contents of the desk drawer. He could use the whole thing, "having already classified and analyzed several thousand pieces of similar folklore, novelties, &c." This was no gag, "but serious interpretation. . . . Won't you help?"[6]

Haldeman-Julius sent "a few to start you off," including a folk gag, a "Peter Meter." He also published a call in his newspaper, the *American Freeman*, alerting "students of folklore" to Legman's project. He quoted "G. Legman Keith, of New York" to his readers: "I wish it were possible to get some of the accumulations of this stuff respectably published . . . so that you could see what a really good cause you've contributed to. But everybody goes into deep shock at the idea of sober print for it. The horrified rejections from the learned journals alone would make an appendix. As a joke, sure—as science, hell no!"[7]

Haldeman-Julius reproduced some of Legman's long folk erotica wish list. "Readers who have unexpurgated versions of any of the poems listed below (and items not listed) are asked to send me copies." For example, "The One-Eyed Riley (As I was strolling round and round) . . . Mary Ann McCarthy (she went out to gather clams)" and more than forty-six other rhymes. He concluded, "Any help you give will be a contribution to education, literature, poetry, science, learning and culture in general." Amateur erotologists should join in the "really good cause."[8] The publication of this exchange brought Legman interested, eccentric, and far-flung correspondents.

In his proposal to Haldeman-Julius (who later refused to publish *Love & Death*), Legman laid out the basic outline of his *Hautes Études* and *Rationale*. His examination of real but unapproachable material would be serious and scientific, classifying erotic stories and jokes as folktales according to the international system of indexing, Aarne and Thompson's *Types of the Folktale*.[9]

Legman's opportunistic method of joke collecting may seem haphazard today, but viewed as a kind of folk historical documentation, it was innovative. His net was wide, and he never missed an opportunity to scoop up materials from any source, especially from print and the files of his enthusiastic correspondents. An Oregon folklorist named Kenneth Larson was one example. He and Legman swapped "barn yard tales" manuscripts. The eminent Vance Randolph, who ghostwrote "Little Blue Books" for Haldeman-Julius, was another.[10]

Legman viewed joke texts as items to be gathered, and he collected jokes as he found them. Judith recalls that Gershon often carried bits of origami paper in his pockets and used paper folding to strike up conversations with strangers, then used the opportunity to exchange jovial stories. He wrote down the jokes in summary form, quoting the punch line exactly, but not trying to document the interaction of the tellers and audience. Nor did he treat joke telling as a performance, as folklorists' standards would later demand.[11] He simply jotted down an outline, a place, and an identity, to be fleshed out and written up later.

Legman saw jokes as part of "the general float," a phrase he found useful for describing oral tradition as it lived. He did not focus tightly on specific joke topics or areas, and it was useful that he did not. Legman gathered mainly English-language materials (and rarely jokes in Hungarian and Yiddish), because like other scholars studying jokes, he saw American humor as a broad current with an English-language core.[12] His twenty-year residence in New York was a superb advantage. Not only was the city densely populated by people from all over the world, but it was also the national center of the entertainment industries and, just as important, the printing and publishing industries. Manhattan was full of playwrights, vaudeville joke men, burlesque operators, and rewrite men, and its clubs were fostering the beginnings of stand-up comedy. Everyone was there, from old-fashioned ethnic vaudeville performers to the Borscht Belt comedians to the young Lenny Bruce.[13] The men who worked in publishing and printing turned out cheap and not-so-cheap semi-erotica, much of it humorous. Just time spent near these characters, most of them now forgotten, was an important source for Legman's joke collections.[14]

A covertly published obscene joke book called *Anecdota Americana* particularly interested Legman during his New York years.[15] It was a privately printed collection of jokes to enliven men's gatherings, on the model of earlier pocket books. It provided a kind of amenable currency for stag parties and smokers. Because *Anecdota* was obscene, it went through numerous publications and was given false locations and several pseudonymous editors; it was copied and appeared in cleaned-up versions. Legman considered the first edition the least censored, but the first and second editions—brought out together circa 1929–32—were an excellent record of the general float of folk stories in the interwar United States (although some more stilted productions, clearly written for publication, were mixed in). He drew heavily on the *Anecdota* for his *Rationale*.

Anecdota Americana I and *II* were written and compiled for men in impolite settings, thus their under-the-counter appeal. Although they seem mild today, most of the jokes would have been considered insulting if told in front of middle-class women. As Legman points out repeatedly, taken as a mass the jokes sound and feel antiwoman, antiwife, and antimarriage. At the same time, they are prosex, presenting a freewheeling, unrestrained male heterosexuality. The *Anecdota* jokes are also frankly antiblack, anti-Semitic, anti-Chinese, and anti-immigrant, full of racist stereotypes that circulated in the 1920s and still do today. The jokes deliver the perspective of the dominant culture; unlike some other folklorists' collections (for example, Zora Neale Hurston's), there are no jokes in the *Anecdota* that seem to come from black or Jewish oral tradition or that aim at white society.[16] If listening to a joke

198 CHAPTER 9

implies acceptance of its little story and agreement with its premise, then a white male audience with conventional prejudices is implied for the jokes.

Legman's *Rationale* organized an unruly range of material. He began with a basic question: What is the joke? How does one understand this omnipresent, powerful, popular, trivial, and shape-shifting form of talk? Certainly, he was not the first person to ask this challenging question, but he plumbed it deeply. He drew on three scholarly traditions in his theorizing, and out of them he invented his own stance.

Bibliography and folktale scholarship were the first two pillars. Legman knew—although it was not widely argued—that the joke is a short oral story (as opposed to a quip) and has a long oral-literary history. Jokes and jest books were among the first items to appear in print in Europe, collated from the notes and private manuscripts of early Renaissance joke collectors.[17] Legman dedicated *Rationale* to "The *Manes* [the spirit or shade] of Poggio," the first European to publish a joke book, his *Facetiae*.[18] Clearly, Legman wanted the *Rationale* to sit on the shelves with the works of the great medieval and Renaissance storytellers.

His knowledge of joke-book publishing history would be on display in *Rationale*. However, he knew that these humorous stories, and even some of the jokes he collected, had a history that reached back before printing, and perhaps before the Common Era. Folklorists had been trying to document the chains of connection between global, Pan-Eurasian oral stories and national linguistic traditions for most of the twentieth century. Their major tool was Antti Aarne's *Verzeichnis der Märchentypen* (*Types of the Folktale*), a classification system for European folktales published in 1910. Aarne's index was later translated, expanded, and revised by Stith Thompson of Indiana University, and it became known as the "Aarne-Thompson Tale Type Index."[19] Aarne and Thompson attempted to give each major tale plot or pattern a name and number. In theory, this allowed folktale scholars to compare them and identify familial relations between stories across languages, cultures, and centuries. Tales were grouped under broad conceptual headings such as "Animal Tales" and then subindexed by variations in plot structure.

Although Aarne, Thompson, and other Scandinavian-influenced folklorists showed that something called the folktale is a world oral literature, the results are more partial than they had hoped.[20] As many scholars have pointed out, there were serious problems with the Aarne-Thompson index. When Legman was working on *Rationale*, the index was beginning to come under withering criticism, not least from Alan Dundes. One point of critique was that the index could not always distinguish a story's structure (type) from its surface features (motifs). And an index had little to say about meaning. By the 1960s, the grand historical indexing project seemed to fall short of the goal of uncovering a unified history of the storytelling imagination.[21]

From early on, the Aarne-Thompson index was compellingly important to Legman as he developed his mode of analysis. There were two reasons. Aarne and Thompson had included jests, making it clear that the facetious story was a folktale with a long history. Not all folktales were funny, but all the old funny stories of tricksters, fools, and surprising reversals were part of the folktale corpus and could be shown to have family relationships to it. Thus, Legman came to see, the much shorter American jokes in his files also had a long history. Just as provocative to him, the magisterial index was almost entirely censored. Where Aarne and Thompson could not excise an erotic or bodily detail, they had changed or bowdlerized it. For tales that were centered upon sex or bodily excreta, they simply made a blank category they called X700 and implied they planned to fill it in later. Legman came to believe that the empty X700 category probably represented the largest part of the index, and its existence signified that many folktales had been discarded or never recorded. As with his dictionary and ballad projects, he aspired to find all the excised material, put it back in, and show the folktale in its full humanity.[22]

Despite its limitations, the index was a useful tool for Legman. Even censored, it was full of bibliographic trails. The index helped Legman connect medieval and Renaissance jests directly to the *Anecdota Americana*, *Immortalia*, and other modern joke books, supplying analogues and dates for his own and others' "orally collected" materials. He could thus verify the jokes' continuity, a much-desired finding for midcentury folklorists, and give many American jokes and their "joke ideas" a lengthy oral pedigree. Perhaps such a history could even improve the joke's lowly social standing.

Legman formed the third pillar of his *Rationale* from the writings of Sigmund Freud. He claimed to have begun reading Freud in the late 1930s, starting with "The Moses of Michelangelo" (1914), an experiment in analyzing the sculptural *Moses*.[23] Legman went on to read everything he could find on psychoanalytic theory, including the early work of Wilhelm Reich on the connections between sexual repression and authoritarianism.[24] Legman was most interested in the Freud who emphasized the turmoil of childhood. Freud theorized that erotic conflicts emerging during infancy and early childhood were foundational processes in the formation of children's hearts and minds, and Legman, who had had such excruciating early years, found this compelling. Freud's shocking assertion of the importance of infantile sexuality resonated with Legman's memories of his precocious fascination with sex.[25]

And there was another dimension of Freud that appealed to Legman. Although the founder of psychoanalysis was no political activist, he argued that there were much broader implications in the child's struggles. Psychoanalysis in its central European beginnings was a political critique with links to socialist youth movements, and in his early writings Freud advocated for the sexual enlightenment and social liberation of youth.[26] As he expressed it in *Civilization and Its Discontents*, Freud thought the world was too harsh in its demands that human beings repress and renounce some of their passions to access society's benefits.[27] Legman agreed intuitively and intellectually that too many people were forced to give up too much simply to be human and that an easing of sexual restraints would make people healthier. Like Freud, he thought civilization must be reshaped if humanity were to survive the twentieth century. And following Freud, Legman wanted to proceed interpretively, placing the theory of eroticism and its repression at the center of an adventurous exploration of culture that would extend in many directions.

Legman knew from reading the work of Friedrich Krauss that Freud was also interested in folklore. Folktales, folk songs and epics, and fairy tales occasionally came up for discussion in Freud's Vienna salon, introduced by Krauss and others. In 1910 Freud had written encouragingly to Krauss about the importance of his folklore collecting, endorsing the *Kryptadia* and *Anthropophyteia* yearbooks.[28]

Krauss had asked Freud to discuss the scientific value for psychoanalysis of "collections of erotic jokes, witticisms, funny stories." Freud underlined that the material "from the standpoint of a psychologist . . . is not only useful but indispensable." He added, "The erotic quips and comic anecdotes that you have collected and published . . . have only been produced and repeated because they gave pleasure to both their narrators and their hearers. It is not difficult to guess which components of the sexual instinct (compounded as it is from so many elements) find satisfaction in this manner. These tales give us direct information as to which of the component instincts of sexuality are retained in a given group of people as particularly pleasurable." Freud saw that in this way, jokes and tales "give the neatest confirmation of the findings reached by the psychoanalytic examination of neurotics."[29]

Freud pointed to his theory that infants progress through a developmental process in which instincts emerge and are mastered. But for cultural reasons—patterns of child rearing, mainly—some "elements" of instincts are retained from infancy, to give pleasure in adulthood. For example, Freud wrote to Krauss that the scatological materials in *Anthropophyteia* that dealt with the anus, excrement, and anal activities were direct evidence that humans universally passed through a stage of anal eroticism and "dwell with pleasure upon this part of the body, its performances and indeed the product of its function."[30] Some people (and not just the disturbed) continued to eroticize this region, if only through talking and joking about it. That this material keeps coming up, as it were, and that collectors innocent of psychoanalytic thought kept reporting it, was evidence in itself for the validity of Freud's developmental schema.

On erotic jokes dealing with "adult" sexuality, Freud wrote to Krauss, "I have shown . . . that the revelation of what is normally the repressed unconscious element in the mind can . . . become a source of pleasure and thus a technique for the construction of jokes. In psycho-analysis to-day we describe a congeries of ideas and its associated affect as a 'complex.'" He continued, "Many of the most admired jokes are 'complexive jokes' and . . . they owe their exhilarating and cheerful effect to the ingenious uncovering of what are as a rule repressed complexes."[31]

For Freud, the fact that "complexive" jokes are in circulation and enjoyed is a source of evidence (although "auxiliary") for "investigating the unconscious human mind." Dreams, myths, and legends provide similar evidence. In closing, Freud wrote that it was "safe to hope" that folklore and psychoanalysis might "soon become more intimate" in the study of the unconscious.[32]

Here in basic form, Freud laid out his perspective on expressive culture and imaginative materials.[33] They were a product of human civilizations and of the civilizing process in interaction with children's development. Jokes and tales were invented and persisted in oral tradition because they spoke to resistances and conflicts—or perhaps unhappiness—in the processes of achieving adulthood. The things people found funny or absorbing were sources of enjoyment, in part, because they represented problems and pleasures that could not be fully transcended. Here Freud advanced a theory of folklore: jokes are not meaningless detritus or cultural trivia. Rather, they persist because they satisfy both tellers *and* listeners. The exchange of jokes is a sociable form of engagement that connects (not always pleasantly) to deep human issues.

As Legman began to focus on the jokes, he realized that he could make a major breakthrough by connecting Freud's insights to the joke's history. He would revise the Aarne-Thompson index of the world's oral traditions by adding back in all the erotic materials that had been suppressed and could reveal so much. He would improve the international study of the tale by reindexing the jokes not by plot or "type," but by the unconscious ideas with which they dealt. Thus, following Freud and Krauss, he would be writing a history of a folk mind as it expressed itself in oral tradition and especially as it expressed itself about the body. The project was wildly ambitious, and he wrote that he knew it was a lifetime's work.[34]

He organized the first volume around the difficulties faced by the modern Western man who progressed through sexual problems from childhood through marriage. A key issue was the child's early acquisition of sexual knowledge, especially in a repressive society. The questions the young child explores, consciously or otherwise, included the following: What are genitals? What is defecation? What is the opposite sex? What do adults do when they have sex? What is marriage? He approved of psychoanalyst Martha Wolfenstein's argument that the child masters these problems in part through the process of learning to tell jokes.[35] As the boy grows up and the *Rationale* progresses, jokes take up problems of sexual approach, angry and violent urges, the sometimes troubled experience of sex with adult women, and the effects of repression on sex in marriage.

Legman argued that jokes approached all these questions and more and that when answers were found in humor, they were filtered by repression into strange, sometimes painful fantasies. An important piece of Freud's theory adopted by Legman was repression within the family, especially as enacted by the father. Parental constraint on sexual knowledge was a miniature of the patriarchal structure of civilization, a censorship that would be reinforced as the child grew by religions, schools, the state, and the mass media.

The problems of knowledge and maturation are linked in Legman's version of Freudian theory to action. Like Freud, Legman presents dirty (or "tendentious") jokes as ways of acting upon others, and he argued that jokes about sex served purposes beyond talk about bodily functions. The teller of the joke is like a child with his bundle of desires and uncivilized impulses, and the joke disguises urges that are totally unacceptable to express. As the young child grabs breasts, plays with feces, and screams, so the joke teller misbehaves and dirties others. Infantile behaviors, Legman thought, are preserved or reworked in jokes—for example, when excrement is used in scatological jokes to abuse the hated and feared object. From Legman's point of view, most adult bawdy jokes actually express a fearful "sex hate" by men toward women, although this is also a childish fear, while dirty jokes from a woman's point of view express female anger and resentment toward men. Men fear and abuse the vagina, while women dislike or "object to" the penis. Jokes are thus symbolic assaults upon genitals. He found this to be sad evidence of the perverse state of contemporary life that makes people so frustrated and full of fear and hate. Further evidence of this was the absence of jokes dealing with tender, erotic love. It seemed to him that obscene humor never took up the most important human experience. He declared: "DIRTY JOKES ABOUT *LOVE* HAVE NOT BEEN ENCOUNTERED."[36] That satisfying emotion does not give rise to internal conflict and thus is not joked about.

Legman's adaptation of Freud's theory offered a grand claim for folklore, showing, in Alan Dundes's phrase, that folklore matters. But Freud and his followers into cultural analysis had left problems unresolved, and Legman imported these unsettled questions into his own work. Unlike the psychoanalysts who probed mythic structures and archetypes, Legman was interested in the relationship between patriarchy and psychic pain.[37] For Legman, folklore was an everyday expression of the conflicts of civilization, not the unities of culture. When Freud referred to "a people's" tastes or traditions, he followed the nineteenth-century romantics who argued for a popular cultural unity based in history and geography. Legman was more interested in how a shared folk way of understanding sex was expressed in people's verbal interactions.[38]

As he applied Freud to folklore, Legman had to confront or finesse theoretical difficulties. If, as Freud argued, the existence of folklore was evidence of psychic structures, this raised all kinds of new questions. Legman's reading of Freud assumed there was a basic set of primal difficulties that every little boy had to master, resulting in unfinished business (complexes) and their expression in stories and jokes. But were the tasks unchanging, or did they vary by social class and culture? The nature of the tie between individual troubles and large social structures remained unclear, and so to later critics Freudian interpretation could seem deterministic, as if it mandated how unacknowledged motives must be identified and named. These problems perplexed careful students of culture, who were right to hesitate.[39]

Such ambiguities of theory did not trouble Legman as he worked out his interpretations of jokes. He was never afraid to be wrong about large questions, and he did not think spending time on such complexities was as important as denouncing the dangerous repressions of the modern world. This may have been a mistake for the later reception of the *Rationale*. Freud died in 1939, and his more radical European followers were dispersed by the war; in the United States, they were silenced by the Cold War.[40] His American interpreters were vigorously revising the critique of civilization to fit an individualistic, consumerist American context.[41] In the United States, simplified neo-Freudian ideas were becoming part of intellectual discourse in the 1940s and 1950s, to the point that complex ideas like "Oedipal complex" and "penis envy" seemed to need no explanation.[42] While Legman was aware of the political dimension in Freud, he also partook of everyday Freudian talk. The idea of hidden motives was a favorite. In *The Psychopathology of Everyday Life*, a short, obscure book, Freud presented evidence for his theories of the unconscious determination of social interactions.[43] *Psychopathology* makes the case for "the slip," Freud's insight that we are not always aware of the motivations for our actions yet manage to reveal them anyway. The book was a favorite of Legman's, confirming his interest in disguised things and people who are not what they seem to be. And jokes certainly managed to reveal plenty of hidden things.

THE GENERAL FLOAT

Legman arranged the books into the ordinary dirty joke, featured in *Rationale*, and the extremely hostile dirty joke, in *No Laughing Matter*, dividing

CHAPTER 9

the materials into the relatively normal bawdy and the extremely perverse. In the first volume, he sorted the jokes by the problems he thought the ordinary person (mainly, the boy) encountered in his "researches" (as Freud called them) into sexuality and in his adult interactions with women. These were problems of sexual information and knowledge, then problems of approaching the opposite sex, and then problems of forming and maintaining sexual relationships. In *No Laughing Matter*, Legman approached (with dread) what he saw as truly horrible psychological predicaments and their sick-humorous presentations. By using "Rationale" in the title, Legman meant to call attention not to structure, technique, or the reasonableness of its humor. Instead, he meant to show that the joke is a part of a rationalizing process: joking is a species of work people do to "rationalize" (or make sense of or deceive themselves about) the irrationally cruel world they live in. Dirty jokes or jokes about unacceptable topics play a paradoxical role in the repressive civilizing process. The joke allows the forbidden to be looked at in disguise and to be laughed away. The dirty joke serves not to help people accept and adjust, or to make the world's horrors go away, but to disguise and displace them so they may be dealt with, but indirectly. Telling dirty jokes is, for Legman, a pleasurable-painful process of dealing with anxieties and wishes while keeping them at a distance. Laughter, he writes, can have a "shriving" or cleansing quality; it relieves both tellers and listeners of their fears. And the butt of the joke can be a scapegoat, carrying away the community's sins.

Rationale I, at nearly nine hundred pages, is impossible to summarize. As Roger Abrahams commented, it is not a book you use so much as one you read, then read around in, and return to.[44] The book has no index, which is odd, since Legman explicitly proposed that he was reworking the Aarne-Thompson folktale index.[45] But in it, Legman suggests intriguing ways of looking at jokes. He points to familiar stock characters as folk types with symbolic associations. In Legman's dirty jokes, there are husbands and wives, mothers and fathers, and children. There are authority figures: policemen, doctors, train conductors, judges, and preachers. There are outsiders: prostitutes and their customers, beggars, homeless people, and criminals. There are animals shifting their shapes and, more rarely, monsters and ghouls. The human cast also features the despised. Women fall here, of course, but also "Negroes," Jews, "Chinamen," Mexicans, Indians, Eskimos, and "Polacks." The identities of joke actors shift and change—but only superficially. Under the surface, the ensemble stays the same: the teller, the audience, the butt of the joke.

Perhaps reflecting his background in burlesque, Legman writes about the joke as if it is a sort of play unfolding on an imaginary stage or street corner. It is a small scene conjured between the teller and his audience. The characters in the joke shift positions and change roles, but they clearly circle a central figure described by the teller: the "I" is a person who is making things happen or, just as often, having things done to him. We might think that the joke teller takes on the central role in the joke, but Legman wonders if the central person might not really be the listener, who identifies as if they were in the story, witnessing or doing bizarre things. When the teller and the listener cannot allow themselves a forbidden thought, the joke sometimes introduces a role for the unconscious—an unexpected voice from offstage or behind a curtain, saying the unsayable. A joke was a complex fictional collaboration, Legman thought, between the teller, the audience, and the imaginary persons.

The question of participation and collaboration led to questions about who the tellers and listeners were. Legman knew (and sometimes acknowledged) that the joke is a complicated little genre, embedded in fleeting social interaction, and that community conventions shape subject matter, styles, and telling.[46] He often argued that the jokes of the "general float" were told and heard by white men. And, he argued, because they were "principally invented by men," jokes largely reflect male anxieties.[47] Legman sometimes wrote that he knew little about the jokes of women. Occasionally, he averred that most women did not tell many jokes. But he also admitted he knew women who were excellent tellers, and he allowed that he occasionally heard women tell jokes that could be seen as expressing a profemale, prosexual attitude.[48]

Legman thought that it was impossible that his collections from the general float of stories did not position the listener as heterosexual. He sometimes said that he knew little about the jokes of lesbians and homosexual men (although he devoted a large part of his second volume to jokes by and about gay men).[49] All this was not to say that the listener or the teller had to be a straight man, but that is the person appearing at the center of the action, and listeners are asked to identify with him. The white heterosexual male dominance in the jokes Legman presented can enact symbolic violence upon audience of the little play. Legman did not discuss racist jokes extensively, but he was aware that black Americans, for example, sometimes told jokes "on" themselves that were painful or hostile to their own community. This illustrated, perhaps, their bitter view of race relations in the United States in the 1950s–'60s. Legman knew this firsthand, he wrote, from conversations and joke-telling sessions with Richard Wright in Paris.[50] And he had heard women tell jokes that he thought were antifemale. Was all of the "general float" disparagement of nonwhites and women, no matter who was telling? He leaves this question slightly open.

If the joke is like a little play, Legman thought it was also distorted and dreamlike. Freud had thought that a joke was very close to a dream in its techniques of disguise and displacement. The forbidden "idea" in the joke has been subject to a process of compression and distortion, and it needs untangling

206   CHAPTER 9

and interpretation before it can be understood as the representation of a human problem. And, like the dream, the joke was properly interpreted with reference to what could not be talked about or enacted—the joke, too, dealt in repressed longings and desires, unexpressed fears, and impermissible angers. Most of these feelings Freud and Legman thought were normal but distorted by social and cultural pressures. For Legman, some of the ideas in the joke were absolutely twisted and fundamentally abnormal. They are less cheerful and exhilarating than grotesque and tragic.

Like the dream, the joke told a story, but it was a story that could not be looked at straightforwardly. One fundamental difference between the dream and the joke, as it concerns us here, is that the dreams Freud analyzed in his case studies were private, interior, and highly individual, and they referred to intimate systems of meaning. Freud interpreted dreams through a complex process of investigating his patients' personal histories and their systems of ideas and images, using the technique of analyzing associations. The dream is tightly connected to the individual's history and memory and often to his or her traumas. Later Freudians, including Legman, might assert "as is well known, the tree in a dream always stands for X," but this was an arbitrary position that Freud apparently did not take. It was a question whether jokes could be analyzed in the same way as individual dreams.

From the perspective of the folklorist, jokes are cultural and less private than dreams; they are interactions between people and depend on shared experience. Joke telling is a social interaction that mobilizes an oral tradition. Both a genre and a form of interactional currency, jokes are borrowed, shaped, and reshaped by each teller and listener and by many tellers and listeners. In Giselinde Kuipers's terms (following Durkheim), a joke is a "social fact." By this, Kuipers means that jokes represent a kind of social agreement about which ideas and problems can be considered, thought over, and addressed even in an indirect or distorted way.[51] In the Freudian sense Legman uses, the joke is a form of disguised wish or fear, shared in conversation. This, not incidentally, is what Legman found most troubling about hostile jokes: from his perspective, they represented a social agreement about whom and what to hate.

In the long introduction to *Rationale*, Legman famously wrote that "behind the mask of humor" society allows "infinite aggressions."[52] The joke is not only a representation of unconscious problems but is (again, following Freud on the tendentious joke) an action upon another person, sometimes a sexual approach or an assault. Legman would say the joke is a socially shared but disguised wish that is acted upon *in its telling*. Sometimes this action upon unacknowledged motivation is quite direct, as when people tell openly racist jokes and then claim to be "just joking."[53]

A few dimensions of Legman's analysis of psychological dilemmas, as expressed in *Rationale*, are worth a closer look. One is the question of knowledge—the child's coming to sexual knowledge as registered in jokes about foolishness, idiocy, and generally non compos mentis behavior by people in pursuit of sex. Legman found in his thousands of jokes a preoccupation with idiots and goofballs, people who make dunderheaded mistakes, and people who are blind because they will not see. As Stith Thompson wrote in *The Folktale*, fools have populated European folktales for as long as there is a record.[54] In the immigrant and multiethnic United States, fool jokes frequently trade in ethnic, racial, or regional stereotypes. For example, take the Yoopers, or Michiganders from the Upper Peninsula, who put fresh air in their tires for a trip to Milwaukee, or the fishermen who make a mark on the water so that they can find the fish again later, or the international female fool, the "dumb blonde."[55]

All fools share generic problems of perception and create problems for themselves based on misunderstanding. Stith Thompson listed the types of errors. There is mistaken identity: "A numbskull is convinced that the pumpkin which he is sitting upon is an ass's egg which he has hatched out." Such misunderstanding "results in inappropriate and absurd actions, like the fool who "sees his cow chewing cud and kills her because he thinks she is mimicking him." Living in a mental world of his own, the fool "may endow objects or animals with any qualities that suit his passing fancy"; for example, he "feeds meat to cabbages because he imagines they must be hungry." A fool may try to dig up a well and take it home or dig a hole "so as to have a place to throw the earth from the excavation he is making," or he may try to send a pair of boots by Western Union by leaving them hanging on the telegraph pole. The fool misunderstands "elementary natural laws" and "sows grain or salt hoping to produce more of the same. Or he sows cheese to bring forth a cow, or plants an animal's tail in order to produce young animals."[56] Of course, he misunderstands human sex and reproduction, too, although Thompson failed to discuss this.

Legman found that ignorance about sex was the subject of many of the jokes he collected. One of Legman's projects was to rescue sexual fools from historical oblivion and show the deep connections over time between them. After the sixteenth century, as late Renaissance elite culture became more polite, most joke collectors censored their own work. Like his hero Poggio, Legman preferred his doofuses unvarnished and presented them as the oral joke tellers found them: oversexed, dirty, and mentally deficient. Legman collected fools who bore the familiar marks of ethnic, racial, and religious stereotype, but he thought this was not especially important. Although fools wear all kinds of disguises, according to Legman, "In fool jokes the surface identity is entirely misleading." The joke may look like it is about dumb blondes or flatlanders, but on closer examination the fool has a core that persists underneath the shifting surface costume, and in real life, "There is no fool to be encountered of quite the sort one meets in jokes."[57]

Like other fools, sexual fools have problems of perception ("Anybody can make a mistake," as the hedgehog said to the hairbrush). They misrecognize the opposite sex. But Legman saw sexual fools as making more disturbing errors. There is the male fool who mistakes female genitals for an animal or a strange man with a beard and becomes alarmed. There are fools who don't realize sexual opportunity when it is offered them. For example, the traveling salesman is told he will have to sleep either with the baby or in the barn. Having visions of the baby crying and wetting him in his sleep, he picks the barn. In the morning, a beautiful young girl comes in to milk the cow.

"Who are you?" he asks.
"I'm the baby of the family. Who are you?"
"I'm the jackass that slept in the barn."[58]

The ultimate sort of fool, Legman thought, is one who does not understand the most basic fact of the adult world: "how to perform sexual intercourse, or who does not recognize it when he sees it being engaged in." This "fool is the child who has grown up"—we might say managed to grow up—"without learning the meaning of sex." Legman surmised that these jokes ridicule "those who have allowed themselves to remain in sexual darkness, to their own detriment," and thus congratulate "both teller and listener on the sexual enlightenment they themselves have achieved."[59]

For example, there is the foolish bridegroom who does not know how to perform intercourse, has to ask for directions, and naturally gets the directions all wrong. Or he takes his instructions literally. The fool wonders what to do on his wedding night: he is told to "watch the animals" for instructions with a variety of ridiculous and unpleasant results, including peeing against the bedpost. There is a lascivious female fool, disguised as an anxious bride who can be tricked into thinking her husband has two penises—a small one for the wedding night and a big one for later. When she asks him to produce the second one, he says he sold it to his friend. Later, he meets her leaving the friend's house—and she tells him he has made a bad bargain. Most dangerously, for Legman, there is the totally befuddled husband who is too foolish to know his wife is in bed with another man. "At the wedding, the fool finds the best man in bed with the bride. He goes downstairs and brings up all the wedding guests to see, chortling, 'Why, he's so drunk he thinks he's me!' Says the fool who has lost his house key to the police, 'Sure, it's my house. This is my hall, that's my carpet, this is my bedroom, that's my bed, that's my wife, and see that man in bed with her? That's me!"[60] Legman thought that monogamy was the most anxiety-producing modern arrangement and found in these kinds of jokes evidence of anxiety about marriage and fidelity.

A key axis of Legman's analysis was the relationship between women and men, which he saw as one of antagonism and inequality. In a familiar, old-fashioned formulation, Legman really did seem to believe that men and women were so different that they almost belonged to separate species. A woman was happiest, he often wrote, when being made love to by a man who was willing to give her a baby. But women were not inferior to men: he believed women are naturally superior but had been made *socially* inferior by patriarchy. At other times, he wrote that women had been horribly exploited by their "liberation" and especially their entrance into the paid workforce, where they worked harder than men and for less money, while imagining they had gained some freedom. This led to delusions of equality, the wearing of trousers and short hair to compensate, and even female attempts to dominate men. Jokes could barely take up this hideous problem: "Dominance is really the nameless sin of women . . . unforgivable and apparently unmentionable."[61]

Legman's writings on how gender might condition jokes and joking are intriguing. One wishes he had devoted an essay to this underexplored topic. Folk thought is all about women's inadequacy, or alternatively their excess, he found. In folk humor, men are unsatisfied and women have *too much* passion. Women are frigid, but also insatiable. Out of two thousand jokes, he finds not one that blames the man for the woman's not having an orgasm. It is always *her* inadequacy, in the joke world. Since this is an "exceedingly common experience," the only explanation is that the man's inadequacy is too threatening to treat, even in a joke.[62]

Legman wondered how women receive and understand jokes about male-female relations. For example, women are asked in jokes to identify with male fears of castration, and thus they are treated to the endless jokes about penis size. But do they identify with this anxiety? In asking this question, Legman suggests an interest in the listener. It is a sociological and philosophical question that leads back to Freud. What does it mean to be listening to all this anxiety and thinly disguised hostility?

Legman also hinted that he had thought about the problem of who the speaker could be in jokes when he commented on the problem of voice. Whether the speaker (either the teller or the role taken by the teller) in the joke is male or female, he argues that the voice in jokes is the "virile prerogative" of the dominant sex. For a woman to speak "forthrightly," whether as the joke teller or a character in a story, is heresy and marks her as immoral in the view of the listening community. Here is a fragment of a perspective on joke telling as an unevenly distributed practice of artful speaking. Legman indicates that the important question is not whether women can be funny, as is often asked.[63] Clearly, they can. Rather, what needs to be explored is how the telling of jokes is learned and how the power to speak humor in public is allocated.

Occasionally, Legman found in his collection and in oral tradition jokes that seemed to address women's own sexuality from a female point of view. He was much taken with a medieval manuscript that described old women sitting around, joking about the size of their well-used vaginas.[64] And Legman occasionally found jokes that expressed frank female admiration for men and male genitalia. An example from another collection tells of a group of men and women out drinking. The men urinate against a billboard, while the women duck behind some trees. A few days later, the women are discussing the fun they had had watching their husbands, and Lena says, "I was so proud when Ole took ours out." Perhaps Lena is a fool to think of Ole's penis as "ours," but could not this joke be considered "loving"? Or consider kilt-tilting jokes told by women: "How do you tell a real Scotsman? You lift his kilt. The McDonald is the one with the quarter-pounder." Or the quip of the orthodox rabbi, consoling a young woman who is suicidal. It turns out she has been told oral sex is immoral. The rabbi advises, "Take it easy, sweet-heart. What do those goyim know about high-class fucking?"[65]

RIPPED OFF

Rationale was brought out in 1968 by Basic Books in the United States and simultaneously by Jonathan Cape in Britain. It was the first published book for which Legman had a contract and an advance. But he quickly lost control of the American publication process. At the time, Legman understood that Basic was going through a merger with Random House, and Basic abruptly decided it could not have a dirty book in its catalog. They arranged to publish under the Grove Press colophon, or with a Grove title page, to conceal it from Random.[66] But then Grove unilaterally went ahead with producing and distributing the paperback.

It was perhaps not a bad thing to be distributed by Grove Press. In the 1960s, its director Barney Rossett was energetically publishing avant-garde works of all kinds, especially in theater and European modernist literature.[67] Grove had previously paid Legman to write an introduction to their 1966 aboveground publication of the erotic autobiography *My Secret Life*—the introduction was based upon the intricate bibliographic detective work on Henry Spencer Ashbee that he had unfolded in *The Horn Book*. Also in 1966, Grove's literary magazine *Evergreen Review* had published Clellon Holmes's profile of Legman, probably to help promote *My Secret Life*. Arguably, this profile boosted interest in *Rationale*. When, without permission or contract, Grove brought out *Rationale* in its popular Black Cat paperback series, the Legmans were "completely cheated" out of considerable royalties. It is not clear whether Basic sold the paperback publication rights to Rossett and Co., or whether Grove simply lifted the book, but according to Judith, the press completely refused "to pay royalties on any of the large printings of the paperback edition, which they claimed had been 'destroyed.'"[68]

In fact, the Black Cat edition sold smartly on college campuses all over the United States. In Judith's words, the Legmans later learned that there was "$17,000-owing on the paperback edition, but we never received any of it." They put their case in the hands of an American lawyer, but in Judith's words, "after sinking three to four thousand dollars into his fees, we realized that Grove was probably just laughing at us, because they could simply deduct any legal expenses, whereas we were paying real money."[69] Gershon and Judith had one baby and another coming. The royalties "would have helped us enormously," she recalled, "considering, what did we live on in those days, eight thousand dollars a year?"[70]

But *Rationale* did bring Legman back into the awareness of the publishing world. The *First Series* received generally interested and friendly reviews in the press and brought occasional interviewers to La Clé des Champs to talk to Legman about his theories of jokes. Although Alan Dundes thought *The Horn Book* was Legman's best work, *Rationale* got more press attention. Roger Abrahams thought the volume was an example of "the best we do." He bought copies for everyone that Christmas, to show friends and family the folklorist's craft.[71] *Rationale* solidified Legman's reputation among scholars as the long-distance expert on materials no one knew how to handle. But unfortunately, it was not going to help him get an academic job or a grant to support his writing.

Rationale received serious notices in the British journals *New Society* and *New Statesman* and, more important, in the *New York Times Book Review*. It was reviewed in the *Chicago Daily News*, the *Washington Sunday Star*, and *Time*.[72] When Joanna Krotz of Grove's publicity department sent some of the clippings on to Valbonne, Legman thanked her warmly. Most of the reviews, he thought, seemed "to have been written by rejected columnists turned down by *Screw* magazine . . .," but "it ain't the wages, it's the integrity you have to go home to at night."[73]

Integrity was what Legman would have to settle for. There was only one initial scholarly notice of *Rationale*, a disapproving overview by Richard Buehler, a young folklorist teaching at Memorial University, Newfoundland. Buehler thought the book's arrival was "an event of the first importance" in bringing uncensored attention to sexual folklore but counted it a failure in its attempt to analyze and classify the dirty joke. Legman's work did not seem objective to Buehler, who suspected that Legman "selects his material to suit his thesis, and that he sees only in his material what he wishes to see." His classification method was no great improvement on earlier ones, because, as with Aarne-Thompson, the same story often appeared in several different categories.[74]

In Europe there were almost immediate offers of translated editions. Eventually, the book would be translated into French, German, and Italian. Foreign and American presses now expressed interest in bringing out a new edition of the long-suppressed *Oragenitalism*; Legman began negotiations with Arthur Ceppos of Julian Press for a revised and expanded American edition to appear, appropriately, in 1969, and with Editions Truong in Paris for a French translation.[75] There was fresh interest in his book on the Knights Templar, and Jonathan Cape asked for the rights to an English edition of *The Horn Book*. Legman's *sitzfleisch*, his ability to stolidly persist, had paid off, though not financially. He was now the premiere expert in the field that he had fought to define. With the opening up of the American publishing industry, his accumulated introductions, short articles, resurrection of lost manuscripts, and his bye-works added to the record of his big books. He really was, as Bruce Jackson would crown him, the king of the censored X700 category. He negotiated seriously with Kenneth Goldstein over the "New Kryptadia," played with typefaces, and dreamed of finally getting his erotic folklore yearbook going.[76]

With attention to *The Rationale* came some gentle criticism from younger scholars. Paris publisher Robert Lafont contracted for a French edition, with a translation by Daniel Dayan, an anthropology student working with Roland Barthes.[77] Young Dayan and middle-aged Legman corresponded about the tricky problem of translating jokes, Gershon advising with great care on how to find dictionaries with the best feel for the American vernacular. Literal translations rarely work, he wrote, because jokes are such sensitive registers of the specific meanings of people's everyday lives and because they so often involve plays with language and larger than linguistic fields of meaning.

Dayan was interested in the way *Rationale* fitted into a new way of looking at everyday communication. He wrote to Legman, "In France, your book has something in common with the Structuralism current, which one could define as bringing to light extremely elaborated systems of communication . . . [of] only accidental arbitrary conglomerations, where one can never see the whole."[78] Dayan thought structuralism was the most important intellectual development since existentialism. He brashly told Legman to read Lacan, Lévi-Strauss, and Foucault to understand this revolution in cultural theory. Legman characteristically mocked the pretensions of the French academics, calling Lacan's work on de Sade *"deux pots de merde et rien dedans"* (two pots of shit and nothing else). Joking aside, he told Dayan to look over *The Fake Revolt* "so that you will see where I really stand on all those intellectual fakers . . . then there will be no struggle between us."[79]

He issued Dayan firm instructions, as he did to all editors: "I cannot accept any sweeping improvement or change in my text and it is important that you should not attempt to Rewrite My Book," but Dayan should take complete liberty in the translation of the jokes themselves. In Legman's view, the anthropologist would translate his analysis but re-create the jokes, "out of the mere clay of my folkloristic materials." The French equivalents of "scenes, conversations, foods, backdrops, oaths, imprecations, repartees" would have to be found or felt for and everything possible reworked into the equivalent French popular argot "to make the FRENCH READER UNDERSTAND THE JOKE."[80] Judith remembered that she and Gershon found Dayan's translation "a marvelously sensitive thing, not too literal but grasping the spirit extremely well." But they did not see much income from the French edition, because translation royalties followed back to the original publisher, who took a cut.[81]

THE NARSTY-NARSTIES

As soon as Legman put *Rationale* to bed with the printers, he began to try to get his second volume into print. Basic and Jonathan Cape, for which he prepared *No Laughing Matter*, found it unacceptable. Even with the new literary freedom, a publisher could go too far. When *No Laughing Matter* was further rejected by Grove, Legman sent it to several psychoanalytic society book clubs, with no luck. Once again, he had written something unpublishable. As Judith recalls, he was "absolutely deflated and depressed" at the thought that half of the work was "dangling over a precipice" and might never make it into print.[82]

Finally, Gershon's friend Osmond Beckwith stepped up and paid for a printing of volume 2, with the publisher named as Breaking Point. As Judith put it, "When it was out and nobody got arrested, then everybody was willing to jump in," and Indiana University Press brought out a two-volume edition of the whole book.[83] There was a seven-year hiatus between the two volumes.

No Laughing Matter allowed Legman to spend more time considering his theories of the joke and contrasting his ideas with the analyses of other scholars. He expanded and bolstered his controversial statements about aggression and hostility in humor. The book is recursive and redundant, circling over arguments already presented, talking back and forth between what he had written in the first volume and the expanded positions he was developing.

The second volume was both a continuation of Legman's arguments and an archive of his approach to even more painful subjects. He continued his thematic organization, now focusing on what he saw as severe sexual distortions and neurotic problems—and organizing the jokes he called "the narsty-narsties" as responses to these psychic difficulties. Fundamentally, he thought, there were some very troubled joke tellers out there—they were not rationalizing "normal" problems but obsessed with troubles they could not resolve. He felt it was his sad duty to explore the folklore evidence of these pathetic and (he would say) nearly crazy people.

Jokes "rationalize" *real* existing perversions such as coprophilia or necrophilia, and laughter shrives our awareness of a "perverted reality" that we all would prefer to ignore.[84] Jokes, seen in this way, are a disguised record of a very dark world, a sort of dirty basement of disavowed desires and acts. This world eroticizes feces, farts, all kinds of excreta and pollution, infections, infestations, accidents, and maimed and distorted bodies. *No Laughing Matter* is at times hilarious, at times bitter. Most often it is disturbing, as it was intended to be. Legman wrote that he felt a responsibility to present his evidence.

As in *Series I*, the cast of joke characters shifts and changes, but only superficially. Under the surface, the central actors are the same throughout. There is more emphasis here on the wretched and despised: women, of course, but also all the familiar ethnic and racial minorities and male homosexuals. It is not pressing a point to say that *No Laughing Matter* is a detailed register of the hatreds and fears of Legman's American joke tellers, at a particular point in time.

Legman understood that *No Laughing Matter* was a kind of historical document. He also noted that while the objects of the jokers' desire and hideous abuse remain the same, they were also changing slowly but not imperceptibly. Legman remembered that in his growing-up years, it was common to tell scatological jokes befouling Catholics and the Catholic clergy. But in the mid-1970s, he thought he noticed that anti-Catholic filth was becoming less common. He wrote, "As centuries pass our cultural scatologica move on to other areas, leaving religion and minstrel shows behind."[85]

While *Rationale* explores what many of us already suspect, that our attitudes toward sex and sexual partners are odd and sometimes obsessive, *No Laughing Matter* is a looser, more uneven unfolding of stuff. As reviewers noted, it is difficult, even nauseating, to read. Legman allows himself to be even more editorial and, in places, more philosophical than in the first volume. He digresses in places on topics he finds important: he reprises his "On the Cause" article to explore the place and role of homosexuals in Western culture, making the heterosexual fear of homosexuals the topic of one long introductory chapter.[86] What he sees as the problematic place of women in Western society, paralleling the destruction of meaningful roles for men under capitalism, comes in for extensive discussion in a chapter on jokes about prostitution. He sees sex work as emblematic of the West's abuse of women. The Second Wave women's movement comes in for a blistering attack, yet, in his critique, Legman allows that he partially understands the motivation of U.S. feminists. In a study of jokes that aim filth and pollution at women, Legman points to the enduring antifemale strains of North American culture as a whole.

Again, Legman traces the history of jokes and is able to show that many of them are quite old. He busily cross-references not only the Aarne-Thompson index but other published and unpublished collections as well. He brings to bear many kinds of evidence about jokes and humor and attitudes toward sex, from art history, comic art, and current news and underground papers. Making no distinction between orally circulating jokes and what he has found in novels, theater, memoirs, and biographies, Legman uses everything that comes to hand to uncover strange attitudes and mental images.

He cites the old joke books and the new crude and tasteless ones. Anything and everything are grist for Legman's mill. He offers frequent examples from his own collecting in England, in the South of France, and by mail. There is a feeling in *No Laughing Matter* that he is piling on every example he can think of, that he is suffering, perhaps, from not being able to stop.

No Laughing Matter received few popular reviews, reflecting how difficult the material was to acknowledge.[87] But in 1975, it was nominated for and won the Chicago Folklore Prize, awarded jointly by the International Folklore Association and the University of Chicago Department of German for the best monograph in any field of folklore.[88] It would have made sense to award the prize to both volumes, but since they had been published over a seven-year span they were not considered as a whole. Bruce Jackson wrote sourly to Legman about how stingy the twenty-five-dollar award was.[89] Legman in turn asked that the prize money be sent to Vance Randolph, who was in even greater financial need. The award nevertheless "pleased him immensely," in Judith's recollection, "and he felt very vindicated, because normally that sort of prize is given to people who have devoted themselves to following a nice neat path in a university or college."[90]

In 1977 Elliott Oring, a young folklorist with a good feel for theory, reviewed both volumes of *Rationale* in *Western Folklore*, edited by Legman's friend Wayland D. Hand. Oring worked extensively on jokes and humor, and, although he generally repudiated ideas of unconscious motivation, he would later write carefully about Freud's *Jokes and Their Relation to the Unconscious* and examine Freud's own favorite jokes.[91]

Oring's review was mixed and dour. He wrote that it made sense to evaluate the volumes jointly now that the long-promised second volume had appeared, but just reading the 1,788 pages was a battle for him. Certainly, Legman had done an amazing job of amassing obscene jokelore into two easily accessible volumes, but he thought the organization was a botch and that Legman fell "flat on his face" trying to analyze. He considered Legman's attempt to develop a psychological index of types and motifs unworkable and his identification of psychological nexuses idiosyncratic. For example, a joke about the immaculate conception has God telling Saint Peter that he cannot go down to earth because he "knocked up a Jewish girl" two thousand years ago. Legman places it under "Rape . . ." But why? Legman asked the reader "to compare a joke involving a man who asks a surgeon to create a new penis from his thigh with the account in Genesis of Jacob's crippled thigh." Yet, Oring charged, "the thigh has already been identified [elsewhere in the text] as a symbol for the arms." Objects were symbolic of too many things. Were jokes about "overlarge vaginas" expressions of fears of castration or of a desire to "return to the womb"?[92] How did Legman decide? Legman's categories seemed arbitrary and shored up with heavy-handed determinism.[93]

Oring's reaction reflected the changes in American intellectuals' attitudes toward Freud.[94] While some anthropologists were interested in testing psychoanalytic concepts in the field, more were suspicious of the idea of the unconscious, and "complexes" were no longer the common coin of well-read conversation. Oring demanded a better justification than general agreement for Legman's analytical strategy. To underscore the need for considerations of validity, Oring tested Legman's system by giving twelve of his students some of Legman's jokes and assigning them to reclassify them, following the *Rationale*. Fewer than half the jokes could be located according to Legman's own system. The system did not work logically.[95]

Oring pointed out that Legman's texts were compressed and abstracted. "Only the essence" of the jokes were presented, and by the standard of 1977 this was insufficient for analysis. Descriptions of the joke-telling sessions and the backgrounds of tellers were also missing. Legman only tossed out "tidbits" of this information. Oring wondered if Legman's psychoanalytic interpretations "might suffer in the face of faithful sociological data."[96]

When he was tracing jokes and giving them a history, Oring thought, Legman did much better. He skillfully located parallels of "patterns, motifs, and theme."[97] No one was better at showing "strong links to the jocular tales and ballads of the past" than Gershon Legman, with his "command of extensive and rare collections." He was to be credited with taking steps to end the isolation of contemporary obscene jokes.[98]

What bothered Oring most was Legman's insistence on jokes as expressions of psychosexual hostility. Legman was "on his own," Oring wrote, when he claimed jokes are disguised aggression against the listener and that the listener "is always really the butt."[99] Oring's refusal to accept a psychological interpretation of jokes was shared in 1977 by most other American folklorists.

The Hell Drawer   **217**

On receiving the review, Legman was stung, but he wrote to Oring, "That is all right. I appreciate the care you have taken with the subject, since it seems obvious that neither you nor any other American folklorist had any intention of doing so until my book forced your hand." Legman suspected that Oring really felt that he should not have written *Rationale* at all. A member of the Chicago Folklore Prize committee, Legman claimed, had told him, "You just got it as a sort of booby-prize for having more guts than anyone else." At least Oring gave *Rationale* to his classes so they could take advantage of all the books that "will otherwise lie dead and dust-covered in Prof. Hand's painfully collected library at UCLA, while the rest of the current crop of 'American study' people kids around with their new dada of 'performance contexts.'"[100]

But Oring had understood him correctly, Legman admitted. "It is certainly one of my main beliefs that *all* forms of human expression (art, dreams, jokes, music, corny post-cards, horror-movies) express exactly the same human problems, with of course certain formal differences." Most of the texts American folklorists worked on were desiccated, their theories futile. But when someone really tried a big important project, they were ignored. He pointed to Vance Randolph, "flat on his back . . . in an Arkansas poor house . . . [surviving] on a World War One pension," hoping the American Folklore Society would make him a fellow. "See St. John, 11:35."[101]

James Leary, another young scholar, also ventured onto Legman's terrain, reviewing *No Laughing Matter* in *Folklore Forum*, a student-run journal of the Folklore Institute at Indiana University.[102] Leary thought the subject was of great importance, and that of all the tales and gibes circulating in the modern world, "perhaps the most prevalent" genre is the dirty joke. Legman's great collection offered clarification and insight. Abundant sources were given, and relevant scholarly materials were referred to in the text. (Perhaps here Leary was being polite, since many scholars found Legman's insistence on weaving full citations into his text, instead of using endnotes, downright infuriating.) *No Laughing Matter* was no mere reference but a presentation of a masterful and decades-long work.

Leary went straight to Legman's central point, his finding that humans devote "so much verbal energy" to the "symbolic degradation" of each other. Then, dirty talk is too often transformed into horrific action, from assault to mass murder. Leary admired Legman's bravery and his willingness, so rare among folklorists, to take an uncompromising stance and to offer social criticism. He agreed with Legman that jokes are often hostilities exchanged as amenities, that laughter expresses immense relief that the catastrophe is happening to someone else, and that the teller is a kind of sacred clown with the courage and power to break taboos.

218   CHAPTER 9

Generally, Leary thought Legman's psychological arguments held together, and he thought that the psychosexual readings of the jokes were plausible. He was aware that Freud's work, with its emphasis on the importance of sexual repression as a feature of modern society, was being drafted anew into the study of culture and history. Herbert Marcuse's *Eros and Civilization*, which in some ways paralleled Legman's arguments, was being read in New Left and antiwar circles and providing a new Marxist-psychoanalytic perspective.[103] Leary agreed with Legman's general negative critique and with his view, now in the context of the Vietnam War, that the world was still going to hell in a handbasket. Injecting profound questions into the dry academic discussions of folktale types and motifs was much needed.[104]

Although the two reviews were substantial and serious, overall academic assessments of *Rationale* and *No Laughing Matter* were sparse. It was as if the folklore journal editors wanted to prove Legman correct: he was dealing with materials no one could bear to discuss. The status of the reviewers was significant, too. Buehler, Leary, and Oring were at the start of their careers; the senior distinguished folklorists who corresponded with Legman and might have had something far-reaching to say about *Rationale* were conspicuously silent. Wayland Hand and Archer Taylor, who among many others had corresponded warmly with Legman, did not find time for a notice of the book. And although Alan Dundes and Roger Abrahams praised the book highly, neither ventured a review. Neither did Richard Dorson. While Legman's epistolary friendships sometimes ended nastily, a larger message was being communicated by the silence of the senior academics: "This work is not important."

Yet the senior scholars and the up-and-coming "Young Turks" agreed in print that jokes were the modern folktale par excellence. Legman had shown how vast and dirty the American hell drawer was, but he had committed the fatal errors of psychological analysis and political critique at a time when folklore study was becoming thoroughly professionalized and shedding its air of political and cultural experimentation.[105] Only a few university-based folklorists, led by Alan Dundes, were interested in Freud's larger critique of social and sexual repression.[106]

Legman's attempts to convince folklorists of the usefulness of psychoanalytic concepts foundered, finally, on a rift he could not close, on the split between humanist and social science approaches to the joke. He insisted on reading large unconscious patterns into the small-scale interaction of joking. He accepted Freud's premises about the nature of the psyche and the importance of repression, but Oring spoke for most American social scientists when he argued that these were impossible to validate.

If jokes expressed individual problems and society's aggressions, how would an analyst show, rather than assume, the connection between the two?

Freud's view of civilization as tragically repressive did not always translate well in the 1960s and 1970s, except among members of the New Left who were committed to the antiwar, anti-imperialist critique of capitalism. Most academics were not so committed, although many had students who were.[107] Legman's critics thought he connected jokes to human catastrophes in a flat and deterministic way. Some, like James Leary, thought he was courageous for trying to make the connection at all.

As Leary's and Oring's readings of *Rationale* show, the younger folklorists demanded Legman go beyond texts to the evidence provided by behavior. Could Legman show that the fears and obsessions he examined were not just his own eccentric selections? How, for example, could one show that the Oedipal situation was the central trouble faced by young boys? Or that monogamy provoked deep anxiety in men? As the ethnographic standard became dominant in academic folklore, scholars became reluctant to assert that they had a firm hold on what a performance or text meant: interpretation should take place, ideally, between the performer and the observer. Legman, who had been busy piling up textual evidence, wasn't interested in testing theories with ethnographic methods.

Then there was the material itself. Jokes seemed too fast moving to present as evidence of the state of something as unchanging as a repressive civilization. The joke was so various, so multifarious and widespread, and joking had so many uses and places, that the "data" was like quicksilver. It could not be made to hold still. Dirty jokes found themselves at home in so many settings that students would need many different interpretive strategies. Folklorists who were beginning to look closely at the social processes of joke telling—as a performance—were arguing that humor could not be corralled into one interpretative frame. Telling a dirty joke could be a hostile act, or a critique of prevailing sexual arrangements, or a political provocation, or a way of ganging up on someone, or a bid for affection and solidarity. The claim Legman made for the dirty joke, that it was always an expression of sexual anxiety and hostility, was difficult to prove, if it could be proven at all.[108]

It was disappointing that the scholarly notice of *Rationale* was so sparse, but it was not surprising. On the other hand, the book was popular, and it brought many people's attention to the joke as a serious subject. The interest Legman spurred encouraged more studies and accounts and occasional tests of his propositions. The series became a standard work for the study of humor, although it served more as an archive than as an analytic tool. Legman's joke studies took part in and encouraged a swell of scholarly interest in humor and play. The 1970s saw an increase in scholarly studies of mass-produced popular culture, including its playful and joking dimensions, led by Ray B. Browne at Bowling Green State University.[109] These were the years of the founding of the several important international associations for the study of humor, including the interdisciplinary Association for the Anthropological Study of Play.[110] At about the same time in England, Stuart Hall and his colleagues at Birmingham University would spark interest in "resistance" through everyday rituals.[111] This attention to popular culture was sometimes less critical than it should have been, but it did reflect a rapidly widening view, driven in part by the influx of new kinds of students into public higher education in the United States and the withering of the censorship regime.[112]

Before the 1960s, the scholarly approach to jokes had been almost entirely the domain of literary historians. Now a scholarly expansion was taking place. Sociologists and anthropologists like Erving Goffman, linguists and sociolinguists like Richard Bauman, as well as folklorists Richard Dorson, Caryl Emerson, and Rayna Green took joke studies in unheralded directions. Rather than view the joke as the descendant of an older oral literature, folklorists were approaching it as a part of a process of communication, as Daniel Dayan had suggested. They noticed that jokes were everywhere, that the "general float" was a current that moved over and penetrated through everyday life. Unlike the European *Märchen,* or folktale, and the Child ballad, which were hard to find in the United States, jokes were everywhere. In the context of the campus counterculture, it was now even fashionable to study the joke: at Berkeley Alan Dundes was becoming known, only slightly disparagingly, as "the joke professor." One could now publish a scholarly, annotated collection of jokes and have it seriously received.[113]

For all the people looking at humor, there were as many fresh questions and methods. Folklorists could get up close and study the small facets of reception.[114] Some asked if women had joking traditions and, if so, how they might be researched and described.[115] Others turned their attention back to children to anthologize, as did Mary Knapp and Herbert Knapp, without cleansing the collection. Sandra McCosh surveyed the lore of playgrounds in one city, over a controlled period of time, in a book for which Legman wrote the introduction.[116]

The Freudian perspective was not entirely neglected in the expansion of joke studies. In 1969 Alan Dundes and Roger Abrahams made a splash with an article in *Psychoanalytic Review* showing that the popular elephant joke fad could be seen as a disguised expression of white uneasiness about black demands in the civil rights and Black Power movements.[117] Further, Dundes and Abrahams insisted, elephant jokes were perceived by black Americans as targeted at them. The study of jokes and joking was not just fashionable; it was a part of the study of social tension and change. Elephant jokes were not really about elephants, and they weren't just silly. Following Freud, the content of the jokes was now treated symbolically rather than taken literally.

Elliott Oring was not alone in his rejection of Freudian approaches to folklore. Over the years, only a few American folklorists, led by Dundes, have wrestled with the difficulties of psychoanalytic theory, especially the problem of the relationship between expressive forms like jokes and the lives of individuals. Of those who have, most accepted some parts of a psychoanalytic perspective while rejecting a great deal more.[118] Folklorists were not convinced of the existence of the invisible entity Freud plumbed, the unconscious (in which Legman believed), nor did they want to see folk productions as evidence of neurosis or troubled behavior. In the United States, psychoanalysis was generally understood as a recondite mind-cure, not a critique of a civilization. A majority of American folklorists ignored psychoanalytic thought altogether, and some were overtly antagonistic to it.[119]

One of the liveliest and most careful scholars testing Legman's proposals about humor turned out to be James Leary, who went on to teach at the University of Wisconsin at Madison.[120] Leary collected and studied the jokes of old-fashioned and socially conservative farmers and loggers. In studying joke tellers' repertoires, he drew some limited and cautious conclusions about the psychological implications of the teller's choice of tale. Leary's appreciation of Legman's theory of the joke recognizes that different social milieus use the joke in varying ways—across not only cultures and social classes, but even within small social environments.

Leary found that his informants could joke about sexual matters anxiously, warmly, affectionately, and in a spirit of social criticism, all within the same conversation. The intimate exchange of the amenity that is the joke is just that, Leary found: intimate, not in the loving sense, but in the sense of "up close." The frame of the joke allows within it the warm and loving and the dangerous and potentially hurtful, all at once.[121]

Overall, despite the upsurge in interest, folklorists were still hesitant about the joke's low prestige. Could one get tenure by specializing in jokes? As Leary's work showed, studying jokes in interaction was difficult and time-consuming.[122] Meanwhile, a new form of collectible text was emerging: the photocopied visual joke (an ancestor of the Internet meme), sent around offices and posted on bulletin boards. Alan Dundes, Michael Preston, and others began to collect and write about this " Xerox lore," and they shared examples with Legman.[123] This was exciting, since he had long envisioned a volume of *Les Hautes Études* on "nonverbal" forms of erotica.

After 1975 Legman had new epistolary and publishing connections, usually with scholars who either had been pushed out of the academy or were secure enough to take up obscenity in their own work. Reinhold Aman, a professor of German at the University of Wisconsin at Milwaukee was starting *Maledicta: The International Journal of Verbal Aggression*. He asked Legman for contributions, and Legman offered his own articles on obscene words, as well as excerpts and translations from others' works.[124] Together they brought out two previously undiscovered and unpublished bawdy manuscripts by Mark Twain, "The Mammoth Cod" and "Address to the Stomach Club."[125]

In 1977 Aman proposed a "Legman issue" of *Maledicta* to Bruce Jackson. For his profile of Legman, Jackson read—or tried to read—everything Legman had published. He was dizzied by the effort, and his article, "The King of X700," was as rich and intriguing as Clellon Holmes's earlier "Last Cause." Although *Maledicta* was a tiny operation, it had a cachet in literature departments, and it helped spread Legman's reputation as the man who knew more about obscene folklore than anyone.[126]

Rationale's publication led to new correspondents, and speaking invitations followed. But it was difficult and expensive for Legman to travel to the United States, and his public presentations were rare. In his sixties, he was now thoroughly overweight and not in good health. Promoting his own work was almost impossible. As a nonplayer of the academic game, he had nothing to offer the younger scholars except his ideas and his materials and sources, which, as Jackson pointed out, he always shared generously. He could not shepherd student articles through journals, or give legs up into jobs, or write recommendations for grants. He pined for a Guggenheim Fellowship, but he could not organize the letters of support.

It is hard to trace scholarly legacies when they are unacknowledged. Legman's work on sexual humor would be cited broadly, and well beyond writings in folklore, but acknowledgment of his ideas was uneven. The lines of argument he laid out in *Rationale* were not always taken up by other folklorists, especially if they eschewed his interest in hostility and unconscious motivations.[127] But the *Rationale* books drew wide attention to this common oral tradition, making space for the occasional study of uncensored, unpleasant, and tendentious jokes. As Jackson pointed out in his profile, if Legman had only published his collections, they would have been seen as scholarly blockbusters. But Legman had noticed early that societies have taboos and unspeakable hatreds, and these can often be examined only in the realm of humor. Legman knew, though these were not his terms, that jokes are social facts, and he was remarkably precise at naming what he saw as these facts. How can our deeper collective problems be aired if no one is willing to publish and argue about their expression? This was a central question that led back to Legman's childhood. How can we discover what is wrong if no one will allow us to speak? As if to confirm this profound question, Emil Legman refused to allow *Rationale of the Dirty Joke* into his house. It was not until after Emil's death in 1975 that Julia was able to hold and appreciate her son's books.[128]

10

UNDER MT. CHEIRON

It ain't the wages, it's the integrity.
—G. Legman to Joanna Krotz, September 16, 1969

From the late 1970s until his final illness, one might have expected Legman to slow down a bit. But he did not. He had many projects on his work tables and felt pressure to say what he had to say and to bring as much as possible into print. Judith worried about his health and regretted that he never took a vacation. The one year she planned a trip for them together, he broke his ankle. His sons, David and Rafael, who were now nearing adolescence, remember him always in his studio, always working. They were out in the neighborhoods, on foot and later on scooters, in David's words, "visiting friends and avoiding our parents, avoiding our father." It was difficult for them socially. The boys could not see where the minimal money was coming from, and "our friends didn't understand what our parents did."[1] Who understands how marginal writers live, off trickles of royalties?

"ROLL ME IN YOUR ARMS"

In the late 1970s, Legman returned to work on his "Ballad" manuscript, writing to Joe Hickerson that he that felt ghastly about his hoard of songs. "I have done wrong, wrong, *multa pecavi*, in collecting so much all these years, and publishing so little." But still he hoped to finish it. Alan Lomax had even promised to write him a bang-up introduction.[2] He was anxious to send the Archive of Folk Song copies of his research, but there were no photocopiers in Valbonne, so everything had to be toted eighteen miles by bus to Cannes.[3]

224   CHAPTER 10

He was still collecting, asking Hickerson to search the archive for unpublished obscene items.[4] He asked Bruce Jackson to search his files and bothered labor folklorist Archie Green for picket-line obscenities that referenced oral sex.[5] He also labored with Kenneth Goldstein on an extension of his work on limericks, producing a study of the history of bawdy monologues and rhymed recitations. They almost got into a dispute over the length of the article, but in the end he was pleased with the outcome, although Goldstein could not find space for Twain's "Mammoth Cod," an example of an erotic after-dinner speech. Goldstein was the first scholar to help him with practical editing.[6] A volume of new limericks was another by-product.[7]

Meanwhile, he was writing to Vance Randolph about bringing the unpublishable Ozark manuscripts into print. Randolph was destitute, nearing the end of his life, and discouraged. He wrote to Legman that he and his wife were in a veterans home, "but otherwise we are paupers." They commiserated about their neglect by the scholarly establishment, and Randolph complained, "I try not to be bitter about the lack of recognition, but it certainly makes one's ass tired. . . . The only honor I ever got was a Litt. D. from the U of Ark in 1951. But you should have had the Nobel Prize years ago. They might have made me a fellow of the AFS but did they? They did not."[8] Randolph signed the rights to all his hell-drawer manuscripts, except the jokes, over to Legman. Meanwhile, Goldstein organized Randolph's jokes into *Pissing in the Snow*, arranging for an introduction by Rayna Green and annotations by Frank Hoffman, which Legman edited.[9] It was a breakthrough book in folklore, and Randolph dedicated it to Gershon.

As Legman pulled "The Ballad" together, it was paralleled and eventually overshadowed by his work on Randolph's manuscripts. The first, "Roll Me in Your Arms," was a collection of songs. A second manuscript that brought together sexual customs, games, and superstitions from the Ozarks, he would call "And Blow the Candle Out."[10] Legman tried to arrange a contract with the University of Illinois Press for the two manuscripts. During a visit to Valbonne, Judith McCulloh, the distinguished music and folklore editor at Illinois, discussed the project with him. Legman asked if she thought she could bring out his "Ballad." She told him sadly, "I just don't know."[11]

By about 1984, Legman decided he now had the "Ballad" as complete as it would ever be, and he wrote an introductory essay for the book, recapitulating his thought on folk song. He began with a tart statement: "Folk song is the voice of those who have no other voice and would not be listened to if they did."[12] But he had been listening: he had been collecting these folk songs for more than fifty years, only to conclude that this important human art form had been systematically deformed by its dedicated students. He repeated his attack on the collectors. From the very moment the English middle class noticed folk songs, there was expurgation—it had been going on for 250 years. What was left was a "faked repertory," "vapid" and "sexless," "only the strangled voice of silence." The prestigious Child ballads were pared down into a folio of songs about rape and grisly murder. What Legman offered was more accurate: "the entire modern repertory of erotic ballads and songs in English . . . from field collection . . . and from the very few privately printed and manuscript records that do exist without falsification."[13]

As he had planned, he opened with the oldest songs, assuming that they were rootstock for the newer ones and trying to show their developing strains. He emphasized that the songs were all alive and could be shown to be sung in the present day. When possible he included tunes, with music editing by his friend Herb Greer. According to Judith, he and Greer huddled for months over Beverley's grand piano, working out what they thought were appropriate melodies.[14]

Legman insisted upon presenting what had been "absolutely and purpose-fully Left Out," the songs overlooked in Malcolm Laws's *Native American Ballads*, for example, and others "filed and forgotten," or simply refused. He included "The Sea Crab," which Bishop Percy had collected for his *Reliques of Ancient English Poetry* in 1640, but Child had refused to edit. It was too crude: An old fisherman puts a sea crab in the chamber pot, for lack of a bet-ter vessel, and in the middle of the night, the crab grabs his goodwife by her crotch. The fisherman tries to help, the crab's other claw grabs his nose, and catastrophe ensues.[15] "The Sea Crab" was too good to ignore, and its absence in Child was a classic example of how the literature of folk song was "faked."[16]

Legman continued his attack on the collectors. He expanded his list of folk song "faker-cleaner-uppers" to include Frank C. Brown, John and (now) Alan Lomax, Cecil Sharp, Maud Karpeles, Iona and Peter Opie, and Peter Kennedy, all of whom copyrighted their sanitized collections. He blasted Bertrand Bronson and the folk music scholars for their persnickety precision about tunes, which to him seemed silly for people who were busy distorting words. No one except Vance Randolph escaped unscathed.[17]

Legman laid out his argument for obscene lore: it is "natural and necessary" and innocent. Obscenity belongs particularly to "country people, children, soldiers, prisoners, students and other isolated work-groups and marginals," and sometimes even to academics. Randolph had never intended the segrega-tion of his manuscripts into printable and unprintable. Indeed, unprintable folklore is "an optical illusion" because it is based on the "skewing" of the whole body of material since at least the 1720s, when "Pills to Purge Melan-choly," the last uncensored collection of songs, appeared.[18]

The same people who collected folk song distorted it, because they could not see the real world. If one does not admit obscenity exists, then there is

226   CHAPTER 10

none to be seen. (And, he admitted, if one only looks for obscenity, one sees nothing else.) The collecting situation itself skewed the record: the more unusual the situation (when an outsider collector visits the singer), the less likely it is that "sexual materials will appear." This is one reason erotic songs seem rare. But in fact, "singers mix together the many things that interest them," including love, work, and drinking. When offered anything bawdy, Cecil Sharp took down only first stanzas and later described texts as fragmentary, as if the problem were the singer's memory. But Randolph never hesitated and never asked for separate materials. He simply took everything he could get.[19] Collectors like Sharp created the pretense that true folk materials are never obscene, and later folk song scholars maintained the fiction. This was a "jolly fraud" all around, Legman wrote, with the effect that folklorists were baffled as to why erotic lore would be worth studying at all. Of course, Legman insisted, it was worth studying because it was part of human life. One could not claim folklore was a science while systematically altering the full picture.[20]

Legman's introduction to "The Ballad" was rewritten as the introduction for "Roll Me in Your Arms," and in the run-up to that publication he also adapted it into a major article for the *Journal of American Folklore*. To this he attached a significant eighty-four-page bibliography, his list of major sources of traditional erotic songs.[21] Remarkably, he allowed Bruce Jackson to edit the article; Jackson did so gently and with a skill that pleased Legman.[22]

Legman was also working on a volume of nonverbal "pictorial humor and similar lore transmitted in ways other than orally." For many years, he had been gathering old-fashioned comic postcards, modern "hostile" greeting cards, and other items in print that make "ever so candid and so unabashed a statement of the aspirations and aggressions of millions of plain people." The cards, he wrote to Hickerson, let people express themselves in "prefabricated symbolisms which speak for them as they themselves cannot or do not trust themselves to speak."[23] He issued a call to collectors. Eventually, this project resulted in a collection of thousands of French and American postcards and greeting cards, as well as boxes of files of photocopy lore and other ephemera.[24] And he experimented with making his own Xerox lore, creating a satire, the FARK, or "Folklore Article Reconstruction Kit," to parody the sludge he thought passed for academic folklore writing.[25] The FARK allows one to assemble an article out of prefabricated chunks of folklorists' jargon.

Amid all these projects, he continued to have health problems. He was in his sixties now, young to be so troubled, but he had been sitting and typing for years. His weight compromised his cardiovascular system, and long years of close reading had strained his eyes. He had had a stroke in 1971, the year his son Rafael was born, and the ministrokes or ischemia continued. He wrote to Jay Landesman that "the gastronomic revolution came too late for me: I never knew animal fat was bad for the arteries until too late."[26]

To friends, Legman claimed that his heart was the problem.[27] He did not want to admit that the trouble was really blood clots breaking free, potentially affecting his brain. According to Judith, "He could not bear the thought of any mental impairment."[28] In 1975 he went to New York, where Clarkson Potter, his publisher, arranged consultations with specialist physicians. He did not offer to give talks on this visit, perhaps because he was not feeling well, but he did visit his parents for what he knew would be the final time.[29]

"AN AUTOBIOGRAPHY OF INNOCENCE"

The last visit to Scranton and his reckoning with his own mortality spurred Legman to begin his autobiography. This would be another major writing project from the early 1980s until he became seriously ill in 1991. He sent an author's query to the *New York Times Book Review*, asking to hear from "acquaintances, correspondents, old enemies, former friends and wives" for his autobiography. He hoped they might be willing to loan him back some of the many thousands of letters he had written over the years.[30] He attended to his card file of names and addresses, compiled over forty years. Now he was using it like an aide-mémoire, reconstructing events and even inventing pseudonyms for people, especially former lovers, whom he feared might not want to be mentioned by name.

He was writing frequently to Jay Landesman, now living in London and producing musicals. They were comparing notes and sharing old letters. Legman wrote, "Memoirs are now in stage of preparation of long lists of people and situations. . . . I was disappointed in the list of women I've slept with (and men . . .). . . . I had to swear my own wife to total calm before I could even consider writing Mems; and, even so, I plan to end them with our marriage. Anyhow, what have I done *since* except sit here and write the books I planned and researched all the preceding years?"[31]

In 1979 Jay sent Legman the manuscript of his memoir, *Rebel without Applause*, and while he took offense at Jay's tone, Gershon critiqued it productively. When Jay was remembering him and the *Neurotica* days fondly, Gershon wrote, "All I remember of the *Neurotica* period was the hard work it was, and the humiliation (by YOU!) *Of never been given any money*, even though you saw that Beverley and I were down to eating ground beef lung, which even most *dogs* refuse to eat."[32]

Legman acknowledged that *Neurotica* was a daring experiment, "an important document and shook the American university—(and C.I.A.)—funded lit mags & rags to their fundament. They have been trying to form a pearl

228 CHAPTER 10

around Freud ever since. But literature and lit rags have never had any human importance, so they don't know that. That's why I always preferred psychology and folklore, which are nothing if not Humanistic!"[33] He did not want Jay to get sentimental. "Please don't love me too much: everybody male who loves me from far away, HATES me from close: especially you! Just love me on paper. It will be good enough."[34]

They fought about the reissue of *Neurotica* that Jay was planning. Gershon reminded Jay that since "*Neurotica* belongs to me, you obviously cannot republish it without some arrangement with me on payment for rights to publish." And, he added, "When do I get copies of Kearney's *The Private Case*? I worked hard on that. I should receive some more fitting reward [than] the usual *Neurotica* poke in the ass with a sharp stick."[35] Landesman never bothered with an advance for the republication.[36]

As they exchanged chapters, Gershon was antagonized by Jay's version of past events. In 1983, Legman wrote, "Your memory often plays you tricks . . . although your writing is sincere and chaste and . . . that has really surprised me." Jay falsely claimed he had gone to Washington for the Post Office hearing in 1950, and "you failed to mention that we paid a bribe to beat the rap in Connecticut." "You have to stop rewriting history," Gershon admonished him.[37]

Legman's most serious objection was to the way Landesman portrayed him: he remained oblivious to what Gershon had suffered. He objected that Landesman sketched his own younger self as a playboy, well dressed in "carefully unpressed seersucker, hand-painted tie, and name brand 'desert' boots." Meanwhile, he showed Gershon in "'smelly' old sweaters . . . pants held up with piece of string, holes in the crotch." Jay described Legman as leering, snarling, and stealing from people.[38] Landesman's writing revealed that he was a snob, forced to eat pastrami with Gershon in Manhattan, all the while "regretting High-Goyishe cucumber sandwiches" that he could have been sharing with Henry and Clare Luce in Westchester County. Jay described himself leaving a fifty-cent tip and Legman snatching it "to eat *next* meal."[39] That was mean.

Legman thought the real problem was with Jay. He could not see the picture he was drawing of Gershon because he did not see himself clearly. Their conflicts were "never caused by my being a resentful poor artist . . . but simply by your unconsciousness, as a rich and pampered mama's boy . . ., of what it means to be poor and exploited." Jay had always had a free ride from one woman or another. He advised, "Think it over, Jay, as you write."[40]

Legman called his memoirs "Peregrine Penis: An Autobiography of Innocence." The title played upon *The Adventures of Peregrine Pickle*, Tobias Smollett's comic novel (1751), and he said that it had been coined by his girlfriend Beka Doherty, because he traveled to so many places to meet her. He began,

Under Mt. Cheiron **229**

as he usually did, by imagining the whole project, making a thorough outline and designing typeface and layout. He outlined "Peregrine Penis" as eight books, each with a title and comprising ninety-eight chapters. For book and chapter titles, he borrowed from "Tom O'Bedlam," an early modern English poem of uncertain origin, but also from A. E. Houseman and Floyd Dell.[41] The "Mad Tom" poems present the begging rants and songs of a homeless man, escaped from London's "Bedlam" hospital. As someone who was often so poor as to be nearly homeless, and who sometimes felt prophetic in a crazy way, Legman found resonance in the poem's psychedelic visions. And it originated in his beloved sixteenth century.

He began filling in the chapter headings on a daily writing schedule. It was graphic: "Like *My Secret Life*, with laughs!" he told Jay.[42] But in the mid-1980s, Legman faced a new problem. He was planning to self-publish "Peregrine Penis," but printers were now demanding digital files instead of typescripts for book production. The Legmans could not afford a word processor, so he solicited a crew of American typists who would each key in parts of the first book. There were "eight apostles" (also known as the Vicious Circle or the Society for the Prevention of Gershon Legman), and they were sworn to secrecy. The reward would be a copy of the very limited published first edition.[43] This seemed like a good idea at the time, but soon it emerged that not all personal computer operating systems were compatible. Endless letters went back and forth about the properties of machines and floppy disks. By the late eighties, "Peregrine Penis" was a mare's nest of typescript, manuscript, printouts, diskettes, and notebooks. It would be unpublished at his death, left for Judith to straighten out later.[44]

"Peregrine Penis" tells at great length of Legman's adventures in Scranton, Ann Arbor, New York, California, and France. It describes the horrible Yeshiva, Lower Manhattan during the Depression, the people he worked with, and the bookstores and booksellers he knew intimately. As an autobiography of innocence, it is far from sexually modest. Legman recounts his childhood, adolescent, and adult sexual life (possibly from the sex-act note-card collection he kept when he worked for Dr. Dickinson) in clinical detail, on the model of Frank Harris's *My Life and Loves*. In making love to women, he is most himself. Mainly, "Peregrine Penis" unfolds Legman's view of his own honorable motives. He is an innocent in that he is always trying to do the brave and right and honest thing in love, in reading and book collecting and in publishing. But like the hero of an eighteenth-century novel, he is undone by the corruption and selfishness of the world. He is sabotaged by his own earnestness.

In the spring of 1986, Legman made what he knew would be his last visit to the United States. He was asked to be the keynote speaker at the World

Humor and Irony Membership conference at Arizona State University in Tempe.[45] From there he made his way through Minnesota, Wisconsin, and upstate New York, stopping to give lectures, see friends, and consult with graduate students. He was miffed not to be invited to Philadelphia and the University of Pennsylvania, where Kenneth Goldstein should have scheduled a talk. Barbara Kirshenblatt-Gimblett drafted him to speak on erotic folklore at New York University, but Legman disappointed her by canceling at the last minute.[46]

At the conference in Tempe, he gave a talk on children's folklore as sex education. He was now being feted as the grand old man of joke studies, and the trip fed his ego and gave him a chance to expound his ideas. When he went on to the University of Minnesota, he gave a version of the same lecture.

He was introduced by Gary Alan Fine, a sociologist who shared many of his interests, including psychoanalysis, humor, and children's folklore. Fine described Legman (drawing on his self-description) as a "fieldworker for Planned Parenthood" and a coinventor of the vibrator.[47] In his presentation "Pecker Pool and Cock-a-lizers," he described the sexual folklore of his child-hood in Scranton, arguing that kids did not get their erotic enlightenment from their parents or teachers, but almost entirely from each other. It was a paradox, he thought, that adults who have forgotten their own childhoods worry about what eight-year-olds do or say. He drew on the recollections he was dredging up for his autobiography to present children's sex riddles and games as age-graded modes of learning. He cited the protective function of play, the way children used it to work out their first loves and aggressions. He remembered show-and-tell games, like urinary contests, that allowed children to learn about genitals and feel tender toward each other. Then there were bodily exploration and rules about touching and who could touch what. Later, there was overt hostility in group play, as in the snipe hunt ("While he's looking for the snipe we pee all over his penis") in a continuum leading to the disgusting initiation traditions of American university fraternities. And he moved toward the sadistic dimensions of initiations, "from forfeits to flagellation," describing a very aggressive card game his friends played called Pecker Pool. They would play Go Fish and beat the loser on his penis with their card hands until he screamed. And he moved on to his main theme, the growing sadism and violence of American culture—which he could see at the community movie house in Valbonne. He denounced the "genocides that are ahead of us" and wondered, "What does it mean that Clint Eastwood is Ronald Reagan's favorite movie star?" There were clubs for watching *The Texas Chainsaw Massacre.* He wondered, "What do we make of that?" He started to tell some jokes about the Space Shuttle Challenger disaster but backed off: "They are too rough for my blood."[48]

He took questions. One man remembered that "everyone at Columbia read *Love & Death*. It was quite an accomplishment. What ever happened to that book?" Legman fabricated a Legman-style answer: a French Arab who fell in love with him had circulated it at UNESCO, whence it filtered into Scandinavia, where it kicked off the pornography boom, which eventually undermined formal censorship in Europe and led to the sexual revolution in America. He had started the whole thing! Pornography, he thought, was perfectly fine. He asked, "If we are willing to do it, why are we not willing to look at it?" Certainly, parts of the industry were perverse, but he thought that the passage of time would allow a wholesome erotic art to flourish.[49]

An additional job for this trip was to promote *Maledicta: The International Journal of Verbal Aggression* he had helped Reinhold Aman start. Aman met Legman at the airport in Madison—an exasperated flight attendant fairly booted him off the plane—and took him back to his home at Waukesha, near Milwaukee, where he stayed for several days, impressing the Amans as the houseguest from hell. He played music at top volume on his new American boom box at four in the morning (a habit from Valbonne) and drank whole gallons of milk, straight from the jug. Mrs. Aman, who kindly did his laundry for him, was amazed at Legman's girth and his gall. He and Rey Aman got into a fight about Aman's childhood in Germany; Legman accused Rey (who had been a child during World War II) of having abetted the concentration camps. That was the end of that friendship.[50]

A few graduate students came to the talk he gave at the Aman house. James Leary was there and remembered Legman advocating his favorite sexual positions and asking for volunteers to demonstrate them. When this suggestion met midwestern reserve, someone thought to substitute forks and spoons for people. Legman used two forks to show "*las tijeras*," the scissors, which he highly recommended.[51]

After Milwaukee he stayed with Bruce Jackson and Diane Christian in Buffalo, giving talks in their classes and sorely trying their patience. At a talk Bruce sponsored at SUNY Buffalo, a young man wanted to discuss jokes about necrophilia. He was floored when Legman insisted he must have a serious problem that needed psychiatric attention.[52] In Diane's class, Gershon was especially rude and hostile to a gay student, but the young man startled him by pushing back against his homophobic pronouncements. Things were changing.

At the Christian-Jackson house, Legman behaved very badly. He argued with and imposed on everyone and insisted on watching video pornography. At dinner he terrified Jackson and Christian's daughter by asking her to imagine him killing her dog. Finally, Bruce lost his temper, physically put Legman and his bags out into the street, locked the door, and called a cab.

PILGRIMS

Visitors still came to Valbonne in the late 1980s, although less frequently than in earlier decades. A new generation, now interested in the history of erotica writing, began asking to interview Legman. Noël Riley Fitch came to consult him for her biography of Anaïs Nin.[54] Historian David Noble and his family met Legman by chance and ended up camping in the olive grove. Noble found Gershon bracing but "really weird."[55]

Writers Eric Laursen and Mary Dearborn visited La Clé des Champs in the autumn of 1988; Dearborn wanted to interview Legman for her biography of Henry Miller.[56] Laursen described the scene to Paris bookseller and publisher Michael Neal. Like Legman's other visitors, they didn't find it easy to get to Valbonne, but once they entered the café where Gershon awaited them, "he was unmistakable—a shortish, fat man with a shock of white hair, sitting at an open-air table with three large loaves of bread in front of him." He "lived up to his legend by ordering coffee for Mary and himself, drinking both cups when Mary couldn't finish hers, and then letting Mary pay for the whole thing." At the house, it turned out that Legman had expected they'd stay and camp, and he was irritated that they planned only a short visit. He advised them to "settle in here awhile like the hippies you ought to be." As usual, he offered an unsolicited opinion about the couple's relationship, telling Eric he suspected he might not be "playing a perfectly traditional 'husband' role vis a vis Mary." Anything else, he told Laursen, and "you're not doing yourself or her any good."[57]

Laursen and Dearborn noted the firm gender division in the household. The studio was a hypermasculine place, Eric felt, "the intellectual equivalent of a Sunday in America watching football with the guys—there he can make sexist jokes and commune with Dr. Freud, without fear of being reined in." Eric thought that Gershon kept Judith confined to the kitchen most of time, although Mary pointed out that she also worked in the studio, typing, proofreading, and keeping his files in meticulous order. It was striking to Eric that Legman had one old typewriter and no computer.[58]

Legman talked during their entire visit, a marathon soliloquy. He told them how he had been driven out of the United States by McCarthyism and offered his opinions on copyright law: writers ought to "pirate everything!" He protested that Philip Roth had hurt the Jews by writing "that book" (*Portnoy's Complaint*). And he was in the habit of propounding his sexism "of the old school that says all women want certain things—a home, babies, domestic tasks to perform. I give them what they want," he told Eric. "'If they want babies I give them babies and a home and the whole thing." Mary Dearborn, a feminist biographer, kept silent on this topic, and what Judith may have said is not recorded. She served a beautiful lunch.[59]

When they discussed Henry Miller, it became clear that Legman didn't care much for him and didn't find Miller's writing erotic. Now "he didn't consider Miller to be as great a writer of the underworld as Celine" and suspected him of being derivative. As for publishing *Tropic of Cancer* in the United States, Legman allowed that he "was young and impressionable." When he told the story of the pornography writing circle that led to *Opus Pistorum* and *Delta of Venus*, Laursen thought he was exaggerating. Many things in Legman's writings and conversation struck Eric "as tongue-in-cheek if not self-indulgent fiction. . . . Come to think of it this applies to some of his conversation as well." Was it true, Laursen wondered, that Legman had twenty-one children? Finally, he wrote, "One of my chief impressions of Gershon Legman is that he's a bitter man" who was surprised to have ended up in rural France after so many adventures.[60]

In 1990 literary historian Jay Gertzman interviewed Gershon about his work with Jake Brussel and Samuel Roth, for a book on the history of smut and its suppression in the 1930s and '40s.[61] Gertzman found Legman "uninhibitedly coarse and virile." From the first moment, Jay was "not even close to being in control of the interview" with the man with a strong, deep voice, "a tight hard smile, [and a] bright, fiercely alert eye." Gershon showed off his library but grew nervous when Jay wanted to examine the books. When Gertzman tried to tell him about Senator Jesse Helms's attacks on the National Endowment for the Arts, Legman accused him of being another wimpy liberal. So many liberals were too weak to "sustain real freedom of expression, or anything else." They just wanted the protection of the authorities, but he'd never had a grant to support his freedoms. At times he growled his opinions, and at times he literally screamed. A dazed Gertzman left the Legmans after dinner, looking back to see their "ancient shadows, indistinguishable from the general gloom."[62]

If Legman was bitter and angry, this was the inevitable result of isolation. He had worked long and hard, in fact endlessly, separating himself from the world to produce his hard-to-assimilate work. He could never have made his folklore and book collections, or written his books, while working an ordinary job; he found no way to insinuate himself into a paid academic position, and near the end of his working life he understood that this was a good thing. He had judged, reasonably, that he would not be able to write what he wanted in the United States, nor would he have survived the university publish-or-perish system. By the time the ice jam of the Cold War broke loose in the

234 CHAPTER 10

United States, he had resettled far away. Now here he was, with his fabled library, but away from the intellectual currents of contemporary life. Perhaps in his ferocious rejection of the counterculture and his attack on American liberals, he was defending against regret.

"BLOW THE CANDLE OUT"

Into 1990 Gershon continued working. He found time to write an article on erotica and libraries for his friend Martha Cornog, and he began a correspondence with David Lister of the British Origami Society on his own role in the history of the introduction of origami to the West.[63] His scholarship nearly came to a halt when, in 1991, he suffered a major stroke. For the first year and a half afterward, Judith tells, Gershon "still had a little bit of his old will to work, and he did dictate three or four or five chapters" of his autobiography to Judith and some parts of other chapters, "things that he was particularly aware of not having gotten down on paper." She sat near his bed and wrote it all out by hand in school notebooks and later typed it up and interfiled it with the rest of the chapters. They also worked together proofreading and indexing Randolph's "Roll Me in Your Arms" and "Blow the Candle Out."[64] When those volumes appeared in the early 1990s, his scholarly marginalization continued: they received few reviews. New bawdy collections from Randolph should have been a major event, but only one folklorist, Erika Brady, reviewed the two volumes for the *Journal of the History of Sexuality*. Brady wrote warmly that Legman's annotations were more than thorough—they were lively, outspoken, and eloquent, although Legman's personality was wildly different from Randolph's.[65] The books were big, and even though they did not come up to Legman's usual standards in typography, layout, and book design, they were expensive.

But other than this, Judith recalls, Legman really did not work much. The few times she helped him to go to his studio, "he didn't have the stamina to stay there terribly long, and the walk was more effort than he cared to make." He had always typed as fast or faster than he could think. But now he was paralyzed on one side, and "he found it impossible to type in any way that satisfied him," in Judith's words. He kept his clarity of mind, but lost interest in his work. "All the will and all the enormous emotional content of him was shrunk away a lot," she recalled. He stopped paper folding and rarely went out of the house. He read "fairly voraciously" in fiction and nonfiction, and "he was still happy to get letters and would read and comment on them," but his answers were brief dictations. The old letter-writing volcano had gone dormant. She regretted that when "people who he was fond of offered to visit him, he refused to see them, saying 'I don't want them to remember me like this.'" She urged physical therapy to help him regain strength, but he was "a rebellious cuss" and refused. There was a second stroke a year later, with similar effects and even less recovery.[66]

Judith cared for Gershon for the next seven years, with help from the two children still at home. It was housebound, difficult work, and she did almost all of it. He declined gradually, and then in February 1999 he had another, more massive, stroke. He was barely conscious for the last few days. Hoping something could be done for him, Judith took him to the hospital in Grasse, where he died on February 23, 1999. She was with him.[67]

For Judith, a long period of strain was ending. The family had a simple secular ceremony with friends and neighbors who had known them all for a long time. Ariëla Legman came from Amsterdam. There were flowers at the funeral and, of course, Mozart. A friend of Rafael's made a speech, mentioning that "he remembered hearing the music come pouring out of the studio" when he walked by as a young boy and "how everybody admired the American writer who was always up so early, the light streaming out the windows at four or five in the morning." The mourners went from the funeral parlor in Grasse to the little cemetery on the steep hillside in Opio and laid him to rest in the grave he had made for Beverley, with roses.[68] His headstone reads,

G. Legman, *Homme des Lettres, La Vie Est Belle*

News of Legman's passing was broadcast unevenly in the barely overlapping worlds of folklore, sex research, and paper folding. The Internet allowed old friends to hear quickly and organize tributes and memorials. Many saw the obituary Janny Scott wrote for the *New York Times*, based largely on interviews given by Judith and Bruce Jackson.[69] Jay Landesman wrote an obituary for the London *Independent* that stressed not only Legman's work on jokes, but his contributions to origami.[70] Martha Cornog and Timothy Perper wrote an appreciation for the *Journal of Sex Research*.[71] Origami master Akira Yoshizawa sent a floral tribute.[72] And Paris bookseller Michael Neal mounted a memorial display of Legman's books in his shop window.

Judith prepared a memorial card and mailed it to hundreds of the people in Gershon's extensive address file. His Scranton family was entirely gone—his sisters deceased and their children beyond reach. Most of his old New York friends were either dead or scattered in retirement. Still, she received hundreds of letters and phone calls and kept track of them all. Alan Dundes wrote a warm condolence to her, saying, "One of the giants of the twentieth century is gone!"[73]

Bruce Jackson proposed an article on Legman for *The Nation*, but he failed to drum up much interest. It wasn't clear if the editors at *The Nation* remembered who Legman was. He then proposed a tribute for the *Journal of American Folklore*, but somehow that fell through the cracks.[74] The journal

236 CHAPTER 10

that Legman had spent so much time pestering and haranguing, and sometimes improving, failed to take any formal notice of his death or to assess his contributions. Perhaps this was to be expected. Most of Gershon's other old folklore friends were gone. Hand, Randolph, Taylor, Dorson, Goldstein, and MacColl had all died before him. Alan Lomax and Hamish Henderson were elderly and ill. No one asked Legman's younger correspondents to produce an obituary.[75]

The most thorough assessment of Legman's contribution to folklore was circulated in Europe. Perhaps nudged by Alan Dundes, *Fabula*, the international journal of folk narrative studies, published an encompassing obituary. After surveying Legman's published work, Uli Kutter wrote:

> Legman did not find in his lifetime the recognition that he deserved. Political and cultural institutions (like universities) never really acknowledged him. It is hard to imagine what Legman could have researched and published if he had had paid help and research funding. Only a few members of the establishment supported him. His trajectory shares commonalities with Vance Randolph, Benjamin Botkin and Ernst Borneman—also engaged researchers who wrote about taboo and obscene topics, who undertook at their own cost and under personal sacrifice that which they felt was important and lived to an extent from hand to mouth. The American Folklore Society never managed to honor him as a Folklore Fellow despite his unquestionable contributions.[76]

Young scholars at the 1999 American Folklore Society annual meeting in Memphis organized a panel of papers in Legman's memory, but with a content warning: "Listener discretion is advised." He would have found this insulting. Meanwhile, the paper-folding community, coming into awareness of its own history, asked on message boards, "Is it true that Gershon Legman is dead?" and "Who was Gershon Legman?"

LEGACIES

Legman left a sprawling legacy consisting of his own books, articles, glossaries, bibliographies, discoveries, and republications, as well as the books that had been plagiarized or reprinted without permission or payment to him. There were his unpublished book manuscripts and his cache of tens of thousands of letters to and from celebrated and unknown writers and thinkers. His seemingly unending research files on popular culture dated back to the late 1930s. There was the remarkable library—toward the end of his life, he had tutored Judith in how to value the rare books as she would need to begin selling them a few at a time to live. There was his unruly, unfinished autobiography.

Intellectual legacies are even more fragile than physical archives, and more conflicted. Writers with long lives outlive their audiences, and their works are at risk of being overwritten by others and forgotten as fashions in scholarship and prose style change. Perhaps this is why Legman insisted that Judith make him a deathbed promise to publish his autobiography without changing a word.

Without patronage or an institutional foothold, Legman left overlapping trails of creative exploration and provocation, writing across many topics related to erotic love and freedom. His memory lives on unevenly today, made up of multiple Gershon Legmans. Sex researchers can find the laborer for Dickinson and Kinsey; historians of publishing can discover the anticensorship crusader and producer of illicit books. Erotica collectors may recognize Legman the pornographer, and they rely upon the bibliographer who rescued rare manuscripts and encouraged younger sleuths. There was Legman the proto-Beat provocateur of *Neurotica,* searching for a language to attack the conformity and terror of the 1950s. Legman the collector, who went beyond amassing texts to probe the roots of repression and wrestle with a Freudian analysis. Legman the introducer of origami. There was Legman the inventor and hero of his own iconoclastic legend, the Count of Valbonne and Vance Randolph's legatee. In this story, he sometimes appeared as an innocent, sometimes as a fallen angel, inventing the vibrating dildo and detonating the sexual revolution, always under surveillance by the FBI.

He had lived through the Great Depression, World War II, and the Red Scare, and he glimpsed the opening of American sexual culture in the 1960s. He had been horrified by the counterculture in which he was a cult figure, and attacked the folk revival. Writing in an engaged and critical vein through all these perplexing cultural shifts took enormous energy, not least because of poverty and exile. It is not surprising that he sometimes got it wrong or turned cranky and bitter. At the end of his life, all of his major books were out of print, and it was not clear whether he would be remembered accurately for his contributions, consigned to the humiliating category "old-fashioned," or just overlooked.

Some of Legman's lack of acknowledgment had to do with his extrusion and departure from the U.S. scene and, in the 1990s, his incapacitation. Perhaps if his "New Kryptadia" project had made it into print, he might have had a stronger impact through the 1980s and onward. If *Maledicta,* so well suited to Legman's varied interests, had appeared more regularly, his name might have remained before his audiences.[77] But he could rarely travel to give talks, and in his seventies he was not well enough to badger editors or arrange deals with publishers. Yet he tried as best he could to keep current. His scholarship—always in a way looking backward—might have narrowed backward to an exclusive concern with the Renaissance and Restoration texts he loved so much. Yet he was vigorously collecting contemporary "nonoral" stuff in print. Bruce Jackson wondered how Legman kept so up-to-date with American popular culture.[78]

Folklore, his claimed scholarly home, had changed dramatically. During the years when his work was most visible, the orientation of the field in North America had moved from the compilation and indexing of texts toward the search for theory and, in method, toward studies of folklore as communication and interaction, "performance in context." His own work on folklore texts was left behind by this shift to a focus on folklore as behavior. Legman called this "dada," just a new fad. He didn't see the point. Roger Abrahams ventriloquized Legman: "What's interesting about that? . . . I take it for granted that everybody is performing always."[79] What was interesting to Legman was *what* was being spoken, its origins, and the deep and slowly changing sexual attitudes it carried. But Legman's analyses of jokes could be pat declarations of meaning that had little in common with the close and careful interpretations of tellings that the younger folktale scholars aspired to pursue.[80]

In Abrahams's words, "What Legman and Dundes were into is the way the personal is deflected" in the play world. When people relate to each other on the basis of aggressive or erotic motives, the traditional oral culture of jokes is drawn on to make that possible. Abrahams expanded: "There are meanings here that need explanation," and "they are obviously carried by people into situations. . . . And that is a good basis for an argument." But it also seemed to Abrahams that in the performance perspective, the argument had been started but not followed through to deeper insights.[81]

Humor studies, and then cultural studies generally, had exploded, and from a distance Legman had played an important part in this. But in the 1990s, with a few exceptions such as James Leary and Elliott Oring, folklorists remained chary toward the joke. It was not a prestigious subject, and as academic careers in folklore became possible, it was perhaps not the genre upon which to stake one's reputation (or at least not one's first book). It was hard to study as performed, and folklorists were resistant to Legman's theses about aggression.[82] There were new and pressing topics for the younger folklorists: the imagined community of the nation, ethnic identity, and the history of tradition as an ideological construction focused their attention.[83] Meanwhile, as Legman found out trying to place "The Ballad," college professors tended to relegate laboriously produced multivolume collections of folk texts to their top shelves. What was in demand were the tightly focused studies that could be presented at conferences, quickly published as articles, and used in the classroom. Just as relevant, more American folklorists were working in the public sector and for governmental agencies. They spent much of their time crafting public festival performances and museum programs. These venues were not friendly to the folklore of sex.[84]

As the field of folklore began to include many more women, this too had consequences for the integration of Legman's work. The American folklore students of the 1960s and 1970s brought with them the concerns of Second Wave feminism. They were unlikely to appreciate Legman's pronouncements on the importance of childbearing for female happiness, and most were put off by the deep sexism and homophobia expressed in his joke collections. They ought to have taken up one of his major points, that most American humor expressed hatred and fear of women. But feminist folklorists were more concerned with tracing the positive contributions of womenfolk, documenting their little-noticed traditions, and exploring the ways they countered the suppression of their own voices.[85] Legman's critique of misogyny slipped by them.

In 2004, five years after Legman's death, Mikita Brottman, a psychoanalyst studying horror movies and car-crash culture, ventured a short book on his arguments about jokes. In *Funny Peculiar*, Brottman sympathetically explored Legman's work in a run-up to her own ideas about the aggressive and terrifying qualities of clowns, humor therapy, and stand-up comedy. She advocated for a recuperation of his broad view of Western culture's troubling uses of laughter.[86] Brottman's salute signaled that more than a decade after Legman's working life had ended, there might be more engagement with his perspective. But as new humor studies were published, Legman was sometimes briefly mentioned in the footnotes and bibliographies, even as just as often he was not. His *Rationale* books formed an important reservoir of interwar American jokes in English, but even when folklorists discussed difficult and unpleasant humor, they were reluctant to take up the gauntlet Legman had thrown down.[87]

Legman's impact on the history of sexuality is less ambivalent. His essays on the history of erotica went on to influence that emerging field, sometimes directly, sometimes indirectly, although this legacy was not usually acknowledged. The ideas Legman presented in *The Horn Book* came into their own as cultural and social historians responded to the European and American women's and gay rights movements. He had early asserted that sex has its own lore and customs and that pleasure has a cultural history. As political activists demanded an opening up of erotic life, it became clear that an examination of sex in the past could reveal a great deal about sex in the present. Suddenly, historians were looking sympathetically at eighteenth-century masturbators and nineteenth-century prostitutes; they unpacked courtship customs, premarital pregnancy, and perversities like flagellation, among many other topics. The past lives of homosexuals, lesbians, transvestites, and transsexuals

240 CHAPTER 10

began to come into view in books and articles. Matters that only a few years before had been utterly taboo were being discussed in college classrooms. A large part of this history of sexuality was new appreciation of the history of pornography, and Legman had directly fostered this.[88] By giving sex collectors like Henry Spencer Ashbee a history, he helped move erotica out of the shadows. In turn, folklorists began to look at the traditions of the body and at neglected erotic folktales and fairy tales.[89]

As the history of sexuality took off, the rhetorical uses of obscenity came into view. Historians went beyond cataloging sexual attitudes and behaviors in the past to explore the ways pornography could attack the sexual status quo and voice a broader political critique of illegitimate authority and corruption.[90] By the time historians were probing the uses of obscenity and scandal in undermining France's ancién regime, for example, Legman was no longer able to respond to their books.[91] But his bibliographic detective work helped make later studies possible.

Without doubt, the study of the history of sexuality that developed in the 1970s and 1980s did not depend upon Legman alone. It was more directly ignited by Alfred Kinsey and supported by the excellent library and archive Legman had helped him build.[92] In fact, the modern history of sexuality was led by theorists Legman declined to read, notably Michel Foucault.[93] But Legman's low visibility and the great difficulty of publishing serious work on erotica until the 1980s had more to do with his marginality than any lack of effort or expertise.

"I AM TELLING THE ROCK-HARD TRUTH!"

The core questions Legman raised in the 1940s have yet to be fully addressed. His argument that sex censorship had to fall if America were to become sane sits oddly in the chaotic twenty-first-century landscape of erotic expression and antagonism to sexual freedom. One imagines him taken aback by the contradictions between the end of formal censorship, the flowering of public sexual expression, and the emergence of new fields of conflict. At the end of his life, if the Comstock code had not completely fallen, the battles had definitively shifted. By the nineties, the unimaginable had happened: pornography had become part of mainstream American culture. Film and video erotica were now such a major industry that porn film workshops began to be subject to governmental health and safety regulations. On the few occasions he had a chance to observe the pornography that flourished on videotape, Legman was amazed at what could be seen and shown.[94] By the time Legman died in 1999, the unregulated Internet was multiplying the bounty exponentially in the United States. At the millennium, pornography delivered over phone lines and the Internet was responsible for fully half the profits of the major telecommunications providers.[95] Even ultraconservative Utah had to allow erotica according to a "community standard" when it was revealed that the Mormon-owned Marriott Inns in Salt Lake City provided pornography via cable to their guests.[96] It would have perplexed Legman to know that erotica was set free not through the triumph of argument but because it was so profitable. In an extension of the commercialization of feeling he had identified in *Love & Death*, repression had fallen not before sanity, but before the market.

The gender expressions in the porn revolution would have perplexed him. As he had told Anaïs Nin, Legman hoped erotica writing would become a feminine occupation. With the sexual revolution, and in better control of conception, women were publicly defining their sexuality and developing their own erotic arts.[97] However, much of the unashamed women's erotica, whether in print or on video, cable, or the Web, was being produced by lesbians, a development he would have found deeply upsetting to his conservative views on gender.[98]

As Legman might have predicted, the collapse of censorship did not meet easy acceptance. As representations of sex flooded the United States, there was outrage from many directions. The main debate became notorious: Did pornography allow a measure of freedom and exploration, or did it incite misogyny and violence toward women?[99] Another question was less frequently asked: In a nation so resistant to formal sex education, online pornography was now the main source of sexual information for adolescents and children. Did porn teach a distorted, unhealthy sexuality?[100] Where Legman would have landed on the question, left, right, or center, is unclear. But the minotaur had escaped from the labyrinth.

Conservative America remained horrified by the visibility of sexual expression, whether in porn, art, or public behavior. Culture warriors denounced open homosexuality and public mention of masturbation, while they stressed the importance of traditional marriage and childbearing for women. As Jay Gertzman had told Legman, the Supreme Court had definitively worn away legal restraints in publishing and rejected the punishment of private consensual acts. Now decency battles shifted from sanctions against immorality to the visibility and civil rights of gays, lesbians, and sexual nonconformists in general. A culture war broke out over the definitions of marriage and gender itself. As the American Right focused its attacks on governmental protections for sexual freedom, erotic expression by minorities remained vulnerable to attack. Would Legman have thought a healthy revolution was being fulfilled or that a "fake revolt" was being rolled back?[101]

Contradicting Legman's hope that lifting sexual repression would reduce brutality in popular culture, violence inundated literature and the media arts, as it did American daily life. From the 1990s onward, all the mass media seemed saturated with war and propaganda for war. Fictional murder and dismemberment were not chased out by erotica; they remained an important form of entertainment. By the 2000s, real sex by celebrities and ordinary people could now be seen on the small screen and even on the big screen.[102] But Legman would have observed, had he been able, that sadism, masochism, and the exploitation of women were even more available in entertainment than before. The racism and woman-hating of much of popular culture persisted, although they moved in and out of public concern.

The "rock-hard truth" about American violence that Legman fiercely insisted on telling, first in *Love & Death*, has become sharper in the years since his passing.[103] He would be unable to ignore the American propensity for extreme violence, and he would relate it to what he saw in comic books as the "universal military training of the mind." Legman's question will not go away: What is the relationship between Americans' acceptance of torture and endless war and their individual and collective mental health? Perhaps he was correct that the violence and hatred in folklore and popular culture stem from deep disturbances of people's minds. But he would argue finally that our collective disturbance and disorientation stem from the cruelties practiced on young people by their elders, at home and in schools, in our courts and the military. In Legman's final years, the United States again asked its young men and women to prosecute war and suffer grave moral injuries, as the atrocities of World War II and the Korean and Vietnam Wars were reprised in Iraq and Afghanistan. Legman would ask how participation in mass killing could fail to influence Americans' sanity. How could the war not come home and work its way into the seams of our lives, even into our stories and songs?

If the questions Gershon Legman raised have not yet been fully addressed, scholars and the public can still use the contributions of this hardheaded, prolific, self-taught man. His work has been hard to absorb, perhaps because his descriptions of "the world they are preparing for us" are harsh and troubling. If he was correct that "very few speak for love," he knew who spoke for death. He wondered, though, who would join him in speaking for his space of authenticity and redemption, "the central mystery and central reality of life."

NOTES

Abbreviations

AC	Arthur Ceppos
ACK	Alfred Charles Kinsey
AFC/LOC	American Folklife Center, Library of Congress, Washington, D.C.
AFS	American Folklore Society
AT	Archer Taylor
BJ	Bruce Jackson
DC	Diane Christian
DE	Duncan Emrich
EC	Ed Cray
EF	Edith Fowke
EH-J	E. Haldeman-Julius
EML	Emil Mendel Legman
FH	Frank Hoffman
FW	Fredric Wertham
GL	Gershon Legman
HH	Hamish Henderson
HMM	Herbert Marshall McLuhan
HS	Harold Spivacke
JCH	John Clellon Holmes
JFL	Julia Friedman Legman
JH	Joe Hickerson
JIL	Jay Irving Landesman
JK	Jan Kindler
JL	Judith Legman
KIRSG	Kinsey Archive, Institute for Research in Sex and Gender, Bloomington, Indiana

LAO	Legman Archive, Opio, France
LF	Leslie Fiedler
MC	Matilda Catalano
MK	Morty Kogut
OB	Osmond Beckwith
PG	Paul Gebhard
RDA	Roger D. Abrahams
RLD	Robert L. Dickinson
RMD	Richard M. Dorson
SEH	Stanley Edgar Hyman
SGDLP	Susan G. Davis Legman Papers, published and unpublished materials by Legman and others, in the possession of the author
SHSM	Western Historical Collection, State Historical Society of Missouri, St. Louis
WCW	William Carlos Williams

Preface

1. Bruce Jackson, "Gershon Legman: The King of X700," *Maledicta* 1 (1977): 112–13.

2. John Clellon Holmes, "The Last Cause," in *Evergreen Review* (1966), reproduced in Holmes, *Nothing More to Declare* (New York: Andre Deutsch, 1967), 21–32; Legman, *Love & Death: A Study in Censorship* (New York: Breaking Point, 1949), 18.

3. GL to JIL, July 4, 1967, Legman Archive, Opio, France.

Introduction

1. See Christine Stansell, *American Moderns: Bohemian New York and the Creation of a New Century* (Princeton, N.J.: Princeton University Press, 2009); Desley Deacon, *Elsie Clews Parsons: Inventing Modern Life* (Chicago: University of Chicago Press, 2008).

2. John Clellon Holmes, "The Last Cause," *Evergreen Review* (1966), reproduced in *Nothing More to Declare*, by Holmes (New York: Andre Deutsch, 1967), 30.

3. Adina Hoffman and Peter Cole, *Sacred Trash: The Lost and Found World of the Cairo Geniza* (New York: Random House, 2011).

4. Mikita Brottman, *Funny Peculiar: Gershon Legman and the Psychopathology of Humor* (Hillsdale, N.J.: Analytic Press, 2004).

5. Ibid., quoting Legman, *Love & Death: A Study in Censorship* (New York: Breaking Point, 1949), 18–19.

6. Holmes, "Last Cause," 25.

7. Christine Nasso, "G(ershon) Legman," in *Contemporary Authors*, ed. Nasso, rev. ed. (Farmington Hills, Mich.: Gale, 1977), 21:525–26.

8. His working definition was close to one used by folklorists now: Cathy Preston, "Erotic Lore," in *Encyclopedia of Women's Folklore and Folklife*, ed. Liz Locke, Theresa A. Vaughan, and Pauline Greenhill, 2 vols. (Westport, Conn.: Greenwood, 2008).

9. On pet names for genitals, see Legman's friend Martha Cornog, "Naming Sexual Body Parts: Preliminary Patterns and Implications," *Journal of Sex Research* 22

(1986): 393–98; and "Idioms and Nicknames," in *Cultural Encyclopedia of the Penis*, ed. Michael Kimmel, Christine Milrod, and Amanda Kennedy (Lanham, Md.: Rowman & Littlefield, 2014), 93.

10. All these usages are cited in a letter from GL to RDA, July 7, 1959.

11. For example, his "FARK: Folklore Article Reconstruction Kit," *Journal of American Folklore* 90 (1977): 199–202.

Chapter 1. The Stranger

1. G. Legman, *I Love You, I Really Do! Part 1: Being Book One of G. Legman's Autobiography of Innocence* (n.p.: CreateSpace, 2016), 18. Legman titled his whole autobiography "Peregrine Penis: An Autobiography of Innocence," but after his death it was partially published and under varying titles. The whole manuscript, written between 1982 and 1992, is in the possession of Judith Legman.

2. Ibid.

3. Ibid., 20–30.

4. J. Harold Brislin, "Portrait of a Champion of People's Causes: Legman, 82, Engaged in 'My Greatest Work,'" *Scrantonian*, January 15, 1967. On the history of Scranton's Jewish population and congregations, see Michael J. Brown, "Toward a History of Scranton Jewry," in *From Ghetto to Emancipation: Historical and Contemporary Reconsiderations of the Jewish Community*, ed. David N. Myers and William V. Rowe (Scranton: University of Scranton Press, 1997), 135–54.

5. Legman, *I Love You*, pt. 1, 30.

6. Mother's story and contraband materials: ibid., 30–36. Legman recalled that his Friedman grandmother and an aunt came from Mono to visit Scranton when he was a small boy, a journey that must have taken significant resources. Ibid., 41–48.

7. Ibid., 33.

8. Ibid., 36.

9. On Scranton's geography and economy during the period of Legman's childhood, see Clifford M. Zierer, "Scranton as an Urban Community," *Geographical Review* 17, no. 3 (1927): 415–28.

10. Ibid., 421–22; Brown, "History of Scranton Jewry," 146.

11. There seems to have been a network of Friedman relatives in Scranton and its surrounding towns.

12. Brown, "History of Scranton Jewry," 146.

13. The picture of the adaptation and economic place of the 1890–1918 generation of immigrant Jews in Scranton is similar to Eva Morawska's description of the ethnic niche economy in early-twentieth-century Johnstown, Pennsylvania. Eva Morawska, *Insecure Prosperity: Small Town Jews in Industrial America, 1890–1940* (Princeton, N.J.: Princeton University Press, 1996).

14. Brown, "History of Scranton Jewry," 147.

15. On the Hungarian Jewish Enlightenment, see Raphael Patai, *The Jews of Hungary* (Detroit: Wayne State University Press, 1996).

16. Legman, *I Love You*, pt. 1, 199. It is less clear that Julia learned to write comfortably in English, as her surviving letters to Gershon seem to have been dictated to her daughters.

17. Brislin, "Portrait of a Champion."

18. The Southside Hebrew School (Talmud Torah) and its "Big Shul" was called Ahavas Achim. The temple was attended mostly by Jews of Hungarian descent. Marian Yevics Lackawanna Historical Society kindly provided this information from Scranton city directories, letter to the author, February 10, 2004.

19. 1910 Manuscript Census, Scranton, Northampton County.

20. Legman, *I Love You*, pt. 1, 30.

21. Brislin, "Portrait of a Champion."

22. Ibid.

23. Marian Yevics to Susan Davis, February 10, 2004.

24. Working for free and buying gold: Gershon Legman, *I Love You, I Really Do! Part 2: Being Book One of G. Legman's Autobiography of Innocence* (n.p.: CreateSpace, 2017), 95.

25. Legman, *I Love You*, pt. 1, 7. "Gershon" is Hebrew for "the stranger."

26. Ibid., 65–67 and passim.

27. Ibid., 174.

28. See Susan Porter Benson, *Household Accounts: Working-Class Family Economies in the Interwar United States* (Ithaca, N.Y.: Cornell University Press, 2007), for a description of these flexible strategies of the working-class family economy. See also Susan A. Glenn, *Daughters of the Shtetl: Life and Labor in the Immigrant Generation* (Ithaca, N.Y.: Cornell University Press, 1990).

29. Obituary, *Scranton Times*, June 24, 1975. Temple Israel was organized in 1921 by "some upwardly mobile Eastern Europeans," according to Brown, "History of Scranton Jewry," 142.

30. Conservative ritual practice sat between that of the German Reform congregations and the proliferating Eastern European Orthodox congregations.

31. Brown, "History of Scranton Jewry," 142.

32. Ibid., 142–44.

33. Everyone's account except his children's: on the occasion of Emil's death, Matilda described the funeral and reflected on how much she hated her father. MC to GL, June 27, 1975; and GL to MC, June 30, 1975, LAO.

34. Legman, *I Love You*, pt. 1; JL, interview with the author, May 9, 2004, Opio, France.

35. Legman, *I Love You*, pt. 1, 7–13.

36. Philip Roth, *Patrimony: A True Story* (New York: Simon & Schuster, 1991), 36, 38.

37. Legman, *I Love You*, pt. 1, 6–8.

38. The Balfour Declaration was "the least well-kept promise in modern diplomacy," he wrote, because the European powers were at the same time "promising the exact opposite secretly to the Arabs." Legman retained a strong sense of himself as Jewish, but he was never a Zionist. Ibid., 16–17.

39. Ibid., 16–17, 114–15.

40. Ibid., 119–21. Indeed, when the family did need it, Gershon refused. When Emil saw that the end of his life was near, he begged Gershon to come from France to his funeral and say the Kaddish. Gershon did not attend. Letters, EML to GL, 1974–75, LAO.

Notes to Chapter 1

41. Legman, *I Love You*, pt. 1, 118–21.

42. Ibid., 16–17.

43. In his article "The Psychopathology of the Comics," *Neurotica* 3 (1948): 3–30; and his introduction to Sandra McCosh, *Children's Humour: A Joke for Every Occasion* (London: Granada, 1976), vii–xlix.

44. Legman, *I Love You*, pt. 1, 16–17.

45. Ibid., 121.

46. Ibid., 116.

47. Early experience of anti-Semitism: ibid., 143–54; "horse-shit juice" incident: 162–63.

48. He couldn't figure out how one could cheat on an IQ test.

49. JL, interview with the author, May 9, 2004, Opio, France.

50. GL to EML, April 17, 1931, LAO. Note that by April 1931, he was already in trouble at yeshiva.

51. Ibid.

52. Gershon Legman, "Bridge of Night," *Brooklyn Bridge Bulletin* (May 24, 1983): 26–27.

53. Ibid.

54. GL to EML, April 17, 1931, LAO.

55. Daniel Gordon wrote his own account of being a student of Rabbi Joseph Jacob during the same year. "Bow Wow, Squinty and Other Feared Teachers," unpublished manuscript, by permission of Daniel Gordon's family. He describes the beating of students at the yeshiva and his own mother intervening forcefully.

56. GL to EML, May 13, 1931, LAO.

57. Gershon, *I Love You*, pt. 1, 447, 468, 466. Heywood Broun, socialist, later the founder of the American Newspaper Guild, wrote "As I See It" for the *New York World-Telegram* in the early 1930s.

58. Ibid., 467.

59. Note on the back of an envelope, n.d., in 1931 letter file, LAO.

60. Note, n.d., in 1931 letter file, LAO; Legman, *I Love You*, pt. 1, 415–68.

61. Note, n.d. in 1931 letter file, LAO.

62. On Jane Jacobs, see Robert Kanigel, *Eyes on the Street: The Life of Jane Jacobs* (New York: Alfred A. Knopf, 2016); on her early life in Scranton, 19–47.

63. His friendship with Endfield seems to be the beginning of his origami interest. On Friday nights, they would fold together and argue politics.

64. See the following chapter.

65. Legman, *I Love You*, pt. 2, 95.

66. Ibid., 96–97.

67. Ibid., 105.

68. Ibid., 105–11.

69. Ibid.

70. Ibid., 108–11.

71. Mr. Wallach mocks radicalism: ibid., 100–105.

72. *Suppressions*: ibid., 117–26.

73. Stück's bookshop and Uncle Joel: ibid., 148–58.

248 *Notes to Chapter 1*

74. He claimed to have had extensive prepubertal sexual relations with neighborhood girls. Legman, *I Love You*, pt. 1, 173–274; pt. 2, 5–93.

75. Legman, *I Love You*, pt. 1, 333–43.

76. Ibid., 180–90.

77. Ibid., 338 (Dreiser), 193 (book a day), 338, 206–7 (Emil).

78. Ibid., 332–33.

79. Ibid., 320–24.

80. His joke collecting: ibid., 322–24; and Legman, *I Love You*, pt. 2, 81–88. His erotica scrapbook: "Ye Olde Scrapbook, 1934," Legman Collection, KIRSG.

81. Be fruitful: Legman, *I Love You*, pt. 1, 334.

82. Legman, *I Love You*, pt. 2, 129–70.

83. Ibid., 199–210.

84. Gershon and Emil came to physical blows when Matilda went into labor—Emil did not want her to be seen outside the house. Legman, *I Love You*, pt. 2, 388–97.

85. Ruth married a labor journalist, Myer Finberg, and moved to Allentown. Matilda Catalano worked as a hatcheck girl in Brooklyn and Manhattan into the 1970s. June Malaken became June Figueroa and lived with her husband, a farmer, near Cuernavaca, Mexico. Daisy and Martin Birnbaum married in 1941.

86. On sexual censorship, see Paul S. Boyer, *Purity in Print: Book Censorship in America from the Gilded Age to the Computer Age* (Madison: University of Wisconsin Press, 2002); and Jay A. Gertzman, *Bookleggers and Smuthounds: The Trade in Erotica, 1920–1940* (Philadelphia: University of Pennsylvania Press, 2001).

87. Legman, *I Love You*, pt. 1, 340.

88. On the American regime of sexual and literary censorship, see Boyer, *Purity in Print*; and Gertzman, *Bookleggers and Smuthounds*. On the federal Post Office Department as censor, see Dorothy Ganfield Fowler, *Unmailable: Congress and the Post Office* (Athens: University of Georgia Press, 1977). The United States Department of the Post Office, established in 1792, was a cabinet-level department from 1872 to 1971 and headed by the postmaster general. It became the independent United States Postal Service in 1971.

89. Upton Sinclair on brothels: *The Goose Step: A Study of American Education* (Pasadena, Calif.: the author, 1923).

90. Christine Stansell, *American Moderns: Bohemian New York and the Creation of a New Century* (Princeton, N.J.: Princeton University Press, 2009); David M. Raban, *Free Speech in Its Forgotten Years, 1870–1920* (New York: Cambridge University Press, 1997).

91. Leonard Wilcox, *V. F. Calverton: Radical in the American Grain* (Philadelphia: Temple University Press, 1992); V. F. Calverton, *The Bankruptcy of Marriage* (London: John Hamilton, 1929).

92. A frequent topic of Broun's was the idiocy of censorship.

93. The spectacle of discussion, controversy, repression, and change was one of several waves of activism for sexual freedom from the early nineteenth century into the late nineteenth and early twentieth centuries in the United States. It featured such colorful characters as John Humphrey Noyes, Frances Wright, Victoria Woodhull, and Ezra Heywood. See John D'Emilio and Estelle B. Freedman, *Intimate Matters: A History of Sexuality in America* (New York: Harper Row, 1988); and Raban, *Free Speech*.

Notes to Chapter 1 **249**

For more on early changes in American sexual expression, see Richard Godbeer, *Sexual Revolution in Early America* (Baltimore: Johns Hopkins University Press, 2003). On Woodhull, see Mary Gabriel, *Notorious Victoria: The Life of Victoria Woodhull, Uncensored* (New York: Algonquin Books, 1998). On Ezra Heywood, see Martin Blatt, *Free Love & Anarchism: The Biography of Ezra Heywood* (Urbana: University of Illinois Press, 1989). On Noyes, see J. H. Noyes, *Strange Cults and Utopias of the Nineteenth Century*, ed. Mark Halloway (New York: Dover, 1966). On early-twentieth-century sex and marriage reformers and their changing attitudes, see Stansell, *American Moderns*.

94. Constance M. Chen, *"The Sex Side of Life": Mary Ware Dennett's Pioneering Battle for Birth Control and Sex Education* (New York: New Press, 1996).

95. David Kennedy, *Birth Control in America: The Career of Margaret Sanger* (New Haven, Conn.: Yale University Press, 1971); Jean A. Baker, *Margaret Sanger: A Life of Passion* (New York: Hill and Wang, 2012); Andrea Tone, *Devices and Desires: A History of Contraceptives in America* (New York: Hill and Wang, 2001).

96. He claimed this many times, but I have not been able to document it.

97. G. Legman, *Mooncalf: Being Book Two of G. Legman's Autobiography of Innocence* (n.p.: CreateSpace, 2017), 180.

98. On collecting as a defense against childhood losses, see Werner Muensterberger, *Collecting: An Unruly Passion, Psychological Perspectives* (New York: Harcourt Brace, 1994), 3–48. See also Alan Dundes, "On the Psychology of Collecting Folklore," in *The Meaning of Folklore: The Analytical Essays of Alan Dundes*, ed. Simon J. Bronner (Logan: Utah State University Press, 2007), 414–21.

99. Thanks to Simon Bronner for this point.

100. Michael Denning, *The Cultural Front: The Laboring of American Culture in the Twentieth Century* (London: Verso, 2000); Franklin Folsom, *Days of Anger, Days of Hope: A Memoir of the League of American Writers, 1937–1942* (Niwot: University Press of Colorado, 1994).

101. John Szwed, *Alan Lomax: The Man Who Recorded the World* (New York: Penguin Books, 2011); Jerrold Hirsch, *Portrait of America: A Cultural History of the Federal Writers' Project* (Chapel Hill: University of North Carolina Press, 2003).

102. John Avery Lomax, *Cowboy Songs and Other Frontier Ballads* (reprint, New York: Macmillan, 1938); John A. Lomax and Alan Lomax, *American Ballads and Folksongs* (New York: Macmillan, 1934); Nolan Porterfield, *Last Cavalier: The Life and Times of John A. Lomax, 1867–1948* (Urbana: University of Illinois Press, 1996); Szwed, *Alan Lomax*; Charles Wolfe and Kip Lornell, *The Life and Legend of Leadbelly* (New York: Da Capo Press, 1999).

103. Robert Cochran, *Vance Randolph: An Ozark Life* (Urbana: University of Illinois Press, 1985).

104. Similarly, Alan Lomax had to invent and feel his way into the techniques of a field collector. He apparently learned a great deal by watching others—his father, Zora Neale Hurston, and his many local consultants. Hurston was making up her field methods as she went along, adopting a participatory, immersive style.

105. JL to Susan Davis, email, May 27, 2002.

106. Legman on Krauss: Legman, *Mooncalf*, 194–95; GL to Alice Loranth (librarian, Cleveland Public Library), March 12, 1972, LAO; *Kryptadia* and *Anthropophyteia*

250   *Notes to Chapters 1 and 2*

could not be printed or published in Austria but had to be printed in France. Bernard Sergent, "Les precurseurs: Histoire de la mythologie Française," http://www.mytho francaise.asso.fr/2_mytho/21_precurs.html.

Chapter 2. Sex Researcher

1. G. Legman, "Road Kid," in *Mooncalf: Being Book Two of G. Legman's Autobiography of Innocence* (n.p.: CreateSpace, 2017), 9–85.

2. Ibid., 12–15. This book was cited in his bibliographies as *Lapses in Limerick* (Ann Arbor, 1938).

3. "That was the real beginning . . ." (notes, correspondence file for 1936), LAO.

4. See G. Legman, "On Sexual Slang and Speech," introduction to *Dictionary of Slang & Its Analogues*, ed. John S. Farmer and W. E. Henley, rev. ed. (New York: University Books, 1966), 1:xxx–xciv. On Farmer and Henley's works, see Julie Coleman, *The History of Cant and Slang Dictionaries*, vol. 3, *1859–1936* (Oxford: Oxford University Press, 2004), 53–73.

5. George and Ira Gershwin, the composers, were first cousins to folklorist Benjamin Botkin. Legman and Botkin corresponded briefly but never met. On the house, see Legman, *Mooncalf*, 85–103.

6. On Jewish youth unemployment in Manhattan in the 1930s, see Beth S. Wenger, *New York Jews and the Great Depression: Uncertain Promise* (New Haven, Conn.: Yale University Press, 1996), especially "Starting Out in the Thirties," 54–79; and Jeffery S. Gurock, *Jews in Gotham: New York Jews in a Changing City, 1920–2010* (New York: New York University Press, 2012).

7. *In the Matter of G. Legman: Post Office Department Fraud Examination*, Fraud and Lotteries Docket, hearing under J. C. Haynes, June 6, 1950, transcript #635, 96; Ellis quoted in Legman, *Mooncalf*, 180.

8. On the publishing industries, see "Book Publishing," in *Encyclopedia of New York*, ed. Kenneth T. Jackson (New Haven, Conn.: Yale University Press, 1995), 124–27. On popular entertainments, see David Nasaw, *Going Out: The Rise and Fall of Public Amusements* (New York: Basic Books, 1993).

9. Christine Stansell, *American Moderns: Bohemian New York and the Creation of a New Century* (Princeton, N.J.: Princeton University Press, 2009).

10. Legman, *Mooncalf*, 103–68. On theater censorship in New York, see Jackson, *Encyclopedia of New York*, s.v. "theater" and "censorship"; and letter from Morton Minsky, http://www.nytimes.com/1981/12/26/opinion/l-the-day-la-guardia-killed-burlesque -147199.html. On 1930s burlesque and its routines, see Andrew Davis, *Baggy Pants Comedy: Burlesque and the Oral Tradition* (New York: Palgrave Macmillan, 2011).

11. Legman, *Mooncalf*, 133–44.

12. Jay A. Gertzman, *Bookleggers and Smuthounds: The Trade in Erotica, 1920–1940* (Philadelphia: University of Pennsylvania Press, 1999).

13. On Depression economics of the book trade: ibid., 15–49.

14. Jacob Brussel (1899–1979): Legman, "On Faking Henry Miller" (unpublished manuscript introduction to a reprint of *Opus Pistorum,* 1983), copy of original typescript provided by Jay Gertzman (*Opus Pistorum* was published by Grove Press in

Notes to Chapter 2

1983, but without the Legman introduction); Legman, *Mooncalf*, 253–349. Legman insisted on calling Brussel "Jake," although he was generally known as Jack.

15. Walter Goldwater, "Obituary Notes: Jacob 'Jack' Brussel," *AB Bookman's Weekly* 64, no. 24 (1979): 4008–9.

16. Legman, *Mooncalf*, 283–349.

17. Jake had a Ph.D. in mathematics and was offered a position at Columbia but said that he knew that they wouldn't want a Jew. Marvin Mondlin and Roy Meader, *Book Row: An Anecdotal and Pictorial History of the Antiquarian Book Trade* (New York: Carroll & Graff, 2004), 222.

18. Ibid., 223–25.

19. Ibid., 226; Legman, *Mooncalf*, 316–18.

20. Mondlin and Meader, *Book Row*, 227.

21. Ibid., 228. In the art field, the Brussels published anti-Nazi art, such as the prints of George Grosz and Kathe Kollewicz.

22. Ibid.

23. Legman, introduction to *Art of Mahlon Blaine* (New York: Peregrine Books, 1982), 7.

24. Ibid., 8–9.

25. Legman, introduction to ibid., 16. Brussel was expurgating *Fanny Hill* to make it shorter and cheaper and just clean enough to skirt obscenity law.

26. There is a short informal history of the Book Mart, but not the life of this influential woman. W. G. Rogers, *Wise Men Fish Here: The Story of Frances Steloff and the Gotham Book Mart* (New York: Harcourt Brace, 1968).

27. Anaïs Nin, *The Diary of Anaïs Nin*, vol. 3, *1939–1944* (New York: Houghton Mifflin Harcourt, 1971), 11.

28. Legman, *Mooncalf*, on Miss Steloff, 202–8.

29. Nin, *Diary*, 179.

30. Ibid.

31. Steloff's late husband, David Moss, had published Norman Douglas's obscene *Some Limericks*, which was of great interest to Legman. She expanded Moss's erotica sales after his accidental early death. Legman, *Mooncalf*, 202–8; Legman, *World I Never Made: Being Book Three of G. Legman's Autobiography of Innocence*, Peregrine Penis (n.p.: CreateSpace, 2017), 67.

32. Legman, *Mooncalf*, 202–8.

33. Ibid., 171–72.

34. His research files at the Kinsey Institute Archives contain parts of these early notebooks.

35. Ibid., 171–211.

36. Ibid., 172.

37. J. A. Dulante and Adolph Niemoeller, *Gods of Generation: On Phallic Cults, Ancient and Modern* (New York: Panurge Press, 1933); Adolph Niemoeller, *Sexual Slavery in America* (New York: Panurge Press, 1935). Niemoeller also wrote many Little Blue Books for E. J. Haldeman-Julius. *Superfluous Hair and Its Removal* (New York: Harvest House, 1938).

38. Adolph Niemoeller to GL, July 8, 1936, LAO.

252   *Notes to Chapter 2*

39. Robert Briffault, *The Mothers: A Study of the Origins of Sentiments and Institutions* (New York: Macmillan, 1927); Legman, *Mooncalf*, 173.

40. Briffault's ideas on the history of the family were at odds with those of his contemporary Bronislaw Malinowski, at midcentury the major anthropologist writing on the topic. The two anthropologists staked out their positions in a major debate in 1930–31, in a series broadcast over the BBC in 1931. The lectures were republished as Ashley Montagu, *Marriage Past and Present: A Debate between Robert Briffault and Bronislaw Malinowski* (Boston: Porter Sargent, 1956), http://www.mailstar.net/marriage-malinowski.html. Intriguingly, Briffault's arguments have been paralleled by the findings of some later-twentieth-century archaeologists. For a summary, see Marija Gimbutas, *The Civilization of the Goddess* (New York: HarperCollins, 1992).

41. Legman, *Mooncalf*, 185.

42. On Dickinson, Janice Irvine, *Disorders of Desire* (Philadelphia: Temple University Press, 1990), 14–15; Judith Allen, "Notes to Finding Aid," n.d., Robert L. Dickinson Collection, KIRSG, 1–5; Vern L. Bullough, *Science in the Bedroom: A History of Sex Research* (New York: Basic Books, 1994), 92–120. In 1943 Dickinson would found the American Association of Marriage Counselors, which he headed until 1950, and become a founding vice president of the Planned Parenthood Federation of America.

43. On the New Woman, marriage and sexuality, see Desley Deacon, *Elsie Clews Parsons, Inventing Modern Life* (Chicago: University of Chicago Press, 1997).

44. Allen, "Notes to Finding Aid," 1–5; Bullough, *Science in the Bedroom*, 111 (vaginal observation).

45. Irvine, *Disorders*, 31–32.

46. Ibid.

47. Legman, *Mooncalf*, 189.

48. Ibid., 193–94.

49. Gershon Legman, November 2, 1936, introduction to "Proposal for the New Kryptadia," LAO. The Kryptadia project would have many other titles and incarnations over the years.

50. Ibid.

51. Ibid.

52. Ibid.

53. RLD to GL, November 13, 1936, LAO.

54. Copy of Adolf Meyer to RLD, May 31, 1937, LAO.

55. Copy of Havelock Ellis to RLD, June 18, 1937, LAO.

56. Copy of Gaston Vorberg to RLD, June 21, 1937, LAO. Magnus Hirschfeld organized the first scientific study of homosexuality. On Hirschfeld's fate, Bullough, *Science in the Bedroom*, 74.

57. Legman, *Mooncalf*, 197–99.

58. "Notes," in 1936 correspondence file, LAO.

59. On the model of the famous Vatican Index Librorum Prohibitorum, but also on the model of Pisanus Fraxi's bibliography. Legman wrote that this had been suggested to him by several Eighth Avenue bookmen. "Notes," 1936 correspondence file, LAO. On Pisanus Fraxi, see Ian Gibson, *The Erotomaniac: The Secret Life of Henry Spencer Ashbee* (Cambridge, MA: Da Capo Press, 2001).

Notes to Chapter 2   **253**

60. Painter would become an important informant to Alfred Kinsey, and Kinsey hired him and Legman to recruit homosexual respondents for Kinsey's Human Male study.

61. Thomas Painter, "Male Homosexuals and Their Prostitutes in Contemporary America" (typescript, New York, 1941, KIRSG). GL to PG, April 13, 1959; PG to GL, May 1, 1959; GL to PG, May 5, 1959, KIRSG.

62. Later, a dispute broke out over publication rights to the "Male Prostitutes" book. Dickinson thought the manuscript belonged to him, since he had commissioned it. Painter thought it belonged to him, since he had researched and written it, and Legman argued that it was partly his, at least morally, since he had helped write, edit, and organize it. But Painter's book would remain unpublishable because of its subject. His detailed research albums of gay pornography and a personal diary and sex-life history survive at the Kinsey Archive. We might know more about the dispute and the relationship between Legman and Painter, but the correspondence between Painter and Kinsey in the Kinsey Archive seems to have been culled. The institute was protective of Kinsey's sexual reputation in the years after his death. One letter between Legman and Painter turns up, accidentally filed in the Legman-Kinsey correspondence. Painter noted in "De Profundis," one of his unpublished writings, that he was intrigued by comic books and that they were erotic to homosexual men. Painter thought comics asked boys to identify homosexually, a point Legman would later make much of.

63. Jan Gay was born Helen Reitman; her father was Emma Goldman's comrade Ben Reitman, the "whorehouse doctor" and Wobbly. See Henry L. Minton, *Departing from Deviance: A History of Homosexual Rights and Emancipatory Science in America* (Chicago: University of Chicago Press, 2002), 35.

64. Minton, *Departing from Deviance*, 43–45. With most other psychiatrists and medical doctors, Henry believed homosexuals were "developmentally damaged individuals, victims of poor parenting and the breakdown of the family in times of rapid social change." Minton describes Henry's attitude as pitying gay men and lesbians as unfortunate targets for a prejudiced judicial system; Henry stressed the prevention of "criminal" or "delinquent" behavior rather than treatment for homosexuality.

65. Minton, *Departing from Deviance*, 40; George Alexander Legman, "The Language of Homosexuality: An American Glossary," in *Sex Variants: A Study of Homosexual Patterns*, ed. George W. Henry, M.D. (New York: Harper and Brothers, 1941), 2:1149–79.

66. Minton, *Departing from Deviance*, 45, 54, 56–57.

67. Legman, "Language of Homosexuality." He later complained in a letter to Alfred Kinsey that Henry and the editors had severely cut the glossary and probably added it to *Sex Variants* only to pump up the volume's sales. The glossary does not appear in later editions of the work. GL to ACK, November 3, 1942, KIRSG.

68. He would later discuss the psychology of word listing and collecting in his "Sexual Slang and Speech."

69. For example, see George Chauncey, *Gay New York: Gender, Urban Culture and the Making of the Gay Male World, 1890–1940* (New York: Basic Books, 1994).

70. Legman, "Language of Homosexuality," 1155–56.

254 *Notes to Chapter 2*

71. In addition to Painter's manuscript, Legman found assistance in Godfrey Irwin's "American Tramp and Underworld Slang" (1931), in "The Underworld Speaks," by Albin J. Pollock (1935), and from David Maurer, a young expert on criminal slang at the University of Louisville.

72. Legman, "Language of Homosexuality," 1159, 1161.

73. Ibid., 1159.

74. Ibid., 1163.

75. Ibid., 1165–66.

76. Ibid., 1161.

77. Ibid., 1157.

78. Ibid., 1160.

79. Ibid., 1155.

80. Ibid., 1155–56.

81. Jackson, *Encyclopedia of New York*, s.v. "lesbians," 733–35.

82. GL probably to Tom Painter ("Dear Tom"), misfiled in the Kinsey Legman Collection, KIRSG.

83. David A. Johnson, *The Lavender Scare: The Cold War Persecution of Gays and Lesbians in the Federal Government* (Chicago: University of Chicago Press, 2006).

84. Gershon Legman, "Poontang," *American Speech* 25, no. 3 (1950): 234–35.

85. Legman later wrote that if he had to do it over, and had had some capital, he would have been a dealer in and master maker of fine books. The design skills would stay with Legman his whole life. Scattered throughout his files are sketches for book projects—title pages, colophons, epigraphs, and experiments with type fonts. JL, interview with the author, May 9, 2004, Opio, France.

86. In "On Faking Henry Miller," Legman traced his path into the underground world of erotica.

87. For example, Margaret Sanger's husband J. Noah Slee smuggled suitcases of German birth-control devices into the United States through Canada, in support of Sanger's birth control movement.

88. On Joyce's *Ulysses*, see Paul S. Boyer, *Purity in Print: Book Censorship in America from the Gilded Age to the Computer Age* (Madison: University of Wisconsin Press, 2002), 247–54; Gertzman, *Bookleggers and Smuthounds*, 172–73.

89. On Miller, see Mary V. Dearborn, *The Happiest Man Alive: A Biography of Henry Miller* (New York: Simon & Schuster, 1991); on the timing of publication of *Tropic of Cancer*, 187.

90. Legman, "On Faking," 10–11.

91. Dearborn, *Happiest Man*; Frederick Turner, *Renegade: Henry Miller and the Making of "Tropic of Cancer"* (New Haven, Conn.: Yale University Press, 2012).

92. Henry Miller to GL, October 20, 1938, LAO.

93. Ibid.

94. George Alexander Legman to James Laughlin IV, November 13, 1938, LAO.

95. Laughlin to GL, October 25, 1939, LAO.

96. GL to Laughlin, December 16, 1938; GL to Laughlin, October 19, 1939; GL to Laughlin, December 6, 1939, LAO.

97. Mary Dearborn's account is based in the Frances Steloff papers and tells the same story except for the role played by Legman. Dearborn writes it was Steloff who helped

Notes to Chapter 2 255

arrange with Brussel and Abramson to secretly publish *Cancer*. They agreed to front Miller money for various pieces of his work. Steloff was "one of Miller's most ardent champions" and "most important American contact," helping him make connections with other bookshop owners, getting him advance orders, and generally spreading the word about his books. Dearborn, *Happiest Man*, 187–88.

98. Henry Miller to GL, March 28, 1939, holograph copy in Legman Archives, with typescript copy.

99. Miller to GL, May 18, 1939, LAO.

100. Legman, *World I Never Made*, 189–240; GL to Laughlin, January 3, 1940, LAO.

101. The full title of the book is *Oragenitalism: Oral Techniques in Genital Excitation*, vol. 1, *Cunnilinctus* (New York: Brussel, 1940).

102. In a second, widely pirated edition, Legman revised *Oragenitalism* to include chapters on fellation and other oral-genital practices, based "strictly" on his own research.

103. Ibid., 5.

104. The research process is described at length in *Mooncalf*. In one place in his memoirs, he says he later destroyed the index upon remarrying to protect his wife, Judith, from distress.

105. The level of sexual detail in his memoirs suggests that he drew on these notes to reconstruct his Manhattan love life.

106. Later, Legman would write a review of the first edition of Alex Comfort's wildly popular *Joy of Sex*, slamming it for its celebration of bondage and mild sadomasochistic play. It was disgusting, encouraging perversion, he wrote. It is unclear whether the review was ever published. "The Joys of Perversion" (copy courtesy of Eric Laursen).

107. Legman, "On Faking," 11.

108. Legman, introduction to *Art of Mahlon Blaine*, 20.

109. Legman never heard from Blaine again. Ibid.

110. Legman, "Fall Guy," in *Mooncalf*, 351–400.

111. Legman, "On Faking," 1: "Wily Jake Brussel always hid half of the printing of everything he issued, to cheat his partners or the public" (or both). Ibid., 11.

112. Legman, "On the Lam in Washington," in *Mooncalf*, 385–460.

113. Ibid., 444–60.

114. Goldwater, "Obituary Notes." In a recent history of the publication of *Tropic of Cancer*, no mention is made of the MEDVSA edition. Turner, *Renegade*.

115. Legman, "On Faking." A few of the volumes of bound typescript by "The Oxford Professor" can be seen in the Kinsey Institute Archives. All the textual and typographic fooling around, and the dating of the books to the late 1930s, seems to confirm Legman's participation or authorship. On Clara Tice, see Priscilla Frank, "Meet Clara Tice, the Erotic Illustrator Who Scandalized 20th-Century New York," *Huffington Post*, April 24, 2017, https://www.huffingtonpost.com/entry/clara-tice-honest-erotica_us_58fa216ae4b06b9cb916396f.

116. G. Legman, "Anaïs Nin," in *World I Never Made*, 99–188.

117. John Clellon Holmes, "The Last Cause," *Evergreen Review* (1966), reproduced in *Nothing More to Declare*, by Holmes (New York: Andre Deutsch, 1967), 21–32.

118. Legman, *World I Never Made*, 99–188.

119. Ibid.

Notes to Chapters 2 and 3

120. Ibid., 125; reproduced as "Erotica of Henry Miller and Anaïs Nin (a Chapter from the Memoirs of G. Legman)," in *Writings about Anaïs Nin: A Sixth Supplement to Rose Marie Cutting's Anaïs Nin, a Reference Guide*, comp. Richard R. Centing (Graduate Library, Ohio State University, Columbus) (Boston: G. K. Hall, 1978).

121. Legman, *World I Never Made*, 127.

122. Ibid., 141–42.

123. Ibid., 135–36.

124. Ibid., 129.

125. Ibid., 187; Nin, *Diary*, vol. 3 (taking on the job); and in Noël Riley Fitch, *Anaïs: The Erotic Life of Anaïs Nin* (Boston: Little, Brown, 1993).

126. Legman, *World I Never Made*, 187.

127. Ibid., 186.

128. "Marianne," in *Delta of Venus: Erotica*, by Anaïs Nin (New York: Pocket Books, 1977), 70–82.

129. Nin, *Delta of Venus*; Fitch, *Erotic Life of Anaïs Nin*, 230–39, 249. Fitch interviewed Legman about the affair and quotes extensively from the manuscript that became *World I Never Made*.

130. Legman, *World I Never Made*, 129–30.

Chapter 3. Kinsey's Bibliographer

1. ACK to RLD, March 23, 1941, KIRSG.

2. ACK to GL, care of RLD, August 31, 1942, LAO.

3. Liana Zhou, head of archives, interview with the author, September 27, 2002, KIRSG.

4. Over the years, Legman wrote that he would will his papers to the Kinsey Institute Archive. This never took place legally, but in the years since her husband's death Judith Legman has been transferring his research files to the Kinsey Institute Archives, which now maintains a Gershon Legman Collection.

5. On Kinsey, see Jonathan Gathorne-Hardy, *Sex the Measure of All Things: The Life of Alfred Kinsey* (Bloomington: Indiana University Press, 2004). (Kinsey, born in 1894, was twenty-three years older than Legman.)

6. On the story of the "Human Male" project, see ibid., 229–54.

7. On Kinsey's method, see ibid., 170–81; and James Gilbert, *Men in the Middle: Searching for Masculinity in the 1950s* (Chicago: University of Chicago Press, 2005), 81–105.

8. Gathorne-Hardy, *Measure of All Things*, 141–42.

9. Ibid., 170–81.

10. Ibid., 146–47.

11. Ibid., 175–77.

12. Ibid., 147, 279–86. See also Julia Ericksen, "With Enough Cases, Why Do You Need Statistics? Revisiting Kinsey's Methodology," *Journal of Sex Research* 35, no. 2 (1998): 132–40.

13. ACK to GL, care of RLD, August 31, 1942, KIRSG.

14. G. Legman, *Musick to My Sorrow: Being Book Four of G. Legman's Autobiography of Innocence, Peregrine Penis* (n.p.: CreateSpace, 2018), 506–7.

Notes to Chapter 3 **257**

15. GL to ACK, November 3, 1942, KIRSG.

16. Ibid.

17. Ibid.

18. Ibid.

19. ACK to GL, January 26, 1943, KIRSG.

20. He discussed this with "prim" Allen Walker Read, author of *Lexical Evidence from Folk Epigraphy in Western North America: A Glossarial Study of the Low Element in the English Vocabulary* (1935), an uncensored study of American graffiti privately published in France. G. Legman, *Mooncalf: Being Book Two of G. Legman's Autobiography of Innocence* (n.p.: CreateSpace, 2017), 208–10.

21. Legman Collection, Folklore, Poems, and Songs (four vertical files) (1943–53). The earliest pieces in the file are dated 1927 and were probably copied from *Immortalia* (1929). KIRSG.

22. ACK to GL, January 26, 1943, KIRSG.

23. GL to ACK, January 28, 1943, KIRSG.

24. ACK to GL, January 26, 1943, KIRSG.

25. GL to ACK, January 28, 1943, KIRSG.

26. Ibid. (emphasis in the original).

27. Ibid.

28. On Roth, see Jay A. Gertzman, *Samuel Roth: Infamous Modernist* (Gainesville: University Press of Florida, 2013). Dickinson exchanged books, drawings, and photographs with Kinsey and sent packages only by private railway companies that did not inspect his outgoing mail.

29. GL to ACK, January 28, 1943, KIRSG.

30. Gathorne-Hardy, *Measure of All Things*, 229–54.

31. GL to ACK, vernal equinox letter, March 21, 1943, KIRSG.

32. Speculator morum [Sir W. Laird Clowes], *Bibliotheca Arcana: Seu Catalogus Librorum Penetralium* (London: George Redway, 1884).

33. GL to ACK, March 23, 1945, KIRSG; GL to "Tom" (Thomas Painter), March 10, 1943, KIRSG.

34. GL to ACK, March 23, 1945, LAO.

35. Ibid.

36. Gathorne-Hardy, *Measure of All Things*, 132.

37. Ibid., 232–33; ACK to GL, June 12 and August 14, 1944, and March 18, 1945, KIRSG.

38. GL to ACK, October 7, 1943, and August 12, 1944, KIRSG.

39. GL to ACK, November 12, 1943, KIRSG.

40. ACK to GL, March 20 and March 26, 1945, KIRSG.

41. ACK to GL, March 15, 1945, KIRSG; GL to ACK, April 5, 1945, LAO.

42. GL to ACK, April 5, 1945, LAO.

43. GL to ACK, March 23, 1945, LAO.

44. Frank Hoffman, interview with the author, September 27, 2002, Bloomington, Ind.

45. JL, interview with the author, May 10, 2004, Opio, France. Judith says that Gershon thought Kinsey was gay and that he was uneasy in Kinsey's research circle of young men.

Notes to Chapter 3

46. Henry Minton, *Departing from Deviance: A History of Homosexual Rights and Emancipatory Science in America* (Chicago: University of Chicago Press, 2002).

47. Robert Laidlaw, M.D., to the Selective Service System Local Board 26, August 19, 1941, LAO. Laidlaw also cited the importance of Legman's work for the Academy of Medicine.

48. G. Legman, "Bridge of Night," *Brooklyn Bridge Bulletin* (May 24, 1983): 26–27; Legman, *Mooncalf*, 75–80.

49. Norman Lockridge [Gershon Legman], *The Sexual Conduct of Men and Women: A Minority Report* (New York: Hogarth House, 1948), with "Minority Report," 13–32.

50. In the opinion of Judith Legman, email, August 10, 2012.

51. Lockridge, *Sexual Conduct*, 144.

52. Ibid., 145–46.

53. Ibid.

54. Ibid.

55. Ibid., 150, 154.

56. On conflict with psychoanalysts, see Gathorne-Hardy, *Measure of All Things*, 60, 152, 167.

57. Legman, "Minority Report," in *Sexual Conduct*, by Lockridge, 13.

58. Ibid. For a recent review of Kinsey's statistical methods, see Ericksen, "With Enough Cases."

59. Ibid., 14. Later critics have pointed out that Kinsey was not attempting proportional sampling. According to Ericksen, he did not understand it, and it would not have been possible in the late 1930s and early 1940s when he was doing his research. Ericksen, "With Enough Cases"; Gathorne-Hardy, *Measure of All Things*, 279–86.

60. Legman, "Minority Report," in *Sexual Conduct*, by Lockridge, 14–15.

61. Gebhard later admitted that the "lower level" data was very poor—it was comparatively sparse and was collected mostly from incarcerated men and boys. Gathorne-Hardy, *Measure of All Things*, 272.

62. Legman, "Minority Report," 17.

63. Ibid., 17.

64. Ibid., 21–22.

65. Ibid., 26.

66. Kinsey even viewed child-adult sexual relations neutrally or at least with less horror than the wider public and establishment. Gathorne-Hardy, *Measure of All Things*, 223.

67. Legman, "Minority Report," in *Sexual Conduct*, by Lockridge, 21–22.

68. Gathorne-Hardy, *Measure of All Things*, 259–61.

69. Legman, "Minority Report," in *Sexual Conduct*, by Lockridge, 29.

70. Ibid., 27.

71. Ibid.

72. Ibid., 31–32.

73. GL to ACK, March 7, 1948, KIRSG.

74. Gorer had worked in the British Depression-era sociology experiment Mass Observation and written about American burlesque theater, strip tease, and the Marquis de Sade. http://en.wikipedia.org/wiki/GeoffreyGorer; Gorer, "Justification by

Numbers: A Commentary on the Kinsey Report," *American Scholar* 17, no. 3 (1948): 280–86.

75. PG to GL, May 1, 1959, KIRSG.

76. Alfred C. Kinsey, with Wardell Pomeroy, Clyde Martin, and Paul Gebhard, *Sexual Behavior in the Human Female* (Philadelphia: W. B. Saunders, 1953); GL to PG, May 5, 1959, KIRSG.

77. Ericksen, "With Enough Cases."

78. Gorer, "Justification by Numbers."

79. GL to ACK, March 27, 1955; ACK to GL, April 7, 1955; GL to ACK, April 11, 1955; ACK to GL, May 4, 1955, and April 6, 1956; GL to ACK, April 17, 1956, all in KIRSG.

80. GL to PG, April 13, 1959, KIRSG.

81. PG to GL, May 1, 1959; GL to PG, May 5, 1959, KIRSG.

82. Wardell B. Pomeroy, *Dr. Kinsey and the Institute for Sex Research* (New York: Harper & Row, 1972).

Chapter 4. *Love & Death*

1. On the left literary scene Legman was trying to join, see Alan Wald, *The New York Intellectuals: The Rise and Decline of the Anti-Stalinist Left from the 1930s to the 1980s* (Chapel Hill: University of North Carolina Press, 1987).

2. Kathleen Beverley Wallace Keith was born in Toronto in 1913 and immigrated to the United States in 1928. She and her brother, Graeme, attended high school in Cleveland, Ohio. When her parents divorced, Beverley and her mother, Kathleen, moved to Manhattan.

3. JL, interview with the author, May 12, 2004, Opio, France.

4. G. Legman, *Musick to My Sorrow: Being Book Four of G. Legman's Autobiography of Innocence, Peregrine Penis* (n.p.: CreateSpace, 2018), 355.

5. Ibid., 308, 357.

6. Ibid., 312, 321.

7. Ibid., 358–59.

8. Ibid., 357; "Columbia University to Confer Degrees on 4,826 at Ceremonies Tonight," *New York Times*, June 1, 1936, 16. In 1943, at age twenty-nine, she was naturalized by petition. Legman describes Beverley's mother, Kathleen, as almost vampiric and certainly crazy. She was interested only in "what she could get out of whom, and how fast, and as much as possible." Legman, *Musick to My Sorrow*, 402.

9. Ibid., 404.

10. Their marriage was a common-law marriage, not legally registered. When Gershon decided in 1964 that he wished to marry another woman, their common-law status posed problems, and he was at pains to prove legally that he had never married.

11. JFL to GL, October 30, 1947, LAO.

12. Ibid. This was a "Lucy Stone" egalitarian marriage, so-called after the feminist who revived the custom of married women keeping their own names. Over the years, Gershon shifted back to using the solitary Legman.

13. GL to JFL, May 20, 1947, LAO.

14. Ruth's death: JFL to GL, May 19, 1947; GL to JFL, May 20, 1947, LAO.

260 *Notes to Chapter 4*

15. Legman, *Musick to My Sorrow*, 407–10; entomological specimen, 410.

16. Ibid.

17. Ibid. Much later some family money was settled on Beverley, which allowed them to buy an old farm in the South of France.

18. Jarry, a largely forgotten Parisian poet, playwright, and artist, was a forerunner of the Dadaist and surrealist movements. His work had been translated into English, in an English edition in 1950, but his poetry and plays were not known in the United States (London: Gabberbockus Press, 1951). Beverley and Gershon's was the first American publication. The translation as "King Turd" was apt: Ubu does look like a large walking turd in Jarry's sketches. Roger Shattuck, *The Banquet Years: The Origins of the Avant-Garde in France 1885 to World War I*, rev. ed. (1960; reprint, New York: Vintage Books, 1968).

19. Legman's translation had a much smaller, less eventful debut in New York in 1960. Arthur Gelb, "'King Ubu' Reigns in Coffee House," review of *Ubu Roi*, *New York Times*, November 24, 1960, 47.

20. Charles Hoy Fort (1874–1932), https://en.wikipedia.org/wiki/Charles_Fort. For years afterward, the Fortean Society bothered Legman, urging him to join them.

21. John Clellon Holmes's profile of Legman, "The Last Cause," *Evergreen Magazine* (1966), is the best description of these evenings; it is reprinted in his *Nothing More to Declare* (London: Andre Deutsch, 1968), 16–20, 21–32.

22. Holmes, *Nothing More*, 22. (Later Legman would object that Clellon Holmes and Landesman had unfairly described him as feeding his wife "on lung.")

23. OB to GL, September 16, 1980 (comments on Legman's draft autobiography), SGDLP. Courtesy of Osmond Beckwith.

24. Ibid.

25. Clellon Holmes, *Nothing More*, 21–22.

26. Ibid., 23–24.

27. Ibid., 25.

28. Ibid., 26.

29. Ibid., 27.

30. Ibid., 25–26.

31. Upton Sinclair to GL, January 18, 1950; Wilhelm Reich to GL, December 31, 1945, and January 22, 1947; Edmund Wilson to GL, January 15, 1947; Dwight Macdonald to GL, November 6 and November 27, 1946, all in LAO.

32. GL to Ewing Baskette, July 20 and October 28, 1955, Ewing W. Baskette Collection, Rare Books and Manuscripts Library, University of Illinois at Urbana-Champaign, folder 107.

33. C. L. R. James, "Notes on American Civilisation," typescript (1950), published as *American Civilization* (Oxford: Blackwell, 1992).

34. Leo Lowenthal, "The Triumph of Mass Idols," in *Literature, Popular Culture and Society* (Englewood Cliffs, N.J.: Prentice Hall, 1961).

35. F. R. Leavis and Denis Thompson, *Culture and Environment* (London: Chatto and Windus, 1933); Q. D. Leavis, *Fiction and the Reading Public London* (London: Chatto and Windus, 1932); Richard Hoggart, *The Uses of Literacy: Aspects of Working Class Life* (London: Chatto and Windus, 1957); Raymond Williams, *The Long Revolution* (London: Chatto and Windus, 1961).

Notes to Chapter 4 **261**

36. On the mass culture debate and Wertham's place in it, see Bart Beaty, *Fredric Wertham and the Critique of Mass Culture* (Jackson: University Press of Mississippi, 2005), 48–73.

37. OB to GL, September 16, 1980, SGDLP.

38. James Agee, writing in *Time* in 1945, noted similarly: "The war was over. The postwar world was born. Everywhere the returning traveler saw signs of change, signs of no change at all, signs of change but too fast, signs of change but not fast enough: signs by the million." James Agee, "The Nation," *Time*, November 5, 1945, 22–24. (Thanks to Lucy Schiller for this.)

39. On E. Haldeman-Julius (1898–1951), see http://en.wikipedia.org/wiki/ E. Haldeman-Julius; and Rolf Potts, "The Henry Ford of Literature," *Believer*, http:// believermag.com/the-henry-ford-of-literature.

40. GL to EH-J, February 4, 1946, LAO.

41. Ibid.

42. Ibid. (emphasis in the original).

43. Bradford Wright, *Comic Book Nation: The Transformation of Youth Culture in American Culture* (Baltimore: Johns Hopkins University Press, 2001), 29. On dime novels and working-class reading, see Michael Denning, *Mechanic Accents: Dime Novels and Working-Class Culture in America* (Brooklyn: Verso, 1998). On print, see Paul Boyer, *Purity in Print* (Madison: University of Wisconsin Press, 2002). On dance halls, see Kathy Peiss, *Cheap Amusements* (Philadelphia: Temple University Press, 1986). On vaudeville and theater, David Nasaw, *Going Out* (New York: Basic Books, 1993). On precode censorship of movies, see Francis G. Couvares, ed., *Movie Censorship in American Culture* (Amherst: University of Massachusetts Press, 2006).

44. Wright, *Comic Book Nation*, 28–29.

45. Sterling North, "A National Disgrace," *Chicago Daily News*, May 8, 1940.

46. James Frank Vlamos, "The Sad Case of the Funnies," *American Mercury*, April 1941, 411–17.

47. Wright, *Comic Book Nation*, 31, 34–36.

48. In 1949 the French National Assembly prohibited the circulation of American crime comics. Joseph A. Barry, "Juvenile Books and French Politics," *New York Times Book Review*, February 13, 1949.

49. Wright, *Comic Book Nation*, 31, 86.

50. James Gilbert, *A Cycle of Outrage: America's Reaction to the Juvenile Delinquent in the 1950s* (New York: Oxford University Press, 1986).

51. David K. Johnson, *The Lavender Scare: The Cold War Persecution of Gays and Lesbians in the Federal Government* (Chicago: University of Chicago Press, 2006); George Chauncey, *Gay New York: Gender, Urban Culture and the Making of the Gay Male World, 1890–1940* (New York: Basic Books, 1994).

52. On moral panics, see Stanley Cohen, *Folk Devils and Moral Panics: The Creation of the Mods and Rockers* (London: Paladin, 1973); for a definition, 9.

53. Wright, *Comic Book Nation*, 86; Gilbert, *Cycle of Outrage*.

54. William Bush, introduction to *Fredric Wertham: The Circle of Guilt* (Jackson: University Press of Mississippi, 2007).

55. Beaty, *Fredric Wertham*, 16.

262 *Notes to Chapter 4*

56. Wertham came out of the tradition of medical psychiatry rooted in the science of the physical brain (neurology). While psychiatry and anatomy are treated as separate disciplines, in the early history of psychoanalysis the distinction was less sharp than it would later become. At Johns Hopkins, Wertham taught both brain anatomy and psychotherapy, but he gradually became more interested in mind and behavior—and left his work as an anatomist to the side. Ibid., 116–17.

57. Ibid., 33–34, 45–46.

58. Henry L. Minton, *Departing from Deviance: A History of Homosexual Rights and Emancipatory Science in America* (Chicago: University of Chicago Press, 2002).

59. Ibid.

60. The training of psychiatrists must be grounded in an understanding of larger social behavioral factors, such as the history of poverty and the interaction of immigration and family history, he thought. Beaty, *Fredric Wertham*, 17.

61. Ibid., 34–35.

62. Wertham, *Circle of Guilt*.

63. He also risked his professional standing by helping victims of the Red Scare, supplying psychiatric support to Ethel Rosenberg on death row and arguing successfully against solitary confinement for her. Beaty, *Fredric Wertham*, 82–86. The Lafargue clinic was so successful that it was certified by the Veterans Administration to treat returning servicemen. Dennis Doyle, "'A Fine New Child': The Lafargue Mental Hygiene Clinic and Harlem's African American Communities, 1946–1958," *Journal of the History of Medicine and Allied Sciences* (2008): 1–40.

64. Fredric Wertham, *Dark Legend, a Study in Murder* (New York: Duell, Sloan, and Pearce, 1949).

65. Fredric Wertham, *The Show of Violence* (Garden City, N.Y.: Doubleday, 1949) and *The Circle of Guilt* (New York: Rinehart, 1956).

66. Dr. Dickinson had consulted Wertham's senior colleague at Johns Hopkins Adolf Meyer for an opinion on Legman's "sex dictionary" project.

67. Bob Lauter, "Do Our Churches Offer a Sound Basis for Faith and Living?," *Daily Worker*, November 25, 1949, 10, in Legman document file for 1949, LAO.

68. Ibid., 10.

69. Gilbert, *Cycle of Outrage*, 91–108.

70. Beaty, *Fredric Wertham*, 171–96. For an example, see the early work of Theodor Adorno on television, "Television and the Patterns of Mass Culture," *Quarterly of Film, Radio and Television* 8 (1954): 211–35.

71. Beaty, *Fredric Wertham*, 161–64.

72. GL to FW, January 4, 1948, LAO.

73. Ibid.

74. Ibid.

75. Beaty, *Fredric Wertham*, 161–64.

76. It was published as "The Comic Books and the Public," *American Journal of Psychotherapy* 1, no. 2 (1948): 472–77.

77. GL to JFL, March 22, 1948, LAO.

78. JFL to GL, March 22 and April 23, 1948, LAO.

79. JFL to GL, April 23, 1948, LAO.

Notes to Chapter 4 **263**

80. I am quoting from the fuller version of his argument, "Not for Children," published in *Love & Death* (1949), from the 1963 reprint; 27–54.

81. Ibid., 27–28.

82. Ibid., 27.

83. Ibid., 31.

84. Ibid., 36–37, 38.

85. Ibid., 31.

86. Ibid., 32.

87. Ibid.

88. Ibid. The Frankfurt School writers, particularly Max Horkheimer and Theodor Adorno in "The Culture Industries" and "Enlightenment as Mass Deception," pointed to mass culture as they tried to identify the roots of fascism in Europe, but their writings, difficult and negative, were not read by many American intellectuals at this point. Legman seems to have come to similar conclusions on his own. See Patrick Brantlinger, *Bread & Circuses: Theories of Mass Culture as Social Decay* (Ithaca, N.Y.: Cornell University Press, 1983).

89. Legman, "Not for Children," 40.

90. Ibid., 40–41.

91. From the point of view of the smut hounds, American youth *did* need to be protected from comic books, because the same people drawing, writing, and publishing the detective and superhero books were the producers of "Tijuana Bibles" and other cheap print pornography. A current view of the Tijuana Bibles is celebratory: Bob Adelman, *Tijuana Bibles: Art and Wit in America's Forbidden Funnies, 1930s–1950s* (New York: Simon & Schuster, 1997). Stylistically and formally, there was noticeable overlap.

92. Legman, "Not for Children," 31. He shared this view with journalists Judith Crist and Marya Mannes, with whom he corresponded, and the children's librarians and educators who had been criticizing comics since the late 1930s. GL to Marya Mannes, March 2, 1948, LAO.

93. Legman, "Not for Children," 32.

94. Draft letter from GL to FW in correspondence file, 1950 (undated and not sent), LAO.

95. "Breaking Point" was perhaps borrowed from a contemporaneous novel and a John Garfield movie, just as Garfield was being hounded by the anticommunist crusade. The name captured the feeling that American culture was breaking with sanity and that Legman had been nearly broken by the process of trying to get his book published.

96. Felix Giovanelli to GL, January 22, 1949, LAO.

97. Giovanelli to GL, January 14, 1948; JCH to GL, September 10, 1949, LAO. Hyman was the husband of playwright Shirley Jackson and author of *The Armed Vision* (1947), which Legman admired. SEH to GL, June 14, 1948, LAO.

98. Legman did save disparaging letters, too, as examples of the idiocy he was up against—but for this article, I found none.

99. Aiken to the poet Weldon Kees, with copy to Giovanelli, August 23, 1949; Giovanelli to Kees, August 27, 1949, LAO.

100. Jane B. Jacobs to GL, February 15, 1950, LAO.

101. Joseph Amber Barry to GL, October 5 and December 11, 1949, LAO.

264   *Notes to Chapters 4 and 5*

102. Louise Doherty to GL, October 21, 1949, LAO.

103. HMM to GL, August 6, 1949, LAO.

104. WCW to book dealer Lawrence W. Maxwell, August 17, 1949; GL to WCW, September 7 and September 13, 1949; WCW to GL, September 13, 1949, LAO. Legman wrote to Williams that "I am very mired in this stuff and have ghosted almost all the things I attack." He was shriving himself by pointing to the audiences' greater crimes. "Very few speak for love."

105. JCH to GL, May 19, 1950, LAO.

106. Robert Gorham Davis to GL, December 2, 1948, LAO.

107. Alex Comfort to GL, November 8, 1949, LAO.

108. Weston LaBarre to GL, April 13, 1949, LAO.

109. Beaty, *Fredric Wertham*, 130–32, 160–61.

110. GL to Keller, August 8, 1949, LAO.

111. GL to Robert Lipson, February 26, 1950, LAO.

112. W. L. McAtee to GL, August 3, 1949, LAO.

113. GL to Maria Leach, November 19, 1949, LAO.

114. *New York Times*, December 4, 1949, 4.

115. Richard H. Rovere, *Harper's* 199, no. 1195 (1949): 114. Rovere was a columnist for *The Nation*.

116. Malcolm Cowley to GL, August 24, 1949, LAO; Malcolm Cowley, "Books in Review: Sex, Censorship and Superman," *New Republic*, October 10, 1949, 18–19; GL to MC, February 26, 1950, LAO.

117. Cowley, "Books in Review," 18.

118. Ibid., 19. The Peekskill Riots (white race riots against singer Paul Robeson and the incipient civil rights movement) took place August 27 and September 4, 1949, in Westchester County, N.Y.

119. Leslie Fiedler, "Come Back to the Raft Again, Huck Honey!," *Partisan Review* 15, no. 6 (1948): 664; LF to GL, October 8, 1949, and January 12, 1950; GL to LF, January 26, 1950, LAO.

120. GL to LF, January 26, 1950, LAO. Ever after Legman would say that Fiedler had stolen his arguments from him and published them in his *Love and Death in the American Novel* (New York: Stein and Day, 1960).

121. Amy Kiste Nyberg, *Seal of Approval: The History of the Comics Code* (Jackson: University Press of Mississippi, 1998). On the Kefauver Committee hearings, see Gilbert, *Cycle of Outrage*, 143–61.

122. Johnson, *Lavender Scare*.

Chapter 5. *Neurotica*

1. John Clellon Holmes, "The Game of the Name," in *The Portable Beat Reader*, ed. Ann Charters (New York: Penguin Press, 1997), 615–22.

2. Carl Solomon (1928–93) met Allen Ginsberg in Greystone Park Psychiatric Hospital in 1949. His "Report from the Asylum: Afterthoughts of a Shock Patient" was published under the name Carl Goy in *Neurotica* (vols. 6 and 8) in 1950–51. James Campbell, *This Is the Beat Generation* (Berkeley: University of California Press, 1999),

Notes to Chapter 5 **265**

96. Naphtali "Tuli" Kupferberg (1923–2010) was a New York poet and founder of the underground band the Fugs. Chandler Brossard's (1922–93) first novel, *Who Walk in Darkness* (New York: New Directions, 1952), was a portrait of 1940s Greenwich Village bohemia. Anatole Broyard (1920–90), writer, literary critic, and *New York Times* editor, was a prominent member of the postwar Greenwich Village scene.

3. Jay Landesman, *Rebel without Applause* (Sag Harbor, N.Y.: Permanent PR, 1987).

4. Ibid., 39.

5. Ibid. Savo Stanley Radulovich (1911–91), painter, and Richard Jay Rubenstein (1922–58), poet, were part-owners of the Little Bohemia bar with Landesman.

6. Ibid., 43.

7. Ibid., 45, 46, 30.

8. Ibid., 46, 49.

9. Ibid., 46, 49–55.

10. Kenneth Patchen (1911–72), experimental poet and novelist who incorporated music, drawing, and painting into his work. Henri Michaux (1899–1984), a francophone poet known for his lyrical, esoteric, dreamlike, and often drug-induced style.

11. Gerald W. Lawlor, "Neurotics, Inc.," *Neurotica* 1, no. 2 (1948): 10–11. Lawlor was a layperson interested in psychodrama.

12. Ibid., 11.

13. Douglas Fitzgerald Dowd, *Blues for America: A Critique, a Lament, and Some Memories* (New York: Monthly Review Press, 1997), 68–75.

14. David K. Johnson, *The Lavender Scare: The Cold War Persecution of Gays and Lesbians in the Federal Government* (Chicago: University of Chicago Press, 2004); Ellen W. Schrecker, *Many Are the Crimes: McCarthyism in America* (Princeton, N.J.: Princeton University Press, 1998).

15. Nathan Hale, *Freud and the Americans: The Beginnings of Psychoanalysis in the United States, 1876–1917*, vol. 2 (New York: Oxford University Press, 1995).

16. Sloan Wilson, *The Man in the Gray Flannel Suit* (1955; reprint, Cambridge, Mass.: Da Capo Press, 1983).

17. John Clellon Holmes, "All the Good Rôles Have Been Taken: The Plight of the Talented Untalented," *Neurotica* 3 (Autumn 1948): 31–35.

18. Landesman, *Rebel without Applause*, 49–70.

19. Ibid., 49.

20. Ibid., 55.

21. Ibid., 86–87.

22. Ibid., 60–62.

23. Ibid., 67.

24. Ibid., 64.

25. JIL to GL, July 29, 1948, LAO.

26. This was the same James Laughlin with whom Legman tangled over *Tropic of Cancer*.

27. JIL to GL, August 10, 1948, LAO.

28. GL to JIL, February 8, 1948, LAO.

29. GL to JIL, October 28, 1948, LAO.

266   *Notes to Chapter 5*

30. JCH to GL, November 9, 1948, LAO.

31. SEH to GL, June 14 and July 28, 1948; Robert G. Davis to GL, December 2, 1948, all in 1948 letter files, LAO.

32. Landesman, *Rebel without Applause*, 69–70.

33. GL to JIL, August 17, 1983, LAO.

34. Landesman, *Rebel without Applause*, 67.

35. Ibid., 67, 70.

36. Gershon Legman, "Institutionalized Lynch: The Anatomy of a Murder-Mystery," *Neurotica* 4 (Spring 1949): 3–20.

37. Philip Marchand, *Marshall McLuhan: The Medium and the Messenger* (New York: Ticknor & Fields, 1989), 129.

38. HMM to GL, December 28, 1948, LAO.

39. Ibid.

40. GL to HMM, January 10, 1949, LAO.

41. Marshall McLuhan, "Dagwood's America," *Columbia* (1944): 23. *Columbia* was an obscure journal of the Knights of Columbus.

42. GL to HMM, February 5, 1949, LAO.

43. When he finally sent the book to Vanguard Press for consideration, it was five hundred pages of clippings and commentary; the editorial staff at Vanguard was not sure what it was and hesitated to open it. Marchand, *Marshall McLuhan*, 117.

44. Siegfried Giedeon, *Mechanization Takes Command: A Contribution to Anonymous History* (Oxford: Oxford University Press, 1948).

45. After Gershon's death in 1999, Judith Legman sent Gershon's early research files to the archive at the Kinsey Institute for Sex and Gender Research at Indiana University. These subject files contain examples of the 1940s advertisements and illustrations Legman studied for *Neurotica* and *Love & Death*.

46. Marshall McLuhan, "The Folklore of Industrial Man," *Neurotica* 8 (Spring 1951): 3.

47. Ibid.

48. Ibid.

49. Ibid.

50. Ibid., 4.

51. Marchand, *Marshall McLuhan*, 117; Marshall McLuhan, *The Mechanical Bride: Folklore of Industrial Man* (New York: Vanguard Press, 1951).

52. Ibid., 115–17.

53. GL to HMM, June 23, 1949, LAO.

54. HMM to GL, June 21, 1949, LAO.

55. GL to HMM, June 23, 1949, LAO.

56. HMM to GL, June 29, 1949, LAO.

57. GL to HMM, June 23, 1949, LAO.

58. HMM to GL, June 29, 1949, LAO.

59. See James Gilbert, *Men in the Middle: Searching for Masculinity in the 1950s* (Chicago: University of Chicago Press, 2005); Joanne Myerowitz, *Not June Cleaver: Women and Gender in Postwar America, 1945–1960* (Philadelphia: Temple University Press, 1994); George Chauncey, *Gay New York: Gender, Urban Culture, and the Making of the Gay World, 1890–1940* (New York: Basic Books, 1994).

Notes to Chapter 5

60. GL to HMM, July 8, 1949, LAO.

61. On Jacobs, see Robert Kanigel, *Eyes on the Street: The Life of Jane Jacobs* (New York: Alfred A. Knopf, 2016).

62. For example, the founding of the Mattachine Society in 1950 by Harry Hay: Stuart Timmons, *The Trouble with Harry Hay: Founder of the Modern Gay Movement* (Boston: Alyson, 1990).

63. Joanne Meyerowitz, "Beyond the Feminine Mystique: A Reassessment of Postwar Mass Culture, 1946–1958," in *Not June Cleaver*, by Meyerowitz (Philadelphia: Temple University Press, 1994), 229–62; Winnie Brienes, *Young White and Miserable: Growing Up Female in the Fifties* (Chicago: University of Chicago Press, 1992).

64. GL to HMM, July 8, 1949, LAO.

65. HMM to GL, August 6, 1949, LAO.

66. GL to HMM, August 6, 1949, LAO.

67. GL to HMM, July 3, 1949, LAO.

68. HMM to GL, October 5, 1949, LAO.

69. "They shall not pass," the antifascist slogan from the Spanish Civil War. GL to HMM, July 8, 1949, LAO.

70. HMM to GL, October 5, 1949, LAO.

71. HMM to GL, July 11, 1949, LAO.

72. Legman had experimented with playful juxtaposition from early on. His high school erotica album had mixed advertising commercial slogans and everyday forms of speech with erotic snapshots.

73. HMM to GL, June 30, 1950, LAO.

74. GL to HMM, August 26, 1950, LAO.

75. Marchand, *Marshall McLuhan*, 118.

76. McLuhan quoted ibid., 119. Marchand writes that *The Mechanical Bride* sold only a couple of hundred copies and that for years McLuhan distributed the remainder, "sometimes selling copies to students who came to see them about their problems with his courses."

77. Ibid.

78. Ibid.

79. Landesman, *Rebel without Applause*, 74, 84–85.

80. Ibid., 77 (quoting Robert Burns, on the eighteenth-century dictionary maker Francis Grose).

81. Ibid., 89–90.

82. William E. Fischer to "Gentlemen," November 22, 1949, LAO.

83. Landesman, *Rebel without Applause*, 90.

84. Ibid., 86.

85. Ibid., 93–100, 169.

86. Morris Ernst (1888–1976), American lawyer, the premier legal writer at the time. Ernst was concerned with obscenity, censorship, and free speech.

87. Ibid., 93–100.

88. Ibid., 162.

89. Landesman remembered Legman very negatively: "I could honestly say that he didn't have a good word for anyone. . . . He needed me to keep him from becoming a literary Gatling gun." Ibid., 77–78.

268   *Notes to Chapter 5*

90. Work by "Towne" is cited in Johnson, *Lavender Scare*, as part of a series of media attacks on homosexuals.

91. Victor Tausk (1879–1919) was a psychoanalyst and an early colleague of Freud who wrote on war neurosis and schizophrenia.

92. William Steig (1907–2003), cartoonist and illustrator.

93. On Legman's troubles with the United States Post Office, see Susan Davis, "Eros Meets Civilization: Gershon Legman Confronts the Post Office," *CounterPunch* (October 2002). The present account is based on the Post Office Department Fraud and Lotteries hearing (transcript 635 of proceedings, June 6, 1950, in author's possession), his FBI file (Federal Bureau of Investigation, Subject: George Legman, File: 71-0-578), and a detailed letter he wrote to legal scholar James C. N. Paul, February 21, 1956, LAO.

94. On postal censorship, see Dorothy Ganfield Fowler, *Unmailable: Congress and the Post Office* (Athens: University of Georgia Press, 1977). Postmaster Summerfield quoted in Jeffrey Werth, *The Scarlet Professor Newton Arvin: A Literary Life Shattered by Scandal* (New York: Anchor, 2002), 148. Recent research has shown that in the 1940s and 1950s, the FBI and postmasters general worked to connect political subversion with pornographers and activists for sexual freedom. Douglas M. Charles, *The FBI's Obscene File: J. Edgar Hoover and the Bureau's Crusade against Smut* (Lawrence: University Press of Kansas, 2012). On the history of the legal definition of obscenity, see Paul Boyer, *Purity in Print: Book Censorship in America from the Gilded Age to the Computer Age*, 2nd ed. (Madison: University of Wisconsin Press, 2002).

95. Jay A. Gertzman, *Samuel Roth, Infamous Modernist* (Gainesville: University Press of Florida, 2013) and *Bookleggers and Smuthounds: The Trade in Erotica, 1920–1940* (Philadelphia: University of Pennsylvania Press, 2001).

96. The Post Office "maintained a long list of proscribed books," from Whitman and Freud to Steinbeck and Simone de Beauvoir. Werth, *Scarlet Professor*, 147.

97. There were many complaints about the process, and from the 1930s onward civil libertarians had been chipping away at the Post Office's censorship powers. According to Jay Gertzman, full judicial hearings were fought so hard by the Post Office bureaucracy that reforms could not be made. Personal communication by email, October 2002.

98. Johnson, *Lavender Scare*.

99. The name of the person who sent the request to the FBI has been blacked out in the redacted Freedom of Information Act version of Legman's file.

100. OB to GL, September 16, 1980, SGDLP.

101. GL to James C. N. Paul, February 21, 1956, LAO.

102. Ibid.

103. Ibid.

104. Just as Legman did not know about his own slim FBI file, he was similarly ignorant of the extent of the dossiers the agency was gathering on other writers, editors, artists, folklorists, anthropologists, and cultural workers, as well as political activists. David H. Price, *Threatening Anthropology: McCarthyism and the FBI's Surveillance of Activist Anthropologists* (Durham, N.C.: Duke University Press, 2004). Politically active teachers and librarians were losing their jobs, college professors were forced to take loyalty oaths, and unions were being purged of radical activists. Legman had prob-

Notes to Chapters 5 and 6

ably heard of the firing of the left literary critic Newton Arvin from Smith College on grounds of sexual perversion (Werth, *Scarlet Professor*). See also Justin Spring, *Secret Historian: The Life and Times of Samuel Steward, Professor, Tattoo Artist, and Sexual Renegade* (New York: Farrar, Straus and Giroux, 2010). Patrick McGilligan and Paul Buhle track the decisions of some Hollywood writers, including some of Legman's friends, to leave the United States in *Tender Comrades: A Backstory of the Hollywood Blacklist* (Minneapolis: University of Minnesota Press, 2012).

105. Landesman, *Rebel without Applause*, 170–71.

106. Elias Wilentz, *The Beat Scene* (New York: Citadel Press, 1960).

107. GL to JIL, December 4, 1979, LAO.

Chapter 6. Advanced Studies in Folklore

1. G. Alexander Legman [*sic*], "Toward an Historical Bibliography of Sex Technique" (unpublished manuscript, 1936), LAO. This proposal saw many iterations.

2. GL to DE, January 1, 1954, LAO.

3. GL to Harry P. Johnson, October 31, 1953, LAO.

4. GL to Mr. John Benson (book dealer), September 5, 1953, LAO.

5. AT to GL, 1954 (letter not dated); GL to AT, January 22 and February 8, 1954, LAO.

6. GL to AT, February 8 and April 29, 1954, LAO. The article became Taylor's book *The Shanghai Gesture*, Folklore Fellows Communication 166 (Helsinki: Suomalainen Tiedeakatemia, 1956).

7. GL to AT, April 29, 1954, LAO.

8. GL to JK, January 30, 1954, LAO. Kindler was a paper-folding fan and collector of rare playing cards.

9. GL to MK, April 27, 1954, LAO.

10. GL to Henry Schuman, April 29, 1954, LAO.

11. Anonymous, *The Limerick*, ed. Gershon Legman (Paris: La Ruche, 1953); GL to SEH, February 19, 1954, LAO.

12. GL to SEH, February 19, 1954, LAO.

13. "Lapses in Limerick" was dated 1935–38. Gershon probably wrote a few limericks for his book, but they are not labeled as such.

14. Roger D. Abrahams, interview with the author, October 17, 2002, Rochester, N.Y. On Abrahams, see note 80 below.

15. Gershon Legman, *The Horn Book: Studies in Erotic Folklore and Bibliography* (New Hyde Park, N.Y.: University Books, 1964; London: Jonathan Cape, 1970); on the history of the limerick, 427–53.

16. *The Limerick*, 24. Legman gave the limericks a date of collection or publication and a reference number. Within each thematic grouping, limericks are arranged mnemonically by the keyword in the first line, usually a place or person's name—for example: "A girl by the green Susquehanna" who "Now must use a banana" appears as #1351 under *S* in the chapter "Substitutes," 278.

17. Ibid., 180.

18. Ibid., 195.

19. Ibid., 30, 31, 27–54.

20. Ibid., 283.

21. Ibid., 256.

22. Ibid., 260.

23. Ibid., 244.

24. "... make me merry." Shakespeare, Falstaff in *Henry IV*, pt. 1. This was a favorite quote of Legman's. On the title of his projected book, he called it "The Ballad Unexpurgated" and, alternatively, "The Ballad." Legman diverged from common scholarly usage, using the term to refer not just to narrative songs but also, following the older English usage, "song ballet," designating any song with or without music. For clarity, I refer to the manuscript as "The Ballad."

25. J. Farmer and W. E. Henley, *Slang and Its Analogues* (1890–1904; reprint, New York: Arno Press, 1970). Farmer also collected and published folk songs. See John Stephen Farmer, *Merry Songs and Ballads, Prior to the Year 1800* (London: privately printed, 1897). On the synonymy, see Julie Coleman, *A History of Slang and Can't Dictionaries*, vol. 3, *1859–1936* (Oxford: Oxford University Press, 2009), 53–73.

26. G. Legman, "The Bawdy Song ... in Fact and in Print," *Explorations* 7 (1957): 139–56.

27. Vance Randolph, *Ozark Folksongs* (Columbia: State Historical Society of Missouri, 1946–50).

28. After Kinsey's death, Legman's requests to work with Randolph's manuscript were routinely brushed off by the institute's director Paul Gebhard. The permission to edit and publish "Roll Me in Your Arms" and "Blow the Candle Out" came to Legman in the mid-1970s. He edited these, and they were published as Vance Randolph, *Roll Me in Your Arms: "Unprintable" Ozark Folksongs and Folklore*, vol. 1, *Folk Songs and Music*, and *Blow the Candle Out: "Unprintable" Ozark Folksongs and Folklore*, vol. 2, *Folk Rhymes and Other Lore* (Fayetteville: University of Arkansas Press, 1992).

29. GL to DE, January 1, 1954, LAO; Emrich to Josiah Coombs, November 16, 1951, Legman, Gershon correspondence folder, AFC/LOC.

30. GL to DE, January 1, 1954, LAO.

31. GL to DE, June 24, 1952, LAO.

32. Emrich suggested Legman write to Randolph and Halpert, then at Murray State College in Kentucky. DE to GL, December 14, 1953, LAO; Herbert Halpert, cited in GL to DE, January 1, 1954, LAO.

33. For example, GL to RMD, March 11, 1955, Richard M. Dorson Collection, Lilly Library, Indiana University, Bloomington.

34. Gordon was the first head of the Library of Congress Archive of Folk Song, and his collections formed the initial core of the archive. On the history of the archive, see Benjamin Filene, *Romancing the Folk: Public Memory and American Roots Music* (Chapel Hill: University of North Carolina Press, 2000), 9–46, 133–82. On Gordon, see Debora Kodish, *Good Friends and Bad Enemies: Robert Winslow Gordon and the Study of American Folksong* (Urbana: University of Illinois Press, 1986). The vulgar Gordon collection was cited as in the Randall V. Mills Archives of Northwest Folklore, University of Oregon, Eugene.

35. Legman had been writing to Dorson since 1953, at the suggestion of Stanley Edgar Hyman. He appears not to have received serious answers. For example, GL to RMD, January 27, 1953, March 11, 1955, and February 1, 1956, Dorson Collection, Lilly Library. See also GL to John Greenway, April 29, 1954, LAO.

Notes to Chapter 6

36. GL to EC, December 25, 1960, SGDLP.

37. He expressed this view many times—for example, to Dorson, GL to RMD, February 1, 1956, Dorson Collection, Lilly Library; and to John Greenway, April 29, 1954, LAO.

38. Alan Lomax to RMD, January 5, 1956, Dorson Collection, Lilly Library. (Thanks to Jim Leary for this.)

39. GL to HS, April 12, 1956, Legman correspondence file, AFC/LOC. Louise Pound (1872–1958) was a renowned American folklorist and linguist. George Herzog (1901–83) was an anthropologist, linguist, and ethnomusicologist. Jameson (1895–1959) was a folklorist, Sinologist, and professor of English. Alan Lomax (1915–2002) was an American folklorist and ethnomusicologist and the son of the folk song collector John A. Lomax.

40. GL to HS, April 12, 1956, Legman correspondence file, AFC/LOC.

41. HS to GL, May 15, 1956, Legman correspondence file, AFC/LOC.

42. Ibid. The Library of Congress Delta Collection is said to have more than ten thousand items (most of which are books and pamphlets) of which there was no published catalog and no shelf list open to the public. Daniel Eisenberg, "Toward a Bibliography of Erotic Pulps," *Journal of Popular Culture* 15, no. 4 (1982): 175–84.

43. GL to HS, May 25, 1956, Legman correspondence file, AFC/LOC.

44. Raye Korson to HS, Legman correspondence file, AFC/LOC, an internal note (n.d. 1956).

45. HS to GL, June 12 and June 21, 1956, Legman correspondence file, AFC/LOC.

46. Legman and Hickerson corresponded regularly from the 1960s into the 1980s.

47. G. Legman, "Who Owns Folklore?" *Western Folklore* 21, no. 1 (1962): 1–12. He became furious with Wayland Hand over the editing of the article. He published a longer version in *The Horn Book*, 505–21.

48. Charles Seeger, "Who Owns Folklore? A Rejoinder," *Western Folklore* 21, no. 2 (1962): 93–101.

49. Legman, "Who Owns Folklore?"

50. Filene, *Romancing the Folk*, 133–82; John Szwed, *Alan Lomax: The Man Who Recorded the World, a Biography* (New York: Viking, 2010), 244–67.

51. Patrick J. Kearney, *The Private Case: An Annotated Bibliography of the Private Case Erotica Collection in the British (Museum) Library* (London: J. Landesman, 1981) and *A History of Erotic Literature* (London: Macmillan, 1982).

52. Legman, "The Bibliography of Prohibited Books: Pisanus Fraxi," in *The Horn Book*, 9–45; Ian Gibson, *The Erotomaniac: The Secret Life of Henry Spencer Ashbee* (Cambridge, Mass.: Da Capo Press, 2001). Legman stayed for six weeks, lodging with publisher Cecil Woolf in what had been Virginia and Leonard Woolf's house in Bloomsbury. GL to AT, April 29, 1954, LAO.

53. The books he offered were not the rarest of his library, but books he had been working over and no longer needed. Judith Legman, email, October 21, 2015. They included erotica and some nineteenth-century pulps, but also writings on feminism and sexual behavior, joke books, collections of riddles, and leaflets of military songs. He included his translation of Jarry's *Ubu Roi*, hoping the museum's catalog entry would help establish him as a serious writer, useful in fighting Customs cases. He later marked which of his donated books had been entered in the Private Case. GL to R.

A. Wilson (Keeper, Dept. Printed Books), July 8 and July 10, 1953; R. A. Wilson to GL, July 17 and July 27, 1953, LAO. Lists of donated books, I and II, Legman Archive documents file for 1953; listed in the British Museum's main catalog: *Curious and scholarly books from a private library*, 1958 (a catalog of books offered for sale by G. Legman). Legman probably hoped to see his own finds included in the library's *enfer* of forbidden works and his own name recorded there for posterity.

54. Eric Dingwall (1890–1986) was a British anthropologist whose research focused on erotica and supernatural phenomena.

55. Margaret Dean-Smith, *A Guide to English Folk Song Collections, 1822–1952* (Liverpool: University Press of Liverpool, 1954).

56. Ewan MacColl (1915–89), born James Henry Miller. Folk singer Peggy Seeger (1935–) is the daughter of musicologist Charles Seeger and composer Ruth Crawford. Lloyd was the author of *Folk Song in England* (London: Lawrence & Wishart, 1967). On Lloyd's importance to the revival, see Michael Brocken, *The British Folk Revival, 1944–2002* (Burlington, Vt.: Ashgate, 2003), 25–27.

57. GL to MK, April 27, 1954, LAO.

58. GL to JK, April 27, 1954, LAO.

59. The story of this homestead is told in the next chapter.

60. On Henderson, see Timothy Neat, *Hamish Henderson: A Biography*, vol. 1, *The Making of a Poet* (Edinburgh: Polygon, 2007), and vol. 2, *Poetry Becomes People* (Edinburgh: Polygon, 2009); on Legman's relationship to Henderson, 2:67–73; and Legman, *Windows of Winter & Flagrant Delectations: Books Five & Six of Peregrine Penis, G. Legman's Autobiography* (n.p.: CreateSpace, 2018), 504–8.

61. Timothy Neat and Hamish Henderson, *The Summer Walkers: A Documentary Study of the Life and Culture of the "Travelling People" in the Highlands of Scotland* (VHS format, Edinburgh, 1977).

62. Quoted in Neat, *Hamish Henderson*, 1:95; "El Alamein" and the "Ballad of Faruk," 1:83–104. A 1940s version of the song appears in Henderson's *Ballads of World War II* (Glasgow: Lili Marlene Club, 1947).

63. Neat, *Hamish Henderson*, 1:83–104.

64. GL to HH, April 1960, quoted in Neat, *Hamish Henderson*, 2:69.

65. Neat, *Hamish Henderson*, 2:69. The quote is from GL to HH, November 7, 1955, Henderson Papers, School of Scottish Studies, Edinburgh, Scotland. "The Bastard King":

> He was dirty and lousy and full of fleas.
> His terrible tool hung to his knees.
> God save the bastard king of England . . .

"The Ballad" manuscript in the Legman Collection at the Kinsey Institute Archive contains typescripts sent by Henderson and other Scottish folklorists, as well as many letters commenting on the songs.

66. For example, Peter Buchan's then unpublished "Songs of Silence" manuscript, in the Harvard University Library. GL to HH, June 1, 1957, in *Hamish Henderson*, 2:69; Murray Shoolbraid, *The High Kilted Muse: Peter Buchan and His Secret Songs of Silence* (Jackson: University Press of Mississippi, 2010).

Notes to Chapter 6　　　**273**

67. This appears to be a later title, added by an anonymous printer.

68. G. Legman, *Windows of Winter*, 428–30.

69. Ibid., 431–35.

70. Legman, *Windows of Winter*, 475–79.

71. Probably at "Ballads and Blues," MacColl's policy club. A policy club was a folk music venue with a roster of approved performers and formal rules as to the style of singing and instrumentation allowed on the stage and from the floor. Brocken, *British Folk Revival,* 34–35.

72. Legman, *Windows of Winter*, 482–89.

73. Stan Hugill to GL, June 8, 1956; GL to Hugill, June 8, 1956. Hugill's letters and uncensored songs are filed under "Hugill" in the chapter "Sailors" in "The Ballad" manuscript, Legman Collection, KIRSG.

74. Ewan MacColl, *Journeyman: An Autobiography*, ed. Peggy Seeger, 2nd ed. (Manchester: Manchester University Press, 2009); on singing in his early life, 3–31.

75. Henderson would become an important leader in Scotland's antinuclear campaigns.

76. JK to GL, 1960 (letter not dated), LAO. Moritz Jagendorf was an amateur folklorist, one target of Richard Dorson's attack on popularizers and "fakelore." An early statement is Dorson, "The American Folklore Scene, 1963," *Folklore* 74, no. 3 (1963): 433–49.

77. GL to RMD, August 12, 1961, LAO, concerning Frank M. Paulsen, "Hair of the Dog and Some Other Hangover Cures from Popular Tradition," *Journal of American Folklore* 74, no. 292 (1961): 152–68.

78. Apart from Alan Lomax, there was no one more central to the folk music revival in the United States. Steve Winnick, "Kenneth S. Goldstein, 1927–1995," *Dirty Linen* 62 (February–March 1996): 11. Goldstein began work for a folklore Ph.D. at Pennsylvania in 1958 and did fieldwork in northeastern Scotland in 1959–60 while a Fulbright fellow. On the Henderson-Goldstein friendship, see Neat, *Hamish Henderson*, 2:159–68.

79. The "New Kryptadia" was announced many times, but it never got off the ground. GL to RDA, May 10, 1965; GL to "The Committee on Folklore," May 10, 1973, Dorson Collection, Lilly Library.

80. Roger Abrahams had been a folk singer in the early 1950s and collected songs in the southern Appalachian Mountains. He studied folklore and English at the University of Pennsylvania with MacEdward Leach and Tristram Coffin. In 1958 he moved into a black neighborhood in South Philadelphia and began collecting there. Abrahams, interview; William Grimes, "Roger D. Abrahams, Folklorist Who Studied African-American Language, Dies at 84," *New York Times*, June 29, 2017, https://www .nytimes.com/2017/06/29/arts/roger-d-abrahams-dead-folklorist.html. On Abrahams's early attention to urban African American folklore, see John Szwed, "Working with Roger: A Memoir," *Western Folklore* 75 (2016): 421–33.

81. GL to RDA, May 2, 1959, SGDLP.

82. Ibid. Goldstein had put Abrahams in touch with Legman while he was working on his dissertation. Abrahams, interview. The collection of slave songs: Guy B. Johnson and Howard Odum, *The Negro and His Songs* (Chapel Hill: University of North Carolina Press, 1925).

Notes to Chapter 6

83. Abrahams, interview.

84. Ibid.

85. GL to RDA, July 7, 1959, SGDLP.

86. Ibid.

87. Ibid.

88. Roger David Abrahams, "Negro Folklore from South Philadelphia: A Collection and Analysis" (Ph.D. diss., University of Pennsylvania, 1961), https://repository.upenn.edu/dissertations/AAI6202817.

89. "Phudnick" (PhD-nik) is a Legmanism for "academic." GL to RDA, October 7, 1961, SGDLP.

90. Ibid. George Lyman Kittredge of Harvard University was the successor to Francis James Child, a masterful teacher of old English poetry and the ballad texts. When Legman wrote "The Text Is the Thing," he meant he focused on texts over performances, but also that he felt the song lyrics should appear beautifully on the page, with no "bug shit" (footnotes or other scholarly marks) to spoil the reader's experience.

91. GL to RDA, October 7 and October 19, 1961, SGDLP.

92. GL to RDA, October 19, 1961, SGDLP.

93. Ibid.

94. Ibid.; G. Legman, "Poontang," *American Speech* 25, no. 3 (1950): 234–35.

95. GL to RDA, October 19, 1961, SGDLP. "The sleeve job" would be an enduring fascination in his books on dirty jokes. Legman thought shaggy-dog stories were always told with hostile intent.

96. Ibid.

97. Ibid.

98. Abrahams was relying on Melville Herskovits, *The Myth of the Negro Past* (New York: Harper and Brothers, 1941). See Pat Mullen, *The Man Who Adores the Negro: Race and American Folklore* (Urbana: University of Illinois Press, 2008).

99. Legman to RDA, October 19, 1959, SGDLP.

100. Ibid.; Legman, "Avatars of the Bitch," in *Love & Death*, 57–82. See also Legman's annotations to the first edition of the book Abrahams made from the dissertation, *Deep Down in the Jungle: Negro Narrative Folklore from the Streets of Philadelphia* (Hatboro, Pa.: Folklore Associates, 1964)—for example, notes 29 and 33.

101. Abrahams felt he had to quote Legman fully or risk a long-distance hail of verbal abuse. Abrahams, interview.

102. John T. Flanagan, review of *Deep Down in the Jungle*, by Abrahams, *Western Folklore* 25 (1966): 58–59.

103. Richard Dorson, review of *Deep Down in the Jungle*, by Abrahams, *American Anthropologist*, n.s., 68, no. 3 (1966): 779–80.

104. Abrahams, *Deep Down in the Jungle*, rev. ed. (Chicago: Aldine, 1970).

105. John F. Szwed, review of *Deep Down in the Jungle*, by Abrahams, *American Journal of Sociology* 77, no. 2 (September 1971): 392–94. The second edition of *Deep Down* is seen as a breakthrough in the study of African American verbal art and literature. John Roberts, *From Trickster to Badman: The Black Folk Hero in Slavery and Freedom* (Philadelphia: University of Pennsylvania Press, 1989); Onwuchekwa Jemie, ed., *Yo' Mama! New Raps, Toasts, Dozens, Jokes & Children's Rhymes from Urban Black America*

(Philadelphia: Temple University Press, 2003). On the differences between the first and second editions of *Deep Down*, see Mullen, *Man Who Adores the Negro*, 131–51.

106. GL to RDA, Thanksgiving Day 1961, SGDLP.

107. Abrahams, interview. Legman joked about his sexual proclivities to Abrahams—for example, GL to RDA, February 17, 1962, SGDLP.

Chapter 7. "The Ballad" and *The Horn Book*

1. This is the size of the extant "Ballad" manuscript in the Legman Collection, KIRSG. GL to EC, January 11, February 19, and March 24, 1960, SGDLP.

2. EC to GL, January 19 and January 28, 1960, SGDLP.

3. GL to EC, January 20 and February 7, 1960, SGDLP.

4. GL to EC, January 1 and "End of June 1962," SGDLP.

5. GL to EC, February 16, 1960, SGDLP.

6. One irritant was a song describing a step-by-step seduction that Sharp bowdlerized and rewrote as "Gently, Johnny, My Jingalo," discussed by Legman in his notes to Vance Randolph, *Roll Me in Your Arms: "Unprintable" Ozark Folksongs and Folklore*, vol. 1, *Folk Songs and Music* (Fayetteville: University of Arkansas Press, 1992), 264, 548.

7. GL to EC, February 16, 1960, and EC to GL, August 18, 1962, SGDLP.

8. GL to EC, August 24, 1962, SGDLP.

9. The poem was "A Talk of Ten Wives on Their Husband's Wares," cited in Legman's *The Horn Book* (New York: University Press, 1964), 414, 443. "Three Old Whores of Canada" turned up in the R. W. Gordon Collection "Inferno," in Burns's *Merry Muses*, and in fragments in Randolph's *Roll Me in Your Arms*. GL to EC, June 16, 1971, SGDLP. On the complexities of its history, see Cray, *The Erotic Muse American Bawdy Songs*, 2nd ed. (Urbana: University of Illinois Press, 1992), 9–10.

10. When he told Cray that he and Beverley were subsisting on rice with an occasional homegrown tomato, Cray may have thought this was exaggeration, but it was not. GL to EC, January 16 and February 7, 1961, SGDLP.

11. GL to RDA, Thanksgiving Day 1961, SGDLP.

12. In the 1950s and 1960s, Oscar Brand issued multiple LPs of "bawdy songs and backroom ballads." See Oscar Brand's partial discography, http://oscarbrand.com/discog.htm. Legman denigrated Brand's *The Ballad Mongers* (New York: Funk and Wagnalls, 1962).

13. On the concept of fakelore, an early statement is Richard Dorson, "The American Folklore Scene, 1963," *Folklore* 74, no. 3 (1963): 433–49. On the folklore-fakelore debates of the 1950s and 1960s, see Regina Bendix, *In Search of Authenticity: The Formation of Folklore Studies* (Madison: University of Wisconsin Press, 1997), 119–54, 188–218.

14. GL to EC, Thanksgiving Day 1960, and February 7 and October 10, 1961, SGDLP.

15. EC to GL, September 21, 1962, January 10, 1961, and January 23, 1962, SGDLP.

16. EC to GL, December 24, 1961, and January 23, 1962, SGDLP.

17. GL to EC, August 5 and August 24, 1962, SGDLP.

18. GL to EC, August 24, 1962, SGDLP.

19. GL to EC, February 25 and March 9, 1963, SGDLP.

276 *Notes to Chapter 7*

20. EC to GL, June 3, 1963, SGDLP. Party records were under-the-counter 78 rpm records of obscene songs and monologues. The genre continued in the LP format in the 1950s and 1950s.

21. Ibid. Richard Dyer-Bennett (1913–91) was an English-born American folk singer. Josh White (1914–69) was an American singer, songwriter, and civil rights activist.

22. GL to EC, June 7, 1963, SGDLP.

23. GL to EC, July 14, 1963, SGDLP; EF to GL, July 25, 1963; GL to EF, August 14, 1963, LAO.

24. He was not alone in this view. In *Folk Song in England*, A. L. Lloyd had suggested that songs about sex were connected to the deep, natural life cycle of the countryside and the peasant community, 199–200, 208–10.

25. The title of *The Horn Book* is an example of Legman's play with language. It refers to an old elementary school primer on slate or horn, to a fugitive late-nineteenth-century erotica publication, *The Horn Book; or, The Girl's Guide to Knowledge* (London or Brussels, 1898), and to the association of "horns" with masculinity. The 1970 London edition alerted Patrick Kearney to the possibilities of erotic bibliography. See also Julie Peakman, *Mighty Lewd Books: The Development of Pornography in the Eighteenth-Century* (New York: Palgrave Macmillan, 2003), 5–44.

26. Osmond Beckwith, "Testimonial" (unpublished manuscript, 1999), copy in SGDLP, 29.

27. Legman, *The Horn Book*, 236.

28. Leslie Sheppard, *The History of Street Literature: The Story of Broadside Ballads, Chapbooks, Proclamations, News-Sheets, Election Bills, Tracts, Pamphlets, Cocks, Catchpennies, and Other Ephemera* (Detroit: Singing Tree Press, 1973). On the emergence in London and other cities of a criminal-recreational sphere, see John L. McMullan, *The Canting Crew: London's Criminal Underworld, 1550–1700* (New Brunswick, N.J.: Rutgers University Press, 1984). On the underworld, the working class, and print, see Peter Linebaugh, *The London Hanged: Crime and Civil Society in the Eighteenth Century* (London: Verso, 2003).

29. Legman, *The Horn Book*, 236.

30. Peter Burke, *Popular Culture in Early Modern Europe* (New York: Harper & Row, 1978); Natalie Z. Davis, "Printing and the People," in *Society and Culture in Early Modern France: Eight Essays* (Stanford, Calif.: Stanford University Press, 1975). Legman would appreciate the recent close examinations of the production and distribution of erotica in England and France. For a summary, see Peakman, *Mighty Lewd Books*.

31. Legman, *The Horn Book*, 290, 292.

32. Alan Dundes, review of *The Horn Book*, by Gershon Legman, *Journal of American Folklore* 78 (1965): 161. Dundes saw Legman as the only other American folklorist besides himself using psychoanalytic thought. Alan Dundes, interview with the author, July 12, 2002, Berkeley, Calif.

33. Alex Comfort, review of *The Horn Book*, by Gershon Legman, *Folklore* 1975 (Winter 1964): 281–82. A less positive review was by Frank Hoffman, who found the book cluttered with Legman's antihomosexual eruptions and complained about the lack of an index. Frank Hoffman, review of *The Horn Book*, by Gershon Legman, *Western Folklore* 26, no. 1 (1967): 61–62. Hoffman would later publish his index with

none of Legman's collected materials referenced as *Analytical Index of Traditional Anglo-American Erotica* (Bowling Green, Ohio: Popular Press, 1973).

34. Patrick J. Kearney, *The Private Case: An Annotated Bibliography of the Private Case Erotica Collection in the British (Museum) Library* (London: J. Landesman, 1981) and *A History of Erotic Literature* (London: Macmillan, 1982).

35. GL to Alan Dundes, March 1, 1964, SGDLP (courtesy of Alan Dundes).

36. Dundes to GL, March 23, 1964, SGDLP.

37. "Sima was born in Brussels to Eastern European Jews. She grew up in the Dutch Indies and survived World War Two, with her mother and two younger sisters, in a Japanese prison camp. After the war, which her father did not survive, they were transported to Holland, where they were 'naturalized.'" Ariëla Legman, email, November 10, 2015.

38. Ibid.

39. Ewing W. Baskette Collection, Rare Books and Manuscripts Library, University of Illinois Urbana-Champaign, folder 107.

40. GL to RMD, February 16, 1964; GL to Roy Morser, February 11, 1964, LAO.

41. GL to FH, May 12, 1964, Legman-Hoffman letters, KIRSG.

42. I cannot locate any record of Legman's marriage to Christine Conrad or its annulment. Christine Conrad may have been a stage name or pseudonym.

43. GL to EC, August 5, 1964, SGDLP.

44. Charlie Seeman, email, June 18, 2001.

45. Dundes, interview.

46. G. Legman, *The Fake Revolt* (New York: Breaking Point, 1966–67). Legman sent a copy to Fredric Wertham, who responded that he thought Gershon's diagnosis of the hippie movement was correct. FW to GL, January 22, 1968; GL to FW, February 9, 1968, LAO. He totally failed to "get" the 1960s, Roger Abrahams later thought. Abrahams, interview. On Legman's objections to the counterculture's "cool" esthetic, see Mikita Brottman, *Funny Peculiar: Gershon Legman and the Psychopathology of Humor* (Hillsdale, N.J.: Analytic Press, 2004), 25–27.

47. On the early antiwar movement and its intersections with free speech and civil rights activism, see Douglas F. Dowd, *Blues for America: A Critique, a Lament, and Some Memories* (New York: Monthly Review Press, 1997). For an international history of the early 1960s as the crumbling of the deadlock of the 1950s, see Ronald Fraser, ed., *1968: A Student Generation in Revolt* (New York: Pantheon Books, 1988).

48. https://en.wikipedia.org/wiki/Make_love,_not_war.

49. GL to FH, December 5, 1965, Frank Hoffman Papers, KIRSG. Robbing the cash drawer: in G. Legman, "A Spiral Universe" and "A Gathering of Rooks," chaps. 89–90, unpublished excerpts from "The Book of Moones," bk. 7 of "Peregrine Penis," LAO.

50. JL, interview with the author, May 8, 2004, Opio, France.

51. GL to Ernest Santini, July 22, 1966; GL to RDA, October 11, 1966. His design for his own headstone predicted accurately that he would join her in 1999. Documents file for 1966, LAO.

52. GL to EC, September 18, 1965, SGDLP.

53. EC to GL, September 24 and November 12, 1965, SGDLP.

54. GL to EC, November 23, 1965, SGDLP.

278   *Notes to Chapters 7 and 8*

55. Ed Cray, *The Erotic Muse* (New York: Oak Publications, 1969) and *The Erotic Muse*, 2nd ed. (Urbana: University of Illinois Press, 1999). Legman style, Cray followed 140 pages of lyrics, music, and notes with almost as much again in scholarly notes and bibliography.

56. In 1971, after Legman had published *Rationale of the Dirty Joke, Series I*, he and Cray were back in touch. Cray arranged with Barre Toelken for Legman to get copies of the bawdy songs from the Robert W. Gordon Collection housed at the University of Oregon. Barre Toelken to EC, May 4, 1971; EC to GL, June 16, 1971, SGDLP.

57. Legman spent a good deal of his own money and time making sure that the fugitive and suppressed songs he worked with would be available to other scholars. See his correspondence from the 1960s and 1970s with Joseph Hickerson, folk music archivist at the Library of Congress, correspondence files, AFC/LOC.

58. Legman would later accuse Cray of violating the songs' integrity by conflating texts from different sources, in the introduction to Randolph, *Roll Me in Your Arms*.

59. More recently, scholars have digitized tens of thousands of broadside ballads in archival collections, making possible new historical uses and comparisons of the songs. David Atkinson and Steve Roud, *Street Ballads in the Nineteenth-Century Britain, Ireland, and North America: The Interface between Print and Oral Traditions* (Burlington, Vt.: Ashgate, 2014). See, for example, Vic Gammon, *Drink, Desire and Death in English Folk and Vernacular Song, 1600–1900* (Burlington, Vt.: Ashgate, 2008).

60. For example, see Henry Glassie, Edward D. Ives, and John F. Szwed, *Folksongs and Their Makers* (Bowling Green, Ohio: Popular Press, 1979); and Edward D. Ives, *Larry Gorman* (Manchester, N.H.: Ayer, 1964).

61. Horace P. Beck, "Say Something Dirty!" *Journal of American Folklore* 75 (1962): 195–99; Herbert Halpert, "Folklore and Obscenity: Definitions and Problems," *Journal of American Folklore* 75 (1962): 190–94.

62. Archie Green, "Hillbilly Music: Source and Symbol," *Journal of American Folklore* 78 (1965): 204–28; Michael Brocken, *The British Folk Revival, 1944–2002* (Burlington, Vt.: Ashgate, 2003), 25–27; Archie Green, *Only a Miner: Studies in Recorded Coal-Mining Songs* (Urbana: University of Illinois Press, 1972).

Chapter 8. The Key to the Fields

1. JL, interview with the author, May 5, 2013, Opio, France.

2. On Ben and Norma Barzman, see Patrick McGilligan and Paul Buhle, *Tender Comrades: A Backstory of the Hollywood Blacklist* (Minneapolis: University of Minnesota Press, 2012), 1–28. Expatriate novelist John Collier was also a friend.

3. JL, interview with the author, May 5, 2013, and May 9, 2004, Opio, France.

4. Ibid.

5. JL, email, June 29, 2018.

6. JL, interview, May 9, 2004.

7. GL to EC, March 24, 1960, SGDLP.

8. JL, interview, May 5, 2013, and May 9, 2004.

9. Henry Herman Evans was born in 1918 in Wisconsin to Russian Jewish immigrants whose family name was Evanchuk. Patricia Healy's family was also from Wisconsin, but they had moved to California when Patricia was two. The couple met in

California and married young. Judith Evans was born in 1940. JL, interview with the author, May 8, 2004, Opio, France.

10. Ibid. "When he felt he could make a living as a printmaker he phased out the bookselling, and in fact in the end he made a better living as a printmaker."

11. Ibid. In the 1960s, Henry shifted his efforts entirely to fine-art printing and specialized in color linoleum blocks of botanical subjects (which are now valued by collectors). http://www.henryevans.com/home.html.

12. JL, interview, May 8, 2004.

13. For example, Patricia Evans, *Rimbles: A Book of Children's Classic Games, Rhymes, Songs, and Sayings* (Garden City, N.Y.: Doubleday, 1961).

14. JL, interview, May 8, 2004.

15. Ibid.

16. Ibid. Her parents divorced in 1959.

17. Ibid.

18. Ibid.

19. Ibid.

20. Ibid.

21. Ibid.

22. Document files, 1966, LAO.

23. JL, interview, May 8, 2004. The book was James Stephens, *The Crock of Gold* (New York: Macmillan, 1912).

24. JL, email, March 19, 2005.

25. JL, interview, May 8 and May 9, 2004.

26. Ibid.

27. Ibid.; JL, email, March 19, 2005.

28. JL, interview, May 8 and May 9, 2004; Gershon Legman, *Mooncalf: Being Book Two of G. Legman's Autobiography of Innocence* (n.p.: CreateSpace, 2017), 171.

29. Ibid.

30. JL, email, January 24, 2016.

31. G. Legman, *The Guilt of the Templars* (New York: Basic Books, 1966).

32. JL, email, January 24, 2016.

33. Ibid.

34. JL, interview, May 9, 2004.

35. JL, email, January 24, 2016.

36. The personal address card file is part of the Legman Archives, Opio, France.

37. Address card for Lomax, Alan, LAO.

38. John Clellon Holmes's profile of Legman, "The Last Cause," *Evergreen Review* 10, no. 44 (1966): 31.

39. And reiterated by Gershon's friend folk song scholar D. K. Wilgus in a presidential address to the American Folklore Society: "The Text Is the Thing," *Journal of American Folklore* 86 (1973): 241–52. Wilgus and Legman were hardly alone in this view.

40. JL, interview, May 9, 2004.

41. GL to Walter Toscanini, July 31, 1969, LAO.

42. JL, interview, May 9, 2004.

43. Ibid.

44. On Jay Landesman's reprint of *Neurotica*, see GL to Michael Neal, October 1, 1988, SGDLP.

45. JL, interview, May 9, 2004.

46. Jay Landesman, *Rebel without Applause* (Sag Harbor, N.Y.: Permanent PR, 1987), 236; Peggy Seeger to JL, April 25, 2000, LAO.

47. JL, interview, May 9, 2004.

48. Helen Dudar, "Love and Death (and Schmutz): G. Legman's Second Thoughts," *Village Voice*, May 1, 1984, 41–43; Jon Vinocur, "Gershon Legman Doesn't Tell Dirty Jokes," *Oui*, March 1975, 94–96, 126–28; R. Z. Sheppard, "The Japes of Wrath," review of *No Laughing Matter*, by Gershon Legman, *Time*, November 10, 1975, 96–97.

49. Kearney, personal communication. For more on Kearney as a bibliographer, see Geoff Nicholson, *Sex Collectors: The Secret World of Consumers, Connoisseurs, Curators, Creators, Dealers, Bibliographers, and Accumulators of "Erotica"* (New York: Simon & Schuster, 2006), 131–52.

50. Martha Cornog and Timothy Perper, interview with the author, February 19, 2004, Philadelphia. They met again in the mid-1980s at a talk Legman gave in Buffalo, New York. At this meeting, Gershon heartily approved of Tim Perper, Martha's second husband.

51. Ibid.

52. Ibid.

53. JL, interview, May 9, 2004; EML to GL, February 10, 1975; MC to GL, June 27, 1975; GL to JFL, June 30, 1975; GL to Daisy Birnbaum, June 30, 1975; GL to MC, June 30, 1975, all in LAO.

54. Ariëla Legman, email, November 10, 2015, and February 7 and February 21, 2016. Never "except one time when I was only 3 years old, had my mother nor anybody else who had met him spoken to me about my father. It's quite a story how my mother managed to keep her mouth shut about him, until he called by phone to the vacation house in the south of France, where we had just arrived the night before."

55. Ibid., November 10, 2015.

56. Ibid.

57. Ibid.

58. Ibid.

59. Ibid.

60. Ibid.

61. Ibid.

62. Ibid.

63. Ibid.

64. See Bruce Jackson, *Get Your Ass in the Water and Swim Like Me: African American Narrative Poetry from Oral Tradition* (1974; reprint, Abingdon: Routledge, 2004).

65. Bruce Jackson and Diane Christian, interview with the author, October 19, 2002, Buffalo, N.Y.

66. Ibid.

67. Ibid.

Notes to Chapters 8 and 9 **281**

68. GL to BJ, October 29, 1975, SGDLP (courtesy of Bruce Jackson).

69. Bruce Jackson, "Gershon Legman: The King of X700," *Maledicta* 1 (1977): 111–24. A few years later, John McLeish, an independent scholar, published a bibliography of Legman's work: J. McLeish, "A Bibliography of G. Legman," *Maledicta* 4 (1980): 127–38. On *Maledicta,* see Martha Cornog, "*Maledicta:* The International Journal of Verbal Aggression," *Journal of Sex Research* 20 (1984): 103–6.

70. GL to BJ, September 15, 1977, SGDLP.

71. David Berenger, telephone interview with the author, November 25, 2015.

72. JL, interview, May 9, 2004.

73. Ibid.

74. Berenger, telephone interview.

75. Ibid.

Chapter 9. The Hell Drawer

1. G. Legman, *Rationale of the Dirty Joke: An Analysis of Sexual Humor* (New York: Simon & Schuster, 2006). The first volume was published in 1968 by Grove Press and reissued by Simon & Schuster in 2006. Because it is more accessible to readers, the 2006 republication will be the reference used here. *Rationale of the Dirty Joke, Second Series: No Laughing Matter* (New York: Breaking Point, 1975) remains out of print. For convenience, the first volume (*Series I*) will be referred to here as *Rationale,* and the second volume (*Second Series*) will be referred to as *No Laughing Matter.*

2. G. Legman, "Rationale of the Dirty Joke," *Neurotica* 9 (Winter 1952): 49–64.

3. *Rationale,* 17. From his annotation, it seems likely that this joke was told by Julia.

4. The card file is thought to be in the Kinsey Institute Archive, but archivists have been unable to locate it. Legman was in the habit of disassembling his research files and working them into his book manuscripts, and this may have happened to his joke files.

5. E. Haldeman-Julius, *My First 25 Years* (Girard, Kans.: Haldeman-Julius Publications, 1949), 7.

6. GL to EH-J, January 4, 1949, LAO.

7. EH-J to GL, January 7, 1949; GL to EH-J, January 11, 1949, LAO. Legman's letter republished in the *American Freeman* 10, nos. 1–2 (1949), Haldeman-Julius's monthly tabloid, the *American Freeman,* continued the name of an important abolitionist newspaper.

8. Ibid.

9. Antti Aarne and Stith Thompson, *The Types of the Folk-Tale: A Classification and Bibliography,* Folklore Fellows' Communications 3 (Helsinki: Suomalainen Tiedeakatemia, 1928). This would become known as the Aarne-Thompson Index.

10. A copy of Kenneth Larson's "Idaho Barnyard" collection manuscript is in the Indiana University Folklore Archives, Bloomington. *Rationale,* 14. Legman and Vance Randolph corresponded but never met. The Legman-Randolph correspondence is part of the Vance Randolph Collection, AFC/LOC.

11. Jeff Todd Titon, "Text," in *Eight Words for the Study of Expressive Culture,* ed. Burt Feintuch (Urbana: University of Illinois Press, 2003), 69–98.

12. On the main currents of American humor, see Constance Rourke, *American Humor: A Study of the National Character* (New York: Harcourt Brace, 1931); and

Walter Blair, *Native American Humor, 1800–1900* (New York: Cincinnati American Book, 1937).

13. Ronald Collins and David Skover, *The Trials of Lenny Bruce: The Fall & Rise of an American Icon* (Naperville, Ill.: Sourcebooks, 2002). On the history of burlesque and cabaret in New York, see David Nasaw, *Going Out: The Rise and Fall of Public Amusements* (New York: Basic Books, 1993).

14. Andrew Davis, *Baggy Pants Comedy: Burlesque and the Oral Tradition* (New York: Palgrave, 2011), gives a strong sense of how much of Legman's joke material must have had burlesque connections.

15. The first series of *Anecdota Americana* was privately printed for J. M. Hall in 1927; a second series was printed by "Humphrey Adams" of Boston in 1934. A later bowdlerizing editor, "Fleisler," made *Anecdota* publicly available but "neutered" it, as Legman put it. The *Anecdota* is available online through the Jack Horntip Collection, http://www.horntip.com/html/books_&_MSS/1920s/1927_anecdota_americana_(HC)/index.htm.

16. For example, Zora Neale Hurston, *Mules and Men* (1939; reprint, New York: Perennial Library, 1990). On Jewish jokes, see S. Felix Mendelson, *The Jew Laughs* (Chicago: L. M. Stein, 1935).

17. Jan Bremmer and Herman Roodenburg, eds., *A Cultural History of Humor* (Malden, Mass.: Polity Press, 1997), particularly Peter Burke, "Frontiers of the Comic in Early Modern Italy," 61–75.

18. Orator, rhetorician, humanist, book collector, and papal scribe Gian Francesco Poggio Bracciolini (1380–1459) is best known simply as Poggio Bracciolini. He was responsible for recovering a great number of classical Latin manuscripts from German, Swiss, and French monastic libraries.

19. It appeared in English as *The Types of the Folk-Tale* in 1928 and again, with a companion history by Thompson, in 1946. Stith Thompson, *The Folktale* (Berkeley: University of California Press, 1946). Citations here are to the 1977 University of California edition.

20. A premier example of historical-geographic folktale study is Walter Anderson, *Kaiser und Abt*, Folklore Fellows' Communications 42 (Helsinki: Suomalainen Tiedeakatemia, 1923).

21. Alan Dundes's influential view is summarized in Dundes, "The Motif-Index and the Tale Type Index: A Critique," *Journal of Folklore Research* 34, no. 3 (1997): 195–202. For a history of nineteenth-century thought on folklore and mythology, see Richard Mercer Dorson, *The British Folklorists: A History* (Chicago: University of Chicago Press, 1968).

22. In 1973 Legman's correspondent Frank Hoffman aimed to remedy some of the North American gaps in the Aarne-Thompson Index in his *Analytical Index of Traditional Anglo-American Erotica* (Bowling Green, Ohio: Popular Press, 1973). Hoffman drew on and cited *The Horn Book* but did not index the material in *Rationale*.

23. Gershon Legman and Mahlon Blaine, *The Art of Mahlon Blaine: A Reminiscence* (East Lansing, Mich.: Peregrine Books, 1982); Sigmund Freud, "The Moses of Michelangelo," in *The Standard Edition of the Complete Psychological Works of Sigmund Freud*, vol. 13, *1913–1914: Totem and Taboo and Other Works*, ed. James Strachey (London: Hogarth Press, 1955), 209–38.

Notes to Chapter 9 **283**

24. On Reich, see Christopher Turner, *Adventures in the Orgasmatron: The Invention of Sex* (New York: Farrar, Straus and Giroux, 2011).

25. Sigmund Freud, "Three Essays on the Theory of Sexuality (1905)," in *The Standard Edition of the Complete Psychological Works of Sigmund Freud*, ed. James Strachey (London: Hogarth Press, 1953), 7:125–245; Sigmund Freud, *The Psychopathology of Everyday Life*, vol. 6 of *The Standard Edition of the Complete Works of Sigmund Freud*, ed. James Strachey (London: Hogarth Press, 1960), 57–214. Here Freud took a close look at slips of the tongue, mistakes, minor forgettings, and confusions to explain the meaning of materials no one took seriously.

26. See Elizabeth Ann Danto, *Freud's Free Clinics: Psychoanalysis & Social Justice, 1918–1938* (New York: Columbia University Press, 2005); Paul A. Robinson, *The Freudian Left* (New York: Harper & Row, 1969), which takes up the left political intersections with Freudian thought in the work of Wilhelm Reich, Geza Roheim, and Herbert Marcuse. But the political tradition of psychoanalysis would be largely ignored in the United States. See Russell Jacoby, *The Repression of Psychoanalysis: Otto Fenichel and the Political Freudians* (Chicago: University of Chicago Press, 1986).

27. Sigmund Freud, *Civilization and Its Discontents*, vol. 21 of *The Standard Edition of the Complete Works of Sigmund Freud*, ed. James Strachey (London: Hogarth Press, 1961).

28. Sigmund Freud, "Letter to Dr. Friedrich S. Krauss," in *The Standard Edition of the Complete Works of Sigmund Freud*, vol. 11, *Five Lectures on Psychoanalysis*, ed. James Strachey (London: Hogarth Press, 1957), 233–35.

29. Ibid., 233–34.

30. Ibid., 234.

31. Ibid., 234–35.

32. Ibid.

33. Earlier, in 1905, Freud had laid out his influential look at jokes and joking. Sigmund Freud, *Jokes and Their Relation to the Unconscious*, vol. 8 of *The Standard Edition of the Complete Works of Sigmund Freud*, ed. James Strachey (London: Hogarth Press, 1960).

34. As will be seen, Legman did not complete this project. Recently, the Aarne-Thompson Index has been extensively reworked and expanded by Hans-Jörg Uther, who has tried to account for and include erotic materials. Uther, *The Types of International Folktales: A Classification and Bibliography, Based on the System of Antti Aarne and Stith Thompson*, Folklore Fellows' Communications 284–86 (Helsinki: Suomalainen Tiedeakatemia, 2004).

35. Martha Wolfenstein, *Children's Humor: A Psychological Analysis* (1954; reprint, Bloomington: Indiana University Press, 1978).

36. *Rationale*, 331, 333.

37. Otto Rank and Robert A. Segal, introduction to *The Myth of the Birth of the Hero: A Psychological Exploration of Myth* (Baltimore: Johns Hopkins University Press, 2015).

38. For thinkers like folklorists and philologists Jacob and Wilhelm Grimm, a deeply shared collective personality could be closely tied to place and the local past. Raymond Williams, *Culture and Society, 1780–1950* (New York: Columbia University Press, 1960); Regina Bendix, *In Search of Authenticity: The Formation of Folklore Studies* (Madison: University of Wisconsin Press, 1997). In this vein, Jungian psychoanalysts and folklor-

ists posit a universal human collective unconscious, which expresses itself through the archetypes of myth and folktale. This was not Freud's position, nor was it Legman's. While Freud had recourse to, and often used, nineteenth-century notions of a "racial mind," Peter Gay writes that this usage was carefully excised by his disciples and followers from the 1930s onward. Gay, *Freud for Historians* (Oxford: Oxford University Press, 1986), 146–48. As the notion of a people's collective mind was reworked into the notion of a national (sometimes racial) mind or personality, with devastating consequences in Europe, Freud's students were anxious to distance their discipline's founder from explicitly racial thinking. Gay, *Freud: A Life for Our Time* (New York: W. W. Norton, 1998).

39. But see Gary Alan Fine, "Evaluating Psychoanalytic Folklore: Are Freudians Ever Right?" *New York Folklore* 10 (1984): 5–20.

40. Jacoby, *Repression of Psychoanalysis*.

41. Ibid. On the translation of Freud to the American context, see Nathan G. Hale, *Freud and the Americans: The Beginnings of Psychoanalysis in the United States, 1876–1917* (New York: Oxford University Press, 1995); Dagmar Herzog, *Cold War Freud: Psychoanalysis in an Age of Catastrophe* (Cambridge: Cambridge University Press, 2017); and Eli Zaretsky, *Political Freud: A History* (New York: Columbia University Press, 2015).

42. On this currency, see Elizabeth Lunbeck, *The Americanization of Narcissism* (Cambridge, Mass.: Harvard University Press, 2014), 1–81. On the multiform post–World War II adoption of psychoanalysis in the United States, see Herzog, *Cold War Freud*.

43. Freud, *Psychopathology of Everyday Life*, 57–214 On Legman's enthusiasm for the book: JL, interview with the author, May 12, 2004, Opio, France. For a critique of the idea of unconscious motivation, see Sebastiano Timpanaro, *The Freudian Slip: Psychoanalysis and Textual Criticism* (London: New Left Books, 1976).

44. RDA, interview with the author, October 17, 2002, Rochester, N.Y.

45. Folklorist Mac E. Barrick, with whom Legman corresponded, created an informal index for the *Rationale*, for his own use. The index is in the collections of the Center for Pennsylvania Culture Studies at Penn State–Harrisburg. (My thanks to Simon Bronner for pointing this out.)

46. Giselinde Kuipers, *Good Humor, Bad Taste: A Sociology of the Joke* (Berlin: Mouton de Gruyter, 2006).

47. *Rationale*, 331.

48. Gloria Dorson, wife of Richard Dorson, was an actress and known as a brilliant storyteller, and he describes his second wife, Christine Conrad, as a good joke teller in Legman, "Bridge of Night," *Brooklyn Bridge Bulletin* (May 24, 1983): 26–27.

49. *Rationale*, 331.

50. Legman seems to have had conversations about racist jokes with Wright, but I have not been able to put the two in Paris at the same time.

51. Kuipers, *Good Humor, Bad Taste*.

52. *Rationale*, 1.

53. Between 2005 and 2015, African American students at the University of Illinois reported to me astoundingly hostile racist jokes told them by white "friends."

(In riddle form: Q. "What's black and would look good hanging from a tree?" A. "You.")

54. Thompson, *The Folktale*, 188–216.

55. James P. Leary, ed., *So Ole Says to Lena: Folk Humor of the Upper Midwest*, 2nd ed. (Madison: University of Wisconsin Press, 2001), 248. See also Elliott Oring, "Blond Ambitions and Other Signs of the Times," in *Engaging Humor* (Urbana: University of Illinois Press, 2003).

56. Thompson, *The Folktale*, 190–92.

57. *Rationale*, 113.

58. Ibid., 123.

59. Ibid., 126, 114.

60. Ibid., 128.

61. Ibid., 349; on female dominance, 347–56.

62. Ibid., 349, 357–58.

63. A recent iteration is Christopher Hitchens, "Why Women Aren't Funny," *Vanity Fair*, January 1, 2007, http://www.vanityfair.com/culture/2007/01/hitchens200701.

64. *Rationale*, 377–84. This joke had continuity with the folk song "The Three Old Whores of Winnipeg." There is a similar female joking session that deals with vaginal size in the film *The Aristocrats*, featuring comediennes Susie Essman and Carrie Fisher.

65. Legman describes the telling of this joke, probably by Christine Conrad, in "Bridge of Night."

66. GL to AC, May 27, 1969, LAO.

67. On Grove and Rosset, see Loren Glass, *Counterculture Colophon: Grove Press, "Evergreen Review" and the Incorporation of the Avant-Garde* (Stanford, Calif.: Stanford University Press, 2013); and Barney Rosset, *Rosset: My Life in Publishing and How I Fought Censorship* (New York: OR Books, 2016.)

68. JL, interviews with the author, May 9 and May 15, 2004, Opio, France.

69. JL, email, January 24, 2016.

70. JL, interview, May 9, 2004.

71. RDA, interview.

72. Ian Hamilton, "Fanny Ha! Ha!," *New Society*, August 28, 1969, 330; Philip French, "Digging the Dirt," *New Statesman*, August 29, 1969, 278; Paul Showers, "Rationale of the Dirty Joke," *New York Times Book Review*, June 15, 1969, 22; Sidney J. Harris, "Strictly Personal: Unmourned Death of the Dirty Joke," *Chicago Daily News*, July 18, 1969; Day Thorpe, "Folklore of Sexual Humor," Washington, D.C., *Sunday Star*, November 24, 1968, G2.

73. GL to Joanna Krotz, September 16, 1969, LAO.

74. Richard Buehler, review of *Rationale of the Dirty Joke*, by G. Legman, *Journal of American Folklore* 83, no. 237 (1970): 87–89.

75. AC to GL, May 23, 1969; GL to AC, May 27, 1969, LAO. On the French edition of *Oragenitalism*, see Truong Cong Thanh to GL, February 10, 1970, LAO. A few years later, Alex Comfort published *The Joy of Sex: A Cordon Bleu Guide to Lovemaking* (New York: Crown, 1972). In a review titled "The Joys of Perversion," Legman blasted

Comfort for his tolerance of kinky sex, including bondage and flagellation. (Unpublished review, kindness of Eric Laursen.)

76. A sheet headed "Legmania," n.d. in the 1969–70 correspondence file, LAO.

77. Daniel Dayan (1943–), a French social scientist, later a major television scholar.

78. Daniel Dayan to GL, October 17, 1969. My rough translation, courtesy of Daniel Dayan.

79. GL to Dayan, October 21, 1969, LAO.

80. Ibid.

81. JL, interviews, May 9 and May 15, 2004.

82. Ibid.

83. JL, interview, May 15, 2004.

84. *No Laughing Matter*, 885.

85. Ibid., 893.

86. Ibid., 55–70.

87. It was reviewed in a profile of Legman in *Time*: R. Z. Sheppard, "The Japes of Wrath," *Time*, November 10, 1975, 96–97.

88. Announcement in the *Journal of American Folklore* 90 (1977): 48. Later, the Chicago Folklore Prize would be awarded by University of Chicago Press and the American Folklore Society.

89. On the prize, BJ to GL, September 8, 1977; GL to BJ, December 14 and December 24, 1977, "Solstix plus 3," all courtesy of Bruce Jackson, SGDLP.

90. JL, interview, May 15, 2004.

91. Elliott Oring, review of *Rationale of the Dirty Joke*, 2 vols., by G. Legman, *Western Folklore* 36 (1977): 365–71. For a strong statement of Oring's theory of jokes as cognitive play, and his firm rejection of Freud's perspective, see *Jokes and Their Relations* (Lexington: University Press of Kentucky, 1992) and *Engaging Humor*.

92. Oring, review of *Rationale of the Dirty Joke*, 371.

93. This is a charge often aimed at Freudian cultural analysis. See Fine, "Evaluating Psychoanalytic Folklore."

94. On the shifts in psychoanalytic thought in the 1970s, see Lunbeck, *The Americanization of Narcissism*.

95. Oring, review of *Rationale of the Dirty Joke*, 367. (Implicitly, Oring raised the thorny problem of what tale type and motif indexes were for.)

96. Ibid., 366.

97. Oring wrote that Legman analyzed folklore genres as though they were identical—as if a joke was no more than its subject matter. But aren't jokes a special form of talk in that they frame wishes, desires, and ideas as "harmless" and "ridiculous"?

98. Oring, review of *Rationale of the Dirty Joke*, 368.

99. Ibid., 369.

100. GL to Elliott Oring, December 23, 1977, copy in the possession of the author. Courtesy of Elliott Oring. It is unclear who could have made this remark to Legman or when.

101. Ibid. "Jesus wept." Later, Randolph would be made a fellow of the American Folklore Society, but probably not due to Legman's hectoring.

102. James P. Leary, review of *No Laughing Matter*, by G. Legman, *Folklore Forum* 9, no. 2 (1976): 85–86.

Notes to Chapter 9 **287**

103. In his wilder moments, Legman would claim that Herbert Marcuse lifted the ideas in *Eros and Civilization* from him and stole his position at the University of California, San Diego, where Marcuse taught in the 1960s and 1970s.

104. Leary review of *No Laughing Matter*, 86.

105. Richard Dorson led the professionalization (and some argue a depoliticization) of folklore study in the academy. See Regina Bendix, *In Search of Authenticity: The Formation of Folklore Studies* (Madison: University of Wisconsin Press, 1997), 188–219; Simon J. Bronner, *Following Tradition: Folklore in the Discourse of American Culture* (Logan: Utah State University, 1998), 349–412; John Alexander Williams, "Radicalism and Professionalism in Folklore Studies: A Comparative Perspective," *Journal of the Folklore Institute* 11, no. 3 (1975): 211–34; and a reply from Richard M. Dorson, "Comment on Williams," *Journal of the Folklore Institute* 11 (1975): 235–39. See also Benjamin Filene, *Romancing the Folk: Public Memory and American Roots Music* (Chapel Hill: University of North Carolina Press, 2000), 133–81.

106. Alan Dundes thought this was evidence of the field's undertheorization. Simon Bronner writes that folklore as a discipline has had an aversion to psychology in "Practice Theory in Folklore and Folklife Studies," *Folklore* 123 (2012): 23–47. Folklorists have hesitated to ascribe meanings outside the awareness of their informants to folklore performances and practices.

107. Ronald Fraser, ed., *1968: A Generation in Revolt* (New York: Pantheon Books, 1988).

108. See Fine, "Evaluating Psychoanalytic Folklore."

109. Browne, a student of Wayland Hand, founded the Center for the Study of Popular Culture in 1968.

110. Founded in the United States in 1973 and led by Brian Sutton-Smith. International societies: International Society for Humor Studies, about 1979.

111. Stuart Hall and Tony Jefferson, *Resistance through Rituals: Youth Subcultures in Post-war Britain* (London: Harper Collins Academic, 1976); Stuart Hall and Paddy Whannell, *The Popular Arts* (London: Hutchinson Educational, 1964); Dick Hebdige, *Subculture: The Meaning of Style* (London: Routledge, 1979).

112. On the American and European expansion of higher education and its accessibility to new kinds of students, see Fraser, *1968*.

113. For example, see Ronald L. Baker, *Jokelore: Humorous Folktales from Indiana* (Bloomington: Indiana University Press, 1986); and Leary, *So Ole Says to Lena*.

114. Thomas A. Burns, *Doing the Wash: An Expressive Culture and Personality Study of a Joke and Its Tellers* (Folcroft, Pa.: Folcroft Library Editions, 1976); Mary Knapp and Herbert Knapp, *One Potato, Two Potato: The Folklore of American Children* (New York: W. W. Norton, 1976).

115. Rayna Green, "Magnolias Grow in Dirt: The Bawdy Lore of Southern Women," *Radical Teacher* 6 (1977), 26–31; Gloria Kaufman and Mary Kay Blakely, eds., *Pulling Our Own Strings: Feminist Humor and Satire* (Bloomington: Indiana University Press, 1994).

116. Sandra McCosh, *Children's Humor: A Joke for Every Occasion* (London: Granada, 1979).

117. Roger D. Abrahams and Alan Dundes, "On Elephantasy and Elephanticide," *Psychoanalytic Review* 56 (1969): 225–41.

288 *Notes to Chapters 9 and 10*

118. For an authoritative collection, see Simon Bronner, ed., *The Meaning of Folklore: The Analytical Essays of Alan Dundes* (Logan: Utah State University Press, 2007).

119. For an example of an attack on the premises of psychoanalysis by a folklorist, see David J. Hufford, "Beings without Bodies: An Experience-Centered Theory of Belief in Spirits," in *Out of the Ordinary: Folklore and the Supernatural*, ed. Barbara Walker (Logan: Utah State University Press, 1995), 11–45; and his response to Utz Jeggle, "A Lost Track: On the Unconscious in Folklore," *Journal of Folklore Research* 40, no. 1 (2003): 73–94.

120. During a visit to Wisconsin, Legman inscribed Leary's copy of *No Laughing Matter*, "To the only folklorist who understood my book."

121. Leary would go on to do analyses of joke tellers' repertoires, especially attending to bawdy jokes, and draw some limited and cautious psychological connections between teller and tale. James P. Leary, "The Favorite Jokes of Max Trezbiatowski," *Western Folklore* 43, no. 1 (1984): 1–17; Leary, "Style in Jocular Communication: From the Cultural to the Personal," *Journal of Folklore Research* 21 (1984): 29–46.

122. But see Barbara Kirshenblatt-Gimblett's study of a humorous anecdote: "A Parable in Context: A Social Interactional Analysis of Storytelling Performance," in *Folklore: Performance and Communication*, ed. Dell Hymes, Dan Ben-Amos, and Kenneth S. Goldstein (The Hague: Mouton, 1975), 105–30.

123. The first of Alan Dundes and Carl Pagter's several volumes was *Urban Folklore from the Paperwork Empire* (Austin, Tex.: American Folklore Society, 1976).

124. G. Legman, "A Word for It!" *Maledicta* 1 (1977): 9–18.

125. Mark Twain, *The Mammoth Cod, and Address to the Stomach Club* (Milwaukee: *Maledicta*, 1976). Legman wrote in his introduction that the publication of *The Mammoth Cod* rested upon a feat of manuscript smuggling. It was found in Yale's Beinecke Library, where a graduate student (name unknown) memorized it, wrote it down later, and sent it to Legman.

126. Bruce Jackson, "The King of X700," *Maledicta* 1 (1977): 111–24. This issue also contained a thorough bibliography of Legman's published and unpublished work by John McLeish, an independent scholar working in Glasgow (127–38).

127. Leary and Dundes are the exception here. Elliott Oring defined the field's theories as frustration-aggression theory, following Legman and Dundes, as well as cognitive-structural approaches (exemplified by his own). He thought the emphasis on aggression had stifled research into jokes, but focused on Dundes and Abrahams's work on elephant jokes and did not discuss Legman's work in detail in *Jokes and Their Relations*, 16–28. Similarly, Legman is cited and then given short shrift in Oring's *Engaging Humor*, 71. Although Legman's work was encyclopedic and masterful, for American folklorists Alan Dundes was the influential man to be challenged.

128. Letter following Legman's father's death. Daisy Birnbaum to GL, July 1975, LAO.

Chapter 10. Under Mt. Cheiron

1. David Berenger, telephone interview with the author, November 25, 2015.

2. GL to JH, January 9, 1973, Legman correspondence file, AFC/LOC.

Notes to Chapter 10 **289**

3. GL to JH, June 17, 1977, AFC/LOC.

4. Hickerson sent a fourteen-page list of the R. W. Gordon collections (it was a collection of collections), and Legman was hoping for a copy of every typed obscene item—205 sheets. He offered to send his own 4,000 pages of manuscript and unique mimeographs to the archive. GL to JH, April 3, 1974, AFC/LOC. Hickerson was interested and in 1977 wrote that he needed an offer in writing to acquire Legman's military song books collection. JH to GL, June 7, 1977, AFC/LOC.

5. Archie Green, interview with the author, July 11, 2002, San Francisco.

6. G. Legman, "Bawdy Monologues and Rhymed Recitations," *Southern Folklore Quarterly* 40, nos. 1–2 (1976).

7. G. Legman, ed., *The New Limerick* (New York: Crown, 1977).

8. Vance Randolph to GL, November 20, 1975, LOC, Vance Randolph Collection; "Joke Book Letters."

9. It was published by the University of Illinois Press in 1976.

10. These were published as Vance Randolph, *Roll Me in Your Arms: "Unprintable" Ozark Folksongs and Folklore*, vol. 1, *Folk Songs and Music*, and *Blow the Candle Out: "Unprintable" Ozark Folksongs and Folklore*, vol. 2, *Folk Rhymes and Other Lore* (Fayetteville: University of Arkansas Press, 1992). The publication process was difficult, and according to one editor at the University of Arkansas Press, several employees tasked with word-processing the manuscript asked to be transferred rather than deal with the salacious materials. Scot Danforth, email, November 29, 2002.

11. Judith McCulloh, personal communication, October 21, 2007.

12. G. Legman, introduction to "The Ballad" (unpublished manuscript), Legman Collection, KIRSG.

13. Ibid., 1–2. For a different perspective on violence and murder in Child's *English and Scottish Popular Ballads*, see Deborah A. Symonds, *Weep Not for Me: Women, Ballads and Infanticide in Early Modern Scotland* (University Park: Pennsylvania State University Press, 1997).

14. JL, interview with the author, May 15, 2004, Opio, France.

15. For "The Sea Crab," "Introduction" to "The Ballad," 4; and Ed Cray, *The Erotic Muse: American Bawdy Songs* (Urbana: University of Illinois Press, 1999), 1–6.

16. "Introduction" to "The Ballad," 4.

17. Ibid., 5–6.

18. G. Legman, introduction to *Roll Me in Your Arms*, by Vance Randolph, 1.

19. Ibid., 2, 4.

20. Ibid. and "Introduction" to "The Ballad," 10–11, 24.

21. G. Legman, "'Unprintable' Folklore? The Vance Randolph Collection," *Journal of American Folklore* 103 (1990): 259–300; and "Erotic Folksongs and Ballads: An International Bibliography," *Journal of American Folklore* (1990): 417–501.

22. GL to BJ, August 20, 1989, SGDLP.

23. GL to JH, November 11 and January 15, 1977, AFC/LOC.

24. In the Xerox lore project, he was joined by Michael Preston and Cathy Preston, "Things Better Left Unsaid: Photocopy Humor," *Maledicta* 5 (1981): 171–76. He described his nonverbal ephemera collection to Alan Dundes in a letter, November 5, 1980, LAO.

25. G. Legman, "FARK ('Folklore Article Reconstruction Kit')," *Journal of American Folklore* 90 (1977): 199–202.

26. GL to JIL, December 4, 1979, Jay Irving Landesman Papers, box 1, folder 24, SHSM.

27. GL to JH, June 17, 1977, AFC/LOC.

28. JL, interview, May 15, 2004.

29. Emil died in 1975, Julia in 1983.

30. Author's query published March 25, 1979, *New York Times Book Review*.

31. GL to JIL, December 4, 1979, SHSM.

32. GL to JIL, April 28, 1980, SHSM.

33. GL to JIL, December 4, 1979, SHSM. He turned out to be right about the CIA funding of the postwar literary magazines. See Joel Whitney, *Finks: How the CIA Tricked the World's Best Writers* (New York: OR Books, 2017).

34. GL to JIL, April 28, 1980, SHSM.

35. GL to JIL, June 1, 1981, SHSM.

36. GL to JIL, February 23 and November 14, 1981, and February 11, 1982, SHSM.

37. GL to JIL, July 15 and August 17, 1983, SHSM.

38. Ibid.

39. Ibid.

40. Ibid.

41. He drew on the poems as edited by Jack Lindsay, *Loving Mad Tom* (London: Fanfrolico Press, 1927); Floyd Dell: *Moon-Calf: A Novel* (New York: Alfred A. Knopf, 1920); A. E. Houseman, "XII," in *Last Poems* (New York: Henry Holt, 1922). Also known as "World I Never Made."

42. GL to JIL, June 11, 1981, SHSM.

43. GL to "The Apostles," sample solicitation letter, LAO (not dated); GL to David Eisenberg, June 21, 1989.

44. JL, interview, May 15, 2004.

45. World Humor and Irony Membership Serial Yearbook, Sixth Annual Conference.

46. BJ and DC, interview with the author, October 19, 2004, Buffalo, N.Y.

47. Legman often claimed to have invented a rotating, vibrating dildo. On the history of the vibrator, see Rachel P. Maines, *The Technology of Orgasm: "Hysteria," the Vibrator, and Women's Sexual Satisfaction* (Baltimore: Johns Hopkins University Press, 2001).

48. A videotape of the presentation survives: "Pecker Pool and Cock-a-lizers," lecture at the University of Minnesota, Spring 1986, VHS tape, LAO.

49. Ibid.

50. Reinhold Aman, interview with the author, July 14, 2004, Cotati, Calif.

51. Ibid.; James Leary, personal communication, January 2, 2018.

52. Martha Cornog, interview with the author, February 19, 2004, Philadelphia.

53. BJ and DC, interview.

54. Noël Riley Fitch, *Anaïs: The Erotic Life of Anaïs Nin* (Boston: Little, Brown, 1993).

55. David Noble, personal communication, October 8, 2004.

56. Mary Dearborn, *The Happiest Man Alive: A Biography of Henry Miller* (New York: Simon & Schuster, 1991).

57. Eric Laursen to Michael Neal, November 20, 1988. Quoted with Eric Laursen's permission.

58. Ibid.

59. Ibid.

60. Ibid.

61. Jay Gertzman, *Bookleggers and Smuthounds: The Trade in Erotica, 1920–1940* (Philadelphia: University of Pennsylvania Press, 1999).

62. Jay Gertzman, "My Visit to Gershon Legman" (unpublished manuscript, 1990). By permission of Jay Gertzman.

63. "The Lure of the Forbidden," in *Libraries, Erotica, Pornography*, ed. Martha Cornog (Phoenix: Oryx Press, 1992), 36–68; David Lister, "Origins of Origami," http://www.britishorigami.info/academic/lister/origins_of_origami.php.

64. JL, interview, May 15, 2004.

65. Erika Brady, review of *Roll Me in Your Arms* and *Blow the Candle Out*, by Vance Randolph, *Journal of the History of Sexuality* 4 (1994): 467–69.

66. JL, interview, May 15, 2004.

67. Ibid.

68. Ibid.

69. Janny Scott, "Gershon Legman, Anthologist of Erotic Humor, Is Dead at 81," *New York Times*, March 14, 1999.

70. Jay Landesman, "Gershon Legman," *Independent*, March 25, 1999, http://www.independent.co.uk/arts-entertainment/obituary-gershon-legman-1083016.html.

71. Martha Cornog and Timothy Perper, "Make Love, Not War: The Legacy of Gershon Legman," *Journal of Sex Research* (August 1999): 316–17.

72. When the 1955 origami exhibit closed, Gershon had carefully packed up Akira Yoshizawa's folds, taken them from Amsterdam to France, and forgotten he had them. In the 1980s, they resurfaced, and he sent them to Yoshizawa, who was amazed to be reunited with his precious exemplars. On Yoshizawa, see "Akira Yoshizawa, Creator of Modern Origami Who Broke Away from the Rigid and Complex Rules Which Had Governed the Art," *Daily Telegraph*, March 30, 2005.

73. Dundes to JL, March 31, 1999, copy in SGDLP.

74. BJ and DC, interview.

75. James Leary remembered proposing a spontaneous memorial resolution at the AFS business meeting that year (1999). It was seconded by Gary Alan Fine. Personal communication, January 2018.

76. Uli Kutter, "Gershon Legman: 1917–1999," *Fabula*, January 1, 2000, 41; translation kindness of Kate McQueen. Dundes remembered that in the 1980s, he had tried to get Legman an honorary degree from Yale and win him induction into the Fellows of the American Folklore Society, hoping to help Legman's book sales and advance the Freudian approach to folklore. Neither Yale nor the AFS was interested. One had to be a member of the AFS to become a fellow—and Legman had never been able to afford membership. Alan Dundes, interview with the author, July 12, 2002, Berkeley, Calif.

77. *Maledicta* was in print between 1977 and 2005, but irregularly after the mid-1980s. It had no university or press backing.

78. GL to BJ and DC, February 18, 1986, SGDLP.

Notes to Chapter 10

79. RDA, interview with the author, October 17, 2002, Rochester, N.Y.

80. Richard Bauman, "Verbal Art as Performance," *American Anthropologist* 77, no. 2 (1975): 290–311; Bauman, *Story, Performance, and Event: Contextual Studies of Oral Narrative* vol. 10 (Cambridge: Cambridge University Press, 1986).

81. RDA, interview.

82. But see Barbara Kirshenblatt-Gimblett, "A Parable in Context," in *Folklore: Performance and Communication*, ed. Dell Hymes, Dan Ben-Amos, and Kenneth S. Goldstein (The Hague: Mouton, 1975), 105–30.

83. Benedict Anderson, *Imagined Communities*, rev. ed. (London: Verso Books, 1991); Charles Briggs and Amy Shuman, "Theorizing Folklore: Toward New Perspectives on the Politics of Culture," *Western Folklore* 52 (1993): 109–34.

84. For a consideration of the problems of presenting and publishing material in "bad taste," see Moira Smith and Rachelle H. Saltzman, "Introduction to Tastelessness," *Journal of Folklore Research* (1995): 85–99 (a special issue on taste and tastelessness).

85. Joan N. Radner, ed., *Feminist Messages: Coding in Women's Folk Culture* (Urbana: University of Illinois Press, 1993).

86. Mikita Brottman, *Funny Peculiar: Gershon Legman and the Psychopathology of Humor* (Hillsdale, N.J.: Analytic Press, 2004).

87. The broader field of humor studies has seemed more appreciative of Legman's work on jokes than the discipline folklore. Simon Bronner, personal communication, January 2018. A major difficulty in using *Rationale* and *No Laughing Matter* is the lack of an index. Legman wanted to force readers to work through the entire corpus. New humor studies include the qualitative and the quantitative, which can now be accomplished via Listservs, email, and metasearch of computerized databases. An example of qualitative work on humor: Moira Marsh, *Practically Joking* (Logan: University Press of Colorado, 2015). Quantitative work on jokes: Christie Davies, *Jokes and Targets* (Bloomington: Indiana University Press, 2011). Internet-based humor research: Bill Ellis, "Making a Big Apple Crumble: The Role of Humor in Constructing a Global Response to Disaster," *New Directions in Folklore* 6 (2015). A study of the humor of contemporary catastrophe that fails to mention Legman: Trevor J. Blank, *The Last Laugh: Folk Humor, Celebrity Culture, and Mass-Mediated Disasters in the Digital Age* (Madison: University of Wisconsin Press, 2013).

88. Julie Peakman connects the history of erotica with the history of sexuality in *Mighty Lewd Books: The Development of Pornography in Eighteenth-Century England* (New York: Palgrave Macmillan, 2003).

89. Folklorists responded to the history of sexuality and new theories of gender by producing work on the lore of the body, although this development was tentative. See Cathy Preston, "Erotic Lore," in *Encyclopedia of Women's Folklore and Folklife*, ed. Liz Locke, Theresa A. Vaughan, and Pauline Greenhill, 2 vols. (Westport, Conn.: Greenwood Press, 2008); and Katharine Young, ed., *Bodylore* (Knoxville: University of Tennessee Press, 1995). In legend studies, there is a more developed treatment of concepts of the body: for example, Gillian Bennett, *Bodies: Sex, Violence, Disease, and Death in Contemporary Legend* (Jackson: University Press of Mississippi, 2009). Legman is not usually acknowledged in work on body lore, but see Inger Lövkrona, "Erotic Narrative and the Construction of Gender in Premodern Sweden," *Journal of Folklore Research* 35 (1988): 145–56. Cristina Bacchilega notes Legman's reintroduc-

tion of the Russian secret tales: "Preface to the Special Issue on Erotic Tales," *Marvels & Tales* 22 (2008): 13–23. See also Cathy Lynn Preston, "'Cinderella' as a Dirty Joke: Gender, Multivocality, and the Polysemic Text," *Western Folklore* 53, no. 1 (1994): 27–49.

90. Lynn Hunt, *The Invention of Pornography, 1500–1800: Obscenity and the Origins of Modernity* (New York: Zone Books, 1993); Catharine Gallagher and Thomas Laqueur, *The Making of the Modern Body: Sexuality and Society in the Nineteenth Century* (Berkeley: University of California Press, 1987).

91. Robert Darnton, *The Literary Underground of the Old Regime* (Cambridge, Mass.: Harvard University Press, 1982); Robert Darnton, *The Forbidden Best-Sellers of Pre-Revolutionary France* (New York: W. W. Norton, 1996).

92. An important overview is Robert Muchembled, *Orgasm and the West: A History of Pleasure from the 16th Century to the Present* (Cambridge: Polity, 2008). Muchembled credits Kinsey as a progenitor of the history of sexuality.

93. Michel Foucault, *The Archaeology of Knowledge* (New York: Pantheon Books, 1972); *The History of Sexuality*, vol. 1 (New York: Vintage, 1978); and *The Use of Pleasure: The History of Sexuality*, vol. 2 (New York: Vintage, 1985); Kathy Lee Peiss, Christina Simmons, and Robert A. Padgug, eds., *Passion and Power: Sexuality in History* (Philadelphia: Temple University Press, 1989); Christine Stansell, *City of Women: Sex and Class in New York, 1789–1860* (Urbana: University of Illinois Press, 1987).

94. BJ and DC, interview.

95. Frederick S. Lane, *Obscene Profits: Entrepreneurs of Pornography in the Cyber Age* (Abingdon: Routledge, 2001).

96. Timothy Egan, "Wall Street Meets Pornography," *New York Times,* October 23, 2000, http://www.nytimes.com/2000/10/23/us/erotica-special-report-technology-sent-wall-street-into-market-for-pornography.html.

97. Barbara Ehrenreich, Elizabeth Hess, and Gloria Jacobs, *Remaking Love: The Feminization of Sex* (New York: Anchor Books, 1987).

98. For an overview of porn on the Internet, see Katrien Jacobs, *Netporn: DIY Web Culture and Sexual Politics* (Lanham, Md.: Rowman & Littlefield, 2007).

99. Andrea Dworkin, *Pornography: Men Possessing Women* (London: Women's Press, 1999); Catherine A. MacKinnon and Andrea Dworkin, *In Harm's Way: The Pornography Civil Rights Hearings* (Cambridge, Mass.: Harvard University Press, 1998). More positively, see Laura Kipnis, *Bound and Gagged: Pornography and the Politics of Fantasy in America* (Durham, N.C.: Duke University Press, 1999).

100. Gail Dines, *Pornland: How Porn Has Hijacked Our Sexuality* (Boston: Beacon Press, 2010). For a recent discussion, see Maggie Jones, "What Teenagers Are Learning from Online Porn," *New York Times Magazine*, February 7, 2018, www.nytimes.com/2018/02/07/magazine/teenagers-learning-online-porn-literacy-sex-education.html.

101. Toward the end of his life, Legman was uncertain of the answer: Helen Dudar, "Love and Death (and Schmutz): G. Legman's Second Thoughts," *Village Voice*, May 1, 1984, 41–43.

102. For example, Stephen Holden, "Film Taboo Is Smashed to General Shrugging," *New York Times*, April 27, 2005, http://www.nytimes.com/2005/04/27/movies/film-taboo-is-smashed-to-general-shrugging.html.

103. GL to JIL, July 4, 1967, SHSM.

WORKS CONSULTED

Unpublished Works

Beckwith, Osmond. "Testimonial." Unpublished manuscript, 1999. SGDLP.

Gertzman, Jay. "My Visit to Gershon Legman." Unpublished manuscript, 1990. SGDLP.

Gordon, Daniel. "Bow Wow, Squinty and Other Feared Teachers." Unpublished manuscript, courtesy of Daniel Gordon's family. Copy in SGDLP.

Laursen, Eric to Michael Neal. November 20, 1988.

Legman, G. Alexander. "Toward an Historical Bibliography of Sex Technique." Unpublished manuscript, 1936. LAO.

Legman, Gershon. "The Ballad." Unpublished manuscript. Legman Collection, KIRSG.

———. "The Joys of Perversion." Unpublished review of *The Joy of Sex,* by Alex Comfort. N.d. Courtesy of Eric Laursen.

———. "On Faking Henry Miller." Unpublished introduction to a reprint of *Opus Pistorum*, 1983. SGDLP.

———. "Pecker Pool and Cock-a-lizers." Lecture at the University of Minnesota, Spring 1986. VHS tape, LAO.

———. "A Spiral Universe" and "A Gathering of Rooks." Chaps. 89–90 in "The Book of Moones." Bk. 7 of "Peregrine Penis." Unpublished manuscript. LAO.

Painter, Thomas. "Male Homosexuals and Their Prostitutes in Contemporary America." Unpublished manuscript, New York, 1941. KIRSG.

Interviews

Abrahams, Roger. Rochester, N.Y., October 17, 2002.

Aman, Reinhold. Cotati, Calif., July 14, 2004.

Berenger, David. Telephone interview, November 25, 2015.

Cornog, Martha, and Timothy Perper. Philadelphia, February 19, 2004.
Dundes, Alan. Berkeley, Calif., July 12, 2002.
Green, Archie. San Francisco, July 11, 2002.
Hoffman, Frank. Bloomington, Ind., September 27, 2002.
Jackson, Bruce, and Diane Christian. Buffalo, N.Y., October 19, 2002.
Legman, Ariëla. Interviews by email, November 10, 2015; February 7 and February 21, 2016.
Legman, Judith. Opio, France, May 8–10, May 12, May 15, 2004; May 5, 2013.
Zhou, Liana. Bloomington, Ind., September 27, 2002.

Archives of Letters and Papers

Gershon Legman's letters number in the tens of thousands, and they are scattered far and wide, in archives, libraries, and private collections. The most important set of Legman's correspondence is located in Opio, France, in his own file drawers. At the time of this writing, the letters have been partially indexed by Judith Legman. The Legman Archive at Opio also contains many of his document research files and some of his published and unpublished manuscripts, as well as the typescripts and notebooks for his partially published memoir, *Peregrine Penis*.

I have also made use of Legman's correspondence with Alfred C. Kinsey, Robert L. Dickinson, and the staff of the Kinsey Institute, in the Archives of the Kinsey Institute for Research in Sex and Gender at Indiana University, Bloomington, as well as other archives and collections listed below. The Kinsey Institute Archive also holds many of Legman's research files for *Love & Death*, some of his notebooks, the unpublished manuscript of "The Ballad," and his high school erotica album. Over the course of this project, many of Legman's friends gave me copies of his correspondence with them, and some people gave me original Legman holographs. In most cases, these letters are not archived elsewhere, and I have described them as belonging to my own Legman Papers Collection (SGDLP). A list of the major archives I have consulted follows.

American Folklife Center, Library of Congress, Washington, D.C.
Dorson, Richard M. Manuscripts and papers, Lilly Library, Indiana University, Bloomington.
Kinsey Archive, Institute for Research in Sex and Gender, Bloomington, Ind.
Landesman, Jay Irving. Manuscripts and papers, Western Historical Collection, State Historical Society of Missouri, St. Louis.
Legman, Susan G. Davis. Papers published and unpublished materials by Legman and others, in the possession of the author.
Legman Archive, Opio, France.
Western Historical Collection, State Historical Society of Missouri, St. Louis.

INDEX

Page numbers in *italics* refer to photographs.

Aarne, Antti, 198–99, 201, 212

Abrahams, Roger D., 141, 144, 155–60, 172, 220, 238, 273n80

Abramson, Ben, 59

Adventures of Peregrine Pickle, The, 228

advertising, 95, 121; violence in, 96, 123

Afanas'ev, A. N., 167

Afghanistan War, 242

African Americans, 100–101; folklore, 155–60; jokes and, 220–21; "Negro folk songs" and, 155–57; oral tradition, 158–59, 274–75n105

Agee, James, 261n38

Age of Anxiety, The, 113–14

aggression: in children, 230; fictional violence and, 110; in humor, 213, 216, 218–19, 226; Legman's theories about, 238, 288n127; society allowing infinite, 206; verbal, 108, 192, 221, 231

Air-Conditioned Nightmare, The, 63

alienation, 115–16, 118, 119

Aman, Reinhold, 221–22, 231

American attitudes toward sex, 1–2, 214–15, 237, 240–41; Legman on, 96–97

American Ballads and Folk Songs, 35

American Birth Control League, 34

American Civil Liberties Union, 130

American Communist Party, 4, 27

American folklore, 4; 20th century revival of, 35. *See also* folklore

American Folklore Society (AFS), 154, 236

American Freeman, 196

American Mercury, 97, 139

American radicalism, 4

American Right, the, 241

American Tragedy, An, 30

American Writers Congress, 35

anarchism: eastern European, 4; movement for free love and, 5

Anecdota Americana, 197–98, 199

Anthropophyteia, 36, 141, 144, 194

anticommunism, 115, 119. *See also* Red Scare

antimilitarism, 28, 113

anti-Semitism, 93

antiwar movement, 170. *See also* "Make Love, Not War" slogan

anxiety: about injury and loss, 146; over castration, 131–32; over homosexuality, in the U.S. government, 111; over homosexuality, Legman's, 107; produced by monogamy, 209, 219; in society, 113–14, 115

"Aphrodite" (poem), 62

Arabian Nights, The, 85

Archive of Folk Song, 148–49

Arzt, Max, 18, 23, 26

Ashbee, Henry Spencer, 150–51, 210, 240; as Pisanus Fraxi, 150, 164, 252n59

Association for the Advancement of Psychoanalysis, 106
Association for the Anthropological Study of Play, 220
atheism/secularism, 1, 12, 15, 23–24
Atlantic, 1
atomic bomb, 101, 139
Auden, W. H., 113–14
authentic folk transmission, 162
authenticity, 173, 188, 242
authoritarianism, 105, 139, 192, 199
autobiography of Legman, 227–32, 245n1; "Peregrine Penis: An Autobiography of Innocence," 228–29, 245n1
"Avatars of the Bitch," 96, 120, 159

Bad Girl, 30
"Ballad, The," 147–49, 194, 238; Ed Cray and, 161–64; Legman's later work on, 223–24
"Ballad of King Faruk and Queen Farida, The," 152, 172–73
ballads, 7, 143–44, 147, 158, 163–64, 184–85, 225; broadside, 150, 161–62, 165–66, 173; Child, 172, 225
Balzac, Honoré de, 30
bar mitzvah of Gershon Legman, 24–25, 25
Barry, Joseph Amber, 27, 151
Barzman, Ben, 175
Barzman, Norma, 175
Basic Books, 210–11, 213
Baskette, Ewing, 169
Bauman, Richard, 220
"bawdy blues," 163
Beach, Sylvia, 43
Beam, Lura, 46
Beat movement, 115, 117
Beaty, Bart, 102, 108
Beckwith, Osmond, 92, 119, 164, 213
Bellamy, Edward, 27
Benson, John, 142
Benton, Thomas Hart, 113
Berenger, David, 186, *187,* 193, 223
Bernstein, Joe, 27, 151
Bernstein, Leonard, 114
Berry, Chuck, 113
bibliographer, Legman as, 65–77
Biblioteca Arcana, 73, 75
Birnbaum, Daisy, 189

birth control, 5, 7, 34, 40
bisexuality, 82
Black Power movement, 220
Blaine, Mahlon, 42, 70
Blondie and Dagwood comics, 120
Blow the Candle Out, 224, 234
Boas, Franz, 36
body, folklore of the, 7–8, 145, 200, 240, 292n89
book-legging, 40–45
book scouting, 41, 47, 142
bowdlerization, 144, 199
"Boy Who Killed His Mother," 131
Brand, Oscar, 163
Bread Givers, The, 20
Breaking Point imprint, 107, 133, 135, 193, 213
Briffault, Robert, 44–45, 151, 252n40
"Brinzi O'Flynn," 163
British Museum, 150, 153, 187; Private Case, 86, 150, 153, 167, 187–88
British Origami Society, 234
broadside ballads, 150, 161–62, 165–66, 173
Bronson, Bertrand, 168, 225
Brossard, Chandler, 112, 128, 139
Brottman, Mikita, 239
Brown, Frank C., 225
Browne, Ray B., 219
Brown v. Board of Education, 100–101
Broyard, Anatole, 112, 128
Bruce, Lenny, 197
Brussel, Jake, 40–43, 47, 54, 56–60, 70, 71, 133, 142, 171, 233
Brussel, Minna, 60
Bryant, Louise, 33
Buehler, Richard, 211
Burns, Robert, 153, 162, 165
Burton, Richard, 85
Busch, Noel, 130
Butzner, Jane Jacobs, 27, 107, 125

California Folklore Society, 179
Calverton, V. F., 5
Cantor, Mel, 27
Capital, 28
capitalism, 28, 95, 126, 214, 219
Captain Billy's Whiz Bang, 30
Carnegie, Dale, 127
Casanova, Jacques, 30
castration, 106–7, 130–32, 194, 209, 216

Catholic Church, 5, 32, 33, 214

censorship, 1, 2, 9, 32–34, 240; advertising and, 121; bowdlerization, 144, 199; collapse of, 240–41; of comic books, 103, 110; entities upholding American, 5; expurgation, 154, 225; free-speech advocates and, 33, 138; *Neurotica* and, 130–31; of *Tropic of Cancer,* 54–56, 60; the unmailable and, 5, 32, 54, 78, 132–40; by the U.S. Post Office, 5, 32, 54, 132–38, 268n94; of violence, 103. *See also* Comstock Laws/Comstockery; *Love & Death: A Study in Censorship*

Ceppos, Arthur, 212

Chicago Folklore Prize, 215, 217

Chicago Tribune, 97

Child, Francis James, 147, 148, 173, 225, 274n90

Child ballads, 172, 225

children: African American, 100; castration issue and, 131–32; comic books and, 98–99, 103, 106, 109, 263n93; education of young, 15; folklore and games of, 151, 156, 158, 163, 179, 220, 230; of Gershon Legman, 169, 179, 186–87, *187,* 189–93, 211, 235; Legman on vulnerability of, 106; mass media effects on, 102, 104; obscenity on the playground and, 8; psychiatry and, 100; rebellion by, 18; sexual enlightenment of, 110, 230

children's folklore, Legman on, 230

Christian, Diane, 191–92, 231–32

Christian American Tract Society, 132

Church of Scientology, 10

Circle of Guilt, The, 100, 101

Civilization and Its Discontents, 200

civil rights movement, 170, 220, 277n47

Clellon Holmes, John, 2–3, 4, 92–94, 131, 139, 178, 186, 193, 210, 222; on *Love & Death,* 108; *Neurotica* and, 112, 116, 118, 119, 128

Colcher, Sima, 168–69, 179

Cold War era, the, 1, 96, 105, 115, 119, 139, 203; Americanism in commercial mass media of, 139; hyperpatriotism and, 113; McCarthyism and, 115, 138, 232; Red Scare, 2, 53, 99, 116, 138, 139, 175

Collected Works of Sigmund Freud, 92

collectors: erotica, 237, 240; folklore, 8, 9, 41, 72, 149–51, 226; "Hell drawer," 1, 7,

148, 162, 168, 195, 218, 224; joke, 195, 198, 207; Legman's attacks on, 224–25; song, 154, 162, 173, 185, 224–25

College Humor, 30

Collier's, 103

colloquialisms, sexual, 6–7

Comfort, Alex, 60, 108, 120, 151, 167

comic books, 95–108; attacks on, 97–98; censorship of, 103, 110; as form of dreaming, 104; juvenile delinquency and, 98–99, 263n91; Legman on, 96–97, 102–7, 109–10; mass culture and, 95, 102, 106; New York Academy of Medicine symposium on, 103–4; as obscenity, 102–3; popularity of, 98; psychiatry on, 99–100, 105; racism in, 100–101; viewed as "lower" social stratum entertainment, 105–6; violence celebrated in, 104–5; Wertham on, 99–103

Commentary, 110, 127

Communism, 27–28, 95, 154

Compleat Neurotica, The, 187

Comstock, Anthony, 5

Comstock Laws/Comstockery, 32, 34, 71, 82, 133, 240. *See also* censorship

condensation (in dreams), 104

Conrad, Christine, 169

conservatism, 241

consumer culture, 4, 96, 111, 121–22, 126, 203; advertising and, 123; sexual symbolism in, 121

contraception, 145

coprophilia, 145

Cornog, Martha, 189, 234, 235

Cowboy Songs, 35

Cowley, Malcolm, 109

Cray, Ed, 161–64, 170, 172–73, 177

Cremorne, The, 144

crime, 3; in children's books, 104; in comic books, 98, 110; juvenile delinquency, 98–100, 263n91; obscenity as, 103, 134, 137

crime fiction, 3–4, 94, 96, 109, 120

Crist, Judith, 103

cultivation theory, 102

cult of hygiene, 122

Cunningham Manuscript (Robert Burns), 153

cursing, 2, 7

300   *Index*

Dadaism, 217, 238, 260n18
"Dagwood-ized" men, 126, 127
Daily Worker, 101
Dark Legend: A Study of Murder, 101
Davis, Katherine Bement, 46
Davis, Miles, 113
Davis, Robert Gorham, 107, 108, 118
Dayan, Daniel, 212–13, 220
Dean-Smith, Margaret, 151
Dearborn, Mary, 232–33, 254–55n97
de Beauvoir, Simone, 151
"Decadent Superman, The," 119
*Deep Down in the Jungle: Negro Narrative
    Folklore from the Streets of Philadelphia,*
    159–60
"Degenerate's Corner," 129
Deitch Landesman, Fran "Peaches," 139
Dell, Floyd, 5, 229
Delmar, Vina, 30
Delta of Venus, 63, 233
Del Torto, John, 131
de Montaigne, Michel, 87
Dennett, Mary Ware, 33–34
detective stories, 79, 96, 98, 109, 120
deviance, 50, 53, 65, 66, 76, 138
Dianetics, 10
Dickinson, Robert Latou, 45–50, 56, 57,
    59, 141, 229, 253n62; Kinsey and, 68–71,
    75, 76
Dictionary of Folklore, 108
Dingwall, Eric, 150
displacement, 96, 145–46, 205
distortions of the body, 145
Doherty, Louise "Beka," 112, 114, 116, 119,
    129, 228
Doré, Gustave, 30
Dorson, Richard M., 8, 148, 154–55, 168,
    218, 220, 236, 270n35, 287n105
Douglas, Norman, 144
dozens, the, 8, 156, 158, 160
dreaming, 104, 122, 205–6
Dreiser, Theodore, 30, 43
*Dr. Kinsey and the Institute for Sex
    Research,* 86
Droll Stories, 30
drug culture, 170
Dudar, Helene, 188
Dundes, Alan, 167–68, 170–71, 202, 211, 218,
    220–21, 235–36, 238, 287n106

Durrell, Lawrence, 118

ego, 124
Eisenhower, Dwight D., 132, 139
elitism, 105
Ellis, Havelock, 37, 44
Ellison, Ralph, 100
Emerson, Caryl, 220
Emrich, Duncan, 147, 148–49, 150
Encyclopedia of Sex, 44
*Encyclopedic Dictionary of Sexual Speech
    and Slang,* 44
Endfield, Cyril, 27
English and Scottish Popular Ballads, The,
    147
*Enormous Changes at the Last Minute:
    Stories,* 11
Erbes, P. H., 38, 39, 54, 144
Ernst, Morris, 130
Eros and Civilization, 218
erotic folklore, 6
Erotic Muse, 172
Evans, Henry H., 179
Evans, Judith. *See* Legman, Judith
Evans, Patricia Healey, 179–80
Evergreen Review, 186, 210
existentialism, 212
Explorations, 127, 147
expurgation, 154, 225

Fabula, 236
fakelore, 163, 275n13
Fake Revolt, The, 170, 213
Farmer, John S., 38, 44, 50, 147
fascism, 28, 47, 80, 96, 126, 263n88
Federal Bureau of Investigation (FBI), 4,
    268–69n104
Federal Writers' Project, 35
feminine hygiene, 121
feminism, 215, 239
Fenichel, Otto, 131
Ferris, Bill, 188
Fiedler, Leslie, 109
Fife, Alta, 188
Fife, Austin, 188
Finberg, Myer, 248n85
Fine, Gary Alan, 230
Fischer, William, 129
Fisher, Vardis, 126

Index

301

Fiske, Marjorie, 168
Fitch, Noel Riley, 232
Fitzgerald, F. Scott, 131
folk epigraphy, 69
folk erotica, 36, 194, 196
folklore: adaptation of, in modern life, 8–9; African American, 155–59, 220–21, 274–75n105; American, 4, 35; of the body, 7–8, 145, 200, 240, 292n89; children's, 151, 156, 158, 163, 179, 220, 230; copyright and public domain, 149–52; fakelore, 163, 275n13; the forbidden in, 34, 204, 205–6; as form of dreaming, 104, 122, 205–6; Freudian perspective on, 199–203; "Hell drawer," 1, 7, 148, 162, 168, 195, 218, 224; jokes (see *No Laughing Matter: The Rationale of the Dirty Joke*; *Rationale of the Dirty Joke: An Analysis of Sexual Humor*); Legman on children's, 230; Legman's love of, 5–8, 35, 237–38; Legman's opening up of, 154–60; obscenities and slang in, 38; scholarship on, 9, 36–37, 238–39, 287n105; of sex, 6, 36, 45, 64, 65, 144, 239
Folklore (journal), 167
"Folklore Article Reconstruction Kit" (FARK), 226
Folklore Associates, 155, 167
Folklore Forum, 217
"Folklore of Industrial Man, The," 119, 121, 122, 127, 131
folk revivals: American, 35–36, 163–64, 237; British, 151–54
folk songs: "bawdy blues," 163; Child ballads, 147, 148, 173, 225; Ed Cray's collecting of, 161–62, 172–73; Legman on necessity of obscenity in, 225–26; Legman's attacks on collectors of, 225; "Negro folk songs," 155–57; "Roll Me in Your Arms," 223–27; soldiers/sailors, 152–54
Folktale, The, 207
folktales, 7–8, 35, 86, 158, 160, 196, 200, 207, 220; modern, 218; scholarship of, 198–99, 204, 238
folktale type and motif indexes, 47, 49, 57, 86, 93, 150, 161–62, 196–99, 201
folk-verse, erotic, 73
Foote, Ellis, 114

"Footprints in the Sands of Crime," 120
forbidden, the, 34, 204, 205–6
"Forbidden Fruit," 153–54
forensic psychiatry, 100
Fortune, 122
Fortuny House, 40, 42
Foucault, Michel, 240
Fowke, Edith, 163, 188
Frankfurt School, 4, 94
free love movement, 5, 40
Freems, George, 39, 40
free-speech activism, 33, 138, 170, 277n47
Free Speech League, 33
Freud, Sigmund, 36, 199
Freudian thought, 3, 36, 79, 82, 92; comic books as form of dreaming and, 104; condensation, 104; displacement, 96, 145–46, 205; dreaming in, 104, 205–6; ego, 124; homosexuality and, 123; jokes and, 199–203, 215–16, 221–22; psycho-analysis, 4, 84, 106, 116, 199–200, 218, 220–21; repression (*see* repression); the unconscious, 119, 122, 201, 205–6, 215–16, 218, 221–22
Friedman, Isaac, 15
Friedman, Joel, 29
Friedman, Julia. *See* Legman, Yolande "Julia" Friedman
Funny Peculiar, 239

Gardner, Martin, 10
Gargantua and Pantagruel, 30
Gathorne-Hardy, Jonathan, 82
Gay, Jan, 49–50, 53
Gebhard, Paul, 84, 85–86, 270n28
gender: American Right and, 241; conflict in family structure, 157; emasculation of men, 126; hidden history of sexuality and organization of, 45; joking about, 209; Legman's opinions on, 77–78, 183, 232; misogyny and, 239, 241; porn revolution and, 241; in the post-war era, 125–26; roles, 33, 125–26, 159. *See also* men; women
Genet, Jean, 142
Gertzman, Jay, 233, 241
gesturing, 142–43
Ginsberg, Allen, 92, 112, 115, 117, 139
Giovanelli, Felix, 107, 118, 119, 120, 125

302   *Index*

glossary, homosexual, 50–54
Go, 139
Gods of Generation: On Phallic Cults, Ancient and Modern, 44
Goffman, Erving, 220
Goldene Buch de Liebe, Das, 70
Goldman, Emma, 5, 33
Goldstein, Kenneth, 155, 159, 163, 212, 224, 230, 236
Goodman, Mel, 39
Goodsir-Smith, Sidney, 153
Goose Step, The, 33
Gordon, Robert Winslow, 148
Gorer, Geoffrey, 79, 84
Gotham Book Mart, 43
graffiti, 69
Great Depression, 1, 5, 14, 19, 24, 237; comic books in, 106
Green, Archie, 173, 224
Green, Rayna, 220, 224
Greer, Herb, 225
Grossman, Manny, 27–28
Grove Press, 163, 171, 210–11

Hacker, Seymour, 142
Haldeman-Julius, E., 95, 195–96
Hall, Stuart, 220
Halpert, Herbert, 148
Hammett, Dashiell, 61
Hand, Wayland, 161, 188, 218, 236
Hapgood, Hutchins, 33
Harper's Magazine, 109, 116, 122
Harris, Frank, 229
Hawes, Bess Lomax, 163, 172, 173
Haynes, J. C., 134, 135
Hays Office, 132
"Hell drawer," 1, 7, 148, 162, 168, 195, 218, 224
Helms, Jesse, 233
Hemingway, Ernest, 43
Henderson, Hamish, 9, 151, 152–53, 154, 188, 236
Henley, W. E., 38, 44, 50, 147, 167
Henry, George, 49, 65
Herzog, George, 149
Hickerson, Joe, 223–24, 226
Hirschfeld, Magnus, 68, 69
Hitler, Adolf, 28, 98
Hoffman, Frank, 169, 171
Hoggart, Richard, 94

homophobia, 76, 125, 231, 239
homosexuality, 115; homophobia and, 76, 125, 231, 239; in jokes, 205; lavender scare and, 53, 98, 115, 125; legislation against, 110–11; Legman on, 77, 106–7, 124–26, 214; Legman's glossary of, 50–54; McLuhan on, 124–26; popular culture and, 124–25; research on, 49–50
"Homosexual Prostitute," 75
Horn Book: Studies in Erotic Folklore, The, 72, 144, 164–68, 172, 184, 188–89, 210–11, 239, 276n25
hostility: American hell drawer and, 7; in children, 230; Emil Legman's, 19; in humor, 209, 213; Legman's, toward homosexuality, 76–77; paranoid, 105; psychosexual, 216, 219, 222; toward men, in women, 91
Houseman, A. E., 229
Hubbard, L. Ron, 10
Hugill, Stanley, 154
humor studies, 292n87
Hyman, Stanley Edgar, 118, 143, 270n35
hypermilitarism, 116
hyperpatriotism, 113
hypocrisy, religious, 33

I Love You, I Really Do! Part 1: Being Book One of G. Legman's Autobiography of Innocence, 245n1
"Immigrant Story, The," 11
Impressions, 29
Index Libros Prohibitorum et Tacendarum, 150
Indiana University, 65, 71
industrial culture, 121–24, 131
Industrial Workers of the World (IWW), 40
"inferno," 72, 148
Ingersoll, Colonel Robert, 26
"Institutionalized Lynch, The," 96, 119
International Folklore Association, 215
Internet, the, 240–41
Iraq War, 242
Ives, Edward, 173

Jackson, Bruce, 191–92, 222, 224, 226, 231–32, 235–36
Jacobs Butzner, Jane, 27, 107, 125

Index

Jagendorf, Mortiz, 154
James, C. L. R., 94
Jameson, R. D., 149
Jarrico, Paul, 175
Jarry, Alfred, 91–92, 260n18
Johnson, Guy, 160
Johnson, Harry P., 142
Johnson, Roy Melisander, 60–61, 63
Jokes and Their Relation to the Unconscious, 215
Jonathan Cape publishing, 210, 213
Journal of American Folklore, 155, 189, 226, 235
Journal of History of Sexuality, 234
Journal of Sex Research, 235
Joyce, James, 32, 43, 54, 133
Joy of Sex, The, 60, 151
Judaism, 18, 21, 78, 80, 110, 168, 204; comics and, 110; jokes about, 216; oral tradition in, 197; Philip Roth on, 232; "Young Turks," 155
Julian Press, 212
juvenile delinquency, 98–100, 263n91

Karpeles, Maud, 225
Kearney, Patrick, 72, 167, 187, 188–89
Kefauver committee, 110
Keith, Beverley, 87–92, *88, 89,* 119, 125, 138, 141, 143, 259n2; death of, 170–71, 174, 179, 180; end of marriage to Legman, 168–69; life in France, 174, 175, 177–78
Keith, Kathleen, 89, 90, 259n2
Keller, Thomas, 108
Kennedy, Peter, 225
Kerouac, Jack, 112, 115, 117, 139
Kindler, Jan, 143, 151, 154
"King of X700, The," 222
King Turd, 91
Kinsey, Alfred Charles, 65, 125, 142, 253n62; background of, 66; blowup with Legman, 73–77; correspondence and work with Legman, 68–72; death of, 85–86; Legman as bibliographer for, 65, 86, 240; Legman's *The Sexual Conduct of Men and Women* in response to, 77–84; response to "Minority Report," 84–86; sex histories project, 66–67
Kinsey Institute Archives, 85, 147, 256n4, 272n65, 281n4

Kittredge, G. L., 35, 186, 274n90
Knapp, Herbert, 220
Knapp, Mary, 220
Kogut, Morty, 143, 151
Korean War, 111
Korson, Raye, 148–49, 150
Kraepelin, Emil, 99
Krassner, Paul, 185
Krauss, Friedrich Salomo, 36, 47, 141, 144, 194, 200, 201
Kroc, Ray, 67
Kroc, Robert, 67
Krotz, Joanna, 211, 223
Kryptadia, 36, 141, 194
Kubie, Ronald, 79
Kuipers, Giselinde, 206
Kupferberg, Tuli, 112

LaBarre, Weston, 108
La Clé des Champs, 178, 184, 232; visitors to, 189–90, *189–93*
Lady Chatterley's Lover, 54, 142, 163
Lafargue Clinic, 100
Lafont, Robert, 212
Laidlaw, Robert, 76
Landesman, Fran "Peaches" Deitch, 188
Landesman, Jay, 174, 187, 188; Legman's autobiography and, 227–29; *Neurotica* and, 92, 94, 107, 112–14, 128–29, 227–28. See also *Neurotica*
Langley Porter Psychiatric Center, 168
Larson, Kenneth, 196
Laughlin, James, IV, 55–56, 107
Laursen, Eric, 232–33
Lauter, Bob, 101
lavender panic/scare, 53, 98, 115, 125
Lawlor, Gerald W., 115
Lawrence, D. H., 32, 142, 163
Laws, Malcolm, 225
Leach, Maria, 108
Leadbelly, 35
Leary, James, 217, 221, 231, 238
Leavis, F. R., 94, 121
Leavis, Q. D., 94
Ledbetter, Huddie, 35
Left-Wing Communism, an Infantile Disorder, 28
legacy of Gershon Legman, 236–40
Legman, Ariëla, 169, 179, 189–91, 193, 235

Index

Legman, Daisy, 16, 32, 248n85

Legman, David. *See* Berenger, David

Legman, Emil Mendel, 5, 11–12, *17,* 64; attitudes toward sex, 29–30, 31–32; final letter to Gershon, 189; Gershon's rejection of, 35; goals for Gershon, 23–26; jobs of, 15–16; life in Scranton, 15–18; marriage of, *13,* 14; relationship with Gershon, 19–26, 37; religious life of, 15, 18, 20–22; socialism and, 27; temperament of, 19–21, 23, 31–32, 66, 123, 222

Legman, Gershon: on American folklore, 4; on America's involvement in wars, 96; in Amsterdam, 168–69, *169;* autobiography of, 227–32, 245n1; "The Ballad" (*see* "Ballad, The"); bar mitzvah of, 24–25, *25;* as bibliographer for Kinsey, 65, 86, 240; birth of, 16; blowup with Kinsey, 73–77; book archive of, 271–72n53; book collecting by, 142–43; as book-legger, 40–45; as a child, *17;* children of, 169, 179, 186–87, *187,* 189–93, 211, 235; on comic books (*see* comic books); comic books and, 95–108; correspondence and work with Kinsey, 68–72; correspondence kept by, 185–86; criticism written by, 44; death of, 235–36; early education of, 21–22; end of marriage to Beverley, 169; failing health of, 226–27; first love affair with "Tia French," 31; freelance work in erotica, 60–64; graduation from high school, 37, *38;* Henry Miller and, 54–56; high school education of, 26–29; homosexual experiences of, 76–77; *Horn Book: Studies in Erotic Folklore,* 72, 144, 164–68, 172, 184, 188–89, 210–11, 239; hostility toward sexual repression, 5; influence of family life on, 19–21; intellectual contributions of, 9–10; Jake Brussel and, 40–43, 47, 54, 56–60; last visit to the United States, 229–32; legacy of, 236–40; *Les Hautes Études,* 141; life after high school, 37–38; life and work in France, 174–88, *175, 177;* life in the Bronx, 92–95; on love and marriage, 78–79; *Love & Death* (see *Love & Death: A Study in Censorship*); love of jokes, 30–31; major stroke suffered by, in 1991, 234; marriage to Beverley Keith, 87–92, *88, 89,* 168–69, 170–71; marriage to Judith Evans, 179–88, *181–82;* Marshall McLuhan and, 119–29; on mass media, 102; "Minority Report" by, 77–84; modern day obscurity of, 3; move to New York City in 1936, 39–40; *Neurotica* and (see *Neurotica*); *No Laughing Matter* (see *No Laughing Matter: The Rationale of the Dirty Joke*); obscene songs collected by, 152–54; opening of folklore by, 154–60; *Oragenitalism,* 56–60, 64, 92, 212; parents of (*see* Legman, Emil Mendel; Legman, Yolande "Julia" Friedman); political stances of, 3, 4–5, 27–28, 230, 233; prejudice against homosexuals, 77, 106–7, 123–24, 214; publishing by, 2–3; *Rationale of the Dirty Joke: An Analysis of Sexual Humor (First Series), The* (see *Rationale of the Dirty Joke: An Analysis of Sexual Humor*); rejection of his father, 35; "Roger-Maxe de la Glannege," pseudonym of, 57, 60; as romantic and modernist, 8; as sex collector, 29–36; as social critic, 1–2, 34, 110–11; study of African American folklore, 155–60; sympathy for working class movements, 5, 34; theories of Robert Briffault and, 44–45; theory of media effects, 108; at the University of California, San Diego, 168–71; at the University of Michigan, 37, 39; unmailable finding and, 132–40; visitors to, in France, 188–93, 232–34; on women, 76, 91; work in Europe, 148–54; work on homosexual glossary, 50–54; work on limericks, 142–46; work with Dr. Robert Latou Dickinson, 45–50; at Yeshiva Rabbi Jacob-Joseph, 23–26. See also *Love & Death: A Study in Censorship*

Legman, Judith, 89, 142, 169, 171, 174, 213, 225; children of, 186–87, *187,* 192–93, 211; early life and marriage to Gershon Legman, 179–88, *180, 182, 187,* 190; later years with Gershon Legman, 223, 232, 234–35

Legman, Matilda, 16, *17,* 31–32, 38, 248n85

Legman, Rafael Amadeus, 186, *187,* 223, 226

Legman, Ruth, 14, 16, *17,* 27, 30, 31, 38, 194, 248n85

Index **305**

Legman, Yolande "Julia" Friedman, 12–13, *17, 90, 103, 222;* attitudes toward sex, 29, 31; life in Scranton, 15–18; marriage of, *13, 14;* relationship with Gerson, 19; temperament of, 19–20
Legman, Yomtov, 11
Lenin, Vladimir, 28
Leonhardt, Karl-Ludwig, 184
Les Hautes Études, 141
Les Temps Modernes, 151
Lewis, Sinclair, 33
Library of Congress, 149, 150
Life (magazine), 114, 116, 122, 130
Life and Death of Great American Cities, The, 27
Limerick, The, 142–46, 155, 163, 184, 188, 194, 269n16
"Limerick, The," 85
Listen, Little Man! 119
Lister, David, 234
Literary Digest, 30
literature as form of dreaming, 104
Little Blue Books, 195
"little romances," 144
Living Theater, 119
Lloyd, A. L. "Bert," 151
Lomax, Alan, 35, 148–51, 153–56, 185, 223, 225, 236, 249n104
Lomax, John A., 35, 150, 160, 225
London, Jack, 33
Looking Backward, 2000–1887, 27
Louÿs, Pierre, 56, 62
love and marriage, 78–79; jokes about sexual fools in, 207–9
Love & Death: A Study in Censorship, 3, 76–77, 94, 151, 159, 160, 170, 196, 242; critics of, 108; establishment of Legman as social critic by, 110–11; on homosexuality, 106–7; John Clellon Holmes on, 108; Legman's last comments on, 231; Marshall McLuhan on, 107–8, 126; on mass culture, 102; published reviews of, 108–10; sales of, 107; as unmailable, 132–40
Lowenthal, Leo, 94, 168
Luce, Clare, 130
Luce, Henry, 120, 129, 130

MacColl, Ewan, 151, 153–54, 173, 188, 236
Macdonald, Dwight, 94, 119

mail standards and censorship, 5, 32, 33
"Make Love, Not War" slogan, 170. *See also* antiwar movement
Malaken, Joe, 31–32
Malaken, June, 32, 248n85
Maledicta: The International Journal of Verbal Aggression, 192, 221–22, 231, 237
"Male Homosexuals and Their Prostitutes," 49
male prostitution, 69, 73, 75, 86, 253n62
Malina, Judith, 119
Malinowski, Bronislaw, 252n40
Mammoth Cod, The, 224
Man in the Gray Flannel Suit, The, 116
Marchand, Philip, 123, 127
Märchen (folktale), 220
Marcuse, Herbert, 218
Marx, Karl, 28, 100
Marxism, 3, 4, 27–28, 94, 95, 218
masculine ego, 124
mass culture, 95, 102, 106, 118, 126; advertising in, 121, 123
mass media: commercial, 139; cultivation theory of, 102; dominance of Americanism in commercial, 139; "Red Channels" and, 115, 150; violence in, 242
Mass Psychology of Fascism, The, 126
material culture, 4, 96, 111, 126, 203; sexual symbolism in, 121
matriarchy, 44–45, 157, 159
McAtee, W. L., 108
McCarthy, Charlie, 122
McCormick, Mack, 159
McCosh, Sandra, 220
McCulloh, Judith, 224
McLuhan, Marshall, 107–8, 112, 118, 140, 147; on industrial culture, 121–24; *The Mechanical Bride* by, 123, 127–28; *Neurotica* and, 119–29
Mechanical Bride, The, 123, 127–28
MEDVSA imprint, 56, 59, 60, 62
Melville, Herman, 131
Memoirs (Casanova), 30
Memoirs of a Woman of Pleasure (Fanny Hill), 42
men: ego of, 124; emasculation of, 126; Legman and McLuhan on role of, 121–24; patriarchy and, 202, 209; prostitution of, 69, 73, 75, 86, 253n62. *See also* gender

Mencken, H. L., 44
Menninger, Karl, 114
mental detachment, 120
mental health, 264n2; comic books and, 99–100, 105; effects of war on, 98, 101; psychiatry and, 151, 262n56, 262n63; psychoanalysis and, 4, 84, 106, 116, 199–200, 218, 220–21; Wertham on, 99–102
Merriwell, Dick, 30, 165
Merriwell, Frank, 30
Merry Muses of Caledonia, The, 153, 162, 165–66
Meyer, Adolf, 48
Michaux, Henri, 114
militarism, 1, 116
Miller, Henry, 142, 151, 179, 232, 233; erotica written by, 61–63; *Tropic of Cancer* by, 54–56, 59–60
"Minority Report, A," 77–84; response to, 84–86
Minton, Henry, 49, 50
"Misconceptions in Erotic Folksong," 154
misogyny, 239, 241
Mistakes of Moses, 26
Modern Quarterly, 5
monologues, 224
monotheism, 83
Mooncalf, 37
moral panic, 98
Morton, Jelly Roll, 149
Moses of Michelangelo, The, 199
Mothers, The, 44–45
murder mysteries, 3–4, 126, 133
My Life and Loves, 229
My Secret Life, 72, 167, 210, 229

Nation, The, 235
National Board of Review, 32
National Committee on Maternal Health, 45
National Endowment for the Arts, 233
nationalism, 192
National Research Council (NRC), 71, 81
Native American Ballads, 225
Neal, Michael, 235
"Negro folk songs," 155–57
Neurotica, 4, 82, 94, 107, 227–28, 237; censorship and, 130–31; content and format of, 114, 118–19; degenerate's corner,

129–32; founding of, 112–14; growth of, 114; impact of, 112, 140; interpersonal issues at, 128–29; Legman recruited for, 117–19; literary world reception of, 119; Marshall McLuhan and, 119–29; Noel Busch Affair, 130; reviews of, 116; topics covered in, 115–16; as touchstone for the early 1950s, 139; as unmailable, 132–40
"Neurotics, Incorporated," 115
New Deal, 28
New Directions Press, 55, 107, 117
"New Kryptadia, The," 47, 155, 171, 212, 237
New Left, 218
New Republic, 102
New Society, 211
New Statesmen, 211
Newsweek, 119
New York Academy of Medicine, 48, 49
New York City, publishing industry in, 39–40
New Yorker, 122
New York Herald Tribune, 103
New York Public Library, 43–44, 48–49
New York Times, 235
New York Times Book Review, 109, 227
Niemoeller, Adolph, 44, 47, 60
Nin, Anaïs, 43, 62–64, 232, 241
Noble, David, 232
No Laughing Matter: The Rationale of the Dirty Joke (Second Series), The, 2, 188, 193, 194, 292n87; arrangement of, 203–4; as historical document, 214; Leary's review of, 217–18; Oring's review of, 215–17; painful subjects in, 213–14
normality, 146, 159
North, Sterling, 97
Notes on Virgil, 87
"Not for Children," 96–97, 103, 107–8

obscenity, 102–3, 132–33, 225–26
O'Connor, V. W., 126
Oedipus complex, 124, 219
"One-Eyed Riley, The," 148, 196
"On the Cause of Homosexuality," 77, 106, 123–24, 214
"Open Season on Women," 106
Opie, Iona, 151, 225
Opie, Peter, 151, 225
Opus Pistorum, 233

Oragenitalism, 56–60, 64, 66, 92, 212
oral sex, 7, 82; *Oragenitalism* on, 56–60, 64
Oring, Elliott, 215–16, 221, 238
Ortelius Bookstore, 42
Oui, 188
Our Lady, 142
"Oxford Discourse on Love, The," 61
Oxford English Dictionary, 38, 50
Ozark Folksongs, 147

Painter, Thomas, 49–50, 52, 59, 69, 71, 75, 76, 86, 253n62
Paley, Grace, 11
paranoia, 105, 109, 111, 115
paranoid hostility, 105
Partisan Review, 109, 116, 126, 127
Patchen, Kenneth, 114, 118
patriarchy, 83, 202, 209
Patrimony: A True Story, 19
Paul, John C. N., 138
Pearce, Roy Harvey, 168
Pearl, The, 144
Peekskill Riot, 140
"Peregrine Penis: An Autobiography of Innocence," 228–29, 245n1
performance in context, 238
Perper, Timothy, 235
photo-copier folkore/Xerox lore, 9, 221, 226
photoplay magazines, 98
Pierre, 131
Pills to Purge Melancholy, 155, 162
Pisanus Fraxi, 150, 164, 252n59
Pissing in the Snow, 224
Playboy, 2
Poggio, (Gian Francesco Poggio Bracciolini), 198, 207, 282n18
politics: communist, 27–28, 95, 154; conservative, 241; Gershon Legman and, 3, 4–5, 27–28, 230, 233; jokes and, 220; porn revolution and, 241; postwar, 139–40, 150 (*see also* Cold War); socialist, 27–28, 40, 126
Politics, 110
Pomeroy, Wardell B., 86
popular culture, 3, 122; commercial culture as, 139; explored in *Love & Death,* 94, 96, 102, 126, 138; explored in *Neurotica,* 112, 118, 122, 131, 139; homosexuality and, 124–25; Legman and McLuhan on, 122,

124; Legman's legacy in research on, 236, 238; mental detachment of American intellectuals from, 120; scholarship on early modern, 166, 219–20; violence and paranoia caused by, 109, 117, 241–42
pornography, 233, 240; bibliographic indexing of, 86, 135, 167; Dickinson's research and, 48; European boom in, 231; Legman's interest in 18th- and 19th-century, 63; Legman's writing of, 60–61; modern porn revolution and, 240–41; online, 241; political, 152; science books bordering on, 41; as unmailable, 132–33
porn revolution, 240–41
Portnoy's Complaint, 232
post-traumatic stress disorder, 116
postwar America. *See* Cold War
Potter, Clarkson, 227
Pound, Louise, 35, 149
Preston, Michael, 221
print culture, 94, 95
Private Case, British Museum, 86, 150, 153, 167, 187–88
Private Case, The, 188
prostitution: of men, 69, 86; of women, 30, 31, 45, 46, 50, 214–15
prudery, 1–2
pseudo-homosexuals, 124
psychiatry, 151, 262n56, 262n63; comic books and, 99–100, 105; forensic, 100; Legman's denouncing of promise of, 105; racism in, 100
psychoanalysis, 4, 84, 106, 199–200, 218, 220–21; *Neurotica* and, 116
Psychoanalytic Quarterly, 220
psychodramas, 119
Psychopathology of Everyday Life, The, 203
"Psychopathology of the Comics, The," 118
Publishers Weekly, 98
Puritanism, 32

racism, 100–101, 242; in comics, 100–101; in jokes, 205
radicalism, sex, 5, 126
Radulovich, Stanley, 113, 115, 140
Ramparts, 2
Randolph, Vance, 9, 35–36, 85, 147, 148–49, 215, 236, 270n28; "Roll Me in Your Arms," 223–27, 234

Index

Random House, 210

Rationale of the Dirty Joke: An Analysis of Sexual Humor (First Series), The, 2, 6, 184, 188, 239, 292n87; arrangement of, 203–4; Freudian perspective and, 199–203, 215–16; jokes in folktale scholarship and, 198–99; Legman's collecting of jokes for, 194–203; oral tradition in, 209–10; psychological dilemmas in, 207–8; publishing and distribution of, 210–11; reviews of, 211–12, 215–18; royalties from, 211, 213; sales of, 211; scholarly legacy of, 222; sexual fools and, 207–9; translations of, 212

Read, Allen Walker, 257n20

Reader's Digest, 103, 122

Realist, 2

Rebel without Applause, 227

Rebhuhn, Benjamin, 40, 133

"Red Channels," 115, 150

"Rediscovery of *The Merry Muses of Caledonia*," 165

Red Scare/McCarthyism, 2, 53, 99, 115, 138, 139, 150, 175, 237; McCarthyism and, 115, 138, 232; psychiatry and, 262n63; repression of, 116

Reed, John, 33

Reich, Wilhelm, 94, 119, 126

Reliques of Ancient English Poetry, 225

repression, sexual: authoritarianism and, 199; easing in the 1930s, 34, 248n93; effects of, in marriage, 202; feeding American violence, 1, 94, 96–97, 109; Kinsey and, 66, 68, 82; Legman's hostility toward, 1, 5, 58, 66, 82, 126, 131, 203, 241–42; prehistory before, 83; psychoanalysis and, 218; religious hypocrisy and, 33; roots of, 237; theory of eroticism and, 200

Reuss, Richard, 163, 171

revivals, folk: American, 35–36, 163–64, 237; British, 151–54

Roberts, Roderick, 171

Robeson, Paul, 100

Rockefeller Foundation, 71, 76, 81

"Roger-Maxe de la Glannege" (pseudonym for Legman), 57, 60

Roll Me in Your Arms, 223–27, 234

Roosevelt, Franklin D., 28

Rosenblum, Lila, 118, 119

Rossett, Barney, 210

Roth, Philip, 19, 232

Roth, Samuel, 40, 59, 60, 71, 77, 91, 133, 233

Rovere, Richard, 109

Rubenstein, Richard, 113–14

Ruder, Bernard, 60–61, 63

Russian Secret Tales: Bawdy Folktales of Old Russia, 167, 171

Sanger, Margaret, 5, 34, 40

Saturday Evening Post, 30

Saturday Review of Literature, 100, 103, 114

Schroeder, Theodore, 33

Schuman, Henry, 143

Scientific American, 96

Scott, Janny, 235

Scranton, Pennsylvannia, 12–15, 37, 229; Jewish immigrants in, 15–16, 18; Legman in high school in, 26–29

Screw, 2, 211

"Sea Crab, The," 225

Second Wave women's movement, 215, 239

Seeger, Michael, 173

Seeger, Peggy, 151, 153–54, 173, 188

segregation, racial, 100–101

self-improvement, 127

Sewall, Alice, 58

Sewall, Bob, 27, 58, 61

sex: American attitudes toward, 1–2, 32, 214–15, 237, 240–41; in ballads, 7; censorship of (*see* censorship); folklore of, 6, 36, 45, 64, 65, 144, 239; growth of Legman's interest in, 29–36; in language of verbal abuse, 7; movements for freedom in, 5; oral, 7, 56–60, 82; public colloquialisms of, 6–7; repression and (*see* repression); research on, 45–50; vernacular language of, 5–7

sex radicalism, 5, 126

sex research, 45–50

Sex Side of Life, The, 33

Sexual Behavior in the Human Female, 84

Sexual Behavior in the Human Male, 66, 77, 79–84. See also "Minority Report, A"

Sexual Conduct of Men and Women, The, 77–84. See also "Minority Report, A"

sexual fools, 207–9

"Sexual Gentlemen's Agreement," 131

sexually transmitted diseases, 146

Sexual Slavery, 44
sexual violence, 109
Sex Variants, 49–50, 65
Shame of the Cities, The, 33
Sharp, Cecil, 162, 225, 226
Sheik, The, 30
Show of Violence, The, 101
Sinclair, Upton, 94
slang, sexual, 53–54
Slang and Its Analogues, 38, 50, 147, 167
Smith, Harry, 9, 168, 173
Smokehouse Gazette, 30
Smollett, Tobias, 228
socialism, 27–28, 40, 126
societal oppression, 115
Society for the Suppression of Vice, 32
soft erotica, 98
soldier songs, obscene, 152–54
Solomon, Carl, 112, 115, 117
Some Limericks, 144
songs. *See* folk songs
soul, 82
Spivacke, Harold, 149
Steffens, Lincoln, 33
Steig, William, 131
Steloff, Frances, 43, 54, 59, 60, 70, 119, 142, 254–55n97
Stevenson, Robert Louis, 30
St. Louis, bohemian scene in, 112–13
St. Louis Post-Dispatch, 116
structuralism, 212
Struwelpeter, 131
Summerfield, Arthur, 132
Superfluous Hair and Its Removal, 44
Superman comics, 105, 109
Suppressions, 29
surrealism, 42, 91, 114, 260n18
Susan Lennox: Her Fall and Rise, 30
synonymy, 38

Tamony, Peter, 170
Tausk, Victor, 131
Taylor, Archer, 142–43, 149, 218, 236
tea-room trade, 69
Temple Israel, Scranton, Pennsylvania, 18, 21
theory of mass media effects, 108
Thompson, Stith, 86, 198–99, 201, 207, 212
Thoreau, H. D., 1
"Tia French," 31

Tice, Clara, 60–61
Tijuana Bibles, 34, 263n91
Time (magazine), 114, 116, 122, 188, 261n38
Toelken, Barre, 172
Toscanini, Walter, 186
Towne, Alfred (pseudonym of Landesman and Clellon Holmes), 131
Triefenbach, Louis, 119, 129
Trilling, Diana, 92
Trilling, Lionel, 92
Tropic of Cancer, 54–56, 58, 60, 61, 62, 66, 233
Tropic of Capricorn, 56
Truman, Harry, 139
Turin Papyrus, 72
Turner, Ike, 113
Twain, Mark, 224
Types of the Folktale, The, 196, 198–99

Ubu Roi, 91–92, 271n53
Ulysses, 54, 133
unconscious, the, 119, 122, 201, 205–6, 215–16, 218, 221–22
University of California, San Diego, 168–71
University of Michigan, 37, 39
unmailable material, 5, 32, 54, 78, 132–40
"Unprintable Songs of the Ozarks," 172
U.S. Customs Office, 5, 32
U.S. Post Office, 5, 32, 54, 132–38, 268n94
Utley, Francis Lee, 171

venereal diseases, 146
verbal aggression, 108, 192, 221, 231
Verzeichnis der Märchentypen. See Types of the Folktale
vibrators, 91, 146, 230
Vietnam War, 170, 218, 242
View, 120, 127
Village Voice, 2, 188
Vinocur, Jon, 188
violence, 4, 97, 101, 102, 110, 230, 242; advertising as, 96, 123; censorship of, 103; in children's stories, 104–5; in comic books, 97, 100, 102, 104, 105, 242; economic, 101; familial, 101; fantasy, 105; juvenile delinquency and, 98–99; in popular culture of the 1930s and '40s, 117; racism and, 205; repression feeding American, 1, 94, 96–97, 109; sexual, 109; toward women, 241; verbal, 108

Index

virginity, loss of, 145
Vlamos, James, 97–98

Walcutt, Charles, 38, 39, 54, 144
"Walking," 1
Wallace, Henry, 140
Wallach, Joey, 28–29
Walt Disney company, 104
war, mental health effects of, 98, 101, 242
Watch and Ward Society, 32
Weckerle, Joseph, 70
Wertham, Fredric, 99–103, 262n56
Western Folklore, 215
"Who Owns Folklore?" 172
Wilentz, Eli, 139
Wilgus, D. K., 170, 172
Williams, Raymond, 94
Wilson, Edmund, 94
Wilson, Sloan, 116
Wolfenstein, Martha, 202
women: feminine hygiene, industrial
    culture and, 121; in jokes, 205, 209, 210;
    Legman on love and, 76, 91; Legman's
    opinions of gender roles for, 77–78, 183,
    232; matriarchy and, 44–45, 157, 159;

misogynistic stereotypes of, 96, 120, 242;
    misogyny toward, 239, 241; post-war
    changes for, 125; prostitution of, 30, 31,
    45, 46, 50, 214–15; Second Wave femi-
    nism and, 215, 239; violence toward, 241.
    See also gender
Woolf, Cecil, 271n52
Woolf, Virginia, 43, 271n52
working class movements, Legman's sym-
    pathy for, 5, 34
World Humor and Irony Membership con-
    ference, 229–30
World War II, 98, 101, 105, 115, 237, 242,
    261n38
Wright, Bradford, 97
Wright, Richard, 100, 151, 205
Writer's Journal, 116

Yeshiva Rabbi Jacob-Joseph, 23–26
Yezierska, Anzia, 20
Yoshizawa, Akira, 235
"Young Turks" (folklorists), 155, 218

Zilboorg, Gregory, 114
zoophilia, 145

SUSAN G. DAVIS is professor emerita of Communication and Library and Information Science at the University of Illinois, Urbana-Champaign. She is the author of *Parades and Power: Street Theatre in Nineteenth-Century Philadelphia* and *Spectacular Nature: Corporate Culture and the Sea World Experience.*

FOLKLORE STUDIES IN A MULTICULTURAL WORLD

The Amazing Crawfish Boat
  John Laudun
  (University Press of Mississippi)

Building New Banjos for an Old-Time World
  Richard Jones-Bamman
  (University of Illinois Press)

City of Neighborhoods: Memory, Folklore, and Ethnic Place in Boston
  Anthony Bak Buccitelli
  (University of Wisconsin Press)

Consuming Katrina: Public Disaster and Personal Narrative
  Kate Parker Horigan
  (University Press of Mississippi)

Czech Bluegrass: Notes from the Heart of Europe
  Lee Bidgood
  (University of Illinois Press)

Daisy Turner's Kin: An African American Family Saga
  Jane C. Beck
  (University of Illinois Press)

Dirty Jokes and Bawdy Songs: The Uncensored Life of Gershon Legman
  Susan G. Davis
  (University of Illinois Press)

Expressions of Sufi Culture in Tajikistan
  Benjamin Gatling
  (University of Wisconsin Press)

Global Tarantella: Reinventing Southern Italian Folk Music and Dances
  Incoronata Inserra
  (University of Illinois Press)

If You Don't Laugh You'll Cry: The Occupational Humor of White Wisconsin Prison Workers
  Claire Schmidt
  (University of Wisconsin Press)

Improvised Adolescence: Somali Bantu Teenage Refugees in America
  Sandra Grady
  (University of Wisconsin Press)

The Jumbies' Playing Ground: Old World Influence on Afro-Creole Masquerades in the Eastern Caribbean
  Robert Wyndham Nicholls
  (University Press of Mississippi)

The Last Laugh: Folk Humor, Celebrity Culture, and Mass-Mediated Disasters in the Digital Age
  Trevor J. Blank
  (University of Wisconsin Press)

Look Who's Cooking: The Rhetoric of American Home Cooking
  Traditions in the Twenty-First Century
  Jennifer Rachel Dutch
  (University Press of Mississippi)
The Painted Screens of Baltimore: An Urban Folk Art Revealed
  Elaine Eff
  (University Press of Mississippi)
The Paradox of Authenticity: Folklore Performance in Post-Communist Slovakia
  Joseph Feinberg
  (University of Wisconsin Press)
Recasting Folk in the Himalayas: Indian Music, Media, and Social Mobility
  Stefan Fiol
  (University of Illinois Press)
Squeeze This! A Cultural History of the Accordion in America
  Marion Jacobson
  (University of Illinois Press)
Stable Views: Stories and Voices from the Thoroughbred Racetrack
  Ellen E. McHale
  (University Press of Mississippi)
Storytelling in Siberia: The Olonkho Epic in a Changing World
  Robin P. Harris
  (University of Illinois Press)
Ukrainian Otherlands: Diaspora, Homeland, and Folk Imagination
  in the Twentieth Century
  Natalia Khanenko-Friesen
  (University Press of Mississippi)
A Vulgar Art: A New Approach to Stand-Up Comedy
  Ian Brodie
  (University Press of Mississippi)
Yo' Mama, Mary Mack, and Boudreaux and Thibodeaux:
  Louisiana Children's Folklore and Play
  Jeanne Pitre Soileau
  (University Press of Mississippi)

The University of Illinois Press
is a founding member of the
Association of University Presses.

Composed in 10.25/13 Minion Pro
with Myriad Pro display
by Kirsten Dennison
at the University of Illinois Press
Cover designed by Faceout, Spencer Fuller
Cover image: Gershon at the time of his marriage to Judith, 1966.
Photograph by John Waggaman.

University of Illinois Press
1325 South Oak Street
Champaign, IL 61820-6903
www.press.uillinois.edu